BUILDING THE OLD TIME RELIGION

Building the Old Time Religion

Women Evangelists in the Progressive Era

Priscilla Pope-Levison

NEW YORK UNIVERSITY PRESS
New York and London

NEW YORK UNIVERSITY PRESS
New York and London
www.nyupress.org

© 2014 by New York University
All rights reserved

References to Internet websites (URLs) were accurate at the time of writing.
Neither the author nor New York University Press is responsible for URLs that
may have expired or changed since the manuscript was prepared.

LIBRARY OF CONGRESS CATALOGING-IN-PUBLICATION DATA
Pope-Levison, Priscilla, 1958-
Building the old time religion : women evangelists in the progressive era / Priscilla Pope-Levison.
pages cm
Includes bibliographical references and index.
ISBN 978-0-8147-2384-5 (cl : alk. paper)
1. Women evangelists—United States--History—20th century. 2. United States—Church history—20th century. I. Title.
BV3773.P58 2013
269'.20820973—dc23
                    2013023718

New York University Press books are printed on acid-free paper,
and their binding materials are chosen for strength and durability.
We strive to use environmentally responsible suppliers and materials
to the greatest extent possible in publishing our books.

Manufactured in the United States of America
10 9 8 7 6 5 4 3 2 1

Also available as an ebook

CONTENTS

Acknowledgments   vii

Introduction: Converted, Called, Commissioned:
A Phalanx of Institution Builders   1

1. Tents, Autos, Gospel Grenades: Evangelistic Organizations   27

2. Mothers, Saints, Bishops: Churches and Denominations   67

3. Biblical, Practical, Vocational: Religious Training Schools   111

4. Soap, Soup, Salvation: Rescue Homes and Rescue Missions   139

    Conclusion   173

    Appendix: Evangelists and Institutions   183

    Notes   187

    Bibliography   233

    Index of Names and Subjects   257

    Index of Scripture References   269

    About the Author   270

ACKNOWLEDGMENTS

A writer takes earnest measure to secure [her] solitude and then finds endless ways to squander it. . . . The work itself, you know—sentence by sentence, page by page . . . comes out of all the time a writer wastes. We stand around, look out the window, walk down the hall, come back to the page, and, in those intervals, something subterranean is forming, a literal dream that comes out of day-dreaming.[1]

As I stare out the study window past my lush garden—even in winter—to the Puget Sound in the distance, random, quotidian memories of "squandered" time pepper my thoughts—weeding, doing laundry, walking our dog on the neighborhood beach, talking with Jack, my spouse, over tea and rosemary crackers, sharing research woes with our dear friend and author, David Laskin, and watching an afternoon sunbreak glisten on the water. These intervals that allowed the ideas in this book to form and percolate are among my fondest.

For allowing me to carve out space and time, enough to squander some in daydreaming, I want to thank the Louisville Institute for a Sabbatical Grant for Researchers, which allowed me to extend my sabbatical during the 2010–2011 academic year. One of the best parts of a Louisville Institute grant is the opportunity to gather with other award recipients to discuss our projects. I profited greatly from my group's insights and suggestions, including the fun we had with the phrase "gospel grenades." Although I did not use it for the book's title, as they lobbied, I made sure to include it as title of Chapter 1. Additional grants from the American Academy of Religion, Association of Theological Schools, and Seattle Pacific University generously provided travel funds for me to accomplish extensive archival research, from the eastern tip of Nova Scotia to the California coast.

I am grateful to many people at Seattle Pacific University who supported me throughout the writing of this book. Let me begin with my colleagues in the School of Theology faculty and my students, who have endured my enthusiasm—and contributed their own—for these women. These student assistants provided many hours of finding resources, checking references, and keeping track of details: Sophia Agatarap, Raygan Baker, Joe Ban, Samuel Ernest, Julie Hubbard, Anne-Marie Hunsaker, Megan Leatherman, Val McLeod, and Rachel Willey. Jacqui Smith-Bates, Director of the Center for Career and Calling, and her spouse, Lorrin, offered me the keys to their picturesque cottage on Lopez Island at two significant bookend points, while I wrote the proposal and again when I finished the conclusion. Librarians Melody Steiner, Johanna Knudson, and Vance Lindahl handled interminable interlibrary loan requests with aplomb and graciously forgave more than a few late fines. Senior Graphic Designer Dominic Williamson ably handled the reproduction of photographs. And Steve Perisho, librarian for the School of Theology, proved heroic over and over again as he scoured the Internet for obscure books and articles, purchased books for the library related to my research, and offered his assistance time and again.

The following archives and libraries provided a hospitable welcome and access to their resources: Apostolic Faith Mission, Beaton Institute, Billy Graham Center, Bridwell Library, Duke Divinity School Library, First Free Methodist Church in Seattle, Flower Pentecostal Heritage Center, Fuller Theological Seminary, John J. Burns Library, Methodist Archives, Nazarene Archives, Pitts Theology Library, Salvation Army Archives, University of Washington, and Vennard College, whose archives are now housed at MidAmerica Nazarene University.

Because lectures on material in the book enabled me to test out ideas along the way, I am grateful to invitations from the Association for African American Historical Research and Preservation Biennial Conference, E. Stanley Jones School of World Mission and Evangelism at Asbury Theological Seminary, Gender Studies Institute of Trinity Western University, Historical Society and the Western Jurisdiction Commission on Archives and History of the United Methodist Church, Justice for Women Working Group of the National Council of Churches, Lilly Fellows Seminar on Gender and Christianity at Seattle Pacific University, McCown Symposium at Roberts Wesleyan University and Northeastern Seminary, Marie NeSmith Fowler Lectureship at Samford University, Wesleyan Heritage Conference at Asbury University, and the Windows on the World Series at Eastern University.

A remarkable coterie of scholars graciously took time from their own work to comment on parts of the manuscript: David Bundy, Michael Hamilton, Bill Kostlevy, David Laskin, Meharry Lewis, Randy Maddox, Susie Stanley, and Diane Winston. Two anonymous readers for NYU Press provided astute comments on the proposal as well as the book at its penultimate stage; I hope someday to thank them in person for their expertise, editorial suggestions, and enthusiasm for the book. Jennifer Hammer, my editor at NYU Press, first contacted me about the project twenty years ago. Not only did she believe in the book and provide wonderful suggestions as a seasoned editor, but she also answered every email I sent within an hour, two at the most.

Two other people worked closely and patiently with me to bring this book to fruition. My incredible spouse of over thirty years, Jack Levison, has lived with these women for two-thirds of our married life. He helped frame the initial proposal to NYU, offered wise counsel about writing from his own vast expertise, edited several times over the book's introduction and conclusion, and buoyed me in times of frustration. I delight every day in our life together at home and as academic colleagues. He is my dearest, huckleberry friend who makes being in love an adventure.

My sister, Deborah, a creative writer, poet, and English professor, read every single word, and to her, I gratefully dedicate this book. She edited the earliest drafts without complaint and somehow found treasures amid the dross. Her pride in me and in this book sustained me throughout. Toward the end, to cheer me on, she even composed a limerick, whose closing lines read as follows:

> For she has been bold
> in quashing the old
> neglect of women who strained
> to get themselves and others trained
> to spread the word.
> Now their story will be heard.
> All hail my sister
> writer supreme
> and patriarchy resister!

Wedding photo of Iva and Thomas Vennard. Courtesy of the Vennard College Alumni Association and the Vennard College Collection in the Marge Smith Archives at MidAmerica Nazarene University.

Iva Durham Vennard and her son, William. Courtesy of B. L. Fisher Library, Asbury Theological Seminary.

Introduction: Converted, Called, Commissioned

A Phalanx of Institution Builders

We learned right there that any work of the Lord should be organized, in order to be a success, because they get scattered and the fowls of the air with the wolves get in and destroy them.

                        Emma Ray, *Twice Sold, Twice Ransomed*[1]

In the spring of 1909, Iva Durham Vennard returned from maternity leave—after having given birth in her late thirties to her only child, William—and stepped into the aftermath of a bloodless coup that had engulfed Epworth Evangelistic Institute, the training school for Methodist deaconesses she had founded in St. Louis.[2] While she tended her newborn, a group of Methodist clergymen and laymen, with the district superintendent as ringleader, seized control of the school, rewrote its charter, overhauled its curriculum, and replaced women faculty with clergymen for Bible and theology courses. Despite this preemptive strike, Vennard magnanimously welcomed the district superintendent, Dr. Wright, onto the faculty to teach the Christian ethics course that fall. In the school's monthly publication, *Inasmuch*, she wrote this notice of greeting: "Especially have we been glad to secure Dr. Wright on our staff, and to welcome him to our city and to the position of President ex-Officio of the Board of Directors of Epworth Evangelistic

Institute."³ While this declaration appears quite generous, and may well have been, Vennard had no choice. By vote of the 1904 General Conference of the Methodist Episcopal Church, district superintendents held official oversight of deaconess institutions within their constituency. To comply with this ecclesial protocol, Vennard had to report regularly to the St. Louis Conference Deaconess Board, a committee chaired by the district superintendent.

Owing to the enforced changes at Epworth Evangelistic Institute (EEI) and challenge to her leadership, Vennard submitted her letter of resignation shortly after she returned from maternity leave. In the St. Louis Annual Conference minutes, the redirection of EEI, including a new name, appeared in this solitary sentence: "Epworth Deaconess Institute is getting a firmer grip on the situation in St. Louis."⁴ Vennard, however, remained undeterred and indefatigable. She moved her family to Chicago, and the next year, in 1910, she opened a new religious training school, Chicago Evangelistic Institute. This school, which would be renamed Vennard College after its founder, lasted as a Christian college for nearly a century until it closed in 2008.

Vennard did not initially plan to pursue the path of institution building. After graduating from Illinois State Normal University, she became a grade school teacher and eventually a high school principal. In 1892, she attended Wellesley College, where she became acquainted with Dr. Charles DeGarmo, professor of modern languages and newly appointed president of Swarthmore College. DeGarmo, recognizing her promise, offered Vennard a scholarship to Swarthmore to complete her senior year as well as an extended stay in Europe with his family. Before embarking in this direction, she attended a camp meeting near her home in Normal, Illinois, as she did every summer. She already possessed strong religious convictions stemming from her conversion at age twelve, membership in the Methodist Episcopal Church (MEC), and experience of sanctification at age eighteen. At this summer camp meeting, she ran into the Reverend Joseph Smith, a well-known Methodist holiness evangelist who had been the preacher when she was sanctified. Her biography records that Smith expressed disappointment over her current spiritual state: "When I knew you a few years ago, I thought you were one young woman who was going to be spiritual; and more than that—a spiritual leader. But I see you seem to have gone mostly 'to top.'"⁵ These remarks "awoke once more the old gnawing restlessness and dissatisfaction of soul," and she worried that she had neglected God's counsel concerning her future plans and educational ambitions. As she wrestled in prayer through the night, she resolved to decline the scholarship.⁶

Doors immediately opened for Vennard to lead evangelistic meetings, first as a singer, then as preacher. One request came from a couple in Lodge, Illinois, thirty-five miles away in the next county, where "there was no pastor and no regular church service. This one Christian man rented an abandoned saloon building, and someone loaned an organ. Miss Durham [Vennard] had to be the entire evangelistic party. She led the singing, played the organ, preached, and conducted the altar service. But the room was filled night after night." Despite the invitations, according to her biographer, she hesitated, since evangelism involved preaching, and "she just did *not* approve of women preachers. It was all right to speak, to lecture, to give messages, but to come out in the open as a *woman preacher*—that did not appeal to her at all."⁷ Vennard prayed for guidance with the hope that God "would excuse me from preaching, and let me be perhaps a singer or a social worker."⁸ That word never came. Eventually she accepted the call to evangelism, and in retrospect, she reflected, "Evangelism has been the chief accent of my ministry."⁹ Vennard then enrolled in a Methodist deaconess training school in Buffalo, New York.

After graduation, her first assignment as a full-fledged deaconess evangelist took her to Methodist churches throughout New York State, where she held evangelistic meetings. Notably successful in her first three years, she was reassigned by her supervisor to travel as an ambassador representing the Methodist Deaconess Bureau. Vennard protested that this promotional work sidelined her evangelistic labors and proposed a compromise: she would create a department of evangelism, under the auspices of the Deaconess Bureau, with a course of study to train deaconesses in evangelism. Her plan involved a division in her time and effort—for two months she would teach evangelism in the new department, for eight months she would continue in her ambassadorial role. When she received a negative response, she quit the Deaconess Bureau and pursued her dream of training deaconesses in evangelism by founding EEI.

A Paradigm Shift in American Christianity

Vennard emblematizes women evangelists who founded evangelistic organizations, churches, denominations, schools, rescue homes, and rescue missions across the country during the Progressive Era. Ill at ease simply to proclaim the gospel message of salvation in Jesus Christ and then move on to the next preaching venue, as had women evangelists in previous generations, women like Vennard undertook the formidable work of building institutions to gather in converts, train them for further work in evangelism and outreach, and ensure the legacy of the "old time religion" for future generations. With this key strategic change, these women transformed the quintessential expression of American Christianity—evangelism—from an itinerant practice into the grand task of institution building.[10]

They were not the first women to evangelize in America. Quaker women preached in public and faced severe persecution, even martyrdom, like Mary Dyer, hanged on Boston Commons in 1660. Three decades earlier, "the most celebrated female evangelist in the seventeenth century," Puritan Anne Hutchinson, incurred the wrath of Massachusetts ministers, including her former mentor, John Cotton, who excommunicated and then banished her to the wilds of Rhode Island.[11] At the turn of the nineteenth century, women evangelists ventured forth in greater numbers as itinerants who "followed their own instincts, or leadings of the Spirit, in plotting their travels."[12] From venue to venue, by foot, horseback, stagecoach, or canal boat, they traveled alone because they viewed themselves as strangers without a community, pilgrims on the move. "As if they knew they would one day be forgotten," writes historian Catherine Brekus, "these women often described themselves as 'strangers in a strange land' or 'strangers and pilgrims on the earth.' Comparing themselves to the biblical heroes and heroines who had lived by faith, they wondered if they would always be exiles who 'sojourned in the land of promise, as in a strange country.'"[13]

This book focuses on the next generation of women evangelists who shifted their tack from itinerancy to institution building. The salient change was this: *the first generation of lone itinerant women evangelists who had once wandered the continent became, in the next generation, a phalanx of entrepreneurial institution builders.* Each of their institutions exhibited a measure of permanency, complete with official incorporation, administrative structure, worker training, membership cultivation, scheduled activities, fund-raising protocols, and an established location for meetings and services. These institutions permeated large American cities, as well as isolated reaches and settlements. In Boston, a Roman Catholic laywoman, Martha Moore Avery, cofounded the Catholic Truth Guild, the first evangelistic organization launched by Catholic laity on American soil. Three thousand miles to the west, Florence Louise Crawford brought the Pentecostal message from Azusa Street to downtown Portland and opened the Apostolic Faith Mission. In Hicks Hollow, an impoverished enclave in Kansas City, a former slave, Emma Ray, turned a ramshackle, two-story wooden building into a rescue mission for African American children, while at a nondescript crossroad along the foothills of the Appalachians, Mattie Perry founded Elhanan Training Institute, even before the first public school opened in Marion, North Carolina. When institution building reached the craggy creek beds of western North Carolina through an ordinary woman like Perry, with no financial reserves, no church standing, and no higher education, the movement can be said to have thoroughly pervaded the entire nation.

Yet, despite their geographical pervasiveness and continued persistence throughout the twentieth century, most of these institutions—the builders as well—have escaped the notice of historians. Despite the marked increase in the last two decades of monographs on American women evangelists, none sheds light upon the capability and proficiency they exercised as fund-raisers, entrepreneurs, publicists, denominational executives, and school principals.[14] None captures women evangelists' penchant for institution building that transformed American religion during the Progressive Era. This book accomplishes this significant feat based largely upon primary sources unearthed in archives stretching across the continent, from Seattle and Portland in the Pacific Northwest to Cape Breton in Nova Scotia. These sources emerge from the women themselves, their sermons, books, articles, diaries, letters, speeches, and autobiographies, as well as their institutions' records, such as letters to supporters, yearbooks, financial reports, and monthly newsletters.

Women, Evangelism, and American Christianity

Just who were these women and what did they believe? Let's take a second look at the conflict at EEI and set it against the sizeable backdrop of

American Christianity. From this vantage point, three significant issues emerge that help us understand these women and the beliefs that motivated them and propelled their detractors. These three issues are conversion, sanctification, and gender. The exploration of each issue will help us to apprehend the commitments of these women. At the same time, each issue also opens a window to view American Christianity in the Progressive Era. In other words, by looking at these women, we garner indispensable insights into the development of American Christianity. In turn, by looking at larger conflicts in American Christianity, we garner indispensable insight into the motivations of these women.

The conflict over conversion in American Christianity. The male leaders of St. Louis Methodism transformed EEI's curriculum by replacing evangelism courses with religious education courses. This seemingly unremarkable curricular change reflected an intense, ongoing struggle within Protestantism over the nature of Christian conversion. Vennard, as an evangelical Protestant, believed that the ultimate goal of religious work should be a demonstrable and prompt conversion of sinners; to that end she established a curriculum at EEI that trained deaconesses to be first and foremost "soul winners."[15] As historian Leonard Sweet quips about evangelicals, "What sinners were supposed to do, whether they felt like it or not, was get converted. Nothing was dearer to the evangelical heart than conversion."[16] Not only did evangelicals embrace a dramatic conversion, but they also galvanized around "biblicism (reliance on the Bible as ultimate religious authority); activism (energetic, individualistic engagement in personal and social duties); and crucicentrism (focus on Christ's redeeming work as the heart of true religion.)"[17]

In contrast, progressives, like Dr. Wright, the Methodist district superintendent, gravitated toward a conversion nurtured gradually in the womb of a Christian family and church; for Wright and others like him, a dramatic conversion seemed an antiquated relic of "old time religion." Even workers in the Young Men's Christian Association (YMCA), an organization initially founded to evangelize young men moving to the cities, put less stock in a definitive conversion experience. "In a 1913 survey, 99 of 127 YMCA boys' workers claimed to have grown 'gradually into the Christian conception of life'; only 47 even experienced a recognizable turning point."[18] The teachings of Horace Bushnell, Congregational pastor and theologian, exercised a significant influence in this direction during the mid-nineteenth century, when he began to criticize "emotional revivalists" for their insistence on the "radical breach-making character" of conversion.[19] Bushnell advocated instead for an imperceptible growth into the Christian life, where "the child is to grow up a Christian, and never know himself as being otherwise."[20] His perspective on conversion, recently described as "organic," relied on a steady, long haul Christian influence at home and church rather than a speedy, spectacular one.[21] To prepare churches and families for this task, the field of religious education emerged at the turn of the century and formalized its own organization, the Religious Education Association, in 1904.[22]

Mainline Protestant seminaries followed suit and advanced a curriculum with religious education as "the new paradigm for ministry" for an educated clergy.[23] "The churches that became 'liberal' in the early twentieth century, in other words, did not simply drift away from an emphasis on the conversion experience," claims historian Ann Taves. "Leading modernists actively promoted a new outlook that replaced evangelism with education within the liberalizing sectors of Protestantism."[24] By changing EEI's curriculum, Wright and his cohort replicated this nationwide transition, at least in certain theological circles, from evangelism to religious education.

Despite these theological and pedagogical developments, evangelicals maintained an unrelenting hold on conversion as the decisive moment of salvation, in large measure because it replicated their own experience. Famed African Methodist evangelist Amanda Berry Smith, for instance, related the moment of dramatic change in her conversion narrative: "In my desperation I looked up and said, 'O, Lord, I have come down here to die, and I must have salvation this afternoon or death. If you send me to hell I will go, but convert my soul.'" A few lines later, she describes the conversion moment: "O, the peace and joy that flooded my soul! The burden rolled away; I felt it when it left me, and a flood of lift and joy swept through my soul such as I had never known before. . . . 'Why, I am new, I am new all over.'"[25] Smith then went forth, galvanized to preach the gospel and bring others to a similar intense and instantaneous conversion.

The conversion of Martha Moore Avery, a Roman Catholic lay evangelist, remains an exception to the extraordinary experiences of evangelists like Smith. Avery's conversion adhered more to Bushnell's paradigm with her lengthy decision process over decades in which she exalted mind over emotion. Even when she reported on her conversion in her diary, emotions did not surface: "April 6, 1904—Wednesday. My birthday—on this day I was pronounced, without reservation, to be competent in the understanding of the doctrine of the Catholic Church. I had been studying with the Prof. of Physics at Boston College, Fr. D.J. O'Sullivan, for two years. And I had found that Catholic theology and philosophy was strictly in harmony with Cosmic Law as far as my knowledge extended." She also noted in similar fashion the occasions of her baptism, first confession, first communion, and confirmation.[26] Reason, Avery's constant guide and measuring rod, figured as the operative word in her conversion. Through reason, not emotion, she sifted through a number of secular and religious philosophies, such as Spiritualism, Unitarianism, Pantheism, Nationalism, and Socialism, and pronounced them void of Truth, a word she always wrote with a capital "T." Only the Roman Catholic Church, she reasoned, held the Truth. Once in possession of this Truth, she developed an evangelistic zeal congruent with her Protestant counterparts and cofounded the Catholic Truth Guild for the purpose of making America Catholic.

This brief discussion of different approaches to Christian conversion provides an apt preamble to this book. This volume will allow us to discover, on the one hand, common ground between disparate forms of Christianity that we might be prone to subdivide and polarize, like evangelical versus progressive Protestant and Protestant versus Roman Catholic. Despite their differences, Vennard, Wright, Amanda Berry Smith, and Avery held to the common ground of a commitment to Christian conversion. On the other hand, this book will not paint only with broad strokes; it will also draw out the nuances that arise genetically from diversities within American Christianity. In this case, probing the various approaches to conversion allows us to perceive how a shared perception could yield surprisingly diverse expressions of faith. Beyond both of these observations, too, lies the realization of just how important rank-and-file Christians can be in helping us tease out the rumblings and permutations that crucially shaped American Christianity during the late nineteenth and early twentieth centuries.

The conflict over sanctification in American Christianity. Another conflict embedded in the crisis at EEI, which shaped these women as well as the larger landscape of American Christianity, revolved around the doctrine of sanctification. Again, the conflict had curricular ramifications. To orient EEI students to sanctification as interpreted by the Wesleyan/Holiness movement, Vennard required students to read J. A. Wood's *Perfect Love*.[27] The book's catechetical format provided tidy answers to common questions about sanctification, and its straightforward approach galvanized more than a generation of Wesleyan/Holiness folk, like William Booth, who bought the book's plates in order to reproduce and circulate it widely among the Salvation Army.[28] To signal their disagreement, the St. Louis Methodist leaders removed *Perfect Love* from the curriculum, and after Vennard's resignation, they determined that "the doctrine of holiness, as a second definite experience, will be dropped from the teaching of this institution."[29]

Vennard promoted Wood's book because, several years after her conversion, she had a second religious experience of "purification and empowerment," known as "entire sanctification" (also referred to as "sanctification," "holiness," "Christian perfection," or "higher life").[30] From then on, she identified with the Wesleyan/Holiness movement and its interpretation of entire sanctification as an instantaneous second moment of grace that, through the power of the Holy Spirit, removed the inbred inclination to sin.[31] The result: the sanctified person possessed the power not to sin. Vennard clarified the point further by exploring the theological difference between two nearly identical yet radically different sentences: "**I am not able to sin.** Notice the position of the negative. That is inability. **I am able not to sin.** That is ability, power, deliverance, victory. Christ by His Atonement does not hamper my will. He does not take from me the power to sin, but praise His name, He puts His power within me, by the abiding presence of the Holy Ghost, thus enabling me to keep from sin."[32]

Vennard traveled every summer to camp meetings sponsored by the National Camp Meeting Association for the Promotion of Holiness, the conduit of the Wesleyan/Holiness movement in America.[33] Founded in 1867, the National Camp Meeting Association directly and indirectly sponsored an extensive network of national, regional, and local holiness associations, periodicals, missions, schools, camps, conferences, prayer meetings, and camp meetings. At its camp meetings, Methodist bishops, district superintendents, ministers, and thousands of laypeople flocked to hear sermons and testimonies on sanctification. Along with Vennard, other women evangelists who circulated in this orbit, some briefly and others for decades, include Mattie Perry, Amanda Berry Smith, Jennie Smith, Alma White, and Jennie Fowler Willing.

By the mid-1870s, serious opposition to the Wesleyan/Holiness movement surfaced over what detractors considered a misinterpretation of sanctification. In particular, they objected to Phoebe Palmer's extremely popular "shorter way" to sanctification. Palmer was the leading Methodist evangelist, author, and editor of the mid-nineteenth century, whom historian Mark Noll refers to as the "majordomo of the holiness movement."[34] Based upon her own experience and following the admonition in Matthew 23:19, "the altar sanctifieth the gift," she taught that one need only consecrate oneself entirely upon the altar, then believe that God promises to sanctify whatever rests upon the altar. According to Palmer, the believer receives sanctification in that moment of belief.[35] She promoted her teaching on sanctification through the national and transatlantic revivals she preached, editorial leadership of the *Guide to Holiness*, several bestselling books, including *The Way of Holiness*, and leadership of the Tuesday Meetings for the Promotion of Holiness.

In defense of this position, Palmer and her associates could appeal to John Wesley, the founder of Methodism in eighteenth-century England, because he insisted that entire sanctification remained, in principle, always instantaneous at least as a work of God. As Wesley wrote, "If sin cease before death, there must, in the nature of the thing, be an instantaneous change, there must be a last moment wherein it does exist, and a first moment it does not."[36] In his writings during the middle years of his ministry, Wesley frequently encouraged followers to seek this experience *now*, no matter how shortly after their justification. However, in his later writings, in part because of turmoil in the 1760s over some who claimed the speedy attainment of sanctification, Wesley more typically maintained that, while God *could* bring entire sanctification at any moment, in the majority of cases, it would be after years of growth in grace, when one had matured into a closer resemblance of Christ-likeness exhibited by a robust love of God and neighbor. Palmer's opponents gravitated to this latter emphasis in Wesley, downplaying (or ignoring) his earlier emphasis on seeking *now*.[37] So the growing split between mainline Methodist and holiness groups intensified over *which* Wesley texts and emphases to prioritize.

As the disagreement deepened in the 1880s, Wesleyan/Holiness leaders struggled to keep the unwieldy movement within established denominations, but to no avail. Between 1880 and 1905, some 100,000 "come-outers," as they were called, broke away to form new denominations specifically focused on this "shorter way" to sanctification.[38] Two women evangelists who left the Methodist Church to spearhead new denominations were Mary Lee Cagle (New Testament Church of Christ, which merged later with the Church of the Nazarene), and Alma White (Pillar of Fire). Women evangelists also gravitated to denominations that sprouted several decades earlier from Wesleyan/Holiness roots, like Martha Lee and Emma Ray, who joined the Free Methodist Church, which broke from mainline Methodism in 1860, and Evangeline Booth, youngest daughter of William and Catherine Booth, cofounders of the Salvation Army in 1865, an outgrowth of British Methodism.

Another segment within Protestantism committed to sanctification, the Keswick movement, emerged alongside the Wesleyan/Holiness movement.[39] The Keswick movement, also known as the higher life movement, provided a transatlantic umbrella for holiness advocates who approached sanctification as a gradual, rather than instantaneous process, which consists of three steps. The first step requires a full surrender or consecration to Christ, in which one relinquishes one's will in order to be replaced by the Spirit's. It happens as a decisive crisis experience after conversion and launches the believer into what Keswick adherents refer to as the "higher life." The second step—the baptism of the Holy Spirit—occurs when the Spirit falls and fills the believer. In the third step, the believer receives power for service, enabling her to continue to progress into a higher life through service to others. This emphasis on service cemented a close connection between the Keswick movement and the global missionary movement at the turn of the twentieth century.[40]

An influential group of Keswick adherents made the connection between sanctification and divine healing at a time when healing shrines, homes, and practitioners had become commonplace. Pilgrims flocked to Catholic healing shrines, such as Lourdes in France and Knock Chapel in Ireland, Mary Baker Eddy's Church of Christ (Scientist) attracted a host of members, and the Emmanuel movement brought divine healing even into the Episcopal Church in America. In this heyday of healing, the atmosphere ripened the link between healing and sanctification. As R. Kelso Carter, mathematics professor, faith-healing advocate, and author of the hymn "Standing on the Promises," explained, "It is a remarkable fact, that no one has been known to seek the healing power for the body, without receiving a distinct spiritual baptism; and further, that everyone known to the writer (a very large number), who has been *entirely healed* in body, is or has become a believer in and professor of entire sanctification of soul."[41] Carter's mentor, A. B. Simpson, founder of the Christian and Missionary Alliance denomination in 1897, believed in divine healing through faith alone, without the interference of medicine or medical expertise. Simpson summarized his teaching in the four-fold gospel: Jesus Christ as Savior, Sanctifier, Healer, and Coming King. A number of women evangelists, including Carrie Judd Montgomery, Mattie Perry, and Emma Whittemore, followed Simpson's teachings and associated with his denomination, at least for a time, after being healed from debilitating illnesses without medicine, only with prayer. In the mid-1920s, evangelist Aimee Semple McPherson would adopt the four-fold reference for the denomination she founded, the International Church of the Foursquare Gospel.[42]

Still another group within Protestantism, Pentecostalism, testified to a baptism of the Holy Spirit that issued forth in speaking in tongues, or glossolalia. Glossolalia broke out prominently in early twentieth-century revivals around the globe, including Bethel Bible School in Topeka, Kansas (1900), Welsh Revival (1904), Mukti Mission in Pune, India (1905), and the Azusa Street Revival, Los Angeles (1906). During these years, significant overlap in terminology, such as "sanctification" and "baptism of the Holy Spirit," yet with widely divergent meanings, exacerbated tensions between holiness folk in the Wesleyan/Holiness, Keswick, and Pentecostal movements. For instance, the phrase "baptism of the Holy Spirit" became problematic because it referred to sanctification within the Wesleyan/Holiness movement and speaking in tongues among Pentecostals. In her 1926 autobiography, Emma Ray, an

African American Free Methodist evangelist, had to clarify that what she understood the phrase to mean was sanctification, not glossolalia: "A great light flooded our souls, and immediately the Holy Spirit began to lead us out into deeper depths. . . . He [the Holy Spirit] didn't give us all the light at one time, but later, little by little, as we were able to receive it. Neither did we speak in tongues, but He gave us a new tongue to testify and tell the glad tidings."[43]

Confusion even confounded the term "sanctification." Did it mean "cleansing and perfecting," as maintained by the Keswick and Wesleyan/Holiness movements, or the more Pentecostal motif of power? As historian Donald Dayton writes, "Often the 'power' themes merely overwhelmed the 'holiness' themes. . . . The mainstream Holiness movement tried valiantly to preserve the classical themes in the midst of the new changes in vocabulary and rhetoric."[44] During these contentious debates, two Pentecostal women evangelists, Florence Louise Crawford and Mary Magdalena Lewis Tate, held on tightly to both terms—"sanctification" and "baptism of the Holy Spirit"—in the holiness Pentecostal denominations they founded, the Apostolic Faith Mission (Crawford) and the Church of the Living God, the Pillar and Ground of the Truth (Tate).

Despite these different perspectives on the particulars of sanctification—instantaneous or gradual, accompanied with glossolalia or cleansing for service—still the shared advocacy of this doctrine draws women evangelists together in an extended family sort of way. They testify that sanctification imparted "holy boldness," as historian Susie Stanley demonstrates, and enabled them to overcome the "man-fearing spirit" that had previously impeded their preaching and evangelism.[45] Evangelist Mary Lee Cagle testified, in her customary third-person narrative style, about the boldness that accompanied her sanctification: "Although of a shrinking, backward disposition, she has never seen a crowd since that day large enough to make her knees tremble, and she has preached to thousands."[46] It is not surprising, then, that of the two dozen women discussed in this book, only Helen Sunday (Presbyterian), and Martha Moore Avery (Roman Catholic), stood outside the wide umbrella of holiness movements.

As we have seen thus far, various peculiarities of vocabulary and interpretations muddied the waters of conversion and sanctification during the Progressive Era. Certainly, even with the explanations blurred, however, this much is clear: by understanding the specific ways in which these women attempted to give expression to their experiences, we apprehend a rich penetration into a formative stage in American Christianity. Further, by looking carefully at various conflicts within American Christianity, we gain a diverse yet comprehensive understanding of theological and experiential expressions during the Progressive Era.

The conflict over gender in American Christianity. The St. Louis Methodist men who ousted Vennard from EEI did so in part over the issue of gender. Their specific complaint: Vennard's supposed duplicity of "training women preachers under the guise of deaconess work."[47] As the district superintendent, Dr. Wright, explained, "Methodist preachers do not want deaconesses who study theology. We can attend to that ourselves. We want women as helpers who will work with the children, care for the sick, and visit the poor. If our deaconesses are trained in theology they will become critical of the preachers, and that will be the end of the deaconess movement." In his outrage, according to her biographer, he then referred to Vennard as "a dangerous and powerful woman."[48] Many clergymen shared Wright's sentiments about deaconesses in particular and women in general.[49] Even though they depended heavily on women's work to keep the church running and bolster membership rolls, since women attended church in greater numbers than men, they became suspicious about any work that approximated women in the pulpit. "Ministers suspected—and rightly—that women had more chance of capturing the church than the Senate; and they reserved their fiercest powers of resistance for such a possibility," explains historian Ann Douglas.[50]

The conflict over gender at EEI replicated a national discussion within Protestantism. Gender issues surfaced, for example, in votes cast at the quadrennial General Conferences of the MEC from 1872 to the 1920s.[51] In 1880, the General Conference voted to rescind all local preacher licenses previously issued to women, including the popular evangelists Jennie Fowler Willing and Maggie Newton Van Cott. The same vote also banned women from all church leadership positions, with the exception of Sunday-school superintendent, class leader, and steward, and it slammed the door shut on women's ordination.[52] Subsequent General Conferences dallied around for another four decades before voting in 1924 to restore women's local preacher licenses. Methodist women would then have to wait another three decades for the General Conference vote to approve full clergy rights for women in 1956, the same year the mainline Presbyterian Church cast a similar vote.

While male church leaders equivocated over gender issues in most Protestant denominations, women forged ahead on their own to establish voluntary religious organizations separate from men's. Their creative ingenuity for circumventing official channels confirms sociologist Mark Chaves's remark that "denominational rules regarding women's ordination—whether those rules are inclusive or exclusive—neither reflect nor shape the tasks and roles women actually perform in congregations as closely or directly as might be expected."[53] Protestant women in a number of denominations, from 1869 into the 1890s, established their own home and foreign missionary organizations, including eight within the Methodist family of churches alone.[54] These organizations enlisted in their ranks a staggering number of members. "More women became involved in women's missionary society work after the Civil War than in all areas of the social reform and woman's rights movements combined. Between 1861 and 1894, foreign missionary societies were organized by and for women in thirty-three denominations and home missionary societies in seventeen."[55] In turn, these missionary organizations opened up myriad opportunities for women missionaries to preach, teach, and plant churches on the mission field, the very activities that women were not authorized to do in their home congregations. Mary Lee Cagle recognized even as a teenager that she would have more opportunities in leadership and ministry on the mission field. "I felt assured of a Divine call to engage in Christian work. On account of the teachings of that time regarding woman's ministry, I decided there would be no opening for me in my home-land. I came to the conclusion that my call was to the foreign field where I supposed a woman would have freedom in preaching Christ to the heathen. Many dreams I had of crossing the waters and preaching to them."[56]

Although Cagle never did cross the waters, many women did. Owing to the substantial influx of women missionaries supported by women's organizations, the Protestant missionary force sent from America grew from two thousand before 1870 to six thousand in 1900. Of the six thousand foreign missionaries at the turn of the century, women constituted roughly two-thirds.[57] Like their counterparts in North America, women missionaries built institutions in foreign lands during the Progressive Era. Take, for example, missionary Eva Swift's Lucy Perry Noble Institute for Women, a school in Madurai, India, that provided evangelistic training for Indian women.[58] The story of this institution and others like it built by women missionaries has been well documented and will not be repeated here, but it is important nevertheless to note the parallel to women's institution building in the United States.

The same impulse for "female institution building," a phrase coined by historian Estelle Freedman, gave rise to the Woman's Christian Temperance Union (WCTU), the largest women's organization in the United States in the Progressive Era, with a membership approaching two hundred thousand by the century's end.[59] From its beginning in the Women's Temperance Crusade of 1873–74 to its expansion into a "Do Everything" policy under Frances Willard's presidency, the WCTU provided women with their own, separate institution for societal and ecclesial reform.[60] Willard purposefully capitalized on the strategy of female institution building, as historian Margaret Bendroth explains: "Preferring 'to keep the dimes and distinctions to themselves,' Frances Willard charged, the denominations had instead classified their women members as mere 'hewers of wood and drawers of water.' Only in their own separate organizations, she argued, could women develop their own latent gifts for leadership."[61]

Despite the obvious success in stature and numbers of female-only institution building, women evangelists embarked on a different strategy. They broke new ground as women religious leaders and built institutions for both women *and* men. They did not adopt the strategy of female institution building. Neither did they follow the strategy typified in many evangelical institutions of "participating in a parallel world of women's ministry groups, where they gain leadership opportunities denied them in their mixed-gender congregations," which still left men in charge as overseers of the women.[62] Instead, women evangelists built the institutions themselves and set the rules from the beginning, and those rules included the presence and participation of both women and men. The evangelistic organizations, churches, denominations, schools, rescue homes, and rescue missions founded by these women attracted male and female converts, members, and students. Church membership rosters listed male and female names. School photographs captured female and male students sitting alongside each other in classrooms. Letters written from male and female workers back to denominational headquarters described their religious service and travel adventures as they crossed the continent to advance the institutional network. Church leadership positions were filled by both women and men. These women evangelists, therefore, rank among the first American women to build—and lead—mixed-gender religious institutions.

To press this further by looking beyond the stigma often attached to the word "evangelist," these women stand as pioneering religious leaders in America who held supreme power and authority over their institution, even over men. Women preached, men listened in the pews. Women set doctrine and interpreted scripture, men accepted their teaching. Women pastored, men joined their churches. Women gave orders, men obeyed. Women made real estate purchases, men contributed money. Women held the power within the institution, men submitted to their religious authority. And the power women wielded within these institutions remained fierce and absolute. They dictated what their followers—male and female—should believe and not believe, wear and not wear, eat and not eat, even when to exercise and for how long. What historian George Marsden observed about institutions of American evangelicalism founded by successful male evangelists applies equally to women: "Usually these institutions have been run autocratically or by an oligarchy; in any case they have typically been regarded virtually as private property. They were designed for a special purpose, which could be defined by the people in immediate command, with no need to answer to ecclesiastical authority. These institutions were thus extraordinarily shaped by the personalities of the individuals who founded and controlled them."[63]

To identify other women religious leaders who accomplished similar achievements of institution building during the same time period, one must look beyond mainstream Christianity to Theosophy, Christian Science, Seventh Day Adventism, and New Thought.[64] Like their evangelical counterparts, Helena Blavatsky (Theosophy), Mary Baker Eddy (Christian Science), Ellen White (Seventh Day Adventism), and Emma

Curtis Hopkins (New Thought) also sought to legitimize their religious movements in brick and mortar, in rules and regulations, in a legacy for the next generation of converts. Mary Baker Eddy, for instance, organized the Christian Science Association in 1876, officially incorporated the Church of Christ (Scientist) in 1879, and opened the Massachusetts Metaphysical College in 1881.⁶⁵ Ten years later, she began construction in Boston on the building which became the movement's Mother Church. Despite many conflicts and several schisms, membership in the Church of Christ (Scientist) grew rapidly in the early decades of the twentieth century, increasing from twenty-six in Eddy's first congregation to eighty-six thousand by 1906.⁶⁶

Eddy's prize former student, Emma Curtis Hopkins, built several institutions for her New Thought movement. In 1886, she launched the Emma Hopkins College of Christian Science, and by the following year, the Hopkins Metaphysical Association consisted of seventeen member groups in cities from coast to coast. She restructured the college in 1888 as the Christian Science Theological Seminary and admitted women and men. From the first graduating class, Hopkins herself ordained twenty women and two men. A historian of New Thought claims that "Hopkins's ordination of women marked the first time in American history (and possibly Western Christian history) that a woman ordained women.... With Hopkins's move, emergent New Thought ceased to be a lay movement of quasi-professional teachers and practitioners. Now it was a religious organization; its leaders were ordained ministers who began to establish churches, hold Sunday services, and preach."⁶⁷

Like these religious leaders, the women you will meet in this book drank deeply of the same draft of institution building.⁶⁸ By and large, they were, like Vennard, theologically conservative, with deeply held views on the necessity of conversion and sanctification and a deep trust in the inspiration of the Bible. Yet—and here lies the utter fascination of these women—despite an entrenched conservatism, which we will note countless times in the pages ahead, these women not only initiated but also stood at the helm of these institutions, which they built to accommodate, to teach, and to equip both men and women. Their evangelistic organizations attracted thousands of women and men to their meetings. Their churches and denominations commenced with a handful of men and women and expanded across the country, some even across continents.

Their training schools and colleges enrolled hundreds of male and female students. Their rescue homes and missions extended humanitarian and evangelistic outreach to men and women in American cities and towns. These women caught the fever rampant in America—and American Christianity—to create institutional legacies during the Progressive Era.

A Remarkable Era for American Christianity

The women in this book occupy a particular niche in American history: the Progressive Era, roughly 1890–1920.[69] These decades of momentous change and foment in America pulsed with the beat of sweeping social change, bold legislation, and audacious innovation, from settlement houses and neighborhood playgrounds to the Nineteenth Amendment for women's suffrage, from the income tax to the Social Gospel, from the assembly line to the movie theater. No segment of American life, no crevice in American culture, no stratum of American society stalled this explosion of innovation. Larger-than-life figures who even today cast their shadows—John Dewey in education, Frank Lloyd Wright in architecture, Jane Addams in urban reformation, Upton Sinclair in journalistic critique, Walter Rauschenbusch in Christian social responsibility, Henry Ford in mass production—emblematize an era in which America accomplished much and dreamed still more.

An unprecedented measure of institution building solidified these movements. The settlement house movement, for example, launched in Great Britain in the late 1880s, took root in the United States at the cusp of the Progressive Era, beginning with New York's Neighborhood Guild and College Settlement and Chicago's Hull House. A handful of settlement houses in 1890 grew to more than four hundred by 1910, each one providing myriad opportunities for urban neighbors to come together across class boundaries through "lectures, classes, plays, pageants, kindergarten, and child care."[70] Along with community-based activism, settlement houses emerged as institutions dedicated to ameliorating the pressing issues of the day, from immigration and urbanization to poverty and health care.

Evangelists, too, joined the Progressive Era's institution-building enthusiasm. While this book focuses primarily on the work of women evangelists, it is important nonetheless to note that Dwight L. Moody, the leading American evangelist of the mid-to-late nineteenth century, had already begun to shift toward institutional evangelism. During the last two decades of his life, along with evangelistic meetings, he devoted resources to institution building. In 1879, he launched a girls school, Northfield Seminary, and allowed his own home to function as the first dormitory and classroom until construction was complete on the seminary's first building.[71] Four years later, the Mount Hermon School for Boys, also in Northfield, opened its doors. These schools, with a core curriculum in Bible and theology, held an evangelistic purpose for Moody, who "hoped that they would become schools for the training of evangelists like himself who would spread the gospel effectively throughout the country."[72] In 1880, he offered the first annual Northfield Conference geared to training laity in evangelism through adult education in Bible study and evangelistic methods. Still another institution, the Chicago Evangelization Society, began in 1887 and developed into the Moody Bible Institute, a training school to equip urban lay evangelists. That same year, he launched a summer-long religious training program, the College Students' Summer School, which prepared and motivated a generation of young men to be leaders in evangelism, ecumenism, and mission.[73] Beginning in the 1880s, institution building for evangelism—evangelistic organizations, churches, denominations, schools, rescue homes, and rescue missions—would intensify throughout the Progressive Era, especially through the efforts of women evangelists.

Along with rampant institution building, the Progressive Era figures as "the most critical time in American religion" according to historian Arthur Schlesinger. He continued, "Perhaps at no time in its American development has the path of Christianity been so sorely beset with pitfalls and perils as in the last quarter of the nineteenth century."[74] Up until this time, evangelicals "had things mostly their own way."[75] Then during the Progressive Era, the evangelical hegemony splintered markedly in reaction to seismic demographic and theological shifts. First, a staggering rate of immigration that reached eight hundred thousand people annually wreaked havoc on every aspect of American life, including religion. Immigrants arrived with their own "dress, language, customs, and religions," which seemed "threatening to older-stock Americans."[76] In reaction, Congregational minister and one-time general secretary of the Evangelical Alliance Josiah Strong ranked immigration as the first of seven perils confronting the United States in his best-selling and influential book, *Our Country: Its Possible Future and Its Present Crisis*. "So immense a foreign element must have a profound influence on our national life and character," wrote Strong. "Immigration brings unquestioned benefits, but these do not concern our argument. It complicates almost every home missionary problem and furnishes the soil which feeds the life of several of the most noxious growths of our civilization."[77] Immigration further exacerbated another peril that worried evangelicals, the rise of Roman Catholicism. In response, evangelicals turned up the exigency of evangelism in an effort to retain the "old time religion" of a Protestant America. Despite myriad entertainment options, from the cheering of crowds in wooden baseball stadiums to the ubiquitous five-cent storefront nickelodeons, Americans turned out in droves to spend a couple of hours at an evangelistic meeting. Evangelism thrived so readily in the Progressive Era that historian William McLoughlin referred to the period as the Third Great Awakening.[78]

Second, the theological challenges that vexed evangelicals emerged from the theories of evolution and higher criticism. Darwin's ideas evoked a scientific account of a world that developed as species evolved as opposed to a "providential explanation for the universe" as held by evangelicals.[79] Higher criticism brought scientific methods appropriate for any type of literature, sacred or secular, to the interpretation of the Bible. These more scientific concepts gained traction in mainline Protestant seminaries and influenced future ministers. In a symposium on higher criticism published in the Methodist periodical, *Zion's Herald*, twenty-five Protestant ministers answered this question, "What should be the attitude of ministers toward the 'Higher Critics,' or 'Criticism,' of the Bible so called?" Without exception, they responded with appreciation, like the Reverend J. R. Day, D.D., a Methodist Episcopal minister, who declared: "Let the higher critics criticize. They are among the best friends of the cause, for when the objections to the Scriptures are examined by scientific methods by the scholars of the land, the easier will it be for the pastors to go on with their work. . . . I hail as a fellow-worker every honest critic in the biblical field today."[80] Following from such sentiments, many ministers utilized the scientific methods of higher criticism in their sermon preparation, and these same ideas thus trickled down to laity listening in the pews.

Evangelicals protested that both evolution and higher criticism inevitably tampered with the reliability, authenticity, and historicity of the Bible. Of the two theories, they saved their fiercest condemnation for higher criticism, referring to it pejoratively as "destructive criticism."[81] In her famous address, "The World's Great Romance," presented in auditoriums throughout the world, Evangeline Booth, longtime commander of the Salvation Army in the United States, delivered a dramatic verbal assault against it. "Destructive criticism . . . the pernicious and seductive teaching of dissection and contradistinction of the Bible, in this day of infidel attack upon the fundamental truths of Christianity, snatching the prop of eternal hope from old age as it stands with one foot in the damp sod of the grave, and robbing youth of its one unerring lamp as it starts down the snare-strewn path of life, in this day of unlimited batterings upon the Christ of the Cross . . . "[82]

Evangelicals also denounced higher criticism for being exclusive and elite, for the well educated and seminary trained; as such, it "threatened the basic assumption of commonsense realism and popular piety—that the Bible was open to the average person."[83] They countered that education, position, class, or wealth did not matter when interpreting the Bible. Evangelist Maria Woodworth-Etter, who could only attend school for a few years because she had to go to work to help ameliorate her family's desperate economic situation, boasted often that she did not need to study or prepare sermons ahead of time; she simply stood on stage and received the biblical text from God, including its chapter and verse, then opened her mouth to preach.

These fancy ideas and "the profound changes and the shocks that accompanied them," observed McLoughlin, "registered most heavily upon those country-bred, evangelically oriented . . . individuals who made up the bulk of the nation's churchgoers."[84] This same audience, longing for the familiar "old time religion," gravitated en masse to hear evangelist Dwight L. Moody and songster Ira Sankey. Moody and Sankey "rejuvenated the revival" by attracting "listeners in the millions, converts in the thousands, their hymns on every lip, their names a household word."[85] Even after Moody retired in 1892, the American populace continued to seek out evangelistic meetings and support them financially. In the year 1911, according to American historian Sydney

Ahlstrom, six hundred fifty full-time and one thousand two hundred part-time evangelists crossed America. Ahlstrom continues with these statistics: "Between 1912 and 1918 they staged at least 35,000 revivals; and according to one careful estimate, the evangelical churches spent $20 million a year on 'professional tabernacle evangelism' during the peak years from 1914 to 1917."[86]

So that they might "confront American life at every level, to permeate, evangelize, and Christianize it," evangelists launched a massive number of institutions in the Progressive Era.[87] From schools to churches, from denominations to rescue homes, these institutions served not only as a conduit for fervent evangelism but also as a safe house from the storms of evolution and perilous biblical interpretations. And women stood at the helm of many of these institutions as founder, administrator, fundraiser, preacher, teacher, publicist, and entrepreneur.

Institution by Institution

Four types of institutions founded by women evangelists are examined in all their intricacies and evangelistic dimensions in the following chapters.[88] Chapter 1 features the evangelistic organizations that arranged, financed, and implemented evangelistic meetings. Some remained small outfits, like Maria Woodworth-Etter's or the Catholic Truth Guild, cofounded by Martha Moore Avery and David Goldstein. Others grew to great proportions, like the Billy Sunday evangelistic organization, ranked among an elite group of American corporations, thanks to the business acumen of Helen Sunday, or the WCTU Evangelistic Department, with its hundreds of women evangelists. Along with their decidedly evangelistic purpose, some organizations, like Florence Crawford's Apostolic Faith Mission, also served as a gathering point for converts who became the nucleus of new churches and denominations.

Chapter 2 investigates these churches and denominations from their initial formation to their development into enduring institutions with established headquarters, printing presses, and full-fledged sets of doctrines and disciplines. Women retained strict control over the institutions as well as their members, often dictating lives down to daily minutiae, like Alma White's insistence on a vegetarian diet and thirty minutes of daily exercise. While the women founders who launched these churches and denominations—like Mary Lee Cagle, Florence Crawford, Mary Magdalena Lewis Tate, Maria Woodworth-Etter, and Alma White—are long deceased, much of their work remains vibrant into the twenty-first century, and second- and third-generation members continue to engage in evangelism across the globe.

Chapter 3 turns the institutional focus to schools. These educational institutions—founded by Elizabeth Baker, Carrie Judd Montgomery, Mattie Perry, Iva Durham Vennard, Alma White, and Jennie Fowler Willing—provided a modicum of training in Bible and practical work for men and women headed into full-time Christian work as evangelists, preachers, Bible teachers, missionaries, and musicians. Despite their own minimal education, women evangelists pioneered a visionary, path-breaking vocational education for men and women that presaged future enrollment and curricular decisions of public educational specialists and seminary administrators.

Chapter 4 introduces rescue homes and missions, which provided humanitarian outreach to the destitute and downtrodden, the prostitute and unwed mother, along with evangelism. The symbiosis between evangelism and humanitarianism, in Vennard's colloquial phrase, was likened to the "bait on the hook" (humanitarianism), whose purpose was to "land the fish" (evangelism). With a similar mantra, Martha Lee, Carrie Judd Montgomery, Emma Ray, Florence Roberts, and Virginia Moss opened rescue institutions in cities like Omaha, Kansas City, and Oakland, while Emma Whittemore launched the Door of Hope, doors really, with an extraordinary national chain—a veritable McDonald's of social outreach—of nearly one hundred rescue homes.

The book's Conclusion teases out these women's legacy as the Progressive Era edged into the Roaring Twenties. At this juncture, Aimee Semple McPherson stood on the giant shoulders of these pioneering women religious leaders and accomplished even more institution building. The women who preceded her had already plowed the hard ground of resistance and opposition to women evangelists. They had already pioneered transportation technology in evangelism, from gospel wagons to decorated autovans. They had already launched every institution in McPherson's repertoire—evangelistic organizations, churches, denominations, religious training schools, and rescue institutions. Women evangelists in the Progressive Era paved the way for McPherson to develop a most extensive, wide-ranging collection of institutions from the 1920s to the 1940s.

Martha Moore Avery and David Goldstein and the Catholic Truth Guild Gospel Car. Courtesy of Goldstein-Avery Collection, John J. Burns Library, Boston College.

Florence Louise Crawford in *Sky Pilot*. Courtesy of Apostolic Faith Mission Archives.

1

Tents, Autos, Gospel Grenades

Evangelistic Organizations

At the appointed hour, on a sultry, mid-July afternoon, the highly decorated, customized Model T autovan, nicknamed "Rome's Chariot," arrived on the corner of Washington Street and Chestnut Hill Avenue in Brighton, Massachusetts. In the autovan rode Martha Moore Avery and David Goldstein, the featured lecturers for the meeting to be held that evening sponsored by the Catholic Truth Guild. The Model T had been modified to hold evangelistic meetings from within its doors. It housed a moveable platform, complete with a stand-up rostrum known as the "perambulating pulpit" that folded out at a forty-five-degree angle from the front of the car. Its four seats could also be removed or stacked on top of one another to form a table, and ample storage compartments carried large quantities of Catholic literature.

Designed as an eye-catching spectacle, the autovan generated a crowd simply by driving into town. Its decorations blended American patriotism and Roman Catholic devotion. On one side, it sported a sentence from George Washington's farewell address: "Reason and experience forbid us to believe that national morality can prevail where religious principles are excluded." A miniature star spangled banner decorated the hood to demonstrate that "this Catholic apostolate campaigns for rendering to America what belongs to America—loyalty."[1] The Catholic nature of the enterprise shone forth in a large crucifix topped by an electric light and in the yellow and white chassis colors, borrowed from the papal flag. In addition, in cardinal red letters, the refrain from the Holy Name hymn, penned by Boston's Archbishop William O'Connell, covered the other side of the car: "Fierce is the fight for God and the right; sweet name of Jesus in Thee is our might."[2] The autovan received a blessing from O'Connell two days before its maiden voyage on July 4, 1917, to Boston Commons, where the first meeting took place.

The Catholic Truth Guild (CTG), the premiere evangelistic organization founded by Catholic laity in America, hosted its inaugural meeting in Avery's Boston home in the winter of 1917.[3] Twenty-five people signed the charter membership list in support of CTG's purpose to "send its members out into the highways and byways in city squares and street corners, proclaiming the truths of Faith."[4] The first name on the membership list and the only woman's name was Martha Moore Avery.

The CTG illustrates the institution building that women evangelists developed around their evangelistic meetings during the Progressive Era. This phenomenon differentiates them from their counterparts in previous generations. Earlier in the nineteenth century, evangelists like Harriet Livermore, Jarena Lee, Nancy Towle, and Zilpha Elaw, the so-called "strangers and pilgrims" featured in Catherine Brekus's groundbreaking study, had labored single-handedly as preachers, publicists, and pastors at the altar.[5] What changed toward the century's end was that women conducted evangelistic meetings, from advance planning to the final offering, under the auspices of an evangelistic organization. These organizations assumed different configurations. Some remained centered on the individual evangelist, like Maria Woodworth-Etter's or the CTG, which never evolved beyond Avery and Goldstein, despite the twenty-five initial signatures. Another evangelistic organization, the Apostolic Faith Mission headed by Florence Crawford, stretched across several cities and states. From each Apostolic Faith Mission (AFM) headquarters, volunteer evangelists, both women and men, departed regularly to hold meetings on street corners and rural crossroads. Still another arrangement took shape in the Evangelistic Department of the Woman's Christian Temperance Union (WCTU). This department within a national organization, headed and staffed by women, depended upon the work of thousands of WCTU evangelists across the country who reported to superintendents at the state, district, county, and local levels.

One might conjecture that these organizations provided untold opportunities for women's involvement and leadership, but the evidence appears mixed. In the multicity-based AFM, some women did participate in local evangelistic meetings, but as it developed into a denomination, as we will see in the next chapter, no woman broke into the top echelon of leadership. Much more beneficial for women at all levels was the WCTU Evangelistic Department, which enlisted a host of women evangelists to plan and lead meetings in keeping with its mission statement: "To enlist more women who shall preach the Gospel, and to train the workers."[6] According to Frances Willard, WCTU president, this department registered "an aggregate of several thousands of women who are regularly studying and expounding God's Word to the multitude."[7] For the evangelistic organizations that galvanized around a woman as the principal evangelist, prospects for other women to gain a foothold in management or to earn the spotlight as the featured speaker did not materialize. Women fared better in Billy Sunday's multimillion dollar evangelistic organization, the largest in the Progressive Era. Along with countless women volunteers, more than a dozen women worked full-time for the organization, including its astute business manager, Helen Sunday.

Evangelistic Meetings

"Catholic Truth Guild"

Through the day and night
Be it dark or bright
The horizon we do scan
For a loving view of the guild so true
For woman, child, or man
Are filled with glee whene'er we see

> The Catholic Truth Guild van.
> The Guild serene with Dave Goldstein
> Mrs. Avery and Corbett
> Should you listen to their pleadings
> The time you'll ne'er regret
> You will thank the God of Heaven
> Who sent his only Child
> To lead us into Heaven
> Through the Catholic Truth and Guild.[8]

This poem, most likely penned by Avery, sketches a general outline of evangelistic meetings: an audience ("For woman, child, or man") gathers around a speaker ("Should you listen to their pleadings") who delivers a religious message to secure a favorable response ("To lead us into Heaven"). Meetings like these stand at the fulcrum of American Christianity, from preaching campaigns in New England churches before the Revolutionary War, to Roman Catholic parish missions in the nineteenth century, to Kathryn Kuhlman's twentieth-century radio and television broadcasts. Remarkably, evangelistic meetings retain a strong ecumenical resonance across churches and denominations, despite differences in theology and polity. Catholic historian Jay Dolan finds these three points of resonance between Roman Catholic and Protestant evangelistic meetings: (1) they are conducted by itinerant evangelists; (2) they incorporate techniques specific to the genre, such as music, publicity, and "how-to" handbooks; and (3) they emphasize a conversion experience.[9] Dolan's conclusion in this regard holds up when we consider the meetings of two women evangelists—Avery, a Roman Catholic, and Woodworth-Etter, an early Pentecostal. Avery, who valued reason and argument, designed the lecture as the centerpiece of the meeting. Woodworth-Etter, in stark contrast, relied on emotion and ecstatic behavior, including body-contorting trances and vivid visions of heaven and hell. Nevertheless, despite what appears on the surface to be intractable differences, Dolan's three elements can easily be identified in meetings sponsored by the CTG and the Woodworth-Etter organization.

The CTG revolved around two itinerant evangelists, Avery and Goldstein, both of whom converted to Catholicism as adults. As already noted, Avery reasoned her way into Catholicism at age fifty-three after considering several religious and secular ideologies, most notably Socialism. Goldstein, who was mentored by Avery, converted to Catholicism shortly after she did, and together they founded the CTG to acquaint the American populace with the Truth of Catholicism. They proposed, through the CTG, the lofty goal of making America Catholic: "Now that America is gradually slipping from its oldtime prejudice against, and people are getting curious to find out all about the Church which they recognize is THE Church after all it would seem as if a magnificent effort should be made to bring the light to those in darkness, and who have no means of finding that light except by the efforts of zealous Catholics. . . . We have our opportunity. Let us not shirk it. The whole country is thinking and thinking hard as to what Catholicity means. . . . The time seems to be ripe. Let us hope that God will send the right assistance to make AMERICA CATHOLIC."[10] During its first summer of operation in 1917, the CTG sponsored eighty meetings in ninety days. As it grew in recognition and popularity, its summer schedule increased to one hundred fifty meetings held in Boston and its suburbs as well as towns throughout New England, like Marblehead, Massachusetts, and Somerville, New York.

Given their proclivity to capture the intellect, Avery and Goldstein designed the CTG meeting around a lecture. They always delivered a prepared speech on a Catholic topic, such as the Catholic perspective on a doctrinal question (the divinity of Christ, sacraments, origin of the Bible), or the Catholic Church's accomplishments (charitable works, contributions to education, service among the poor), or contemporary issues (Socialism, democracy, the economy, women's roles) presented from a Catholic perspective. In a favorite lecture given countless times, Avery made the connection—albeit quite circuitously—between the Catholic Church and democracy. She opened with the claim that democracy can be traced to the Ten Commandments, the Israelite law code recorded in Exodus 20 and Deuteronomy 5, and from there to the advent of Christianity, specifically the birth of Christ. From this pronouncement, she traced the origin of democracy not to America's Declaration of Independence but two millennia earlier to Bethlehem's cradle. According to Avery, "this is the democracy upheld and fostered by the Catholic Church."[11] Based upon this established link between democracy and Catholicism, she continued with the main assertion of her lecture, namely that "America is the fruit of the Catholic Church on civil ground" because both the nation (America) and the Church (Roman Catholic) embrace democracy. Or, in a nutshell, "true Catholicism . . . inspires true Americanism"; thus the Catholic Church is the "true exponent" of democracy.[12] It was this symbiosis between Catholicism and American patriotism that the CTG autovan embodied with its vibrant decorations.

Long before Avery spoke at CTG meetings, she had already gained a reputation as a seasoned lecturer, earning $3 a day plus expenses while on the lecture circuit.[13] She first gave public lectures under the auspices of the First Nationalist Club when she moved to Boston in 1888.[14] At the pinnacle of her Socialist phase, several Socialist groups in the Midwest invited her to give a lecture tour.[15] She also lectured several times a week in her Karl Marx class, which she began in order to educate Boston Socialists on the philosophical and economic underpinnings of Marxism.

After she quit the Socialist Party and converted to Catholicism, she, along with Goldstein, joined forces with an anti-Socialist organization in Boston, the Common Cause Society, founded in 1912 at the height of the party's popularity, when 6 percent of American voters cast ballots for the Socialist presidential candidate, Eugene Debs.[16] The Common Cause Society (CCS) adhered to Pope Leo XIII's sociological principles, particularly his anti-Socialism, as evident in the preamble adopted by the organization: "To defend our national inheritance, and advance the cause of equity within the sphere of economics upon the basis laid down by Pope Leo XIII in his encyclicals on the social problems of our times, especially to bring forth by argument and given facts the falsity of Socialist principles and their treasonable use of the ballot."[17] Support of these principles stood as the only membership requirement, thus allowing Max Mason, a charter member and a Jew, to retain his membership despite opposition.[18] With few exceptions, however, the CCS maintained a strong Catholic identity, with close to 80 percent Catholic members in 1913.[19]

During the winter months, the CCS sponsored hour-long public lectures on Sunday evenings in Franklin Union Hall, and in the summer, open-air lectures on Boston Commons on Sunday afternoons. For both venues, more than one thousand people regularly gathered to hear lectures on "The Dangers of Socialism" or "The Origin of Civil

Authority."[20] Following the lecture, opponents were invited up to the platform to voice objections and engage in public debate with the lecturer for another hour. Avery and Goldstein quickly rose to prominence in the CCS as featured lecturers, and Avery served as president from 1922 to 1929. Yet this avenue for lectures and leadership did not fulfill Avery's and Goldstein's ardor to make America Catholic.[21] To that end, they founded the CTG.

The lecture format of a CTG meeting fit the well-established template of Roman Catholic evangelism to non-Catholics. In the parish mission, instituted by priestly orders in the mid-nineteenth century, for example, the morning service consisted of an address on a Catholic doctrine or devotional practice. In his mission manual, Father Walter Elliott, a Paulist priest and leading evangelist to non-Catholics, explained that the forty-five minute talk should not only clarify confusion but also answer "in a kindly manner" any questions or "difficulties" raised by the audience.[22]

Elliott, like Avery, held to the grand design of making America Catholic, and he exhorted all Catholics, especially the laity, to be missionaries to the American people.[23] To inaugurate his campaign to "win America for Christ," Elliott resigned as editor of the *Catholic World* in order to work full-time holding missions aimed at non-Catholics. His 1893 speech, "The Missionary Outlook in the United States," given at the Columbian Catholic Congress held in conjunction with the Chicago World's Fair, invigorated Catholic lay evangelism in America at a time when other leading Catholics sounded the same call. Several years earlier in 1889, at the First Lay Catholic Congress in Baltimore, Henry Brownson, son of the well-known Catholic convert and writer, Orestes Brownson, insisted that laity bear the Catholic message wherever they go. Brownson explained, "A layman can often get the ear of a non-Catholic that the priest cannot reach, and an intelligent explanation of Catholic doctrine and practice by a layman will, in many cases, carry more weight than that made by a priest, because it is in a language and form of thought better understood and appreciated, and is less likely to be thought insincere." The previous day and in another part of the country, Archbishop John Ireland expounded the same message: "Laymen are not anointed in confirmation to the end that they merely save their own souls and pay their pew rent. They must think, work, organize, read, speak, act, as circumstances demand."[24]

However, these advocates of lay evangelism, who had charged Catholic laity to make Catholicism at home in America, stood on the wrong side of the Americanist controversy. Pope Leo XIII condemned Americanism, the inculturation of Catholicism into America, in his 1899 encyclical, *Testem Benevolentiae* ("True and False Americanism in Religion").[25] The encyclical also clarified the "division of labor" regarding lay and clergy participation in mission. Catholic laity could only witness to their faith by "integrity of life, by the works of Christian charity, by instant and assiduous prayer to God," a marked contrast from Archbishop Ireland's call to the laity, as quoted above, "to think, work, organize, read, speak, act, as circumstances demand."[26] Nonetheless, several decades later, spurred on by the rise of Socialism, two Catholic laity, with the blessing of Archbishop O'Connell, went on the offensive to demonstrate through the CTG their twofold devotion to Catholicism and America.

Another technique adapted by Avery and Goldstein was the Quiz Period, an informal question and answer time with the audience. The Quiz Period replicated the Question Box, developed by the Paulists for their lecture courses to non-Catholics.[27] The Paulists set up the first Question Box in the Assembly Hall at the 1893 World's Fair, and every day fairgoers dropped in hundreds of questions on all sorts of topics: "Is the Pope the Antichrist?" "The Fable of Pope Joan," "The Crusades," "The Ouija-Board," "Theatre-Going," and "The Morality of Strikes." Due to its success, the Question Box remained a regular feature of a Paulist mission. Avery and Goldstein altered the technique in one significant way; they solicited questions on the spot rather than selecting them beforehand. Both speakers enjoyed volleying spontaneous questions and debating such controversial topics as the Catholic teaching on hell and confession to a priest for the forgiveness of sins.[28] Both relished the verbal brawl, and turned the opposition into publicity. Avery had already perfected this attribute during her Socialist days. At a strike meeting of shoemakers, for instance, she climbed onto the platform and proceeded to address the crowd, even though the organizers had already rebuffed her initial request to speak. As she began to talk, the meeting turned unruly, so the organizers shut off the lights, and everyone dispersed. A month later, when she returned to address the strike rally again, the crowd attacked her with spit, fists, mud, and snow. Instead of leaving town at the suggestion of the police chief and mayor, she rented a hall and delivered a series of lectures.[29] Her ingenuity in capitalizing on opposition benefited CTG meetings as well, like the occasion when she redirected negative publicity about the Ku Klux Klan to promote the CTG. She wrote to her daughter, Katherine, about the incident: "The K.K.K.'s had so stirred up things that we had an immense audience, and Fr. ____ was glad to have us there—he is not afraid of them and he means to route them out."[30] Avery handled the outrage that sometimes erupted during the Quiz Period in her inimitably forceful way.

After the Quiz Period, CTG speakers distributed Catholic literature. This technique also developed in parish missions as a means to educate and enlighten people further about Catholicism. As Walter Elliott commented, "We allow the supremacy of the spoken word. But suppose it could be remembered as if it were *printed* on the memory? In truth the spoken word applies the healing ointment: the printed word sinks it in. Book preaching is persistent."[31] Literature available at a CTG meeting included Catholic pamphlets, subscriptions to Catholic magazines and newspapers, and clothbound books written by Avery and Goldstein. Some literature they handed out at no cost, but they preferred to sell it, even for a pittance. Not only did the profits help with the meeting and travel costs, but also they surmised that "when the printed word is paid for it is better appreciated than when taken as a gift."[32]

Lastly, in keeping with Dolan's observations, CTG meetings emphasized conversion in keeping with Avery's and Goldstein's experience. To that end, while one handled the Quiz Period, the other held one-on-one conversations in a more private setting behind the autovan. Even this aspect demonstrated a wholesale borrowing from the Paulists, who referred to this time as Personal Work, when the priest held personal interviews with interested non-Catholics or lapsed Catholics. Avery recalled for her daughter the people who came around back to talk. "I receive a variety of visitors at the back of the van. These on last Sunday! A beautiful girl actress—N.Y. a member of the Actors Catholic League there. One horrid old blaspheming atheist. One genial old Socialist Labor 'comrade.' An old Yankee Bible-reading Christian. A young lady Theological college student with a keen appreciation of the several times that she was forced by the logic of the points I made to take back water—all in good spirit. Two girls from Maine having Catholic friends down there to whom they would give my message."[33] Because

Avery and Goldstein were laity, not clergy, they referred some conferees to the local priest for further guidance. Still, historian Debra Campbell suggests that behind the van, they "exercised at least a quasi-pastoral function from time to time," which, for Avery, as a Catholic laywoman in the early twentieth century, was most remarkable.[34]

In an anonymous history of the CTG, probably written by Avery, because it contained unusually high praise for her role in particular, the writer suggested that judging "actual results" from a CTG meeting would be tricky. Even so, the writer managed to cite this numeric assessment of Avery's work: "This was the Confirmation of 1500 converts, over half of whom were women, and for whom Mrs. Avery stood sponsor at the request of the Cardinal. She is now godmother for about two thousand persons, and it is not extravagant to say that many of these conversions are due to the work to which she has devoted her life."[35]

Similar to the CTG's capitalizing on the tried-and-true practices of Catholic evangelism, so Woodworth-Etter followed the well-developed format of Protestant evangelistic meetings. They opened with preparatory music and prayers to warm up the crowd in anticipation of the evangelist's sermon. After the sermon, the evangelist offered a plea-filled exhortation for sinners and backsliders to come to the altar where, hopefully, they would experience a dramatic conversion. To spice up the meeting's atmosphere, Protestant evangelists throughout the nineteenth century leaned heavily on emotions, spontaneity, even ecstatic behavior, like this description of an 1885 Woodworth-Etter meeting: "Dozens lying around pale and unconscious, rigid and lifeless as though in death. Strong men shouting till they were hoarse, then falling down in a swoon. Women falling over benches and trampled under foot. Children crying and weeping as though their parents were dead. Aged women gesticulating and hysterically sobbing, as though their sons and support had been cruelly murdered. Men shouting with a devilish, unearthly laugh, jubilant as if the arch angel had been conquered."[36] This depiction recalls frontier camp meetings earlier in the century, where religious enthusiasm displayed itself in shouting, jumping, laughing, crying, shaking, moaning, and other physical and verbal contortions.

Beginning from her home in rural, central Ohio, Woodworth-Etter traveled first to preach in small towns and crossroads in Ohio and Indiana. She worked her way up to mid-size cities, like Kokomo and

Hartford City in Indiana. As the crowds increased, she bought an eight-thousand-seat tent, formed an evangelistic organization with a handful of workers, and journeyed across the country to Oakland, California, then back to St. Louis and the Midwest. As an itinerant evangelist, she worked tirelessly, holding three meetings per day—morning (10:00 a.m.), afternoon (beginning at 2:00 or 3:00 p.m.) and evening (7:00 p.m.). Considering that each meeting lasted several hours, she literally spent more time on stage than off in a twenty-four-hour period, and she maintained this pace for several weeks at a time. Not surprisingly, reporters commented frequently on the fatigue etched on her face, but once on stage, she "soon became animated in her speaking."[37]

During the meeting, Woodworth-Etter preached for over an hour. She refused to prepare the sermon in advance; instead she "would take a text and trust God to lead me in his own way."[38] Ironically, by adopting this practice, she served as a mouthpiece similar to Spiritualist mediums, who invited spirits to speak through them as they stood before a gathered audience. Early on in her work as a lecturer, leading suffrage and women's rights activist Susan B. Anthony expressed that she too would like to receive speeches in a similar fashion. In a letter to Elizabeth Cady Stanton, her close friend and colleague in the work, Anthony wished that "the spirits would only just make me a trance medium and put the right thing into my mouth. . . . You can't think how earnestly I have prayed to be made a speaking medium for a whole week."[39]

While preaching, Woodworth-Etter punctuated her words with repetitive physical gestures, striking her hands together, moving her arms in wide arcs, and stomping her feet on the floor. Several newspaper reporters observed that her hands never stopped moving, even when at her side, they ceaselessly opened and closed. Earlier in the century, evangelist Charles Finney had developed "a theology of gesture," according to historian Martin Marty, who cited this quote from Finney: "Gestures are of more importance than is generally supposed. Mere words will never express the full meaning of the gospel."[40] Along with gestures, Woodworth-Etter repeated certain phrases, such as "his damnation is sealed." These phrases peppered her speech, particularly at the end of a sentence when "she cannot resist the temptation to 'ring it in' with a staccato movement that has a telling effect on those in front."[41] All in all, her preaching resembled this description of evangelist Dwight

Moody's sermons, offered by one of his biographers: "extremely diffuse ... unconnected, rambling and given to repetition."[42]

However, what really drew crowds to Woodworth-Etter's meetings was her reputation as the "trance evangelist." While preaching, she would fall into a trance and remain rigid in a semi-conscious state for an extended period.[43] A newspaper reporter published this description of one of her trances: "Mrs. Woodworth's face is working strangely and its color has changed to a grayish white. Suddenly she drops into a chair. Her face is turned upwards, her eyes open, staring, the pupils dilated." For forty-five minutes, she held her right arm raised high overhead, waving it slowly back and forth, while the index finger pointed upward and pulsated. One of her workers explained to the reporter the religious significance of her stance: "The rigid evangelist was pointing heavenward with one finger and toward hell with the other, and 'Oh, dear friends, which way will you go?'"[44] Trances fell on her in a variety of positions, as she recalled in her autobiography: "Sometimes standing with my face and hands raised to heaven, my face shining with the brightness of heaven; other times the tears streaming down my face with mute preaching, pleading with sinners to come to Christ; other times lying for hours, sometimes as one dead, and diverse operations of the Spirit, conscious all the time, but entirely controlled by the power of the Holy Ghost."[45]

A heated debate erupted in newspapers over trances, as reporters and physicians weighed in on their legitimacy. Many considered them a hoax, like this front page opinion in the *Indianapolis Times*: "It is absolutely, undoubtedly and beyond per adventure a stupendous deception. There is evidently nothing of divine interposition in it. It is simply as a leading physician of the town told the *Times* reporter, a state of comatose into which any person is liable to fall whose nervous system is severely strained. The evangelist apparently has but little personal magnetism. She relies wholly upon the fear and terror which she instills into the minds of her usually ignorant audience. Almost every one who has been stricken is illiterate."[46] An alternative opinion by Dr. T. V. Gifford appeared the same day in another Indiana newspaper: "While in the trance, that portion of the brain through which God's spirit comes to us and teaches us of Him is in supreme control, and all the rest of the brain is dormant, or is held more or less inactive for the time.... And to you, Christians of the Methodist and Quaker order, who have been praying so long and loud for the fullness of that religion of which you have been permited [sic] to have a little taste, let me say that this woman only has that fullness for which your souls have long panted; so be careful how you treat her when she comes among you."[47]

Debates did not solve the veracity (or not) of trances, but they certainly prompted a dramatic attendance increase, much like Avery's ability to turn volatile responses to her advantage. Whereas Woodworth-Etter first preached to crowds that fit into small-town churches, by the summer of 1885, when trances became highly publicized, she had to purchase a large circus-style tent, forty by sixty feet, as well as several smaller tents to accommodate the overflow crowds. Workers in her organization would pitch the tents outside of a town, like Muncie, Indiana, where an estimated twenty thousand people traveled thirteen miles to her campground in a ten-acre grove.[48] In order to be seen and heard while preaching, she stood on top of two chairs placed in the center of a two-foot high platform and held steady by two men.

To accompany the evangelist's message, Protestant meetings incorporated upbeat, energetic music as a technique to energize the audience. During Moody's large-scale meetings, for instance, a sizeable choir performed several songs, then the congregation, led by his intrepid musician, Ira Sankey, sang hymns and gospel songs. "All this was a way of warming up in an impersonal atmosphere. . . . In a yet more practical manner the musical preliminaries helped to muffle noise and confusion as latecomers searched for seats," explains historian and Moody biographer James Findlay.[49] The Woodworth-Etter organization, which did not employ a full-time musician, utilized local talent at each venue, like Mrs. Boyer of Noblesville, Indiana, who "attracted thousands of people, with her singing."[50] Sometimes even Woodworth-Etter sang her favorite song, "The Lily White Robe." One observer, writing for the *Anderson Bulletin*, characterized the music in this manner, "The metre is of a peculiar and exciting nature, such as is heard in the country churches or among the colored people of the south."[51] After the music came prayers and a short message by a local minister or one of Woodworth-Etter's workers, like Miss Posther, who recounted her healing from blindness. All this prepared the audience for Woodworth-Etter, the main attraction.

After the sermon came the moment, as Dolan notes, when the evangelist pressed for conversion. Often in Protestant meetings, musicians provided soft background melodies or sang hymns about coming home to Jesus, like a prodigal son, to encourage a greater response. Instead of music, at a Woodworth-Etter meeting people prayed aloud simultaneously in an impulsive manner. The atmosphere, as one reporter confessed, "is very confusing to the disinterested listener, but apparently has a strong effect upon those who are engaged and the voices of the contestants rise higher and higher, and they become more and more excited."[52] During this cacophony, conversions happened at an accelerated rate, spurred on by ecstatic signs and wonders that erupted in the audience, like trances, visions, healings, and speaking in tongues.

In two versions of her autobiography published before the turn of the century, Woodworth-Etter described conversion experiences in which the newborn convert spoke in tongues. One instance, related in her first autobiography published in 1885, involved her husband, Philo: "About this time my husband was converted in the Methodist Church, where my little girl had been converted. He was very bright and seemed to speak with other tongues."[53] In the 1894 version, she recalled another post-conversion celebration, the same year as Philo's, when Brother Vaughn spoke in tongues. "He dropped on his knees and began to pray. I felt if he was ever saved, it must be there and then. As I prayed, it seemed as though heaven and earth came together, and in a few minutes he was on his feet, speaking as if it were with other tongues, exhorting sinners to come to Christ."[54] Woodworth-Etter dropped both of these references from subsequent versions of her autobiography, but she nevertheless pressed the point that speaking in tongues occurred at her meetings prior to the 1906 Los Angeles Azusa Street Revival. In her 1916 autobiography, she reminisced that twelve years earlier, during her St. Louis meetings in 1904, "one sister spake in unknown tongues all night. This was before the Holy Ghost fell at Los Angeles, California."[55]

Woodworth-Etter believed these signs and wonders provided visible manifestations of God's power as happened in the apostolic age, when the apostles, the earliest followers of Jesus, healed the sick, raised the dead, spoke in tongues, and received guidance through visions. She rejected the opposing argument, known as the "limited age of miracles," that claimed the cessation of the miraculous at the close of the apostolic age.[56] Advocates of this position insisted that God gave the apostles power to perform miracles only to confirm to others their apostolic authority on which stood the church's foundation. Once the apostles died, so did miraculous deeds. Woodworth-Etter completely disagreed and supported her claim by announcing the arrival of the "latter rain" that brought with it an even greater demonstration of God's power. The latter rain metaphor, which would become commonplace in Pentecostal circles, first appeared in her 1894 autobiography, when she recalled the outbreak of trances in 1883 at her meetings in Fairview, Ohio: "It is now twelve years since that meeting; the Lord has poured out the Holy Ghost as he promised he would in the last days, with signs and wonders following. He said he would give the *latter rains* of the Spirit before the notable day of the Lord came."[57] These signs and wonders both accompanied and fueled conversions in her meetings. As Woodworth-Etter explained, "These outpourings of the Holy Ghost were always followed by hundreds coming to Christ."[58]

While evangelistic meetings relied on accoutrements and techniques to stir up an expectant atmosphere, still the evangelist remained the celebrity. People lined up far in advance for a seat in the tent or tabernacle in order to get as close as possible to the famed preacher. Even Goldstein studied intently several leading Protestant evangelists with an eye to incorporating their techniques. Letters written to Avery during the 1920s related his impressions of Aimee Semple McPherson and the British evangelist Gipsy Smith. For instance, Goldstein had carefully scrutinized Smith's orchestrated voice mannerisms and their visible impact upon the crowd's emotions and proposed that the Catholic church send a commission to study evangelists in action "to learn what to do to touch the hearts of the class of persons who can be reached by the evangelical system."[59] Avery, however, had a far less appreciative reaction to Billy Sunday during his Boston meetings. In an article in the Catholic paper, *America*, she poked fun at Sunday's less-than-eloquent rhetoric: "It would seem that bad taste is the guiding star of the evangelist who fights the devil with language most befitting the presence of his satanic majesty." Yet the overriding issue, what trumped all for her, was Sunday's Protestantism because he failed to embrace the inextricable link between true Christianity and the Truth of Catholicism. "He came, but he could not conquer. He cannot conquer because he does not see the Protestant mote in his own eye." She concluded with this final declaration, "For what is Christian comes from Rome and must in time lead back to Rome. Needless to say, Catholic Boston is taking no part in the tabernacle service: to do so would be adding to the fascination of a man who has no commission to preach."[60] Despite, however, Avery's intractable view of Protestant evangelists and her desire to distance Catholicism from Protestantism, CTG evangelistic meetings, like Woodworth-Etter's, revolved around three common factors: itinerant evangelists who utilized various techniques designed to encourage a conversion experience.

Material Concerns

Even a two-person evangelistic organization like the CTG had myriad material concerns to tackle, from packing literature to sell to setting up the summer schedule.[61] Before confirming each meeting, Avery and Goldstein worked to secure approval from the bishop as well as the local priest. They put a high premium on the priest's cooperation because he could enhance the meeting's effectiveness, as this newspaper article recounted: "The past week's successes have been greatly due to the practical interest of the priests who have advertised the coming of the autovan and to their being seen upon the perambulating rostrum welcoming the speakers to their districts."[62] Ideally, the priest would provide assistance with these four tasks: (1) choose an appropriate place for the meeting; (2) publicize the meeting in local newspapers and the parish newsletter; (3) convene a committee to sell literature during the meeting; and (4) put in a public appearance at the meeting. Each of these practical considerations required time and effort, ideally by someone other than the evangelist, so he or she could concentrate on the spiritual efficacy of the meeting.

Similarly, Dwight Moody's evangelistic organization, which managed meetings with thousands in attendance, followed this same basic protocol.[63] The first step was to enlist the backing of leading pastors in the city and work with them to set a suitable date. Then, more than a year in advance, the organization set up a host of working committees—finance, executive, prayer, home visitation, charitable work, temperance, ticket arrangement, choir members and ushers, and publicity. Publicity also commenced with a year-long blitz in newspapers, churches, handbills, and personal invitations. Along with these assignments, the organization worked to secure financial contributions from prominent businessmen.

Moody had a peculiar knack in this regard; no matter the city, wealthy, influential men signed their support on the dotted line. In Philadelphia, for instance, John Wanamaker donated downtown land with an abandoned railroad depot that was remodeled into the main auditorium for the campaign. After the campaign ended, he renovated it once more into a department store. Wanamaker also contributed to the campaign by encouraging his store employees to sign up as ushers for the campaign. The young men selected to be ushers wore a special colored ribbon and carried long, wooden poles, known as "wands." Moody's workers trained them how to "handle unruly crowds politely, how to care for fainting women, and how to silence crying children."[64]

By tracking these tasks, Moody's efficient evangelistic organization systematically occupied one metropolis after another for weeks at a time, including what several scholars reference as the "greatest single effort of Moody's evangelistic career," the 1893 World's Fair Campaign.[65] Throughout the weeks of the campaign, his organization sponsored as many as five meetings a day in scores of venues that added up to ten churches, seven halls, two theaters, and five tents. Determined to "beat the World's Fair" with electrifying, crowd-pleasing events, Moody, along with his hand-picked team of evangelists and several hundred workers, kept up a breakneck pace. On a day touted as the campaign's best, September 23, 1893, the organization scheduled "sixty-four different meetings held in forty-six places, with an estimated attendance of from sixty-two to sixty-four thousand people."[66]

Within a decade of Moody's death on December 22, 1899, as the twentieth century dawned, evangelist Billy Sunday commenced his rise to national renown. At the height of Sunday's popularity, he preached in a colossal tabernacle, acclaimed as "the largest structure for public meetings ever erected in New York," built in 1917 exclusively for his New York City meetings. Its seating capacity of sixteen thousand, with standing room for four thousand more, housed the crowds that totaled nearly one and a half million people.[67] To administer these massive meetings, the Billy Sunday evangelistic organization replicated the same procedure as had Moody's and, on a much smaller scale, the CTG. Directing the business side of the organization was Billy's spouse, Helen Sunday. She took responsibility for all the material concerns—schedule, publicity, finances, staff, and each city's local committee.

A particularly wrenching assignment for Helen involved securing the date and venue for the ten-week long New York City campaign because it required rescheduling the campaign in Chicago, her hometown. Soon after the Chicago Committee had secured the spring of 1917, the New York City Committee contacted the Sunday organization demanding the earliest possible date. When Helen, nicknamed "Ma," offered New York a block of weeks the following year, they "argued and insisted . . . and would not go away." Helen recalled the intricate diplomacy required to solve the conundrum:

> Finally someone suggested, why not try to get Chicago to wait until 1918 and then give New York their ten weeks of time in April, May and June of 1917. . . . Mr. Sunday said—"Ma is the only one for that job." I looked at him aghast, the very idea of me having to ask my own home town to give way to New York. I knew how every Chicagoan felt about New York, but the job was finally saddled upon me and letters were sent to Chicago stating that Mr. Sunday was sending me on an important mission, and he requested them to notify all the Committees and Preachers of Chicago to meet me at a certain hour on a certain day. I really was overwhelmed with the terrible responsibility and I slept very little.

Still, she managed to secure a unanimous vote from the Chicago Committee.[68]

With a firm date in hand, Helen then entered into a prolonged negotiation for the best location in New York City for the tabernacle to be constructed. She turned down the first two sites suggested by the committee, one due to noise from a nearby baseball park, the other to a scarcity of parking spaces and its proximity to a neighborhood she considered questionable. The third site also had disadvantages, particularly its distance from the city center, yet she recognized its commendable features; it had "plenty of room and the subway had a station at Broadway and 168th Street at the corner of the property . . . and the City Council would vote to extend the Charter to the Fifth Avenue bus line company if we decided on that location." She approved the site "amid great rejoicing on the part of all present."[69]

Helen's business savvy catapulted the Billy Sunday evangelistic organization to new heights, as one of Billy's biographers explains: "There is no way that he [Billy] could have vaulted himself and his infant organization to national fame, material wealth, and numerical success without Nell's administrative skills. An inherently able woman who had picked up some of her father's business acumen, Nell was one of the few people in America who could have kept Billy calm and happy and at the same time reshaped his ministerial team into a nationally renowned phenomenon."[70] Under her capable management, the Billy Sunday evangelistic organization rose to the heights of an elite group of Progressive Era businesses, alongside the Standard Oil Company, United States Steel, and National Cash Register.[71]

Compared to these impressive financial and attendance statistics, the evangelistic organizations of women evangelists had substantially fewer coins to rub together, often only a few pennies and dimes. Fund-raising efforts became a necessity. Like many evangelists throughout the nineteenth century, they raised money by selling songbooks, photographs, and their autobiography.[72] Woodworth-Etter astutely revised and updated her autobiography, publishing at least seven editions between 1885 and 1922, thus providing incentive for people to keep purchasing the latest version.[73] Evangelists also depended heavily on freewill offerings collected after the meeting. For that reason, when Boston police halted vending on Boston Commons, the location of the first and last CTG meetings, which always attracted the largest attendance, Avery and Goldstein had to tap their own personal finances. Even with financial backing from Archbishop O'Connell, who held tightly the archdiocese purse strings, they nearly depleted their respective bank accounts to make up the deficit between his contributions and CTG expenditures.

Sometimes fund-raising efforts displayed creative ingenuity, like those of Woodworth-Etter's business manager and her first husband, Philo Woodworth. He set up a refreshment stand alongside the meetings to sell food and trinkets. As he announced his wares to meeting goers, reporters likened his voice to a "circus ring master advertising the grand concert," and they characterized him as a mercenary who preyed on people's emotions during the meetings in order to turn a profit:[74]

> The husband of the evangelist is of a thrifty turn, and while the meetings are in progress he and his two assistants operate a peanut, candy and lemonade stand within sixty feet of the pulpit. The other day, as men and

women were shouting and going into trances, old Woodworth sat beside an ice cream freezer and cranked it unconcernedly, preparing a supply of the popular refreshment for the weary, sinsick crowd. Sunday morning he was dispensing cigars and plugging watermelons for the million, and the nickels, dimes and quarters flowed into his till in a steady stream, while the wife was laboring with care-burdened sinners.[75]

To deflect criticism, Maria offered this justification: "The only money we receive is from the refreshment stand Mr. Woodworth runs on the ground. . . . He also serves meals to any who desire them. This has been characterized as a money-making scheme, but it is the only means in the world we have of keeping up expenses."[76]

Philo's business ventures persisted with plans to develop a Christian compound on fourteen acres of land he purchased in north-central Indiana, along the shores of Manitou Lake, a popular spot for fishing and boating. He envisioned a hotel, gardens, campground for tent meetings, and a home where Maria could rest and recuperate between meetings. None of these plans materialized, however, because of their ongoing marital conflicts, which erupted visibly in a fight during the 1890 Oakland meetings over ownership of the eight-thousand-seat tent. One reporter observed and then publicized Maria's punching Philo.[77] Philo quit the meetings early and returned to the Midwest. In retaliation, Maria sued for divorce on the grounds of his adultery with several women.[78] Within a month after their divorce on February 26, 1891, Philo married a teenager, sixteen years old, who had been married once already. A year later he died from typhoid fever.

Every evangelistic organization, no matter the size, took advantage of newspapers' free publicity to advertise upcoming meetings and report on past ones. This practice commenced in America with British evangelist George Whitefield in the mid-eighteenth century, who "learned to exploit the emerging world of print journalism to promote his tours." Subsequent evangelists since then had come to rely on the power of the press.[79] Avery developed a particular knack for generating publicity in the press not only for the CTG but also for herself. She found innumerable ways for newspapers to promote her articles and opinions, even her actions. For instance, her resignation from the Socialist Party became a multiweek newspaper feature. Along with the *Irish World*'s published account of her dispute and resignation, she penned countless letters to the editor over the next several weeks to keep the event before the public.[80] In similar fashion, she filled pages of the *Pilot*, Boston's Roman Catholic newspaper, with reports on CTG activities and its upcoming meeting schedule. Her belief in the power of the press knew no bounds, as she expressed in this statement:

> Above all the natural powers of wind and stream: above all the mechanical devices by which steam drives the loom and electricity draws the load; above all ingenuity of man in multiplying the material goods which feed, clothe and shelter the body, is the power of the press. It feeds the intellect and it takes possession of the human will. Turning out its hundreds of thousands of copies of its hundreds of thousands of editions of newspapers and books and magazines, pamphlets and leaflets of all kinds, the press floods the entire civilized world with literature—good, bad, indifferent. The power of the press is incalculable.[81]

An evangelistic organization that took a different tack with regard to material concerns was the Apostolic Faith Mission (AFM), founded in Portland in 1907 by the Pentecostal evangelist Florence Crawford. Rather than setting up a schedule in advance, the AFM held spontaneous street meetings advertised on placards attached to automobiles parked by a city park or on postcards dropped from an airplane. To pull it off with aplomb, the AFM exceeded other evangelistic organizations in its cutting edge use of multiple forms of transportation for advertisement and evangelism. Crawford's impulse for transportation technology remained unbridled, as she deftly embodied what historian Grant Wacker singled out as paramount for many first-generation Pentecostals—the pragmatic use of "the limited resources at their disposal to gain their purposes, sacred or otherwise."[82] Further, she accomplished this without financial solicitation beyond AFM members.

The AFM's reliance on transportation technology began modestly enough with a gospel wagon purchased for $250 in 1908. The organization only owned the wagon; horses had to be hired for each meeting. White canvas stretched tautly over each side of the wagon provided a surface for gospel slogans printed in large capital letters: PREPARE TO MEET THY GOD and TURN YE FOR WHY WILL YE DIE.[83] Within four years, the AFM traded the wagon for a Federal brand truck, complete with detachable seats for carrying literature. A dozen workers took the truck on its first evangelistic trip in 1913, driving more than three hundred miles from Portland, Oregon, to Vancouver, British Columbia. They followed the Oregon coastline, "distributing the papers through the mountain towns and isolated homes," then proceeded north into Washington, stopping in Tacoma and Seattle before heading across the Canadian border.[84]

Two years later, in August, 1915, four workers headed out from Tacoma in an Oldsmobile, nicknamed "Pathfinder," loaded with camping equipment strapped to the running boards, a trunk made for carrying large quantities of food, and a canvas sack holding over a thousand pieces of literature. For the six-thousand-mile transatlantic trip, they headed west to Salt Lake City, across to Chicago, over to Cincinnati and Pittsburgh, then to Washington, DC. On the way, they held evangelistic meetings and distributed literature hand stamped with these words: "This paper is handed to you from a Gospel Auto from the Apostolic Faith Mission, Front & Burnside Streets, Portland, Ore. Read Contents carefully." A different kind of automobile, a two-seated Dodge roadster known as "Scout," provided transportation throughout Oregon's and Washington's mountainous, rural districts, around horseshoe curves, and over rock slopes. Along the way, they placed literature into every mailbox, and at each schoolhouse and logging camp, the pair of workers stopped to hold an evangelistic meeting; one played the banjo and sang, the other told the gospel story. In all, Crawford's organization would purchase more than a dozen automobiles, enough to spread across multiple cities with an AFM mission—Seattle and Tacoma in Washington and Eugene, Dallas, and Portland in Oregon.[85]

To this fleet of cars, the AFM added a twenty-eight-foot motorboat, the *Morning Star*, used in harbor evangelism. Merchant ships with sailors from many countries docked in Portland's harbor, located about one hundred miles from the Pacific Ocean on the Willamette River. Apostolic Faith Mission workers steered the *Morning Star* alongside docked ships and used an extension ladder to climb aboard, when given permission, to distribute literature and invite sailors to nightly services at the downtown Portland mission. When captains prohibited their access on board, workers launched "gospel grenades," or "waterproof packets of papers and tracts in the language of the men on that ship."[86]

Factoring in the height differential between the *Morning Star* and a seagoing freighter, the grenades had to be thrown as high as fifty feet in the air to land on deck. Through harbor evangelism, the AFM sent the gospel message across the ocean, as sailors from other countries took the packets back home.

In addition to automobiles, trucks, and boats, the AFM purchased a three-passenger Curtiss Oriole biplane, *Sky Pilot*, in 1919 and pioneered aerial evangelism. Crowds gathered as the plane looped across the sky and wound down to land on a vacant field near a town. The pilot, Raymond Crawford, Florence's son, would then preach from the cockpit, which, like the CTG autovan, doubled as a pulpit. Once the plane was airborne, Crawford let loose thousands of pieces of AFM literature or copies of John's gospel over targeted areas that included Oregon's state penitentiary, reform schools, poor farms in Multnomah and Clackamas counties, and public parks throughout greater Portland on a Saturday afternoon. This practice only lasted for several years, until 1922, when "restrictions were made prohibiting the dropping of literature from the air" and the *Sky Pilot* was sold.[87]

Also different from other evangelistic organizations, the AFM played down material concern over fund-raising. Again, Crawford determined this practice. After preaching her first sermon in a Portland church, the pastor asked her to take over the congregation. Before agreeing, she stipulated that all requests for money cease immediately. The pastor was said to respond, "'Who is going to be responsible for the upkeep of this place if no collections are taken?" In sheer faith, she said, "'I will be responsible.'"[88] From then on, Crawford determined that the work would proceed entirely "on faith," meaning that she trusted God to supply all necessary funds through people's unsolicited generosity. She had a box mounted by the mission door to receive tithes and offerings, and the AFM became known as "a church without a collection plate," a practice that continues to this day.[89]

In keeping with Crawford's insistence on proceeding by faith, rather than by selling religious literature for profit to finance meetings, as other evangelistic organizations practiced, the AFM distributed its literature freely and widely by dropping it from the sky, launching it onto boats via gospel grenades, and mailing it across the world. Through its publication in many languages and distribution around the world, they believed that religious literature would act as a "silent missionary," making its way into places where an evangelist might not have access.[90] Literature distribution remains a characteristic of the AFM over a century later. According to a 2001 survey, more than 80 percent of the members in the Portland AFM church had participated in passing out religious literature.[91]

Material concerns, whether printing religious literature, changing the oil in a gospel car, writing an autobiography, or purchasing a plane, necessitated someone's attention. Certainly the more personnel available to carry out these tasks, the better, and the larger organizations fared better in this regard. Different from itinerant evangelists in the early part of the century who wandered alone from town to town, evangelists like Avery, Woodworth-Etter, and Crawford enlisted personnel to help with the many facets of an evangelistic meeting.

Personnel

The CTG initially recruited more than two dozen people, yet it never grew beyond the intrepid duo of Avery and Goldstein. Partly to blame, from all accounts, was Avery, who, paradoxically held herself aloof from and in charge of every organization she frequented. A 1922 photo in the *Boston Post* of an annual ball sponsored by the Philomatheia Club, a Catholic women's auxiliary for Boston College, captured Avery's dominant personality trait. In the photo, taken at Copley Plaza, all but one of the 1,799 guests line up shoulder to shoulder on the dance floor. One guest stands markedly apart and out in front. "Mrs. Martha Moore Avery is shown in the foreground," reads the last line of the photo caption."[92] Her physical stance in this photo replicated her approach to organizations and their members because, from her own admission, she felt duty bound to "mould" them to her opinions. When she perceived that Philomatheia Club members looked too longingly at Boston's Brahmin organizations, she curtly reminded them that their allegiance belonged only to Catholic clubs. When she wrote about this occasion in a letter to her daughter, she declared, "Sentiment for Harvard and for Radcliff not to mention the Women's City Club comes to the fore in our Philomatheia Club which is strictly Catholic. Our dear Lord gives me hard work to do—not to beat, but *to mould* the Club membership into a Catholic influence of so high an order that it shall impose Catholic culture upon an unwilling Boston."[93]

Avery's strident personality made it difficult for her *not* to be in charge. Because of this, rather than join a well-established Catholic organization with leadership solidly in place, she devoted her considerable energy—and hubris—to launching or expanding three organizations: Common Cause Society, Philomatheia Club, and the Catholic Truth Guild.[94] Tellingly, Avery never mentored another woman to succeed her in leadership or to lecture regularly at CTG meetings. It appears that only once, in September 1925, did a woman besides Avery address a CTG meeting; the speaker was Maud Green, a Fordham University graduate. A newspaper article commented that Green was only the second woman to lecture for the CTG.[95]

From a close read of Avery's voluminous writings, both fiction and nonfiction, I find that she held an innate belief in women's intellectual inferiority.[96] In a pamphlet written during her Socialist days, she divided women into two categories: "women of the heart and women of the intellect." Most women, she argued, fit the "heart" category; only a few could be cast as "of the intellect." To quote her, "There are few women of commanding greatness; few who stand at a mental elevation high enough to gain a vision of the new and necessary fraternal relationships, which alone will support an environment that will admit of the future advance of the race. While the great multitude of women ever dwell in the world of personal relationship, in the realm of the heart's emotion; live lives which are expressed through those they love, rather than in their own individuality."[97]

However, at least one woman, in Avery's estimation, combined both heart and intellect. Curiously, this woman, Mrs. Fanshaw, was a fictional character in a short story, "A Suggestion of Indian Summer." Fanshaw was "gifted with the deep heart of a woman, and the fire brain of a man." Purportedly, a man called Marcus O'Brien, Ph.D., wrote the short story; however, from all indications, including the fact that Avery often wrote under a male pseudonym, the story reads exactly as an autobiography of Avery in three respects: Mrs. Fanshaw, like Avery, was a former Socialist who converted to Catholicism; her daughter was a nun, like Avery's, who even had the same name in the convent as Avery's daughter (Rev. Mother St. Mary); and Mrs. Fanshaw's speech contained Avery's favorite phrases, such as "elevation of the race," "law of contrast," "light of reason," "First Cause," and the two types of women—"women of the intellect" and "women of intuition."

The story opens with Mrs. Fanshaw perusing a book on Marxian Socialism while she smiles inwardly because "at each successive point the author's 'good reasons' perforce gave way before her own better ones." Then comes a knock on the door, and Professor Strassor, the book's author, enters the room. From the ensuing dialogue, the reader quickly learns that these two previously enjoyed a romantic acquaintance, which might have led to a "sympathetic life together," but circumstances prevailed against the match. The rest of the story details their heated debate on Socialism versus Catholicism. Their irreconcilable differences on this subject diminish any hopes, on the professor's part, of rekindling their previous affection. In closing, Mrs. Fanshaw reflects on the difficulties facing a woman of intellect: "She knew, too, that intellectual women are too often tense—quite unlovely. That women should as a rule see intuitionally, from being pure in heart."[98]

Like her Mrs. Fanshaw character, Avery considered herself to be a woman of intellect, and as such, she distanced herself from ordinary women. In several letters to her daughter, Katherine, Avery expressed disdain for women's intellectual abilities. "Today twelve of the leading women of the most exclusive set of the 400 are to take a course on Political Economy with me. . . . Of course *I much prefer a class of men,* but these women ought to feel the weight of their responsibility sufficiently to learn what to do and how to do it."[99] She also made clear to Katherine her resentment toward women who attended Common Cause lectures because of their inattentiveness.

> At the Common Cause Sunday night my lecture was somewhat too philosophical for the bulk of the audience. I should like to keep at home some of the giggling women who insist upon having the front seats to the exclusion of the men who would like a fair chance. When the first negative said that I had "assasinated [sic] truth" these women giggled and kept it up. At last I arose and asked the Chairman if he would request the audience to treat our opponents [sic] with "Christian Courtesy." . . . They kept still after the Chairman put my request to them.[100]

At the same time, Avery recognized that intellectual women—like herself—did not enjoy access to opportunities afforded to men. Even though intellectual women, in her opinion, "are never at heart's ease outside an environment which gives them free and equal opportunities with men," they still faced gender restrictions.[101] She took it quite personally when Goldstein, her male protégé, had more occasions for speaking and writing than she did. To make matters worse, she served as a ghostwriter for his speeches and several articles published only with Goldstein's name. As she recounted to Katherine, "Today I wrote the last words of an article—*of course to go out in the Secretary's* [Goldstein's] *name* about lay street preaching for one third of a book gotten out by Father John A. O'Brien, Ph.D."[102] For several months, she even kept track in her diary of days she devoted to work on Goldstein's material:

Tues, Jan 1, 1907 . . . Edited work for Goldstein.
Fri, March 8, 1907 Edited Goldstein's letter to the Journal.
Sat, April 6, 1907 Edited Goldstein's article to the "Journal," in the morning
Sun, May 5, 1907 . . . Goldstein came in with his sketch of the Western Federation of Miners—worked from four o'clock until half past eight on it.
Mon, May 6, 1907 Edited Goldstein's article
Sun, July 14, 1907 At 12:00 I went over his speech with Goldstein for the Women's Trade Union Convention[103]

Her editing and writing for Goldstein continued until her death. In a letter to Katherine two months before she died, she wrote, "This is to tell you that I've just finished D.G. [David Goldstein] Fourth of July address—oration."[104]

Avery clearly begrudged praise heaped on Goldstein for something she had crafted. In one diary entry, she complained, "Boston Pilot referred editorially to my 'admirable lecture,' and to Goldstein's 'remarkable book.' I must exercise self-control when the credit of my book is given to another."[105] And she raged in letters to Katherine as well. About an article on lay street preaching published under Goldstein's name, she wrote, "A letter comes saying that the M.S. 'reads well' . . . Father wants personal data from the author. Sometimes it is hard to maintain the equities, since the author is really the woman not the man whose name is attached."[106] Again, about Goldstein's use of diagrams that she had created, she confided to her daughter, "Goldstein lecture at Fordham was a good success—it was hard that he should be the first, not myself, to use the diagrams which having originaled [sic] are dear to me, but I have been able to take it with a good grace."[107] Several years later, her resentment spilled out vehemently in this letter: "Next Sunday I give the opening lecture at the Common Cause. Please pray for me? I have not one single thought worked out as yet.... Drilling Goldstein in his new lecture takes not alone a lot of time but it is rather wearisome work when one must keep up an enthusiastic interest for so long a time—weeks, months even. I sometimes wonder what sort of an address I could give if I were to spend as much work over my own as upon Goldstein's lectures. But then, *he has a hundred opportunities to my one*; so I must be content to do my best work for another's credit—in this world."[108]

For his part, Goldstein readily acknowledged his indebtedness to Avery and often expressed it in his own correspondence with Katherine. "You know how dependent I am on your mother in order to carry out my part of the work we are doing."[109] Yet his most poignant statement about Avery appeared after her death, in his autobiography dedicated to "The Memory of Martha Moore Avery": "Is it any wonder that years of association with such an accomplished and generous person should make one, who never had the advantage of any formal education, fitted to play the part in public life that is to be recorded in this Autobiography of a Campaigner for Christ? I am eternally indebted to Mrs. Martha Moore Avery for the understanding and appreciation of the intellectual and moral standards and example, that have made many years of my life a joy and given to me the hope eternal that I pray will be realized."[110]

While Goldstein benefited from their work together, so did Avery. With him, she enjoyed a devoted *male* disciple, who had more occasions than she, especially on the lecture circuit, to express publicly the views they held in common. Further, beyond their work in common, she enjoyed his companionship; they were friends who went on excursions and even rented a house together in Maine for a summer. She accompanied him on visits to his parents, and he, in turn, corresponded regularly with her daughter. Goldstein's long-lasting friendship remained unique in her life because she had no other close relationships. Even her marriage to Millard Avery showed signs of strain long before his early death. During their ten-year marriage, he worked much of the time away from home as a traveling salesman. When Martha and Katherine moved to Boston in 1888, Millard did not accompany them; he died two years later. Considering her voluminous writings and letters, the silence surrounding her marriage speaks volumes. There is only one reference to her marriage. In her lengthy, rambling autobiography, she included this cryptic allusion to marital difficulties: "Still deeper currents of life's meaning were set running in my heart's blood. Heaven and hell mixed up together in hopeless confusion. No solid ground was under my feet, though an appearance of permanence was preserved and a most decorous quiet. 'My dear Mrs. Avery, your home life is delightful, so serene in its atmosphere' said Mrs. Lombard, the minister's wife."[111] Otherwise, she never mentioned her marriage again.

Avery appeared compliant with only one person—Boston's archbishop, William O'Connell. Being a woman of intellect, no doubt she recognized the benefit of securing the good graces of the Catholic hierarchy in Boston, which began and ended with O'Connell.[112] Avery and O'Connell met for the first time on May 7, 1911, and she raved about it in a letter to Katherine: "I had a red-letter day, yesterday. After coming from the Cenacle I called upon the Archbishop of Boston: 'Why have you not been to see me before? Mrs. Avery. I have missed seeing [sic] very much' said His grace. . . . His Grace and I talked of Catholic affairs most intermately [sic]."[113] Within a year, Avery described their association in familial terms: "As though I were his own sister the Cardinal wanted me to put his mind at rest regarding any possible time when I should be in financial stress. 'I have the money and you should not want, but should come and tell me if you ever need anything.'" She attached a postscript with the same warm sentiments: "With our great Cardinal it is like being with my very own—somehow my spiritual family connections are much closer than my blood relations."[114]

Avery's and O'Connell's agreement on every contemporary issue cemented their mutual regard, particularly their shared antipathy toward Socialism, the source of blatant evils, like feminism and women's suffrage. Both balanced their Socialist attacks with fervent appeals to patriotism. Certainly Avery concurred with O'Connell, who held that "devotion to God and loyalty to the country were indivisible in the hearts and souls of American Catholics."[115] Avery and Goldstein expressed a similar opinion about patriotism and religion in *Bolshevism: Its Cure*: it is "within, *not without*, love and loyalty to God reside love and loyalty to country."[116] O'Connell, in turn, approved the CTG's blend of patriotism and Catholicism and bestowed on it its motto, "For Faith and Fatherland."[117]

Throughout the tenure of the CTG, Avery and Goldstein held on to the reins of leadership. They gave the lectures and counseled behind the van; they wrote the publicity pieces, newspaper articles, and set up the meeting schedule. Other personnel had little to do besides put up and take down the autovan's moveable parts and distribute literature after the meeting. One can imagine that this limited role dampened the interest of potential workers in the CTG. The one exception, Arthur B. Corbett, held the position of CTG chairman for several years. Corbett also traveled as Goldstein's associate on CTG cross-country tours in the winter and handled the speaker's introduction. However, the expressed intention at the CTG's formation had been to train laymen and laywomen for open-air speaking. A letter sent out soliciting interested persons received good response, and some talk surfaced of a training course, yet nothing developed. Instead, the CTG revolved entirely around the efforts, even the finances, of Avery and Goldstein.[118] A comparable organization, the Catholic Evidence Guild, proved more successful in expanding the roster of speakers by establishing a training course with lectures on Catholic doctrine followed by oral and written examinations.[119] This course attracted enough participants to expand its number of locations. Eventually the Catholic Evidence Guild, not the CTG, spread into a handful of American cities in the 1930s.[120]

Similar to the CTG, Woodworth-Etter's evangelistic organization remained quite small, never more than a handful of personnel. Two men had prominent roles in the organization after Philo Woodworth's departure. Samuel Etter, her second husband, worked for twelve years until his death in 1914 as her ghostwriter, business manager, and assistant during the meetings. She commented that "it makes no difference what I call on him to do. He will pray, and preach, and sing, and is very good around the altar. He does about all of my writing, and he also helps in getting out my books, and looks after the meeting, in and outside."[121] However, Samuel, like Philo, also embarrassed her publicly, though for a very different reason; he battled chronic illnesses, quite an albatross for a faith-healing ministry. On one occasion, he accompanied her to Atlanta but remained housebound during her meetings because his acute rheumatism made it difficult to walk. When a reporter queried her inability to cure her own husband, she blamed him and exonerated herself. "He lacks faith. . . . Yes, I have tried to give him faith, and I think I have kept him alive by working over him and have kept his mind clean." She even pointed to God as a culprit: "Why hasn't he been cured? Well, God works in mysterious ways, His wonders to perform; and He must have some purpose in keeping my husband sick. I can't attempt to say why God does some things."[122] Eventually Samuel's condition made traveling with her impossible, so that when he died in Indianapolis on a Sunday afternoon, she was away from his bedside holding meetings in Philadelphia. She made a quick trip back for the funeral but returned to Philadelphia in less than a week to preach on Saturday evening. Even after his death, she reported that "carrying and caring" for him "from the Atlantic to the Pacific," while holding evangelistic meetings, weakened her own health and rendered her susceptible to pneumonia.[123]

Then August Feick took over as business manager, ghostwriter, and assistant pastor at the Woodworth-Etter Tabernacle in Indianapolis. He displayed the opposite personality of his mentor; unlike her on-the-spot preaching, he adopted a formal style complete with well-crafted sermon notes. These notes became sacrosanct. Once when the wind blew the "treasured sermon notes and scattered them along the countryside," in a panic, "he turned to Lydia Paino, a member of the gospel team, and broke the news she would be the speaker since he never preached without notes."[124]

A handful of women also participated in the Woodworth-Etter evangelistic organization over the years. They came up on stage during the preliminary singing and praying, sometimes giving a short talk before the sermon, then worked the altar as people came forward. One name, Emma Eisenberg, appeared several times in Woodworth-Etter's 1894 autobiography. Eisenberg had traveled with the organization for a year and a half, and Woodworth-Etter likened her to a daughter. "I believe God raised her up especially for me. No daughter could be more loving, kind and thoughtful of my comforts than she is. There is never anything too hard for her to do for me or the salvation of the people. God has wonderfully blessed her labors in bringing sinners to the fold."[125] Eisenberg undertook a variety of tasks, from calming a hostile mob before a meeting in a St. Louis tenement to nursing Woodworth-Etter during a bout of seasickness while traveling by steamer from Jacksonville to New York City. Then something bizarre occurred in the autobiographical narrative between the 1894 and 1912 versions; someone excised the name of every female worker. The 1912 edition reads as if women never worked for the organization, which, in Eisenberg's case, given Woodworth-Etter's expressed feelings about her, is extraordinary. Yet this practice of expunging names had happened before. The 1888 edition of Woodworth-Etter's autobiography, to cite one example, includes this description of a baptismal service at Boiling Springs, Illinois: "On the last day (Sunday) *we* baptized nine persons in a beautiful stream of water near the camp ground."[126] The "we" referred to Woodworth-Etter and a man named Smith, who had worked alongside her throughout the meeting. In the next edition, the "we" had been changed to "I," and the sentence read instead, "On the last day (Sunday) *I* baptized a number of converts, *assisted by Elder Smith.*"[127] This was not a onetime editorial mistake or oversight because nearly all of the "we" pronouns in the 1888 edition appeared as "I" in 1894.

A rationale for these changes would be to create an appearance of self-sufficiency, as if Woodworth-Etter required no one else's assistance. This would explain the wholesale change from "we" to "I." While plausible, it does not answer why some names were eliminated, particularly women's names, and not others. Considering the specific deletion of Eisenberg's name, most likely it can be traced to the difference in opinion between the two women regarding their denomination, the Churches of God, General Conference (Winebrenner). Whereas Woodworth-Etter severed the denominational connection in the face of mounting opposition against her, as discussed in the next chapter, Eisenberg remained a loyal supporter and an ordained minister in the denomination. Regardless of the reason, the elimination of Eisenberg's name implies that Woodworth-Etter, like Avery, had a prickly personality that rendered associations with co-workers, especially women, problematic.[128]

At the same time, we cannot overlook that Woodworth-Etter inspired the leading woman evangelist in the first half of the twentieth century and one of the most successful evangelists in America, Aimee Semple McPherson. On her cross-country trip to Los Angeles, she planned a stop in Indianapolis to visit with Woodworth-Etter. In a diary entry, McPherson wrote, "For years I have been longing to meet Sister Etter, and have been talking about it more in recent months. I have longed to hear her preach and be at her meetings. . . . Tomorrow Mrs. Etter's tabernacle will be open and I will have the desire of my heart. Glory!"[129] An influenza epidemic in the city nearly prevented the anticipated meeting, but officials lifted the ban shortly before the service, and the two women "rejoiced and praised the Lord together."[130]

Forging a different path from the CTG and Woodworth-Etter in terms of opening doors for women stood two other organizations: the Evangelistic Department of the WCTU and Billy Sunday's evangelistic organization. The WCTU, during Frances Willard's presidency, enlisted thousands of women as evangelists under the Evangelistic Department. This department, one of six established at the 1880 WCTU national convention, the year after Willard became president, sponsored evangelistic meetings, religious visits, church services, and Bible readings. In 1896 alone, Jennie Fowler Willing, a WCTU evangelist and secretary of the Department of Evangelistic Institutes and Training, gathered these statistics of the department's work from its many superintendents around the country: seventy-five thousand evangelistic meetings held, ten thousand religious visits made, six thousand church services given under the auspices of the WCTU, three thousand Bible readings given, four million pages of Christian temperance literature distributed, twenty thousand pledges made, and six thousand conversions.[131]

Willard made the case in *Woman in the Pulpit* that the Evangelistic Department provided an avenue for women who felt called to preach but were forbidden by their church. Speaking of these women, she observed:

> Nearly all of this "great host" who now "publish the glad tidings" are quite beyond the watch-care of the church, not because they wish to be so, but because she who has warmed them into life and nurtured them into activity is afraid of her own gentle, earnest-hearted daughters. The spectacle is both anomalous and pitiful. It ought not to continue. Let the church call in these banished ones, correlate their sanctified activities with her own mighty work, giving them the same official recognition that it gives to men, and they will gladly take their places under her supervision.[132]

For women tentative about preaching, like Elizabeth Baker, becoming involved in evangelism through a local WCTU unit provided a means of testing the waters. Newly married, Baker heard God ask an unsettling question: "Will you go into pulpits and preach for Me?" She responded negatively at first. "I had a great aversion to women in a pulpit. I had always felt that they were out of place, and that the many other spheres of usefulness in home, schools and church were quite sufficient, but now the Lord was asking me to do the thing I had so disliked in others." Eventually, after a back and forth struggle, she yielded. "'Lord,' I said with tears, 'if You can ever bring me where You can use me in speaking for Thee, I am willing to be brought.'"[133] Through her work in the WCTU Evangelistic Department in Rochester, New York, she began to speak at evangelistic meetings, then stepped into the leadership role of evangelistic superintendent for Monroe County. Eventually, she left the WCTU to develop, along with her sisters, a compound of fledgling Pentecostal institutions in Rochester, including Rochester Bible Training School, which is discussed in Chapter 3.

Woman's Christian Temperance Union evangelists pursued a variety of venues to share the gospel. Two African American women, Emma Ray and Amanda Berry Smith, engaged in interracial evangelism through the WCTU.[134] Amanda Berry Smith joined the WCTU in 1875, the year after it began, and quickly became a prominent national and international evangelist and singer for the predominantly white WCTU rallies. Her voice was the first "raised in prayer and praise within the walls of Willard Hall" at its dedication service. For an international WCTU gathering at Faneuil Hall in Boston, she sang "a weird plantation melody, full of the hope and heart-break of slavery days" whose effect, according to an observer, "was utterly indescribable."[135] She drew the attention of Lady Henry Somerset, the British WCTU leader, who invited her to speak in Great Britain and included her on the platform party at the 1893 WCTU world conference in London. In these venues, Smith's interracial cooperation in the WCTU ranged across the country and the ocean.

Emma Ray and a dozen women from Seattle's African Methodist Episcopal church launched a WCTU unit named after Frances Harper, a poet, writer, lecturer, abolitionist, women's rights activist, and first superintendent of colored work for the WCTU. Along with promoting temperance, they ministered to people living in the Yesler-Jackson area, a working-class, transient neighborhood south of downtown Seattle, replete with rooming houses, saloons, gambling spots, movie houses, and brothels. Despite, or perhaps because of, the women's creditable outreach, their minister complained about the "class of people" who received their ministrations. Evidently he wanted the women to focus on helping their own church, whose heavy debt needed their capable fund-raising activities. The minister's criticisms eventually prevailed, to the demise of the WCTU unit.

Although that unit disbanded, Ray remained active in WCTU work by attending meetings at a white unit. "I would attend the white unions," she recalled. "The women all seemed nice and sympathetic, and did all they could to help me. They said they were sorry, because we had sent in better reports than any other unions in the County."[136] Along with a few white workers and her husband, L. P. Ray, an honorary WCTU member, she visited in the jail and held evangelistic meetings using a bathtub as an altar. In recognition of this work, she was elected county superintendent of jail and prison work for the WCTU. She attempted one time to restart an African American WCTU unit at the suggestion of Lucy Thurman, national superintendent of colored work of the WCTU, who came to Seattle for the WCTU national convention, but this unit did not last long, either.

Another WCTU evangelist, Jennie Smith, served as the WCTU's national superintendent of the railroad department, which reached out to men in uniform, such as firefighters, police, streetcar drivers, postal workers, and railroad men, in particular. The department, among other activities, sponsored an annual, all-day reception for railroad workers with food, flowers, special music, scripture cards, and religious literature. For the reception hosted by the Philadelphia WCTU, the B. & O. Railroad offered "their dining room, table cloths, dishes, kitchen, cooks, and everything needed." A choir, quartet, soloists, and a series of speeches filled out the entertainment.[137] Smith had developed an affinity for railroad men thanks to their many courtesies when she, an invalid for sixteen years and restricted to a specially designed, moveable bed, traveled extensively by train. After her healing, she held meetings for railroad workers, often preaching in a freight yard during the lunch hour and distributing religious tracts in depots and baggage cars. Even at her meetings in churches or town halls, she invited men in uniform to sit in the front rows. Her uplifted hand indicating God's blessings on a passing freight train became her well-known gesture. Through the

WCTU's Evangelistic Department, evangelists like Jennie Smith, Emma Ray, Amanda Berry Smith, Elizabeth Baker, and Jennie Fowler Willing, both African American and white, volunteered their time to preach, teach, sing, visit, and supervise evangelistic work.

The Billy Sunday evangelistic organization, which at its apex required several thousand workers to carry out a campaign in an urban metropolis, enlisted women for a variety of volunteer and paid positions. Women in each city volunteered to sing in the two thousand to three thousand member choir or to write down the names of those who came forward during the altar call. In addition, nurses staffed the temporary hospital set up adjacent to the tabernacle. Along with these local volunteers, for the largest campaigns, like New York City, the organization hired seventy-five clerks and stenographers to manage the preliminary correspondence and preparatory details beginning a year in advance. Further, at least fifteen women through the years, according to historian Margaret Bendroth, joined "the Sunday party," the closest associates of Billy Sunday's who traveled with him and Helen.[138] Most worked as musicians or Bible teachers, like Grace Saxe and Virginia Asher, who regularly spoke to crowds of several hundred women. At a meeting led by Asher, "One observer recalled with evident pleasure a meeting in Atlanta where 'there wasn't a man in sight, except the janitor.'"[139]

Helen Sunday held a unique role in the organization as business manager and Billy's spouse and closest confidante. At first, she stayed home with the couple's four children and advised Billy and the organization from afar, but this entailed a triple-shift for her as a single parent, long-distance administrator of the campaigns, and counselor to Billy, whose spirits often dipped when away from home. After several years of juggling these demands, Helen fell prey to exhaustion and hives. In 1907, Helen and Billy decided to travel the campaign circuit together; Billy preached, Helen managed the organization. A beloved nanny stayed with the two younger children still at home. During the summers, the Sunday family traveled together to evangelistic meetings.

In an interview, Helen catalogued the different strengths that she and Billy brought to the organization:

> You know, we have thought of coming [to New York] many times before this, but I never would consent until I was sure everything would be

done properly. It wasn't enough to have a committee of one hundred. It wasn't enough to have the influential men in New York give us their money or even their sympathy. They had to be willing to work. I knew what it meant to tackle New York. Mr. Sunday didn't. He is always so wrapped up in the campaign of the moment that he can't make any plans for the future. I'm the one that has to look ahead.[140]

After the New York City campaign, Billy's popularity waned, the campaign schedule slowed, the size of the hosting cities decreased, and the organization required fewer paid staff. Helen continued to manage the campaigns and travel with Billy, but she had more time for their now adult children, who struggled with a myriad of financial, marital, emotional, and health issues. She lived long enough to bury Billy and their four children. At Billy's deathbed in 1935, Helen experienced her own call to preach when, at age sixty-eight, she beseeched God for direction:

I put my head on Billy's forearm as he lay there dead, and I said, "Lord, if there's anything left in the world for me to do, if you'll let me know about it, I want to promise you that I'll try to do it the best I know how." I want to admit to you that I didn't see one single thing left for me to do! Billy was my job. We had lived together for forty-seven years—we had traveled together for thirty-nine years in the work—and he was *gone!* There just didn't seem to be anything left for me to do!

When requests came for her to speak at several memorial services for Billy, on first impulse, she wanted to decline, though before she did, her prayer came to mind:

So, I just stood there and shut my eyes, and I said, "Lord, is this You speaking to me through these two men from New York State?" . . . It just seemed as though I heard Him say, "Why, certainly! Why not? Of course!" So I opened my eyes, and I said to one of the men, "When do you want me?" And he said, "I'd like to have you come a week from Tuesday night." I hurriedly counted the days and the dates, and I said, "Why that's dad's birthday! That would make it the nineteenth of November." He said, "I know it would. That's why I want you to come to Buffalo then." And so I told him I'd be there.[141]

She then embarked on twenty-two years of preaching at evangelistic meetings. In 1935, the Presbyterian Church granted her official permission to work as an evangelist. The document's wording recognized Helen Sunday, who "assisted her husband in his evangelistic meetings in all parts of the United States, organizing the committees and directing the business, and preaching whenever Mr. Sunday was unable to do so."[142] The Interdenominational Evangelistic Association also certified her as an evangelist, and she served as a member of its board of directors. As she preached across the country, she shared the platform with the next generation of American evangelists, including Billy Graham. Before she died in 1957, she expressed delight that "God has let me do my little part here and there."[143]

Helen Sunday simultaneously exemplified and defied women's roles as defined by the most conservative wing of American Protestantism, known as Fundamentalism.[144] On the one hand, she demonstrated sacrifice and devotion to her family, from birth to death. Even her autobiography, *"Ma" Sunday Still Speaks*, centered mostly on Billy's career. Some have said she only preached on two subjects: Billy Sunday and Jesus Christ.[145] Beyond her own family, she extolled women to take care of the home front in an article, "The Woman Who Didn't Like to Cook," featured in her newspaper column, *Ma Sunday's Column*, published during 1917–18. "It seems to me that it is as important for a woman to cook well for a man as it is to pray well for him."[146]

On the other hand, she moved beyond familial expectations when she left the children with a nanny so that she could travel with Billy. This decision, according to historian Michael Hamilton, reflected the priority accorded to full-time Christian service among Fundamentalists. "The Fundamentalist imperative to service always implied that, beyond earning a livelihood and attending to family responsibilities, more was required of both women and men."[147] In her article, "Having Faith in Women," Helen directed women to obey God, not a man: "The world's ideas about women are changing rapidly. The old question used to be: 'What does the man want the woman to be?' The present question seems to be worded: 'What does a woman want herself to be?' But, in the future, we shall come to asking the right question: 'What does God want a woman to be?'"[148]

Helen Sunday's situation highlights the multiple demands on women who engaged in public evangelism and institution building while simultaneously tending to family matters. Particularly with young children, women could not easily demarcate the private from the public, as did their male counterparts, because they had dual responsibilities. At home, women were expected to raise the children, support their spouse, keep domestic affairs running smoothly, and maintain a religious atmosphere. The sacredness of the family in both Protestantism and Roman Catholicism, particularly in its impartation of "domestic values [that] were eternal, unchanging and God-given," depended largely on the woman's efforts.[149] At the same time, as evangelists, they had to reckon with the call to be a religious teacher beyond their home. Evangelism and institution building required an arduous schedule of traveling, preaching, fund-raising, and overseeing property away from home, all of which conflicted with the religious nurture of their own family. No doubt this multipronged exertion by women, who had to negotiate their roles as evangelists, mothers, and wives, helps to understand the difficulties that emerged in their marriages, as we discover in the next chapter.

Male evangelists, in contrast, did not have to manage the home front while simultaneously preaching and overseeing evangelistic meetings in the public square. They were free to travel as their itinerary unfolded, without family encumbrances; their dependents simply conformed to their schedule, even as Helen and the children accommodated Billy's campaigns. Similarly, Dwight Moody never had to consider child care, because Emma Moody took care of their children, whether the family was at home in Massachusetts or traveling on his preaching tours in America and Great Britain.

Still, for all the accomplishments of women like Avery, Woodworth-Etter, and Crawford, who founded and led evangelistic organizations, they neither specifically mentored nor purposefully paved the way for women to succeed them. Avery clearly preferred a male disciple like Goldstein, though she resented his easy access to writing and speaking opportunities. Likewise, Woodworth-Etter had a more successful track record with male workers. Crawford, as we see in the next chapter, groomed her son, not her daughters, to assume leadership of the AFM. This checkered history will continue to unfold as we now turn to churches and denominations.

Bishop Mary Lena Lewis Tate. Courtesy of the Lewis-Tate Foundation and Archives, The Church of the Living God, the Pillar and Ground of the Truth, Inc.

Pillar of Fire workers outside of the Zarephath Post Office. Courtesy of the Pillar of Fire Archives.

2

Mothers, Saints, Bishops

Churches and Denominations

And the one and only mother of the Church at present and in the future shall be Saint Mary Magdalena, the first mother and Chief Overseer of the present and future Church, through whom this Church is resurrected and established. Therefore she alone shall ever be recognized and called the mother of the Church. During life and after her death she shall be remembered as the mother of the Church of the Living God, the Pillar and Ground of the Truth. And no mother nor father shall be named for this Church nor reverenced as such after her.[1]

When Mary Lena Lewis Tate, whose titles extended to "mother," "Saint Mary Magdalena," "chief overseer," "first revivor," "president," and "bishop," first "felt moved by the Holy Spirit of God to go out into the world and preach the gospel," she began close to home, journeying thirty miles away from Dickson to Steel Springs, Tennessee.[2] Soon, however, the miles this African American woman traveled extended to several hundred as she crossed state lines into Kentucky and Illinois. Along the way, she gathered converts first into "Do Rights" bands, then into a church, which came to be called the Church of the Living God, the Pillar and Ground of the Truth. As the churches continued to multiply in several states, in 1908, she held a general assembly in Greenville, Alabama, where she, now as Bishop Tate, presided over a denomination.

Certainly women evangelists in the generation before Tate traveled as extensively. From her home base in Philadelphia, African Methodist Episcopal evangelist Jarena Lee itinerated to preach throughout New

England, north into Canada, and west into Ohio. She traveled by foot, stagecoach, and boat to preach in churches, schools, homes, camp meetings, and town halls. In her autobiography, she paused at several points to catalogue her ministry in numerical terms, adding up miles traveled and sermons preached: "That year I traveled two thousand three hundred and twenty-five miles, and preached one hundred and seventy-eight sermons. Praise God for health and strength, O my soul, and magnify his name for protection through various scenes of life."[3] Yet Lee kept itinerating and never stopped to set up any association for converts after the altar call. She established no Sunday School, no prayer group, no church or denomination. After a series of meetings, as she explained in her autobiography, she left those affected by her preaching "in the hands of God" and moved on to the next venue: "I was next sent for by the servant of a white gentleman, to hold a meeting in his house in the evening. He invited the neighbors, colored and white, when I spoke according to the ability God gave me.... I tried also to preach three times at a place 14 miles from here—had good meetings—backsliders were reclaimed and sinners convicted of sin, *who I left in the hands of God*, with the hope of meeting and recognizing again 'when we arrive at home.'"[4] Lee's statement reveals complete trust and confidence in divine providence, but it also underscores the absence of any post-meeting association. In this regard, Lee exemplified other nineteenth-century women evangelists— "strangers and pilgrims"—such as Harriet Livermore, Nancy Towle, Zilpha Elaw, and Julia Foote.[5] In their zeal to preach the gospel, they braved opposition and ridicule from family and strangers, dangers along their travels, hunger and thirst, and sporadic sleeping arrangements, but they did not extend their evangelistic work beyond the meeting. Those touched by the message were on their own reconnaissance to locate a nearby church or prayer meeting for further fellowship.[6]

In the Progressive Era, women evangelists, like Tate, shifted this practice markedly and convened an association as the finale to the evangelistic meeting. Maria Woodworth-Etter first formed a Sunday School or prayer group, then transitioned to planting churches in strategic midwestern cities like Indianapolis and St. Louis. Mary Lee Cagle founded churches in southwestern states for the New Testament Church of Christ, a small Wesleyan/Holiness denomination started by her first husband. Alma White's vision for an independent association commenced as a downtown Denver rescue mission and multiplied into a multifaceted, international denomination, the Pillar of Fire. At its apex, White had incorporated into the denomination more than eighteen schools, fifty pieces of property, several radio stations, and many churches. Florence Crawford moved to Portland, Oregon, to spread Azusa Street's apostolic faith message to the Pacific Northwest and launched the Apostolic Faith Mission (AFM), now a denomination that extends around the globe.

Theirs is a mixed legacy that prompts both admiration and apprehension. Each of these women heard God's call to evangelism and institution building in the midst of severe sickness or wrenching personal experiences, like Woodworth-Etter's burying five of her six children. Her interpretation, that God purposefully removed them because they blocked her ability to obey the call to evangelism, is alarming, yet she channeled her grief into preaching the gospel and church planting throughout the Midwest. Most held complete authority over their followers, like Alma White, who micromanaged every detail of the Pillar of Fire, yet she established a string of churches and schools from New Jersey to Los Angeles, even across the Atlantic into greater London. Most had tortured marriages, like Tate who divorced three husbands, yet she persevered to start a denomination and become perhaps the first African American woman bishop. In the pages ahead, I do not leave their flaws unearthed or foibles untended. At the same time, I highlight the accomplishments of these women religious leaders who pioneered mixed-gender churches and denominations across America.

Churches

After her first marriage ended in divorce, Tate took her two young sons and traveled from Tennessee to Paducah, Kentucky, where her sister lived. There her call to preach became even stronger, so she embarked on her first preaching tour—alone. A dramatic scene ensued when she parted from her sons, as reported in the denomination's official account: "Being poor and financially unabled [sic] to carry her two little sons with her, she left them standing on the banks of the Ohio River gazing with eyes filled with tears as she sailed on the Ohio River from Paducah to Brooklyn, Illinois. The two little boys wept and looked on that old vessel that moves with their mother, who is now the mother and Chief Overseer of the Church until in the distance and dense fog of the Ohio River, the vessel finally disappeared with mother on board."[7] Tate gathered converts into small groups or bands known as the "Do Rights," so named because members responded to her message by wanting to "do right." These associations in Illinois, Missouri, Kentucky, and Tennessee began to purchase property in order to have a meeting place for their worship services of song, testimony, Bible study, and preaching. In 1903, a new name for the organization was revealed to Tate's younger son, Felix, and the "Do Rights" became the Church of the Living God, the Pillar and Ground of the Truth.[8]

Even though a church emerged from her itinerant evangelism, Tate did not leave home with this goal in mind; she simply made her way initially, like Lee, beyond hearth and home out of obedience to the call to preach. And she found success. As people gathered around her preaching, she faced the dilemma of what to do with the converts. She had not even found a church suitable for herself. Although she married into Methodism with her first husband, David Lewis, she experienced a critical divergence between "the precepts of organized religion and the observable inconsistent practice of its proponents."[9] To put it simply, she found churchgoers hypocritical and churches apostate. Thus, she neither remained long within Methodism nor joined any other existing organized church. Now, however, she had followers to consider, and no church consistent enough with her belief and practice to keep them on track. Historian George Marsden finds this scenario to be true for each generation of reformers within American Protestantism "since the first reformers set foot on Plymouth Rock." They faced the pressing question: "Must they separate from corrupted denominations?"[10] Tate answered the question, as did Crawford, Cagle, White, and Woodworth-Etter, by quitting "corrupted denominations" and beginning anew. In this regard, each one embraced a restorationist vision that aimed "to recover some important belief or practice from the time of pure beginnings that believers are convinced has been lost, defiled, or corrupted."[11]

The institution building of churches and denominations by these women coincided with the precipitous growth of voluntary associations across the country. Many constituencies—women, men, youth, blue-collar workers, trade unionists, African Americans, and adherents of Judaism, Catholicism, and Protestantism—either formed a new association or markedly increased membership in an existing one. "From the Red Cross to the NAACP, from the Knights of Columbus to Hadassah, from Boy Scouts to the Rotary club, from the PTA to the Sierra Club, from the Gideon Society to the Audubon Society, from the American Bar Association to the Farm Bureau Federation, from Big Brothers to the League of Women Voters, from the Teamsters Union to the Campfire Girls," these stalwart associations exemplified the Progressive Era proclivity to gather like-minded people around a common goal.[12] In statistical terms, the growth rate of voluntary associations exceeded even the nation's rapid rise in population, in the range of twenty-five million, between 1870 and 1914, largely due to immigration. As impressive, the highest growth rate in voluntary associations occurred in midwestern and western towns and cities with fewer foreign-born residents, like Kokomo, Denver, St. Louis, and Cincinnati, where women evangelists most often established their post-meeting associations.[13]

Before proceeding further, we pause to consider a long-standing difference among scholars about whether churches and denominations actually qualify as voluntary associations. C. R. Henderson, writing during the Progressive Era, specifically excluded the church, family, and state from consideration based upon his definition of a voluntary association as "that form of social cooperation in which the conscious choice of each member determines his membership." The absence of "the self-determining element" in the church, family, and state, according to Henderson, precluded them from consideration as voluntary associations. Perhaps an additional rationale, at least for excluding the church, can be traced to his opinion that it is a static, fossilized body, legendary for "rigidity and conservatism," which "can readily be made over by the combined efforts of a small circle of advanced thinkers."[14] More recently, in their book on voluntary associations, Constance Smith and Anne Freedman upheld Henderson's assessment that individual choice ranks as the deciding factor in what constitutes a voluntary association, and being born into an association negates choice. "Members are not born into such associations as they are into the family or the church."[15] Curiously, Smith and Freedman *do* consider religious organizations as voluntary associations within ethnic communities, yet they offer no reason for this amendment.[16]

An opposing opinion, proffered by historian Arthur Schlesinger and upheld by contemporary historians, such as Gerald Gamm, Robert D. Putnam, and Mary Ryan, claims religious associations to be voluntary owing to the constitutional separation of church and state.[17] Thus, they argue that unlike one's birth into a family or a state, church membership occurs by choice. Truly, personal choice by the first generation of members did circumscribe the churches formed by Tate and the other women evangelists because these were brand-new associations. No one was born into them; rather, individuals voluntarily chose to congregate with others who shared similar religious experiences during the evangelistic meeting.

Once safely ensconced in their own church, founders turned with animosity toward other churches. They critiqued the encroaching middle-class values invading the churches as represented, in their view, by liturgical services held in Gothic Revival sanctuaries from the mid-nineteenth century, whose style was both "splendid, [and] expensive."[18] Historian Ann Taves enumerates this "ever widening gulf" in the late nineteenth century as that between "religion of the church and the religion of the camp meeting."[19] Woodworth-Etter labeled the first kind of church as worldly because it had obviously "lost its power." "Oh, the spiritual death that has come over the churches in this part of the country! They have drifted into formality and gone out after the world," she complained."[20] Tate went so far as to pronounce "damnation in wearing the wrong church name" and "salvation in wearing the right church name." She condemned as false any other name for a church besides that "revealed by brother Paul to his Bible student, Timotheus, in 1 Timothy 3:15" and those who promoted other names she considered to be "wicked men and women." And what name did Paul choose? In the King James Bible, the verse in Paul's first letter to Timothy reads this way: "But if I tarry long, that thou mayest know how thou oughtest to behave thyself in the house of God, which is the church of the living God, the pillar and ground of the truth" (1 Tim. 3:15). In her biblical literalism, the belief that "exegesis is best when it is as literal as credibility can stand," Tate simply connected the phrase, "house of God," to the rest of the verse.[21] From this simple equation, she claimed that the church called by this name—Church of the Living God, the Pillar and Ground of the Truth—is "the House of God."[22] There is none other.

One of the so-called apostate churches to come under fierce attack by these founders was Catholicism, especially from Alma White, whose anti-Catholicism and racism prompted her support in the 1920s for the Ku Klux Klan. She published three books—*The Ku Klux Klan in Prophecy* (1925), *Klansmen: Guardians of Liberty* (1926), and *Heroes of the Fiery Cross* (1928)—that simultaneously drew the Klan into the deep waters of "Protestant American identity" and "demonized Catholicism," according to historian Lynn Neal. Scores of visual images throughout these books drawn by the Pillar of Fire artist, the Reverend Branford Clarke, cement White's holy trio—the Klan, the Bible, Protestant America—which would prevail against "the enemies threatening Christian civilization (the United States)," that is, Catholicism.[23] Her biographer, historian Susie Stanley, also characterizes White's Klan involvement as "an unholy alliance," though she cites anti-Catholicism more than racism as the motivating factor.[24] Still, White's racism and anti-Catholicism, as Neal argues, demonstrate a "religious intolerance" for anyone outside of Protestant America, and within Protestantism, for any church besides the Pillar of Fire.[25]

Methodism also came under critical scrutiny. Each woman founder had attended a Methodist church previously, and each found much to disparage. White declared that God had in former times raised up Methodism as the true church, but its holy zeal had dwindled; it no longer held the apple of God's eye. Using a boat metaphor, she described Methodism as "an old painted hulk, with no power, no fire, and no steam, —simply a towed-in vessel that will never plow the billows of the story deep again."[26] Her ideas filtered down to Pillar of Fire members, as evident in letters sent back to the denomination's headquarters. One member reported a conversation she had with a Methodist woman in Pikesville, Maryland, who "sees a good bit of what is wrong with the churches. She says she is going to stop eating meat, since talking with us, and would like very much to visit Zarephath. I wish you would pray for her."[27]

A very different encounter occurred between a Pillar of Fire member and a Methodist minister in Kansas: "Xmas. day I went in a resturant

[sic] selling the litature [sic]. Two men were playing checkers. One subscribed for the Metropolitan and I found the other was the Methodist preacher. I was honestly so shocked I could hardly say a word for a second. I finialy [sic] talked to him about it and told him if he would read our litature [sic] awhile he might find he needed good genuine salvation."[28] Seemingly, this member had also taken to heart White's antipathy toward mainline Protestant ministers. White likened them to "great vampires" who "fasten themselves on the public and draw large salaries."[29] She criticized them for leading their congregations astray by introducing them to popular, theological innovations spawned by Charles Darwin or Horace Bushnell, rather than sticking to the long-standing, often unpopular message of what she considered to be "true religion." As she explained, "The modern pulpits are largely occupied by men who refuse to preach the truth themselves or let others do so. They and their official boards would no more let fire-baptized ministers of the Gospel preach to their worldly congregations than the Pharisees and masters in Israel would have allowed John the Baptist to preach in their synagogues in his day."[30]

White's first stirrings to separate from Methodism awakened in reaction to Methodist ministers in Colorado who, in her opinion, opposed women preachers as well as the doctrine of sanctification, two issues she held sacrosanct. She and her husband, Kent, a Methodist minister, relocated to Denver in 1896 to set up their own work: a downtown rescue mission that sponsored street meetings, distributed clothing to the poor, and opened a school to train workers for the mission. After five years of running the mission and preaching in nearby states, Alma decided over Kent's objections to break from Methodism and form an independent church with converts from her evangelistic work. She organized the Pentecostal Union Church, later to be renamed the Pillar of Fire, on December 29, 1901, in Denver. Because she now had responsibility for churches and mission work in four western states and oversight for forty pastors and evangelists, she set up her ordination the following year; three signatures appear on the official paper: Kent White, Seth Rees, and Frida Rees, an evangelist and Seth's wife.[31]

In her rationale for a separate church, White included several statements that divulge a great deal more about her marriage and her self-perception:

During the weeks of my absence the Lord spoke to me definitely about organizing an independent church. The difficulties of such an undertaking were inconceivably great, especially since my husband and many of our people thought it would be a great mistake. The experience I had had in missions where false shepherds would use every available means to carry off the lambs—capture my converts—was sufficient to show me what we should have to contend with in taking a definite step toward organization. . . . The question of how to save those who were converted under my ministry had been a great problem for seven years. In spite of all efforts to keep them satisfied with mere membership in the missions where most of them had been converted, some had been persuaded by false shepherds that this was not sufficient and were drawn away into the cold, formal churches where they soon died spiritually.[32]

First, the reference to Kent's objection underscores their marital discord and eventual estrangement for many years until his death. When Kent embraced Pentecostalism, he separated from Alma and the Pillar of Fire because she refused to endorse speaking in tongues. After he left her and their two sons to work with a Pentecostal mission, she retaliated by publishing *Demons and Tongues*, in which she assailed the evils of the signature Pentecostal doctrine—speaking in tongues. In a poignant passage, which again referenced their alienation on account of Kent's Pentecostal experience, at least from her perspective, she wrote: "I know of some who have been so hardened under the influence of this demoniacal power that they are entirely unlike what they once were. They turn away in cold indifference from those who are suffering on their account, and manifest no sympathy toward those whose hearts they are breaking or have broken."[33] Believing it to be God's will, in 1921, eleven years after Kent moved out, Alma filed a complaint against him for desertion. The case was eventually dismissed, according to her, after he "had been required to make certain promises in the restoration of his family relationships."[34]

Another statement in the rationale reveals White's self-perception as a Christ figure who, like Jesus, the Good Shepherd (John 10:11–18), had responsibility to tend her lambs, her converts. Just as Jesus had to watch out for thieves, bandits, strangers, and wolves who enter the sheepfold to injure the lambs, so she had to contend with "false shepherds [who] would use every available means to carry off the lambs—capture my converts." These false shepherds led cold, formal churches, which sapped spiritual vitality from her converts when they left her fold for one of these. Repetitive of Tate's vision, White believed that in these last days, God had raised up the Pillar of Fire as *the true* church. Supplanting old time Methodism, only the Pillar of Fire held the beacon of gospel light in the midst of apostate churches and a world gone awry. "We knew God had placed the Pillar of Fire in the breach for the last days, to fill a place that no other Church could fill. The old denominations had lost their efficiency and power to be a vital force in the winding up of the Gentile Age. A new movement was necessary to enlighten the people on spiritual and national issues. We had been doing this for twenty-one years."[35]

A similar refrain about Methodism sounded from Woodworth-Etter, who early in her evangelistic work held many meetings in Methodist churches, which she stamped with unflattering adjectives and phrases, such as "dead," "very weak," "contentious," "few in working order," and "a valley of dry bones."[36] She relished holding meetings at these churches, particularly if no evangelist had succeeded previously, because she wanted to be the change agent to revive it with an influx of energetic, spiritually alive members, such as the Methodist church in Pleasant Mills, Indiana. "I could only find six who had any experience; they were discouraged. Even the minister had no hope of it being built up again. The Baptists were strong there, and there was contention between the churches. A good many of the brethren advised me not to go; but I thought if it was such a hard place, work was needed there worse than anywhere else."[37] As a result of her meetings, new members joined the Methodist church. Likewise, in Van Wert, Ohio, not only did the large, forsaken-looking Methodist Church, surrounded by weeds several feet high and ready for the real estate market, blossom with her converts, but the resultant attendance boost also secured the appointment of a new minister.

After a season of reviving "dead" churches, Woodworth-Etter, who understood well "the value of conserving the results of evangelistic efforts," established her own associations apart from an existing church.[38] She first organized Sabbath schools and prayer meetings. After two weeks of meetings six miles from her home in "The Devil's Den," notorious for its "infidelity and skepticism," she organized "a Sabbath-School of one hundred and fifty scholars, and put in a man for superintendent who had been a noted drunkard; appointed two prayer-meetings for each week, and established meetings every Sabbath. Different ministers promised to furnish them with preaching."[39] She maintained regular communication with these associations, reuniting with them as she traveled nearby and tapping them for workers at her meetings.

She then shifted her institution-building strategy to starting churches in midwestern cities like St. Louis in Missouri and Indianapolis, Anderson, and Kokomo in Indiana. An article in a Kokomo newspaper described the protocol she followed when setting up a church:

> When the series of meetings were nearing their close, there was a feeling entertained by many that there should be a church formed for the benefit of those who were without a religious home. There was, accordingly, a mass meeting held by those interested in the work to consider this question. This meeting appointed a committee of thirteen to formulate resolutions, and this committee brought in a report recommending the organization of an independent church... the Bible to be its only creed, and Christian character its only test of fellowship. This report was adopted by the mass meeting, which at once appointed a committee on the reception of members.[40]

If religious terms are excised from this account, it reads like an organizing session for any voluntary association: a planning meeting to appoint a committee charged with the task of forming resolutions for an association that will receive members once a second committee has been formed to decide the basis of membership.

To cement a new church, Woodworth-Etter instituted a baptismal service at the close of her meetings. In Anderson, Indiana, she held a group baptism for 194 converts in the White River. With arms locked together, the baptismal candidates formed a procession and marched four abreast from the campground to the river, where they gathered on a pier of wide planks extending thirty feet into the river. She led each one to the end of the pier, then handed them over to a minister who performed the immersion baptism. A crowd of several thousand lined both banks of the river to witness the event.

She did not settle in to pastor these fledgling churches, even though she was an ordained minister for over two decades with the Churches of

God, General Conference (Winebrenner). She either left behind one of her workers who had helped with the meeting or requested the denomination to appoint a minister. However, these churches quickly developed the reputation within the denomination of being difficult to pastor. Whereas the presence of ecstatic phenomena became customary at her meetings, as we saw in Chapter 1, the stationary pastor responsible for membership cultivation did not necessarily relish such eruptions. Conflict often broke out between her converts and the pastor once she left town. In an 1889 issue of the denomination's journal, the phrase "herculean task" appeared in a discussion about how to pastor a Woodworth-Etter church: "Touching the revival work of Sister Woodworth I have this to say: 1. In her revivals she gathered people of all mental and moral grades, and of all religious beliefs, as well as many who were avowed skeptics. 2. To harmonize these in one Church of God is a *herculean* task. It requires patience and special tact. Where men took hold of this work with these qualifications they have succeeded admirably. Where men failed to possess qualifications to harmonize contrary elements they most signally failed."[41]

The push/pull between stationary pastor and itinerant evangelist raged elsewhere. In an editorial, titled "More Pastors Needed," in a Wesleyan/Holiness newsletter, the anonymous author praised pastors and vilified evangelists:

> The woods are full of evangelists, but what a great help it would be to the work if it had a few more good pastors. Most any person, if he can be anything at all, can be an evangelist; but not so with a pastor. If a man can lead a meeting and can talk a little and give out an invitation, he can be an evangelist.... An evangelist holds meetings from place to place to place; in fact, it is this moving about that saves the people and the man from desperation and ruin. A pastor has to stay by the flock in time of trouble, and live down and pray out of the bother that he or the devil may stir up. When things go hard, an evangelist can move on and get away from the battle. Not that all do that, but as a usual thing, it is considered an indication that their work is done in that place; and so they leave.[42]

In Woodworth-Etter's case, eventually the setbacks and challenges of argumentative churches overshadowed the membership gains from her evangelistic work, and the denominational hierarchy revoked her ordination credentials.

Further complicating matters, a social class divide in the Churches of God, General Conference (Winebrenner), at the end of the nineteenth century separated the increasingly respectable, upwardly mobile, middle-class core members from the unsavory, living on the fringe characters attracted to Woodworth-Etter's rapturous meetings. The official word from the denomination claimed that she attracted "heterogeneous elements" of a "proverbially inferior order," which explained why, in their estimation, her churches exhibited "little cohesion."[43] A contemporary denominational historian offers this explanation: "In the 1880s the Churches of God were much more zealous to convert doctors and lawyers than to convert coal miners and factory workers. In her selection of audiences, Mrs. Woodworth's taste was as bad as John Wesley's or George Whitefield's."[44] The reason notwithstanding, it is true that some of her churches remained vibrant only for a few years, like the church in Anderson, Indiana. Within a decade after the impressive baptismal service, the church incurred a large debt owing to a dwindling membership. The denomination published this official report: "The church at Anderson in 1898 had become so weakened that an appeal was made to the Board of Missions of the General Eldership to appoint a missionary to Anderson, Greensburg and Williamstown. The mortgage on the Anderson property was foreclosed and its sale finally effected." This same situation recurred elsewhere. In Indiana alone, where "eleven fields of labor" once existed in 1895, within three years only seven still operated.[45]

The one exception to Woodworth-Etter's pattern of founding a church then moving on remains to this day her most enduring one. The nondenominational Lakeview Church in Indianapolis, which started in 1918 as the Woodworth-Etter Tabernacle, continues as a thriving congregation.[46] She stayed on to pastor the congregation and lived next door until her death. As with many momentous decisions in her life, she claimed to receive a vision for the exact location to build the five-hundred-seat Tabernacle: "God showed me one night that I was to build a tabernacle here at West Indianapolis, Indiana, so that people from all parts of the country could come in and spend some time in a good spiritual mission, and get established in God. He showed me that the meetings should be of oldtime fashion and power, where people can get spiritual food to supply their needs for soul and body."[47]

While White and Woodworth-Etter found mainline Methodism insufficient in spiritual power, the Free Methodist Church, a Wesleyan/Holiness denomination that broke from mainline Methodism in 1860, also came under scrutiny by R. L. Harris and Mary Lee Wasson Harris Cagle. Mary grew up in a Methodist church in rural Alabama and experienced conversion as a teenager. Immediately, she became a successful evangelist to her fifteen classmates. From this experience, she discerned a call to Christian work, but her family's hostile response eventually quelled her enthusiasm. Her mother "bitterly opposed her," and her brother-in-law declared that if she ever followed through on her call to preach, his children—her nieces and nephews—would be prohibited from acknowledging their aunt. Five years later, when she heard the Free Methodist evangelist R. L. Harris, the "Texas Cow-Boy Preacher," expound on sanctification, not only did "Holy Ghost conviction" seize her, but also her "old time call to preach" reawakened.[48]

Mary married Harris, and together they held evangelistic meetings in Tennessee, Mississippi, Alabama, and Texas. He preached; she assisted by singing and working the altar. Harris eventually left Free Methodism because he believed it had relaxed the standards for holy living by allowing the wearing of jewelry, smoking, and other such taboo habits. Shortly before his death from tuberculosis, he formed a new church, the New Testament Church of Christ, in Milan, Tennessee. After his death, though reluctantly at first, Mary accepted his mantle to develop the new institution. Eventually her timidity turned to boldness when God "absolutely broke every fetter. . . . It was the first time in her life that she could turn the pulpit loose. . . . It was a permanent loosing from that day."[49]

She, along with several women evangelists, itinerated to preach and plant churches throughout rural Tennessee and Arkansas. "Women preachers were not popular," recalled an early pioneer in one of her churches, "and all hell tried to stop them, but they went forward with a determination to win, and God mightily blessed their labors."[50] Even in her hometown Methodist church, "where she had been a member in girlhood and where her father had put in as much money in the building of the church as any one man and where she had worked with her own hands and helped to paper it," she was not allowed to preach due to opposition against her holiness message and to women preachers.[51] Because of such occurrences, she and the other evangelists decided to hold tent meetings instead. "This made them independent of churches, which so often refused them their houses."[52] They continued to stir up controversy by holding meetings among the poor and marginalized, including African Americans in the South.

Mary ventured into Texas when she received a letter with money enclosed from an immigrant settlement of Swedes, Norwegians, and Germans asking her to organize a holiness church in their town of Swedonia. She responded and founded the Swedonia Church in December 1897 with thirty-one charter members. Similarly, at Buffalo Gap, Texas, she founded a church after holding meetings for three weeks: "There was a church organized with thirty-five charter members. A church was built—an annual campmeeting set on foot; the first one to be held west of Waco, and for years before the auto was heard of in this country, the people came for miles, sometimes for more than a hundred miles in a covered wagon, and camped the ten days through."[53] In the midst of her journeys, she met and married another cowboy, Henry C. Cagle, known prior to his conversion and sanctification as "Battle Axe" because he insatiably chewed large quantities of that tobacco brand.

The New Testament Church of Christ grew by a handful of churches, then merged in 1904 with another small group of holiness churches to form a denomination, the Holiness Church of Christ. The Reverend Fannie McDowell Hunter, editor and primary writer of *Women Preachers*, a collection of women's narratives, served as host pastor at the merger convention in Rising Star, Texas. This denomination, with its larger collection of personnel and resources, including eleven churches, sixteen ministers, and several foreign missionaries, extended its outreach with a rescue mission, training school, church paper, and yearbook.[54] Within four years, in 1908, it merged again as a charter member of the Church of the Nazarene. At its formation, women constituted 13 percent of the ordained ministers in the Church of the Nazarene, a statistic due largely to the assiduous preaching and church planting of women evangelists like Mary Lee Cagle.

Similar to sentiments expressed by Cagle, Tate, Woodworth-Etter, and White, Florence Crawford also deemed existing churches to be lacking in spiritual mettle. She had attended many Los Angeles churches—Methodist, Presbyterian, and Christian and Missionary Alliance—after her conversion. She stayed longer in the Methodist church and even rose to the position of class leader, but her request to be baptized by immersion led to an irreparable conflict with the pastor, who insisted on sprinkling instead. "I had been in this church and that one," she explained. "I stood there on that day, my heart aching. I said, 'Is there no place where they believe the whole Word?'"[55] Further searching brought her to the Azusa Street Mission in the early days of the revival, and there she found the "whole Word," including the baptism of the Holy Spirit and divine healing. After several months of worshipping in such a heady revival atmosphere, she—like scores of people, including as many as thirty-eight missionaries who crossed continents headed for Africa, India, and China—left to carry the Pentecostal message to other locales.[56]

From the beginning of her work in Portland in 1907, Crawford instituted a group baptismal service in the waters of the Columbia River to mark the close—and climax—of the summer-long camp meeting. After several months spent together in close quarters on the campground, they traveled to the water's edge by the church's fleet of cars or, when the crowds attending exceeded their capacity, by the "Bluebird," a barge accommodating a thousand passengers. There, on the banks, underneath the interstate bridge spanning Vancouver, Washington, and the Oregon state line, hundreds of newly minted believers stood in two lines—one for women, one for men—waiting for as long as two hours to be baptized.

The following day, all the members celebrated a more intimate ritual, the ordinance service, in the downtown Portland church. The service, consisting of the Lord's Supper followed by a foot washing, commenced with a procession into the church accompanied by a loudly sung refrain: "When the saints are marching in, / When the saints are marching in, / Joyful songs of salvation thro' the sky shall ring, / When the saints are marching in." They gathered first for the Lord's Supper, men and women together, filling the large room, cloakroom, and prayer room, and sitting on chairs, suitcases, and large boxes from the business office. For the foot washing, as with the baptism, the genders separated to opposite sides. To ensure complete modesty, considering ankles and legs would be partly exposed, they lowered to the ground a large white canvas partition attached to the ceiling. Each gender group accompanied the washing with song: "Not for ease or worldly pleasure, / Nor for fame my prayer shall be; / Gladly will I toil and suffer, / Only let me walk with thee."[57] In 1907, at the very first foot washing, Elsie Ott reminisced that the women gathered in a circle around Sister Crawford, and "she showed us how to gird ourselves with a towel and wash each other's feet."[58]

Tate's church observed an identical service, the Lord's Supper followed by the "sacred order of feet washing with the church" with each gender group forming a separate circle around a basin. Tate's paramount concern for cleanness circumscribed the description of the foot washing. Cleanness was to mark not only the towels and the water, which must be fresh and clean, not dirty or stained, but also the thoughts of those gathered, particularly the men's. The official account continues with these admonitions: "Let the Deacons quietly and peaceably see that no men stand upon seats or elsewhere and gaze upon the women's undressed feet. Let such be strictly forbidden not with masculine temper, but with sobriety, and calmness, and coolness of mind and with command and sound judgment in order that the sacredness of the feet washing be not turned into a frolic."[59]

As Tate's churches expanded in number and location, she set up the more formal arrangement of a denomination. In American Protestantism, the term "denomination," from the Latin *denominare*, which simply means "to name," refers to a group of churches sharing the same doctrine and polity (organizational structure), who band together into one larger institution. "Denominations help to provide some type of religious identity amid the pluralism of belief. They also provide needed resources for local communities of faith, such as facilities for training ministers, for publishing curriculum resources, and for overseeing certification procedures."[60] It is to the establishment and growth of denominations founded by women evangelists and the authority afforded to them as denominational leaders that we now turn.

Denominations

After nearly a decade of preaching and forming "Do Rights" bands, Tate fell seriously ill, became immobile, and "was pronounced incurable."

While convalescing in Greenville, Alabama, she experienced "the baptism of the Holy Ghost and fire" and "sprung up from that bed of sickness where she had lain for some time, and leaped and shouted and spoke in unknown and other tongues and was healed and sealed."[61] The timing of her healing replicated the common scenario of many Pentecostal leaders, who experienced "stunning divine healings in their own bodies" that "brought physical restoration" along with "renewed vigor."[62] In the wake of her physical transformation, in 1908, she convened a general assembly for her churches. During the ten days, ministers were ordained, the denomination became officially incorporated, and she was pronounced bishop of the Church of the Living God, the Pillar and Ground of the Truth. The denomination grew rapidly throughout the next decade and spread into twenty states, prompting her to appoint state bishops to oversee churches within state boundaries. To solidify further the denomination, she assembled doctrines, rules, rituals, and governing structures into the "Decree Book" and distributed it to the churches.

At the core of Tate's denomination, consistent with each one discussed in this chapter, stood the doctrine of holiness, also known as sanctification, or by Tate's word, cleannness. She taught that cleanness must direct "one's entire life-system"—"what one eats and drinks, how one dresses what one wears, how and what one talks about, marriage and the family, courtship and dating, attending church and other services, participating in social and community affairs, politics and government."[63] In the "Decree Book," she listed sixteen injunctions concerning cleanness. Most mirrored the standard fare of the Wesleyan/Holiness movement, such as refrain from alcohol, cigarettes, sexual relations outside of marriage, cards, horse races, fraternal societies, and jewelry. While this list might appear lengthy, it did not disintegrate into banning what Grant Wacker refers to as "blameless indulgences," such as "chewing gum, soda pop, ice cream, Cracker Jack candy, and neckties."[64] One positive directive on Tate's list encouraged attendance at "health resorts, parks, live stock and agricultural shows" because these promoted healthy living.[65] It is curious, though, given her reference to cleanness in marriage, that she did not cite a prohibition on divorce. Perhaps this omission can be explained by her own decision to divorce three husbands, while both of her sons also divorced and remarried.

Tate's grandson, Meharry Lewis, refers to this state of affairs as "the multiple marriages crisis."[66]

White reiterated similar holiness admonitions for the Pillar of Fire denomination, with one addition. In 1914, she inserted vegetarianism and, from then on, insisted that no Pillar of Fire member eat meat, including fish. A former member recalled that beans ranked highest as the most frequent protein staple of the Pillar of Fire diet. "We were told how fortunate we were. We always had some kind of food. A person couldn't starve on beans."[67] For biblical corroboration, White appealed to the Bible's opening page, where God commanded Adam and Eve as well as animals of the earth and air to eat vegetation: "God said, See, I have given you [humankind] every plant yielding seed that is upon the face of all the earth, and every tree with seed in its fruit; you shall have them for food. And to every beast of the earth, and to every bird of the air, and to everything that creeps on the earth, everything that has the breath of life, I have given every green plant for food" (Gen. 1:29–30). From this text, she extrapolated that human beings who ate meat occupied "a lower plane than the animals" and thus exhibited a lower moral standard.[68] "By the eating of flesh, man takes on the nature of a brute.... For the cravings of the lower nature make a person much like a ravenous beast, and there is always danger, for when once vent is given to passion, often crimes are committed that take the victim to the prison or the gallows."[69]

She further deduced that humans who slaughter animals will be more likely to do the same to other humans, a belief she held to be true for individuals as well as nations. This perspective fueled her condemnation of "civilized" nations for their participation in World War I: "The so-called civilized nations of today will be looked upon by future generations as having been half-barbarous or savage, and not far removed from cannibalism. And until they suppress this organized, systematic taking of life to satisfy the desires of the flesh they may expect to see their subjects slaughtered in just such wars as are now raging between the great powers."[70] Not surprisingly, then, she embraced pacifism for her denomination and forbade members from engaging in "earthly warfare... the conduct of war is to be left to those who have not consecrated their lives to the cause of the Gospel."[71]

She further linked vegetarianism to her understanding of history as divided into two dispensations—the old and the new. The old dispensation covered the time period from the Old Testament to Pentecost, which occurred fifty days after Jesus' crucifixion when the Holy Spirit descended (Acts 2); the new dispensation began at Pentecost and lasts until Christ returns.[72] Even in the old dispensation, she reasoned, Jews did not eat pork, so how much more in the new dispensation, when a higher standard of morality and conduct is expected, should Christians refrain from every variety of meat, including fish? To seal the point and tap into the era's eschatological fervor, she claimed that the way people currently devoured meat provided a conclusive sign of the imminence of Christ's return.[73] Additional reasons she cited for vegetarianism sound remarkably modern, including cruelty inflicted on animals, illnesses contracted from eating animal flesh, and the elimination of poverty by feeding grain to hungry children instead of cattle.

Crawford, like Tate and White, also focused on holiness, though she most often used the term sanctification. She set sanctification in the middle of her *ordo salutis* between justification and baptism of the Holy Spirit. Justification marks the born-again moment through the forgiveness of sins when one becomes a child of God. To remain at this point and proceed no further, she cautioned, becomes a serious matter because a "justified soul" could easily "get into trouble," make mistakes, or have doubts. Sanctification, the next step, removes such danger because it eradicates inbred sin, which plagues everyone on account of the Fall. Because of sanctification, Crawford explained simply, "You don't have to go on and make the same mistakes all the time."[74] Sanctification then prepares one to receive the baptism of the Holy Spirit, "a gift of power upon the clean life" demonstrably evident in speaking in tongues, as happened at Pentecost (Acts 2).[75] Crawford herself experienced this baptism when she attended Azusa Street, a narrative she recalled often for her followers. She had only been sanctified for three days when "the power fell while I was sitting there, and my lips began to speak a Chinese dialect. A Chinese brother came rushing over and stood in front of me. I was so lost in the Spirit that I didn't know whether I was on earth or in Heaven . . . and then the power fell!"[76]

On the basis of her *ordo salutis*, Crawford answered affirmatively this question: Were the disciples sanctified prior to Pentecost? In her explanation, she moved sequentially through the three moments—from justification to sanctification to the baptism of the Holy Spirit. "Yes," she said:

> Jesus witnessed that they were saved, telling them to "Rejoice that your names are written in heaven." (justification) . . . He prayed for them in the power of the Spirit in the Garden, "Sanctify them through Thy truth." (sanctification) Then when He appeared unto them as they sat at meal after His resurrection, He showed them His hands and His side and breathed on them and said, "Receive ye the Holy Ghost." (baptism of the Holy Ghost) He cleansed them of all doubts. We know they were sanctified and . . . were ready for the baptism of the Holy Ghost.[77]

She also argued from Acts 1:13 that Mary the mother of Jesus experienced sanctification when she, the eleven disciples, Jesus' brothers, and a group of women waited in an upper room in Jerusalem. In her explication of this verse, she wrote, "They were all in one accord, Mary the mother of Jesus was there, and nobody would dare to say that the mother of Jesus was not a sanctified woman, and if she was sanctified these disciples had to be sanctified in order to be one with the mother of Jesus . . . and the Holy Ghost fell upon them."[78] Again, from a canonical perspective, the sanctification in the upper room (Acts 1:13) occurred before the baptism of the Holy Ghost at Pentecost (Acts 2).

Certainly adherence to common-core religious experiences like sanctification and the baptism of the Holy Spirit galvanized these newly formed institutions. Yet as multiple churches spread across state lines, the country, even countries, the need for more structure emerged, so founders turned their attention to issues of authority and governance. In each of these denominations, authority rested ultimately in the founder herself. Tate made clear her sole wielding of power in the titles she accrued: "chief overseer," "president," "bishop," "one and only mother of the Church at present and in the future," and the one "through whom this Church is resurrected and established." In practical terms, per the "Decree Book," Tate's authority dominated every denominational nook and cranny; even her grandson calls her power "plenipotentiary."[79] She, as the "general moderator of each and every meeting held in any of the churches," had authority to "approve or disapprove of and annul any rule or decree made by any person or persons in the Church." As chief overseer, she held simultaneously the positions of chief editor and general manager of the *Official Organ*, the denominational periodical. All official business, including every property deed, must include the chief overseer's name. Even the "Decree Book" itself stood subject to the chief overseer who could make changes to it "in the way it seems best."[80] In addition, only the chief overseer had power to ordain a minister, bishop or elder, to appoint bishops, to decide whether and where denominational schools would be established, and to set the salaries of teachers in the schools. In other words, Tate held dictatorial power over every person, institution, and decision—even the "Decree Book" itself—pertaining to the Church of the Living God, the Pillar and Ground of the Truth.

Although she did not attach a string of titles to herself, White, also a bishop, nevertheless held as tightly as Tate to authority. Letter fragments from her New Jersey headquarters give deliberate, detailed orders to Pillar of Fire workers across the country. To workers in Denver, Colorado, she wrote a letter ordering that they eat biscuits on Friday afternoon. The letter back from the Denver workers indicated their attempt to obey despite severe financial hardship: "We are praying today and fasting per force. Mrs. White said we were to have biscuits on Friday afternoon but we haven't anything to make them out or money to buy anything, unless the Lord comes to our aid we will not have any bread for breakfast. But that is looking too far ahead."[81] To workers in Los Angeles, she wrote demanding an account of how they reused old shoes. Again, their letter back demonstrated their compliance: "We wear them out so close that even the junk man refuses to take them. I am afraid they would not be worth sending across the continent and as for our uniform suits, what's left of them, we make them up for the children."[82] Additional directives ordered workers to buy materials only from the denomination's store, not to rent the third floor of a Wichita building for meetings because of accessibility issues, and to remove a worker's uniform for a disciplinary infraction. Return letters from workers in Denver, Los Angeles, Cincinnati, Jacksonville, and London reported on daily details with a repetitive refrain of financial accounting down to nickles and dimes.

A close read of the volume of letters back and forth from the Pillar of Fire headquarters in Zarephath, New Jersey, to workers across the country evokes the strong impression that White treated them like commodities, ordering them here and there at a moment's notice or assigning them to jobs whether or not they had training, talent, or inclination. For example, when the first group of settlers moved to Zarephath from Denver, White simply announced that a school would open for the children. To the task, she assigned her niece Gertrude, who had always said, "I would never be a teacher." Initially White determined that Gertrude would share the assignment with White's son, Arthur. Then she changed her mind and sent Arthur to work in California instead. Gertrude recalled, "This left the responsibility of the school on my shoulders. It came like a thunder-clap and I staggered beneath the burden. During the following days I frequently went alone to have a good cry."[83]

Another last-minute decision left the Denver headquarters in a panic when White ordered a trusted and tested worker, Brother McRobbie, to come to Zarephath immediately. McRobbie had worked diligently to form an instrumental band to play for services, and he also taught morning classes at the Pillar of Fire school and preached evening services at the mission. Within the week after she issued the first order, White changed her mind. The deleterious impact of her impulsiveness on the Denver Pillar of Fire community as well as McRobbie personally emerged in three letters sent in rapid succession back to Zarephath. The first letter on November 10, 1916, described White's decision as "rather a shock to us." Five days later, the letter from Denver opened with these lines: "Mr. McRobbie threw up everything when he heard he might go to Zarephath. Stopped working in office and teaching in classes." Then, on November 17, a week after the first letter, a Denver worker wrote,

> There was some excitement this morning when we found out that Mr. McRobbie's plans were changed and that he would not go at present. I think he feels the disappointment very keenly. I told him several times that I did not believe he would go soon, but he was quite sure of it, and was ready to leave us just as soon as the mail came this morning. He had let go of everything and now seems not to know what to do. He was praying today about going to the missionary field. Unless Mr. McRobbie gets interested again we have no one to teach the morning classes. Mr. Bradwell never comes in the morning. Wish there was someone who could do it.[84]

Despite the upheaval, however, McRobbie remained a prominent Pillar of Fire member.[85] For her part, White continued to issue authoritative instructions, meted out in the many letters to workers written from her top floor, three room, wood-paneled corner apartment in the administration building at Zarephath. From this place, according to a reporter, White did "all the work connected with the *control* of her multitude of converts."[86]

A programmatic mandate leveled by White across the denomination regarded the duty for all young people in the Pillar of Fire to receive a Christian education separate from public schools. White decided that she did not want these youth, who possessed high, Christian morals, to share the playground or sit in class beside youth with perhaps questionable morals. "The power of association cannot be overestimated," she reasoned, "therefore the rule of separation must be operative in educational institutions." Pursuing this opinion to its extreme, she declared unequivocally that *no* education remained preferable to one obtained under improper conditions: "It would be better for them to be illiterate and have their spiritual interests looked after, than to acquire much learning and lose their souls."[87] Her unyielding position on a mandatory Christian education created difficulty for Louisa Gilman, a Pillar of Fire worker and mother of two, who had been sent to Salina, Kansas, in late summer just prior to the first day of school. Gilman became embroiled in a conflict with the superintendent of the Board of Education because she would not send her school-age children to public school. She wrote several letters to Zarephath explaining the situation and asking for prayer support. These excerpts are reproduced here as written by Gilman without spelling or grammatical corrections: "I have been making a protest about the Public School. Never since I got the light in the Bible School have I been willing to send the children to Public School that is the reason I have tried so hard to get them in the Bible School for the School Season at least for a while. The Supt. Board of Education told me I was compelled to either send them to Public School or hire a teacher with a State Cirtificate. He said it was the law and I'd have too." Evidently on the opening day of school, their first-grade teacher told a story about bears. On the morning of the second day, Gilman reported that "we could not get either one to eat breakfast, said they were going to fast and ask the teacher to read the Bible instead of telling bear stories. Mildred ask her but she said not today. So they prayed for the Lord to shake her up and make her read it." Unexpectedly—no doubt considered an answer to prayer—the school promoted Gilman's children to the second grade with a different teacher, and they came "home feeling fine. This teacher reads the Bible and ask questions, opens School with prayer and Singing."[88] To support White's separatist educational mandate, the denomination established a string of Christian elementary schools from California to Florida. Of the several secondary educational institutions she founded, both Belleview College near Denver and Alma White College (now Somerset Christian College) at Zarephath continue to enroll students nine decades after their founding.

Despite holding positions of power within their own institution, they remained susceptible to criticism and opposition for being women religious leaders over women *and men*. Even though women in the Progressive Era had gained significant ground through increased opportunities in many societal and occupational venues, most churches and denominations dragged their heels rather than promote women in leadership. They held to a hermeneutic that interpreted the second creation story (Gen. 2:4b–25) and scattered Pauline texts (1 Cor. 14:33b–36 and 1 Tim. 2:11–15) through the lens of prohibiting women from exercising authority over men. Because of this staunchly held interpretation, these women evangelists had their exegetical work cut out for them. They rose to the occasion. First, they turned to prominent biblical women who exercised leadership within the Israelite community and the early church. Their list ran long—Deborah, Miriam, Huldah, Anna, Esther, the four prophesying daughters of Philip the evangelist, Mary who first proclaimed the risen Lord, Phoebe, Priscilla, the women in Acts 1 who prayed alongside the disciples, and the Samaritan woman in John 4 who testified about Jesus to her people.

Second, they appealed to biblical texts that supported their position, such as the baptismal confession in Galatians 3:28: "There is neither male nor female . . . for all are one in Christ Jesus"; Paul's exhortation in Philippians 4:3: "Help those women which labored with me in the gospel"; and Peter's quote from Joel 2:28–32 in his Pentecost sermon in Acts 2:16: "This is what was spoken through the prophet Joel: 'In the last days it will be, God declares, that I will pour out my Spirit upon all flesh, and your sons and your daughters shall prophesy, and your young men shall see visions, and your old men shall dream dreams. Even upon my slaves, both men and women, in those days I will pour out my Spirit; and they shall prophesy.'" Particularly this last text had long fired the imagination and impulse of women evangelists, like Phoebe Palmer, who drew from it an inextricable link between sanctification, power, women's preaching, and eschatology, or what she referred to as the new dispensation. Palmer believed that the fulfillment of Jesus' promise in Luke 24:49—that believers would be clothed with power from on high—occurred in the Holy Spirit's descent at Pentecost. This "endowment of power" fell on both men and women, who received the command and ability to prophesy. It is the "promise of the Father" to impart to women, in the last days of this present age—the new dispensation—the power to bear witness to the saving and sanctifying gospel of Jesus Christ.[89] Sanctified women's preaching, she declared, will be a leading feature of the new dispensation.[90]

Women interpreters also dared to tread on two biblical texts that would seem, at first glance, to undercut their activities: "I permit no woman to teach or to have authority over a man; she is to keep silent" (1 Tim. 2:12) and "Let your women keep silence in the churches" (1 Cor. 14:34). On the interpretation of 1 Timothy 2 in a tract on women preachers issued by Crawford's Apostolic Faith Mission, the author concluded that the biblical writer only had those women in mind who "'usurped authority' and assume their office without a divine call'"; the text does not apply to women called by God.[91] This liberative word for women, however, becomes muted when the context in the tract shifts from church to family. Although man is not the head of woman in the church, the man *is* and must remain the head of the woman at home. "He [the writer] is not there [1 Tim. 2] speaking of the order in assemblies. Man is the rightful head of the family and the woman is not to usurp authority over her husband in the government of the home."[92] Others did not agree with Crawford's strong sentiments on this matter. Woodworth-Etter, for instance, might well have uttered this retort: "If some women had to depend on their husbands for knowledge, they would die in ignorance."[93] Cagle approached the 1 Timothy 2 conundrum from a different perspective by emphasizing the fourteenth verse instead of the twelfth: "The Bible says, 1 Tim. 2:14, that the man was not deceived, but the woman. It was one single transgression by one person that opened up the floodgates of depravity and damnation that has been sweeping souls to hell for the last 6,000 years. If one woman under the power of the devil did so much to damn the world, it stands to reason that woman, under the power of the Holy Ghost, can and will do much to save the world."[94]

Turning to 1 Corinthians 14:34, proponents of women preachers mounted the argument that Paul's command must not be universalized but considered within the specific context of the Corinthian church, the recipient of Paul's letter. That church had become mired in a state of confusion, where people spontaneously and simultaneously shouted out a psalm, gave an interpretation, or pronounced a prophecy. Using this hermeneutical strategy, advocates argued that Paul's injunction did not apply universally to all situations in all subsequent generations; it only addressed this one situation in ancient Corinth. Crawford, for one, adopted this explanation and claimed that the problematic verse referred only to Corinthian women "who obviously were causing confusion by talking and asking questions"; it is these women—and these alone—who were enjoined by Paul to remain silent until their husbands answered their questions at home. Rather than silencing women, she contends that the "Holy Ghost makes everyone a witness."[95]

White tackled Genesis 1–3 and wrestled it into a declaration of gender equality. As opposed to interpreters who found male headship in the creation of the sexes, particularly in the King James Bible version of Genesis 2:18, where woman is called a "help meet," she interpreted God's original design as the establishment of a "copartnership" between the genders. White blamed the Fall for destroying this copartnership and for relegating woman to her present-day subservient role. As a result, "the social fabric is going to pieces and the world is well-nigh wrecked. Before lasting peace can be expected, woman must be accorded the place designed for her."[96] Thus, she traced a direct line in the following poem from the "social evils" currently plaguing the American church and society to the loss of the original equality between the sexes:

> If social evils they'd correct,
> Men on this subject should reflect,
> And learn from Genesis, the Book
> Where God would now have all men look.

> 'Tis there equality is taught
> For which the women long have sought;
> To this end then we will contend
> Till men their rights to them extend.
>
> Then will a change be brought about,
> And God's word men no more will doubt;
> The nations all shall be at peace
> When inequality shall cease.

In the same poem, White also turned her attention to Eve and described her, from Satan's perspective, as "the stronger citadel."

> Secure her first, he would prefer,
> So as not to risk losing her;
> She was the stronger citadel,
> And what she'd do he could not tell.[97]

This last stanza echoed Elizabeth Cady Stanton's interpretation of Eve in the first volume of *The Woman's Bible*, published in 1895, several decades earlier than White's poem. Despite their disagreement on many issues, particularly their contrasting hermeneutical approaches—biblical inerrancy (White) and higher criticism (Stanton)— it is noteworthy that they expressed similar opinions about Eve. Stanton, like White, considered Eve's demeanor to be heroic because she exhibited "courage, dignity, and lofty ambition." She applauded Eve's ambition for extending, not to riches or trivial luxuries, but instead to knowledge and wisdom. Like White, Stanton elevated Eve to a higher plane than Adam and concluded that the tempter "roused in the woman that intense thirst for knowledge, that the simple pleasures of picking flowers and talking with Adam did not satisfy. Compared with Adam she appears to great advantage through the entire drama."[98] Along with their shared perspective on Eve, both women championed the equality of men and women not only in theory but also in institutions—political, religious, familial, social, and economic. White, born a generation later, carried on Stanton's work for women's suffrage, and after the passage of the Nineteenth Amendment, White supported women's equality and the platform of the National Women's Party with its equal rights amendment introduced to Congress in 1923.

Turning to the Pillar of Fire's stance on women in ministry, White staunchly upheld the full equality of men and women in the church as in society. For biblical corroboration, she strongly endorsed the favorable exposition on women in ministry and church leadership presented in scholarly detail in *The Bible Status of Woman*, published in 1926, by the Reverend Lee Anna Starr, a Greek and Hebrew scholar and Methodist Protestant minister.[99] After the initial print run, the Pillar of Fire acquired permission to reprint the book, and a current resident kindly gifted me with a copy. Pillar of Fire women workers traversed the country, and into England, carrying the gospel message, selling religious literature, and building up the denomination. Jennie Garretson, for example, had charge of Pillar of Fire work in California for many years. At the same time, however, evidence of women serving as ministers proves to be elusive, even though current members claim they did. In Stanley's biography of White, she writes, "In interviews, Pillar of Fire members consistently emphasize that their church has ordained women since its inception."[100] Yet, in an illustrated book on the Pillar of Fire published in 1920, only men, twenty-six of them, posed in a photo of ministers and ministerial students. On the next page, twenty-four women gathered for a photo with a caption that reads "Pillar of Fire Deaconesses and Home Missionaries."[101] Undoubtedly, White oversaw this publication, as she did every aspect, which prompts consideration of whether these photos captured accurately the gendered dimension of Pillar of Fire ministers. Eventually, however, in the third generation, a woman assumed leadership as bishop, third president, and general superintendent of the Pillar of Fire. She was White's granddaughter, Arlene White Lawrence.

Crawford and the AFM had little to say about women in ministry, only a short article in the *Apostolic Faith* in 1918, which answered affirmatively the question, "Does God Call Women to Preach the Gospel as Well as Men?" and a tract on women preachers issued in 1932. Unfortunately, the tract does not list an author's name, but one can extrapolate that Crawford, if she did not write it, at least agreed with its conclusion. Even more telling than a dearth of written material on women in ministry, there is no evidence of women ministers or any other woman in leadership besides Crawford. She did not usher her colleague from

Azusa Street, Clara Lum, who joined her in Portland, or either of her daughters, Mildred and Virginia, into church positions. Further, Crawford's strict adherence to gender hierarchy in the home—the man is the head of the woman—would hardly encourage bold innovations by women in other areas of their life.[102]

Among these denominational founders, Tate provided by far the most open and visible access for women's leadership. She purposefully used generic language when referring to church positions to keep them open for both genders. Her grandson, Meharry H. Lewis, claims that some men left because of this premise. Perhaps these might be those Tate had in mind when she wrote about "the so called men leaders of today are flesh people and all they who follow their pernicious ways are lost." She went on to highlight the need as never before for "mourning women," since only "a few humble men who as helpers, will assist in leading the people of God."[103] Women answered her call, and she found time and occasion to mentor personally many of them. In a book compiled by Tate's grandson on women in leadership throughout the denomination's first century, the names of women evangelists, ministers, and bishops number several hundred.[104] Currently, the denomination over which her grandson presides as bishop unequivocally supports women ministers, as this core statement from its catechism attests: "That God is no respecter of persons and that He calls women into the preaching ministry and leadership positions in the church just as He does men (Acts 10:34; Galatians 3:28)."[105]

More than gender, however, the attribute that paved the most direct way to influential positions revolved around family connection. In each denomination, a relative succeeded the founder. Sometimes, this worked out to the promotion of a woman, like White's granddaughter. Similarly, a member of Tate's family, a daughter-in-law, Bishop M. F. L. Keith, held the positions of chief helper and general secretary in the Church of the Living God the Pillar and Ground of the Truth.[106] In the aftermath of Tate's death and the 1931 Decision to split the denomination into three parts, Keith became one of the Triumvirate directed to oversee the work in sixteen states.[107] Another of Tate's daughter-in-laws, Bishop Helen Lewis, served as chief overseer of the Lewis Dominion, an offshoot of the original denomination.[108] In similar fashion, White's granddaughter, Arlene White Lawrence, became head of the Pillar of Fire in the third generation.

Otherwise, the trajectory to leadership promoted the founder's son. Here's the common scenario: the son (or sons) came alongside his mother as her marriage dissolved either into divorce or long-term estrangement, which coincided with the denomination's expansion; the son served in various capacities and then stepped into his mother's leadership position at her death. This happened in the Pillar of Fire. When the Whites separated, their sons, Ray and Arthur, moved with Alma to New Jersey. Both sons assumed leadership and oversight tasks within the denomination and became the first and second assistant superintendents in the 1920s, though Alma still retained control; even at age seventy-five, she traveled forty-five thousand miles, purchasing property along the way and sometimes preaching more than twenty sermons in a week.[109] In 1946, the year both Alma and Ray died, Arthur became president and general superintendent of the Pillar of Fire.

The same sequence occurred in the Church of the Living God the Pillar and Ground of the Truth. Tate's two sons, Walter and Felix, left home with her after the divorce. As finances allowed, the boys traveled the evangelistic circuit as her co-workers. In 1914, she ordained each son a state bishop. Walter, who worked to build up the church on the Eastern Seaboard, died at age thirty-one from pneumonia contracted while he worked by day in the Pennsylvania coal mines. Felix helped to establish the publishing house and Nashville headquarters and became one of the Triumvirate leaders of the denomination.

Like White and Tate, Crawford also had a checkered marital history. Before age eighteen, she had already married and divorced a man.[110] She then moved from Oregon to Los Angeles and quickly married Frank Crawford, and they had three children, Raymond, Mildred, and Virginia, their adopted daughter. Florence's religious awakening at Azusa Street in 1906 and her subsequent headlong immersion in evangelism up and down the West Coast stretched an already difficult marriage to the brink. Raymond recalled that, because the family now revolved around his mother's full-time religious activities, tension escalated even more between his parents. Raymond continued with this assertion: "She had much opposition in that home." At the same time, his father "did not want her to leave, and break up the home and go preach the gospel, leaving us to shift for ourselves."[111] Finally, because she believed her call to preach came from divine authority, she decided to leave the

Azusa Street mission, Los Angeles, even her family, despite opposition from her husband and from William Seymour, leader at Azusa Street.[112] The Crawfords' marriage ended in divorce within four years. Florence never remarried, and the AFM, with her stringent insistence, prohibited all second marriages as long as the first spouse remained alive.[113]

The Crawford children got caught in a tug of war between their mother in Oregon and their father in California. From a young age, Mildred worked alongside her mother in religious work. At age ten, she posed for a photograph alongside her mother and other leaders at Azusa Street. She then traveled with her mother while Raymond initially remained in California with his father. As Mildred grew into adulthood, however, she drifted in and out of the AFM before leaving it altogether.[114] Raymond became more active once he joined his mother in Portland. Ordained at nineteen, he headed up the various transportation carriers, including the cross-country automobile tours and the aerial component. He became assistant overseer and then general overseer after his mother's death, a position he occupied for the next thirty years. The AFM, unlike Tate's and White's denominations, has yet to appoint a woman to the highest leadership position.

Headquarters

Bishop Tate chose Nashville for her denominational headquarters, and in 1923, she directed two bishops, B. L. McLeod and her son, Felix, to find property. With her approval, they purchased eleven city lots at 1915 Heiman Street for $5,000, including a large brick building with five rooms. The publishing house opened in the building after it was renovated and equipped with "two large printing presses, paper cutters, print type and type-setting equipment."[115] Part-time workers hired from several African American schools in the area staffed the publishing house. For two decades from this location, the New and Living Way Publishing Company printed Sunday School literature, music, and several periodicals. Unfortunately, this same "ambitious endeavor" depleted finances severely, forcing Tate to make frequent monetary appeals in letters to her "dear followers": "But you probably don't know just how I, your dear Mother, have suffered and tugged and worried and begged to get the saints to send the money to pay on their own property here. Then after all, I had to pay the interest all myself which was $95.50 . . . and I need it on my own personal expenses for food and other bills." She ended the letter with this charge: "You are showing no mercy for me at all . . . I took up the last note all right, but you are still hardheartedly doing nothing while some are doing all they can!"[116] Financial distress further catalyzed dissension, and some of Tate's opponents quit to start other denominations, which factored into the "startling number of schisms" within Pentecostalism in the two decades between 1915 and 1935.[117]

From her first days in the Pacific Northwest, Crawford set a high premium on extending the gospel message through literature. She saw this practice firsthand at Azusa Street as thousands of inquiry letters asking for news of the revival arrived from around the world. The publication and dissemination of newspaper reports about the revival seemed a most expedient response. Crawford, Clara Lum, and William Seymour collaborated on the *Apostolic Faith*, first published in September 1906. Within two years, Lum abruptly left Los Angeles, taking with her the *Apostolic Faith* mailing list and her editorial expertise, and she joined Crawford who had already moved to Portland. Conflict then erupted between the apostolic faithful in Los Angeles and Portland, both of whom blamed the other and exonerated themselves.[118] Nonetheless, by 1908, the first Portland issue of *Apostolic Faith* came off the press. Crawford quickly increased the print run to one hundred fifty thousand bimonthly issues and launched German and Norwegian editions.[119] Apostolic Faith Mission workers typed the tracts and other religious literature on typewriters with foreign language characters. By 1920, the AFM published religious material in ten languages and mailed it to destinations across the globe from Panama to China.

For the first decade, the AFM relied on a commercial plant for the printing. When the printed literature came back to the Portland headquarters, workers folded and readied it for mailing. In 1917, the AFM bought its first printing equipment and continued to upgrade the machines until 1919, when the purchase of a large Miehle printing press allowed them to handle all the printing in house. An AFM newsletter noted that, whereas "sinners" had printed the papers previously, "Now no hands but the saints of God will rest upon them [the literature] as it never has before."[120] Literature outreach continues on the south side of Portland, in the basement of the three-story, brick headquarters building at the intersection of Southeast 52nd Avenue and Duke Street.

Currently, the publishing department churns out over two million pieces of literature annually in three main languages—English, Spanish, and Portuguese. It also stocks literature in Chinese, French, Burmese, Russian, and Kiswahili, while its international contacts in Africa and India print their own literature in other dialects.[121]

On eleven acres across the street from the AFM headquarters stands the campground with its imposing wooden tabernacle, built to seat roughly two thousand people. Across the front of the tabernacle in large letters reads the denomination's motto, "Jesus the Light of the World"; a ten-foot-high gold star rests above the word "Jesus." The same message lit up the forty-eight-foot-high by fifty-foot-long electric sign erected on top of the AFM mission in downtown Portland. The sign flashed in coordinated three-part rhythm, illuminating first the gold star, then the word, Jesus, and finally the phrase, "The Light of the World."[122] In the intervening nine decades since Crawford purchased the campground property in 1920, workers have renovated and improved the facilities, replacing canvas tents with more than six hundred tiny wooden cabins, building community kitchenettes around the grounds with running water and refrigeration, and constructing a restaurant and snack bar.[123]

The annual summer camp meeting, the pinnacle of the AFM calendar, began in 1907, the year Crawford moved to Portland. Initially it lasted from five to seven weeks with singing, Bible teaching, and preaching throughout, often in several languages. On weekend afternoons, first the Gospel wagon, then the autos, carried workers from the campground throughout Portland neighborhoods to hold street meetings and advertise the camp meeting. Crawford considered attendance at the camp meeting to be mandatory for AFM ministers because she provided further instruction in denominational doctrine and practice. She encouraged laity, too, to attend no matter the distance, expense, or number of children to look after.[124] Elsie Ott, an early member, wanted to camp all summer long at the meeting, but she worried over the logistics of child care and laundry: "I did not see how I could possibly camp this time, as John was a baby now, only about six months old; and with the four small children and all of that washing to do, it did not seem possible for me to go. Besides, it was a long way to move and money was pretty scarce in those days, as my husband only got small wages—about $65.00 per month." When she showed up for the opening Sunday service, one member offered to do laundry and another provided a horse and wagon to move the family's belongings to the campground. Ott wasted no time in her deliberations, "As the Lord had opened the way, I packed up and was soon on the campground."[125]

Ott reminisced that, in the early years, participants camped in tents and ate meals for twenty-five cents at the restaurant on the grounds. They piloted an "all things common" approach to meals with the expectation that people would contribute enough to cover expenses by way of a freewill offering. "We have had many a laugh since," wrote Ott. "It seems I can almost see those bachelors yet, who had been doing their own cooking, moving to the restaurant with their few cooking supplies as an offering . . . but the offering box did not fill up accordingly, so things didn't go so good. That was the last time we had an 'all things common' restaurant."[126] These days, the annual camp meeting lasts for two weeks each summer and closes, following the century-long tradition, with immersion baptisms followed by an ordinance service.

White established more than a denominational headquarters on an extensive tract of farmland in rural New Jersey, adjacent to the Delaware and Raritan canal and three and a half miles from the nearest town of Bound Brook. She formed a utopian-like, communal village named Zarephath, where residents did all things together—ate, worshipped, exercised, farmed, ran a printing press, went to school, raised families, and were buried in the cemetery. White's early involvement with a Wesleyan/Holiness group, the Metropolitan Church Association, which had formed a self-sufficient community in Waukesha, Wisconsin, most likely influenced her to establish at Zarephath what historian William Kostlevy calls "holiness communalism."[127] Kostlevy references John Humphrey Noyes, a radical antebellum perfectionist and founder of the Oneida Community, who observed that "the immediate response to the pouring out of 'the Spirit of truth' at Pentecost was the introduction of community property."[128] Noyes's followers abided by this practice at Oneida, as did White's at Zarephath. These two holiness communities exemplify a dozen other similar expressions, all with ties to the Wesleyan/Holiness movement.

White chose the name Zarephath after the village where a widow and her son, down to their final crumbs on account of a severe famine, miraculously fed the prophet, Elijah, when he showed up on their doorstep asking for hospitality (1 Kings 17:8–9). She linked the biblical story to the religious climate in America and her community's role to be a standard bearer in the midst: "The famine in Israel in Elijah's time is a symbol of the spiritual famine in Christendom today. There is also significance in the name as it relates to the work of our society in trying to raise the old standards of true religion that have been broken down."[129] She claimed to recreate these "old standards of true religion" in a living, working, praying, and worshipping community, which held all things in common.

To accomplish this vision, forty-seven people, adults and children, moved in the summer of 1906 from Denver to a New Jersey farm belonging to the Garretson family. The highly contested deed transfer of the farm to the Pillar of Fire instead of the Metropolitan Church Association ruptured relations between their formerly "close-knit ministries."[130] Undaunted, Pillar of Fire pioneers lived in makeshift tents without electricity, ate farm produce, and commenced the arduous task of constructing a town. The daily chores of cooking, washing, darning, and ironing proceeded under primitive conditions. When the kitchen stove began to smoke, workers moved it out to the lawn "with its pipe running straight up in the air. The girls with their ironing worked right out in the open until the boys erected a shed in which the stove and ironing facilities were installed."[131] Others planted crops and milked cows. Long-range construction plans commenced without money in hand, so workers made bricks on the property to reduce costs. A current Zarephath resident who came to the community as a child relishes memories of those first settlers with their can-do spirit: "I was raised by the giants. Sacrifice seemed to be the norm," he explained proudly. A case in point, his grandfather, an early Zarephath settler, had already kept up a demanding schedule while living on the Colorado frontier. After he was graduated from high school in 1890 and earned a Methodist exhorter's certificate, he served as the only teacher for a six-school circuit. During the two months spent at each school, he taught by day, preached by night, and launched a church in the community if enough people gathered for the evening services.[132]

Within a few years of breaking ground, the community at Zarephath had the capacity, like Tate's and Crawford's organizations, to produce its own books and written materials on a large Miehle printing press, a folder, power cutter, and book-binding machine.[133] By 1913, the town had its own third-class post office and a power plant with an engine and boiler. Its dairy farm received the highest marks for cleanliness from state inspectors at their annual visits, and the homemade apple butter and whole wheat bread produced in its kitchens and the sweet corn grown on the farm remained legendary. Counterfeits were quickly spotted: "One grocer who was offering sweet corn for sale had a sign: ZAREPHATH CORN. A purchaser, observing that the quality was not up to the standard asked, 'Is that really Zarephath corn?' The man, not daring to falsify too openly, replied, 'Well-uh-uh don't you suppose I want to sell my corn?'"[134]

White enforced a strict schedule at Zarephath with ordered times for prayer services, meals, work, even midday exercise. A letter mailed to workers around the country in 1916 detailed the schedule: "These are busy days at Zarephath. Mrs. White is here and is working out several reforms. We now have breakfast at 7:30. People are only allowed 30 minutes from their work at noon. Supper at 4:30. Meeting in the chapel from 5 to 6, then services again at 7:30. This is a wonderful move for Zarephath. No more meals at all hours about here. Farmers and all have to eat at the same time. Miss Huffman says this is the biggest move for women's rights Zarephath has ever made."[135] However, all activities ceased immediately with the announcement of a prayer siege because it signaled that the community faced an acute need, most often a financial one. The community dropped everything to gather for a long, fervent prayer meeting.[136] On one occasion, a prayer siege commenced when no merchant in town would extend any further credit to Zarephath. As a result, the Pillar of Fire leadership expected residents to pay $1.50 per person toward the grocery bill. Considering they had no personal finances, it is not surprising that residents prayed *and* fasted to increase their prayers' efficacy to settle the credit issue. One Zarephath resident recalled prayer sieges over the breakfast meal when they ate only bread and cocoa instead of the regular fare. He quipped, "It seems like I was fasting half the time."[137]

White enforced a uniform for Pillar of Fire workers whether or not they lived at Zarephath. The uniform, she believed, signaled their religious purpose and separation from the world. The men's uniform consisted of dark knickers and jackets and London bobby-style hats; the women wore long black dresses, trimmed with deep pockets and round collars, and wide-brimmed black hats. Pillar of Fire seamstresses kept the members in uniform, alternating lightweight or heavier material depending on the season. In her reminiscences about the uniform's unflattering cut, a longtime member joked that "Omar the tentmaker" made them. To make them more fashionable, she explained, "We learned how to make a seam for a princess waistline."[138]

The women's uniform also served as a reprimand to the fashion industry, whose male hierarchy, White believed, perpetuated women's oppression by marketing flimsy, provocative, and unhealthy clothing. Her disdain for women's fashions appeared frequently in *Woman's Chains*, such as these stanzas critiquing the power men exercise over the fashion industry:

> The fashions men design and make,
> And then the blame must women take
> For garments Satan could not beat,
> For winter's cold or summer's heat.
>
> The skirts are short, the necks are low,
> You'll see it ev'rywhere you go;
> No matter what a woman thinks
> Of fashions bold from which she shrinks,
>
> She must the latest "togs" all wear,
> Must paint her face and bob her hair,
> So that a market may be had
> For ev'ry vain and foolish fad.
>
> Her neck and arms they would have bare,—
> A place for jewels rich and rare;
> And thus you see that woman's made
> The dupe of all the tricks of trade.
>
> But what has she to do or say?
> When man decrees she must obey.
> He is the power upon the throne,
> And naught can she say is her own.[139]

White's connection between fashion and women's oppression presaged by decades what second-wave feminists, like Naomi Wolf, would later critique as the "beauty myth."[140]

The Pillar of Fire uniform also served as a means of disciplinary action. When a member committed an infraction, White ordered them to remove the uniform. Sometimes just issuing the order secured the intended result: "I was glad to get a letter from Mrs. White saying I could keep the uniform on," wrote a worker who had previously received White's order to remove her uniform. "I thank the church for this."[141]

Another disciplinary action involved an injunction against a worker to stay away from Pillar of Fire property. White issued such a restraining order in 1916 against a woman with the initials M. G. in Jacksonville, Florida. M. G. responded in a letter addressed to Dear Mrs. White, excerpts of which are included here without corrections:

> I am told that you ordered me to stay away from the home. I would like to know the reason for it as I havent bin doing anything that would cause you to order me away. . . . I havent ate any meat or anything cooked with it or fish either since you first gave light on the meat question. I thought you might of herd the same reports that I herd was circulating around in the home that immoral things had transpired between me and P. but it is not so. He has never said a word out of the way to me as I would not stand for it. He is the young man that is staying in my home. He is a good boy the only thing is that he smokes and has'ent got salvation but he is a good boy other wise. He belongs to the Navy. He doesent run around like other boys, he is home here every night but drill then he comes right home. Don't think that I am in love with him as I am not. Well I will close hoping to get an answer from you as soon as possible.[142]

In this letter, it remains quite evident that Pillar of Fire workers attempted to comply with White's authority as head of the church, despite receiving very upsetting directives from her. Otherwise, they left the denomination.

Workers also adhered to a common purse, in keeping with the early church's practice following Pentecost (Acts 2:44–47). Per White's instructions, no worker earned a personal salary; all monies collected or donated benefited the denomination for real estate purchases, building renovations, workers' living allowances, and radio broadcasts. Most of the denomination's capital came in through the nickels and dimes earned by workers moving from town to town like traveling salespersons, selling religious literature on the streets, in homes, and in businesses. These workers, who lived away from Zarephath, could keep a fraction of their earnings for room and board, but they had to be frugal, as Louisa Gilman explained in this letter back to Zarephath:

> Yes it pays to sacrifice. The morning the Lord gave me the $10.00 and the .25 cents of tooth paste we only had rye bread, a little caned [sic] milk and a little sugar for breakfast. We would not go into the Church money for it. I told Miss Sharp our bread and water was sure and we got so blest. We are both dead to our appitites [sic] and economize all the time. I had 30 cents handed me not long ago for Chololates [sic] and ice cream but I did not feel like doing so that I gave Miss Sharp 10 cents for that purpose and put the rest where it was needed. I had a dollar handed me before that most of it for ice cream but I spent 10 cents and put the rest on the bills.[143]

While the Pillar of Fire rules and regulations might appear excessively strict, members in other Progressive Era voluntary associations—like fraternal societies, one of the most popular and rapidly growing groups—also willingly adhered to stringent behavioral expectations.[144] For instance, the Workmen's Circle, a Jewish fraternal socialist society, "laid out strict guidelines for personal, moral, and political behavior." Rules included not "working during (or otherwise impeding) a strike, charging 'usurious interest rates,' or supporting candidates of the 'capitalistic' parties, the Republicans or the Democrats." Punishments for a rule violation ranged from fines averaging $99 per individual to outright expulsion.[145] In terms of advantages, members in good standing with a fraternal benefit society enjoyed the security of sick benefits, funeral benefits, even care for orphaned children in a society-sponsored orphanage.[146] Such incentives spawned a furious influx of new members, particularly from the working class, who came to depend on these benefits. In a 1908 article likening fraternalism to an "enormous army," the author compared the army's foot soldiers to "the middle-class workman, the salaried clerk, the farmer, the artisan, the country merchant, and the laborer" who enlisted in the fraternal society. They did so to "insure their helpless broods against abject poverty. . . . Rich men insure in the big companies to create an estate; poor men insure in fraternal orders to create bread and meat. It is an insurance against want, the poorhouse, charity, and degradation."[147]

Likewise, the mostly working-class Pillar of Fire members also had assurance of being looked after from cradle to grave, particularly at Zarephath. Residents had access to food, housing, clothing, employment, a church, and educational institutions from elementary school through college. As Helen Swarth, former Pillar of Fire worker, explained, "We never had to worry about a home, taxes, or even death. We had our own cemetery!"[148] In return, members relinquished personal possessions and savings, abided by Zarephath's regimented schedule, and obeyed White's commands. A community still lives at Zarephath more than a century after its founding. Residents still gather for a common noon meal—not strictly vegetarian these days—along with students enrolled next door at Somerset Christian College.

The Pillar of Fire continues, albeit in a miniature version of its size when White died in 1946. As the entrepreneur of the denomination's formation stage as well as the master organizer and motivator of its growth and development, she exercised an overbearing and autocratic managerial style, making every decision, down to choosing the floor covering for the Denver dining room after construction workers spilled oil on it. An exercise of tight control might be understandable, perhaps forgivable, when a voluntary association expands into the thousands with extensive property holdings from coast to coast, even across the Atlantic. Yet her micromanagement was obsessive. As a former Pillar of Fire member related about White, "She knew if a chair had been moved, even though she never spent a night in many of the communes in years."[149] Still, the admiration for her among current Pillar of Fire members remains palpable, even decades after her death. She possessed an impressive ability to inspire greatness in people who accomplished tasks beyond their training, ability, or even interest. In an interview with a current Zarephath resident, he paid her this tribute: "Alma was dynamite. She would say she was a shy girl from Kentucky, but when she turned her life to Jesus, something happened."

Each woman—Alma White, Florence Crawford, Mary Lee Cagle, Maria Woodworth-Etter, and Mary Magdalena Lewis Tate—left behind a conventional, domestic life and obeyed the call to venture out and preach the gospel. These powerful and persuasive preachers held evangelistic meetings wherever they could gather an audience. As success mounted, they shifted from itinerant evangelist to institution builder. They gathered converts into a new church and then formed multiple churches into a denomination over which they presided. From their followers, they demanded financial support, holy living, obedience, and countless hours of volunteer work to build up the institution. Proceeding in this way, the founders retained a tight hold on the institution throughout their lifetime and groomed a close relative as successor.

Further, as we have seen, their large personalities came filled with incongruities. Alma White championed women's equality but failed to extend the same to African Americans. Instead, she supported the Ku Klux Klan's racist policies and actions. Twice-divorced Florence Crawford commanded any divorced and remarried AFM member to return to their first spouse and family, but she excused herself from abiding by her own regulation. Mother Tate, a champion of holy living, managed to divorce three husbands so as to disassociate herself from each man's uncleanness. It is precisely here in the incongruity of the use and sometimes abuse of women's religious power that historian Robert Orsi encourages us to stop and explore, to zero in on precisely what is confusing, disappointing, uncomfortable, and frustrating about these women. He writes, "We should be able to study how women use religious power to destroy themselves and others as well as to heal, how women manipulate other women [and men] in religious settings; we should begin to think in more complicated, ambivalent, even contradictory ways about power and powerlessness, especially in religious contexts, and to recover dimensions of religious life disallowed by the canons of modernity."[150] Instead of interpreting American religious history to mirror an imagined Lake Wobegon, where "all women are empowered, all men improved, children nurtured, the universe rendered meaningful," Orsi commends writing an historical narrative that is "more complex than mastery and triumph."[151] Following this advice, I have endeavored to unveil "the everyday tragic" in these flawed yet accomplished women who pioneered mixed-gender religious institution building.

Elhanan Training Institute, Marion, North Carolina. Courtesy of the Flower Pentecostal Heritage Center.

Mattie Perry, founder of Elhanan Training Institute. Courtesy of the Flower Pentecostal Heritage Center.

3

Biblical, Practical, Vocational

Religious Training Schools

With empty coffers and a faith promise, thirty-year-old Mattie Perry opened the doors of Elhanan Training Institute in Marion, North Carolina, a sparsely populated farming community at the foot of the Blue Ridge Mountains. She confessed in her autobiography that she never expected, as a woman, to begin and oversee a religious training school. "I was an evangelist and still hoped to go to China as a missionary, but during the three years of waiting on God for a man to open an institution of this kind, the call sank deeper and deeper into my own heart. No man seemed forthcoming to take up the work, although I met perhaps eight or ten people who claimed that God had given them a plan for a school like this, and had called them to it, but that they could not begin because they had not the funds." As she continued to pray and plead "most earnestly for the school," she believed that God entrusted her with the call: "My tender, loving Father responded softly, 'My child, if you will trust and obey me I will let *you* do this work.'"[1] She got to work quickly. Working with her father and brother, she refurbished, furnished, and readied twenty-five rooms of the former Catawba Hotel in time for the watchnight dedication service on December 31, 1898.

Perry believed Elhanan would appeal to students with little money for books and tuition but great eagerness for Bible study and practical training before they headed into evangelistic work. She had once been that student, setting her "one thought" on attending Scarritt Bible and Training School in Kansas City, Missouri.[2] Despite being accepted to matriculate, she could not afford the train ticket to Kansas City from her South Carolina home. As the years passed and she heard many at her evangelistic meetings mention their interest in some practical training, Perry decided not to keep waiting for a man to step up. Ever resourceful, she tapped into the wave of religious training schools sweeping the country, establishing Elhanan, meaning "gracious gift of God," before the first public school had even opened in Marion.

A similar resolve ignited in twenty-six-year-old Iva May Durham (Vennard) during a summer camp meeting in 1897 at Mountain Lake Park in the Allegheny Mountains of western Maryland. She had come to this Methodist campground, bordered by Victorian-style cottages topped with gingerbread trim, set amid eight hundred acres of mountain scenery and pristine air, to find respite from her grueling travel schedule as an ambassador for the Methodist Deaconess Bureau. She also took the opportunity to work as the stenographer, recording in shorthand the first Itinerant Institute on Evangelism, a set of lectures given by a leading evangelist of the Wesleyan/Holiness movement, the Reverend Joseph H. Smith. Through these lectures, Smith provided a modicum of practical training before people went into evangelistic work.[3] He addressed a host of practical issues, such as crafting evangelistic sermons, working the altar, and raising money. As Vennard's pen flew across the page, capturing Smith's words in every shorthand dot and line, her own "illumination," as she would later refer to it, took shape for a religious training school steeped in evangelism. Five years later, in 1902, she opened Epworth Evangelistic Institute in St. Louis.

Religious training schools, like Perry's and Vennard's, delivered a curriculum of "brevity, practicality, and efficiency" in Bible study and practical work intended for students heading into full-time Christian work as evangelists, missionaries, pastors, and Bible teachers.[4] Other types of training schools also proliferated in the Progressive Era, like the National Training School for Women and Girls in Washington, DC, founded by Nannie Burroughs under the auspices of the Woman's Convention of the black Baptist Church. This industrial school enrolled African American women with the vocational aim of preparing them for paid work, particularly in domestic service. According to Evelyn Brooks Higginbotham, a historian of the black Baptist church, now the National Baptist Convention, "The domestic science department became the school's most extensive and well-funded program. Courses in the department included homemaking, housekeeping, household administration, interior decorating, laundering, home nursing, and management for matrons and directors of school dining rooms and dormitories."[5] Even though the school's curriculum included Bible study as a part of its "School of the 3B's ... the Bible, bath, and broom as tools for race advancement," its purpose differed from religious training schools.

Alongside Perry's and Vennard's religious training schools stand a number of similar institutions founded by women evangelists in the late nineteenth to early twentieth centuries, such as Union Missionary Training Institute (Lucy Drake Osborn), Shalom Training School (Carrie Judd Montgomery), New York Evangelistic Training School (Jennie Fowler Willing), Pentecostal Mission Home, Belleview College, Alma White College, Zarephath Bible College (Alma White), Bethel Bible Training School (Minnie Draper), Rochester Bible Training School (Elizabeth Baker), and Beulah Heights Bible and Missionary Training School (Virginia Moss).[6] Curiously, not one institution from this list figures in monographs, articles, or dissertations on religious training schools.[7] Instead, historians consider only the schools associated with a renowned male evangelist or minister, such as Moody Bible Institute (Dwight L. Moody), Missionary Training College for Home and Foreign Missions in New York City (Albert B. Simpson), Bible Institute of Los Angeles (R. A. Torrey), Gordon Bible College (A. J. Gordon), Northwestern Bible and Missionary Training School (William Bell Riley), and Philadelphia School of the Bible (C. I. Scofield). Based upon this second group, historian Virginia Brereton developed the thesis of an "increasing masculinization" in these schools that replicated the gender-stratified curriculum and career path of vocational education in the public schools.⁸ What Brereton failed to consider is that the first group of schools, those founded by women, defied a separate, gendered curriculum and educated women alongside men for vocations in religious work as pastors, Bible teachers, evangelists, musicians, and missionaries. Because of this, women evangelists stand at the forefront of a visionary, path-breaking vocational education for men and women that presaged future enrollment and curricular decisions of public educational specialists and mainline Protestant seminary administrators.

Called to Evangelism

Perry identified herself as an evangelist first and foremost at a heady time for evangelism in America. Neither the whirring of the new electric machines at home—appliances like vacuum cleaners, toasters, and washing machines, all of which were invented during the Progressive Era—nor cheering crowds in outdoor, wooden baseball stadiums kept Americans from record attendance at evangelistic meetings during the Progressive Era. Evangelism thrived—whether from nostalgia, curiosity, or a search for meaning—and sparked resurgence in "the vitality of religion among ordinary people."⁹ Perry's meetings, along with awakening a religious moment, also stirred in many a vocational call, prompting shopkeepers, schoolteachers, and farm laborers to approach her afterward to inquire about becoming an evangelist. For these would-be evangelists, Perry founded Elhanan Training Institute.

Elhanan's cornerstone, laid in 1898, places it in the third decade of religious training schools in America. In the 1870s, several opened in New York City to prepare lay workers for city mission work. A prominent male minister sponsored each one, like the Reverend Stephen H. Tyng, who founded the Home of the Evangelists as "a short cut to the ministry."¹⁰ The next decade witnessed more than a handful of schools up and running, including three in Chicago: the Baptist Missionary Training School (1881), Chicago Training School (1885), and Moody Bible Institute (1886). Also in the 1880s, Methodist evangelist and former missionary Lucy Drake Osborn founded the Union Missionary Training Institute, perhaps "the first school for adults in America in which a female administrator supervised a mixed-gender faculty and student body."¹¹ Religious training schools would continue to proliferate and numbered at least two hundred and fifty by the mid-twentieth century.[12]

According to Brereton, when Moody set his influential imprimatur on religious training schools "as the training ground for lay Christian workers," he gave them "a visibility and a legitimacy [they] would otherwise have lacked."[13] Yet, although his name became attached to Moody Bible Institute (MBI), the vision and initial impetus belonged to Emma Dryer. Dryer already had considerable experience in educational institutions, including six years as dean of women and instructor in grammar and drawing at Illinois State Normal University. After recovering from typhoid fever, she moved to Chicago in order to reach out with a religious message to prostitutes. She became associated with Moody, who encouraged her to begin a "Bible Work," so she set up social and educational outreach programs as well as an institute designed to train women as Bible teachers and urban missionaries.[14] After completing the institute's training, graduates were poised to "organize prayer meetings in various homes, establish sewing schools, and make house-to-house visits to read Scripture to women and children."[15] Dryer envisioned that with Moody's backing, she could inaugurate a permanent training school for women patterned after Mildmay, a renowned deaconess training school in England she had visited to observe firsthand. However, with the initial seed money in hand, Moody dashed her hopes to train women and committed instead to equip "gap men," who could step into the ever-widening breach between ministers and the unchurched masses in Chicago.[16] Dryer resigned from Moody's employ and incorporated her institute—the Bible Work of Chicago—into the Chicago Bible Society, where she worked until retirement in 1903.

Nevertheless, a women's training institute had already been launched a few miles north from Moody's church in 1885, when Lucy Rider Meyer founded the Chicago Training School for City, Home and Foreign Missions (CTS). Meyer, like Dryer, also traced the influence of a visit to Mildmay and other European deaconess schools.[17] In turn, CTS served as the prototype for subsequent deaconess training schools, particularly within Methodism. When Meyer retired after thirty years as the chief fund-raiser, Bible teacher, and principal, forty agencies, including hospitals, orphanages, training schools, and homes for the elderly had been established either directly by CTS or its graduates.[18]

Along with training nurses and pastoral assistants, CTS also provided academic courses and practical work for deaconess evangelists. During weekday mornings, every student enrolled in the required courses in Bible and church history. In the afternoons, students could choose from elective courses that corresponded with their intended field of work. Electives offered by the Department of Instruction for Evangelism included "Individual Evangelism," "World Wide Evangelism," and "The Psychology of Evangelism."[19] According to Meyer, training in evangelistic work held premium importance: "It is not a light matter to undertake in any degree to be the spiritual guide and help of an immortal soul; and those who are to make this their constant work should be as well prepared as possible, by qualities both natural and acquired."[20]

Yet the religious training school with the clearest priority to train Methodist deaconesses in evangelism, as its middle name indicated, was Vennard's Epworth Evangelistic Institute (EEI).[21] Vennard found an ally early on in Bishop James Thoburn of the Methodist Episcopal Church (MEC). He became a leading advocate for deaconesses through the influence of his sister, Isabella, an early Methodist deaconess, who worked in the United States and India. Bishop Thoburn brought the resolution to the 1888 MEC General Conference to establish an office of deaconess.[22] The conference, which approved the resolution, enumerated these duties for deaconesses: "minister to the poor, visit the sick, pray with the dying, care for the orphan, seek the wandering, comfort the sorrowing, save the sinning, and relinquishing wholly all other pursuits, devote themselves, in a general way, to such forms of Christian labor as may be suited to their abilities."[23] Working within these parameters, deaconesses served as nurses, teachers, settlement workers, pastor's assistants, evangelists, missionaries, and house-to-house visitors.

Bishop Thoburn, like Vennard, articulated an expansive vision of deaconesses as a mighty evangelistic force. He expressed the hope that one day a legion of five hundred Methodist deaconesses "will bring more souls to Christ and add more members to our Church in this city of New York in one year than all the Churches in the city to-day have added during the past ten years."[24] For that reason, he refused to countenance the restriction of deaconess work to a separate, gendered sphere. Thoburn declared,

> The deaconess is not set apart for any one special form of work, but rather for any work which the Church can find for her. . . . I notice a persistent inclination on the part of the public generally to regard the work of the deaconess as simply and solely the duty of visiting the poor and nursing the sick; *but this is limiting her sphere in the most arbitrary way* . . . this is but a small part of the work which is to be done. A deaconess may be set aside for any form of work to which she is adapted.[25]

Even more provocative, he launched the argument that deaconesses should be allowed to preach. He appealed to the phrase, "forms of Christian labor," cited above in the official description of deaconess work, and reasoned that it could apply to preaching. In other words, he suggested that preaching, as a Christian labor, be considered appropriate for deaconesses. For biblical validation, he turned to the story of Pentecost, a favorite text for advocates of women preachers, as discussed in Chapter 2. Thoburn first pointed out the inextricable link between women, prophesy, and the pouring forth of the Spirit in this verse: "In the last days it will be, God declares, that I will pour out my Spirit upon all flesh, and your sons and your daughters shall prophesy" (Acts 2:17). He then defended the words "prophesy" and "preach" as interchangeable. This move was foundational to his argument because he noted biblical examples where women prophesied, like Philip's daughters (Acts 21:9). To conclude, he reasoned that if women have received a divine commission to prophesy (Acts 2:17–18), and if prophecy is preaching, then "women are anointed for this kind of service," that is, preaching.[26]

In Thoburn's obituary, a Methodist colleague, Bishop William F. Oldham, told this story about Thoburn's advocacy for deaconesses, which extended beyond preaching, even to their ordination: "He tried to secure their ordination that they might exercise a fuller ministry among the shut-ins of India. It is laughable to recall that a General Conference sought to censure him for allowing the tips of his fingers to rest on the heads of some of them when being 'consecrated.' It might be mistaken for ordination! And, now, to see that even this is coming!"[27]

Thoburn championed Vennard's deaconess training school, the Epworth Evangelistic Institute, before the Methodist Board of Bishops, and it received episcopal approval with the proviso that it be located in St. Louis. Vennard advertised EEI as "a School of practice for

Deaconesses, Evangelists and Missionaries" whose design was "to give the impulse of direct soul-winning to every department of Christian service."[28] Into every curricular and cocurricular aspect, she poured her conviction that deaconesses had a primary vocation as evangelists.[29] As part of the required theology curriculum, students read *Binney's Theological Compend*, which, in its final pages, offered biblical support for women's preaching. In the section "Woman's Sphere in the Church," Amos Binney dismissed the separate-sphere arrangement that relegated women to household domesticity. Woman's sphere, he argued, must not be "limited to the duties of the family or household, since she is often by nature and grace pre-eminently adapted for a wider service."[30] Continuing on, he tackled 1 Corinthians 14:33b–35, a text commonly interpreted as Paul's prohibition of women from religious leadership. In his exegesis, Binney took the same tack as the women biblical interpreters discussed in Chapter 2 and denounced a universal application of the text: "To say that his [Paul's] prohibition applies alike to all times and conditions of society, is to say that the prudential regulations of a degraded heathen people, eighteen hundred years ago, are universally binding, and that Christianity in this respect has wrought no change in the world it came to reform. Paul surely had a different estimate of woman service. Rom. Xvi, 1–7, 12–15. His first public discourse in Europe was at a meeting of women, and his first convert and host was a woman. Acts xvi, 9–15."[31] In a closing, sweeping statement, Binney sanctioned not only women engaged in public prophesying, preaching, and teaching but also women serving in positions of "the higher ministerial duties, as appears from the rank next after apostles."[32]

In their cocurricular placements in practical work, women training to be deaconesses gained firsthand experience in evangelism at myriad venues throughout the city, sponsored by EEI's Evangelistic Department: city missions, the jail and juvenile court, work at Bethesda institutions, American Bible Society, city hospitals, the workhouse, Mid-Night Rescue Home, Old Ladies' Home, Sunday Schools and other classes, Jefferson Barracks, Book Depository, Thursday Afternoon Prayer Meeting, Workers' Conference, class meetings, student volunteer band, and field evangelism. Students took part in every aspect of evangelism, from visitation to preaching to altar work.

Epworth Evangelistic Institute alums sent in reports from their church work to be featured in the "personals" column of the school's newsletter, *Inasmuch*. Many of these women served as evangelists and ministers, like Miss Rebecca Bell, who "visited Epworth a few days before going South for a three month revival campaign. Her first engagement is with Rev. Wm. R. Chase's church in New Orleans, La," and Mrs. Cooper, "a Deaconess who has been acting as Pastor of the Methodist Episcopal Church of Harrisonville, Mo., by appointment of the Presiding Elder of that District, spent the week after Conference resting at Epworth."[33]

In her role as newsletter editor, Vennard filled out the copy with her own articles in support of women evangelists. In "Help Those Women," for instance, she took to task opponents who unfairly assessed women evangelists as overly masculine. "Instantly people jump to the conclusion that a woman in public work will become masculine, that she will lose her love for domestic life, etc. But in spite of all this prejudice, and in spite of the fact that even the church endures her by mere sufferance, rather than give her recognition, yet the fact remains that some women are called of God to labor in a public capacity for souls." Continuing on, with theological acumen, she charged critics with a lack of trust in God's sovereignty. "Are you prompted to say that you do not believe it? Then you must doubt the whole proposition of Divine calls." After all, she reasoned, surely God must possess the requisite power and authority to call women to public evangelism if that be God's inclination. Therefore, she concluded, "we must respect the conviction of women called of God to public evangelism."[34]

Vennard's unrelenting advocacy for deaconesses trained in evangelism raised the ire of Methodist clergymen and laymen in St. Louis who, as recounted in the introduction, ousted her as principal of EEI.[35] Bruised but not defeated, in 1910 she opened a second religious training school in Chicago, Chicago Evangelistic Institute (CEI), which welcomed its first class of ninety-two female and male students representing seventeen states, two foreign countries, and fourteen denominations.[36] At CEI, as we see below, Vennard supervised for nearly four decades the vocational education of women and men training for full-time Christian work.

Vocational Education

Students at Perry's Elhanan Training Institute typified the enthusiasts enrolling in religious training schools across the country. Converted or reclaimed at evangelistic meetings, they emerged eager and fired up to save souls. To expedite matters, they looked for an abridged training in Bible and practical work before embarking for home or foreign mission fields. A seminary curriculum did not fit the bill for several reasons. Most could not have matriculated at a seminary because they had not earned a high school diploma, let alone the requisite college degree.[37] Those enthusiasts who were women, the "largest single group of potential lay workers," were already excluded from seminary classrooms because of their gender.[38] Further, the seminary's academic curriculum rendered it overly cumbersome in biblical languages and woefully lacking in practical training. Leading evangelical pastors, like Presbyterian minister and mission theorist Arthur Tappan Pierson, worried over the dampening impact of the multiyear educational hiatus. "We have often observed that the seven years of our college and seminary life not infrequently leave candidates with a chronic chill. Long withdrawal from active work, and absorption in mere study, are not favorable to burning zeal. Intellectual standards often displace the higher spiritual ideals."[39] Similar sentiments showed up in a very different venue, in this last verse of the gospel song, "May I Know Thy Voice," written by Henry H. Hadley, a rescue mission worker: "No Greek or Hebrew can I speak, / Nor learned questions scan; / But when He speaks I know His voice: / For Jesus talks with man."[40]

Rather than a seminary, religious training schools most closely resembled a normal school, whose curriculum offered a secondary education along with a practical training component to prepare and graduate teachers. "Many prospective teachers, consequently, went to normal schools where they were not only drilled in academic subjects but also taught such practical matters as the theory and practice of teaching. The normal school was thus something new in American education: it offered education on an advanced or collegiate level and, at the same time, offered very practical work that related directly to the job at hand."[41] The student profile at normal schools replicated that of religious training schools; both attracted students from a "modest educational background" and "unexceptional social origin," whose family's limited financial means barely covered the reduced tuition.[42] Vennard typified these students. When her father died from tuberculosis he contracted while a soldier in the Civil War, her mother struggled to support the family through various business ventures, including renting rooms to students at nearby Illinois State Normal University, also Vennard's alma mater.

Normal schools presaged the vocational education movement that rose to prominence during the Progressive Era. Education became the "mirror of the progressive hope for national reformation," and progressives brandished a comprehensive list of educational improvements.[43] "Along with efforts to replace one-room country schools with 'consolidated' schools, there were attempts to raise spending, lengthen school terms, increase attendance, improve school buildings, raise teacher salaries, strengthen vocational training for working-class children, and add high schools."[44] Although some rural and southern areas lagged behind, these educational crusaders still made their numerical mark: "From 1900 to 1909, the enrollment rate for children aged 5 to 19 in all types of schools rose from 50.5 per 100 to 59.2; public secondary-school enrollments grew from 519,000 to 841,000; expenditures per pupil in public schools increased from $14 to $24; and the average public school term lengthened from 144.3 days in 1900 to 155.3 days in 1909."[45]

However, many eligible elementary and secondary school-age children could not enjoy these unfolding opportunities owing to social class, ethnicity, or even geographical region. Public high schools, for instance, increasingly dotted city landscapes, yet their student population drew from predominantly white, middle-class, native-born Protestant families. Students on the margins of this privileged constituency frequently dropped out before graduation. To minimize this trend, reformers turned their prodigious attention and abilities toward the development of a vocational track in public high schools to train these youth for productive work, thus spawning the vocational education movement.[46] A broad and unlikely coalition of supporters—settlement workers, women's club members, businessmen, labor leaders, and agrarian groups—galvanized a national push for vocational education, packaging it in nearly millennial rhetoric. They championed it as a panacea for pressing social issues that would "integrate immigrants into the labor force, slash worker turnover, lessen labor conflict and social alienation, reduce unemployment, and increase occupational opportunities for poor and working-class youth."[47] Backed by such rhetoric as well as passage of the 1917 Smith-Hughes Act, which provided federal funds to states to develop vocational curriculum and programs in public high schools, vocational education emblematized the promise and progress of the Progressive Era.[48]

Important as this legislative event became for the curricular development of America's public schools, the establishment of vocational education in religious training schools superseded its passage. Decades in advance of the Smith-Hughes Act, religious training schools already provided vocational education in the truest sense of the word for men and women heeding a call to religious work. From its Latin root, *vocare*, which means "to call," vocation is inextricably linked to a calling in the sense of a divine directive to religious work. For men and women called to work as ministers, Bible teachers, missionaries, evangelists, and gospel musicians, religious training schools supplied the requisite vocational education. Cecelia Cross, a missionary in Africa under the Woman's Division of the MEC, offered this testimonial about the vocational education she received as a student at Vennard's CEI: "This training was my background for the varied program of a missionary—teaching, preaching, farming, building, road making, settling quarrels, caring for the sick, helping little ones into the world, praying with the dying, burying the dead, weeping over the erring, rejoicing over the redeemed, sharing the burdens of the sad and sorrowing; mothering girls of all ages . . . following them with loving prayers as they go out into the harvest field to lead others to Christ, directing their love affairs and planning their weddings. In short, being all things to all men."[49]

To prepare students for their vocation in full-time Christian work, the religious training school's curriculum revolved around Bible study. Students at CEI, for example, could choose from a range of biblical courses covering individual books of the Bible, topics (biblical archaeology and geography, hermeneutics, biblical criticism, Old and New Testament apologetics, and Bible as literature), genres (poetical books, Wisdom literature, and Gospels), and biblical languages.[50] In these courses, the Bible itself remained the primary textbook—sometimes the only one—thus reflecting the tacit understanding that "the Bible is its own best interpreter."[51] Even more extreme, at Rochester Bible Training School, a Pentecostal institution founded and led by former Methodist and Woman's Christian Temperance Union (WCTU) evangelist Elizabeth Baker, the decision was made in the school's sixth year, in 1912, that the Bible would be the only curricular subject—no more history or English classes—in order to maximize students' biblical knowledge during their brief course of study. As Baker explained, "Formerly we have had classes in History and English and Rhetoric, but we feel very clearly led of God, in view of the shortness of time and the shortness of our course of study to confine ourselves wholly to the Book of God. . . . Here we see that a knowledge of God's word is in itself a liberal education, and is the only safe ground worth further research."[52]

Bible teachers at religious training schools advanced the spiritual application as the most common interpretative method. They instructed students to read the biblical text carefully and repeatedly, then to ask questions of it to draw out "the spiritual interpretation and lesson."[53] Sometimes they provided students with the exact questions to ask, like these taken from a CEI course booklet:

> a. When and by whom are the following traits of character shown? (1) Generosity; (2) Courage; (3) Prayerfulness.
> b. How is it demonstrated that material good often leads to spiritual danger?
> . . .
> c. How is it shown that selfishness leads to spiritual poverty and often to material loss?
> d. How is illustrated Paul's saying, "Godliness with contentment is great gain?"
> e. Is there anything in this lesson that brings to mind the saying "The meek shall inherit the earth?"[54]

From these questions, students developed answers about whether a biblical character exemplified suitable values for application (or not) to their own spiritual life.

While the spiritual application method assumed the Bible's authority and veracity, another interpretative method—historical criticism—created a stir at these schools. Historical criticism entailed a purely academic inquiry into the biblical text, void of all spiritual influence, using the same critical tools applicable to the study of any literature, either sacred or secular. This method approached the biblical text with a rigorous skepticism of its innate accuracy and authority.[55] Most Protestant denominational seminaries in North America had already adopted this interpretive method by the turn of the twentieth century, which only cast aspersion on it in religious training schools. In order to distance their institutions from seminaries, religious training school founders repeatedly advertised this refrain: "free from the taint of higher criticism and evolution."[56]

Vennard expressed her own concern over the proliferation of the historical critical method. In an article for CEI's newsletter, she wrote, "We seem to be in a time of unusual activity and aggressiveness among the Higher Critics. There is so much of it in schools and even in the pulpits."[57] Her staunch rejection of higher criticism complicated the completion of the few courses remaining for her undergraduate degree. Certainly she could have enrolled nearby at the University of Chicago Divinity School; in fact, she debated the pros and cons of this option in a letter to her mentor, John Paul, who served as president of Taylor University in the late 1920s. On the pro side, Vennard believed that CEI's academic respectability would be enhanced if she, as principal, had her bachelor's degree. On the con side, she did not relish studying with the Divinity School's faculty, especially the dean, Shailer Mathews, a well-known supporter of historical criticism. As she wrote to her mentor, "But this I hesitate to do for I do not want Shailer Mathews' teaching, and I would hesitate to have my name associated with the Divinity Department of Chicago University. However I would like your advice on this. I am not afraid to take a few courses with him even though he teaches *Destructive Criticism*, but as I see it at present it looks to me like a waste of time. I would very much rather be studying on something that I could accept with my whole heart and could use in my own teaching."[58]

Lucy Rider Meyer, in contrast, relished Mathews's courses with their scientific examination of the biblical text, and she eagerly passed it on to CTS students and faculty.[59] Following her lead, most CTS instructors enrolled at the Divinity School.[60] Even when CTS's impending demise might have been slowed had Meyer relinquished her favorable opinion of historical criticism, thus quieting critics who found her too liberal, she remained adamant: "I can never consent that the historic method of Bible teaching shall be given up. It is reasonable and sensible. I could no more go back to the old way than I could put myself into the little calico dresses I used to wear when I was ten years old."[61]

The Chicago Training School eventually became subsumed under Garrett Bible Institute, a Methodist educational institution whose personnel, Vennard complained to John Paul, had treated her with disdain. Vennard conjectured to Paul that the Garrett community would never agree to grant her a degree, even though she, like Garrett, was Methodist. "I do not wish to take it to Northwestern for the Methodists have opposed me so many years, and the Faculty at Garrett are so prejudiced against our Institute work that it would only be giving them another opportunity to humiliate me by refusing."[62] She never did complete her undergraduate degree; instead, she received an Honorary Doctor of Divinity Degree from Taylor University when Paul was president.

Despite Vennard's strong opinion against historical criticism, at least one CEI instructor opted to introduce students to it with a measured approach, not simply to condemn it. In the Old Testament apologetics course, the instructor assigned James Orr's *Problem of the Old Testament*, which won the first Bross Prize for the best book investigating a topic of the Christian religion. Orr set about to examine various theories of Old Testament criticism, even higher criticism, in an even-handed manner. As Orr explained in the book's introduction, "Those who expect to find in it a wholesale denunciation of critics [higher criticism] and of everything that savours of criticism will be disappointed. The author is not of the opinion that much good is accomplished by the violent and indiscriminating assaults on the critics sometimes indulged in by very excellent men. The case which the critics present must be met in a calm, temperate, and scholarly way, if it is to be dealt with to the satisfaction of thoughtful Christian people."[63]

Quite the opposite approach presided in the New Testament apologetics class at CEI. The course description for this class conjured up battle imagery and turbulent weather to warn students of the enemy's ferocity: "The storms have ever raged around the Gospel of John, because of the strong emphasis he placed upon the deity of Jesus Christ. In recent years the enemies of the faith have made a fresh and more vigorous assault upon this bulwark of Christian revelation. A study of Prof. Sanday's book, 'The Criticism of the Fourth Gospel,' will help to keep one calm and confident in the face of the storm."[64] This second course reflected more accurately the common opinion in religious training schools that historical criticism remained an enemy to vanquish.

For nonresidential students, most religious training schools offered a Bible study curriculum through correspondence courses, a format that enabled anyone "to make a Bible School in their own home," as Perry explained.[65] Through Elhanan's Correspondence Bible School, Perry mailed students the reading materials, and they sent examination papers to her to be graded. Similarly, Jennie Fowler Willing's New York Evangelistic Training School, opened under the auspices of the WCTU, offered a correspondence course through its publication, the *Open Door*, "a pocket magazine for tram and train."[66] The correspondence course, which appeared alongside essays, short stories, poetry, and general interest articles, listed propositions for which students were to write concise and competent answers. Willing recommended students read the biblical text in several different versions and consult footnote references and background material as they prepared their answers. The propositions for each lesson could be found in the *Open Door*, such as these for Genesis 1-11:

> a. Give the commonly received date of the creation of man.
> b. Relate the events of creation in their order. Were they probably by evolution, or instantaneous production?
> c. Describe its crowning event.
> d. Is the account of the Fall of Man allegorical or literal? Give an account of it.
> e. What were the morals and civilization of the world, just before the Flood?
> f. What was the extent of the apostasy, and of its punishment?
> g. Are there proofs of a general Deluge outside of the Bible?
> h. Give the proximate date of the Flood. Relate its events in their order.
> i. When and where was the tower of Babel built?
> j. What was the purpose, and what the result of its building?[67]

Students assessed their own work to see "how nearly they have hit our mark" by comparing their answers to those supplied in the next issue of the *Open Door*.[68] Once students completed the yearlong Bible study course, they could take correspondence courses in theology, church history, Christian living, and evangelism.

Along with Bible study, practical work was the other integral component of vocational education at these schools because it balanced classroom learning with a real-life setting where students gained hands-on experience, like an internship. To provide multiple sites for practical work, most training schools originated in high-density, urban locations. Willing, for example, set up her school on New York City's Thirty-second Street near Tenth Avenue, in the vicinity of "three or four thousand factory girls within easy reach" and "scores of young men racing to ruin at breakneck pace."[69] Opportunities in practical work to reach these populations involved many different activities, as outlined by Willing: "Each student has been required to give an hour a day to visiting in the tenement houses in the vicinity. Each has had to assist in Mission service in the chapel nearly every evening in the week, help in the open airs, teach in the Sunday School, give Bible readings, or preach sermons, as there is ability or demand. Each has been expected to lead children's, young men's or young women's meetings, care for the sick, feed the hungry, and clothe the shivering poor, as each day has brought the need."[70]

Similarly, Vennard located CEI on Chicago's West Side, "about a mile from the heart of the commercial district, in the midst of a teeming population of the middle and lower classes, wage-earners, foreigners, and in conditions representing almost every race and nation of the world."[71] Within a twenty-minute walk from campus, students had access to urban churches, rescue missions, and a settlement house, run by CEI, that offered a kitchen garden, sewing school, industrial school, Young Ladies' Club, Boys' Club, Mother's Sewing Club, a free dispensary, a Sunday School, and a mid-week prayer meeting. Practical work in these settings provided vocational education for students headed into full-time work as evangelists, ministers, missionaries, deaconesses, Bible teachers, and musicians.

To finance even a basic curriculum of Bible study and practical work for a small number of students and faculty required relentless fund-raising, perhaps the most difficult task for the founder because individual monetary donations rarely topped two dollars, with most ranging from pennies to fifty cents. To attract more substantial gifts, Lucy Drake Osborn offered the option of naming a room at the Union Missionary Training Institute after a benefactor—$1,000 for a large room, $500 for a small room.[72] Gifts to these schools also arrived in the form of food and household goods, such as this list of donations to CEI: "One crate of celery, two barrels of pears, one barrel of nuts and popcorn, four comforters, two wash cloths, and three iron holders."[73]

Stories of financial desperation, particularly at the outset, became legendary. The property Alma White purchased for a religious training school four miles outside of Denver housed a defunct college with a vandalized central heating plant and a basement full of farm machinery and 2,000 chickens. With no money left to buy fuel for the classrooms' woodstoves, one resourceful teacher relocated class to the kitchen to keep students warm through their language recitations.[74] Osborn recited similar hardships in the first year of her school when the one and only room served multiple purposes as parlor, recitation room, and nursery for her young children. Even the dining table had to accommodate students and her family at one sitting. One evening, when the student cook inquired about meat for dinner, Osborn retorted, "We cannot have any, as I have no money; but we can sing the doxology without it."[75] At Elhanan, Perry had the good fortune to hire volunteer teachers "who loved God and souls more than salary" and to secure free labor from her brother, who hammered and sawed to ready schoolrooms, and her father, who solicited donations of "three car loads of beautiful long leafed pine lumber" for remodeling the unfinished building.[76] Even so, the school barely scraped by from meal to meal. On a morning when only enough flour for one biscuit remained, Perry claimed that the number of biscuits "multiplying in the pan in the stove" miraculously fed all the students.[77]

At these times of acute financial crisis, when insurmountable debt required an intervention—human or divine—the principal canceled classes to gather the community for prayer, like the prayer siege at Zarephath (recounted in Chapter 2). Then, when the necessary funds appeared, a written testimonial account celebrated the event in the school's newsletter, like this report from CEI's newsletter: "A few months ago a note of one thousand dollars was almost due. . . . Only a few days remained before the money would have to be forthcoming, and still it had not come in. In this crisis Mrs. Vennard took the whole family into her confidence, and the Thursday afternoon prayer meeting was made an especial time of prayer for the definite sum of one thousand dollars. Victory came and there was a 'shout in the camp' that continued in the dining room all through the supper hour."[78]

Clearly, women founders of religious training schools went to inordinate lengths to keep the institutions afloat. They felt pressed by the need they perceived to equip evangelical Protestants with a modicum of Bible and practical work before they headed into vocations in Christian work. Different from Protestant mainline denominational seminaries, these schools aimed for a quick turn-around between admission and graduation in order to maximize the number of workers spreading the gospel. They also welcomed women, as discussed below, who felt called to ministry and had nowhere else to enroll.

A Place for Women

Perry waited for a man with initiative to begin a religious training school, but none did, at least in her neck of the woods. Elsewhere, particularly in large cities, men already headed up religious training schools. Most of them, like the Reverend A. J. Gordon, benefited not only from steady employment as pastor of an affluent urban church but also from the church's monetary resources to finance the school. Under Gordon's twenty-five-year visionary leadership, Clarendon Street Baptist Church in Boston supported twenty-four foreign missionaries and local evangelists, a women's missionary organization, and an industrial temperance home for the unemployed.[79] The church also funded the Boston Bible Training School, opened in 1889 and later renamed Gordon College after its founder.

Women who founded religious training schools could not count on such largesse from a church or denomination; in fact, ecclesial connections often proved more obstructive than beneficial. Willing received a preacher's license in 1873 from the MEC, only to have it revoked by vote of General Conference seven years later.[80] Whether this debacle influenced her to place her training school under the umbrella of the

WCTU rather than the MEC is not clear, but as discussed in Chapter 1, the WCTU possessed a strong track record for supporting women evangelists. Likewise, after Vennard's discouraging experience with St. Louis Methodism, she resolved that her second training school, CEI, would be nondenominational and therefore not accountable to the MEC or any other denomination. As she explained, "Let us be frank enough to say that the history of this work proves that the spreading of holiness is more often hindered than helped by ecclesiastical authority and that this full salvation ministry cannot be bridled and held by any one humanly organized company. It must find the hungry soul in any church regardless of church form."[81] Despite denominational obstacles, however, women evangelists persevered to open religious training schools and offer vocational education to men and women students.

The number of women students in educational institutions positively boomed after the Civil War. Women rushed to occupy the majority of classroom desks as soon as construction ceased on the growing number of coeducational public high schools. Statistics on the disproportionate gender enrollment evoked widespread concern about the feminization of the high school and arrested the U.S. commissioner of education's attention when, in 1888, male enrollment in public high schools only reached 25 percent in the ten largest cities. This trend continued into the next decade, when female high school graduates outnumbered males by a two to one ratio.[82] Colleges experienced the same influx of women students. The founding of a handful of eastern women's colleges, including Vassar (1865), Smith and Wellesley (1875), Radcliffe (1879), and Bryn Mawr (1885), bolstered the feminization trend.[83] In midwestern states like Wisconsin, Iowa, and Michigan, women enrolled at coeducational land-grant colleges, built on public lands established through the Morrill Act of 1862, and required to be "open for all."[84] Colleges also opened for African American women, like Bennett College (1873), originally founded as a coeducational institution, and Spelman College (1881),which began as the Atlanta Female Baptist Seminary in a church basement.[85] For Roman Catholic women, the College of Notre Dame in Maryland opened in 1899; fifteen years later, the number of Catholic women's colleges had jumped to nineteen.[86] Historian Kathryn Kish Sklar marks the phenomenon of women and education in the Progressive Era with these words: "The generation of educated women that emerged in the United States in response to these opportunities had no equal in other industrializing nations."[87]

At the same time, there occurred a significant demise in coeducation in the early twentieth century concomitant with the rise of vocational education in public high schools. Bowing to growing pressure for education to coincide with a student's presumed vocational destiny, public high schools took the step of segregating males and females into separate curriculums and classrooms for gender-specific vocational training.[88] Males received manual training for jobs in factories, industry, and labor; females studied "a distinctively *female* curriculum" in home economics in preparation for domestic-type work whether on the job or in the home. In 1910, a report issued by the National Education Association stated two primary aims in "The Vocational Education of Females": "(1) It is to enable them, thru the right sort of homemaking training, to enter homes of their own . . . (2) The courses of instruction should also train for work in distinctly feminine occupations."[89] Again, the rhetoric ramped up to grandiose proportions when advocates, like Albert Leake, in his 1918 publication, *The Vocational Education of Girls and Women*, insisted that women's homemaking would have a direct impact on the nation: "We should not lose sight of the fact that the character of our people will depend even more in the future than it has done in the past upon the education we give to our girls and to our women. Notwithstanding the new avenues of employment opening up to them in industrial, commercial, and professional life, owing to reorganized schemes of education, lessening opportunities of marriage, and the withdrawal of men from industrial occupations, homemaking is and will become more and more the one industry the character of which will determine the caliber of the nation."[90]

Bucking this trend, religious training schools did not ascribe to gender-segregated vocational tracks but educated men and women together in the same classrooms and with an identical curriculum of Bible study and practical work. Through these open doors, women came in droves. At Shalom Training School near Oakland, California—opened in 1894 by Carrie Judd Montgomery, a leading faith-healing advocate who transitioned from the Christian and Missionary Alliance denomination into Pentecostalism—an equal number of men and women students enrolled from across the country and several foreign nations.[91] Likewise, at Osborn's Union Missionary Training Institute, the gender ratio reached an exact 50/50, with twenty-five women and twenty-five men.[92] According to alumnae records at religious training schools, women completed the coursework and headed out to work as evangelists, missionaries, ministers, Bible teachers, and frontier preachers. Historian Janette Hassey confirms even MBI's substantial contribution to women's vocational education: "Moody Bible Institute at the turn of the century trained and motivated women to publicly minister in Evangelical churches and applauded such efforts. MBI leadership may not have explicitly encouraged women to preach, pastor, or seek ordination, but their implicit endorsement of women in those authoritative roles for over forty years cannot be denied."[93] By offering the same training for both genders, religious training schools occupied a unique coeducational and vocational niche among educational institutions in the Progressive Era.

After this first generation of students were graduated, as historian Virginia Brereton, author of the most comprehensive work on religious training schools, argues, the once-open doors began to close for women under the pressure of an increasing masculinization. In her three-stage developmental typology of these schools, she found the initial period, roughly 1882–1915, most amenable to women, because schools needed any kind of student in order to bolster enrollment and tuition dollars. As faculty and students increased in the second stage, 1915–30, so did the number and variety of courses in church history, comparative religions, Christian ethics, and social sciences, yet Brereton found evidence to suggest a marked curricular separation between the genders. For instance, MBI's curriculum diverged into a pastor's track for men and a home economics track for women, thus replicating the configuration of vocational education at public high schools.[94] Similarly, at Gordon Bible College, trustees voted in 1930 to restrict women students to less than one-third of the student body.[95] Brereton found comparable statistics at the five most prominent schools in her study, which prompted her conclusion that all religious training schools eventually restricted women's vocational education to home economics.[96] Finally, in the third stage, from 1940 on, administrators pursued accreditation for a bachelor's degree program, which in turn required more faculty with advanced degrees. This adjustment coincided with an increase in the number of male faculty. In many training schools, the student body also became proportionally more male, and the gender-stratified curriculum a fixed entity.

While Brereton's thesis about an increase in masculinization, confirmed as well by Hassey, applied to many schools, it did not include any founded by women.[97] This is a significant omission, because schools like CEI do not corroborate her thesis; they challenge it. A close analysis of CEI documents demonstrates a continued commitment to a coeducational, vocational training when the schools in Brereton's study had long forfeited theirs. Chicago Evangelistic Institute continued to admit women into the 1940s in even greater numbers than men, to train both genders under the same curriculum, to hire a majority female faculty, and to be led by the woman founder for thirty-five years. This claim becomes evident when one considers CEI personnel (faculty, students, alums, trustees), curriculum (both formal and informal), and practical work opportunities.

When CEI opened in 1910, its seventeen faculty members consisted of ten women and seven men, five of whom were local ministers and part-time teachers. Women faculty remained in the majority and taught most courses, including Bible and theology. Also in the majority were women students. Posed pictures of student groups in CEI yearbooks bear this out, including a photograph of thirty-one students, where women outnumber the men three to one.[98] When the gender-ratio approached a 50/50 balance in 1926, the board of trustees meeting minutes noted the unusual occurrence.[99]

Students became accustomed to seeing women in religious leadership because CEI alumnae working as pastors, evangelists, missionaries, and Bible teachers regularly returned to campus to preach in chapel and to guest lecture in classes, like the Reverend D. Willia Caffray. Caffray studied first at CTS under Meyer's tutelage. After a decade as a Methodist deaconess evangelist, she enrolled as a postgraduate student at CEI, where she and Vennard became close friends. Caffray went on to become an international missionary evangelist, preaching in over fifty countries on fourteen trips spread over thirty years. She also pressed forward the fledgling movement toward women's ordination in the early twentieth century. In 1919, she signed on as a charter member of the American Association of Women Preachers, an organization that Vennard also supported by serving on its executive board. Caffray relentlessly tracked Methodism's halting progress toward ordaining women. Within seven minutes after new guidelines went into effect, she received a Methodist local preacher's license and became a fully ordained MEC minister in 1929. By preaching from the pulpit of CEI's chapel or telling students about her missionary endeavors, Caffray provided a living illustration of women's calling to any type of Christian vocation.

As the finale to the academic year, CEI students competed for awards in preaching and exposition. Women often won first place in these competitions, as in 1940, when only one award went to a man; women collected every other one, including Best Sermon in Defense of the Christian Faith.[100] For the practical work component, students ran the radio ministry, preached from the gospel auto, or worked in city missions, depending upon talent and interest, not gender. Considering the majority of women students, CEI sent out scores of women to preach in Chicago churches and rescue missions and to hold evangelistic meetings across Illinois. Well into the 1940s, CEI occupied a distinctive place among religious training schools through its coeducational, vocational curriculum devoid of gender-specific tracks.

Chicago Evangelistic Institute pioneered women's higher education in Bible and theology at a time when Protestant seminaries rarely admitted women as students. Perhaps this realization contributed to Vennard's protracted contemplation of adding a seminary track to CEI's curriculum. In her correspondence with John Paul, she raised this possibility: "I told the Board that for years I have had in my thought that the logical development of our Institute would be an orthodox Theological Seminary." Her letter continued, "I sounded them out a little bit to see what their attitude would be. There was not a dissenting voice but quite a genuine response."[101] She then outlined three potential problems with this idea: (1) finding a suitable faculty of "men and women thoroughly equipped and capable of teaching the seminary grade of work who would be orthodox and evangelistic," (2) expense, and (3) attendance. Of the three, attendance troubled her the most because she questioned whether students would enroll in a nondenominational seminary.[102] Also problematic for attracting potential students was Chicago's already saturated educational market, which, by the 1920s, had nearly twenty schools within close proximity to the city or easily accessible by direct railroad lines.[103] Eventually, Vennard decided against the addition of a separate seminary track, vowing instead to offer seminary-level training in every degree CEI offered.[104] Her intentions remain noteworthy, nevertheless, because she fully intended to enroll women students *and* hire women faculty, an innovative plan at the time for theological education.

Then, in 1945, Vennard died. Without the founder and longtime principal at the helm, CEI underwent two significant changes. First, it abruptly moved from its urban location to the rural, Iowa campus of Kletzing College, a small, Wesleyan/Holiness school that had closed its doors due to economic difficulties. Vennard had contemplated the possibility of a move whenever financial pressures mounted, yet she always resisted departing from Chicago with its abundant educational, cultural, and practical work sites. After her death, when donations dwindled rapidly and the financial crisis could not be averted, the board of trustees made a contested decision to relocate over the protests of prominent faculty and the board's chair. The first van load of equipment left Chicago on July 30, 1951, in time for CEI to begin the academic year in Iowa. For eight years, the school retained its original name, despite its distance from Chicago. Then in 1959, the institution became Vennard College to honor its founder and longest serving principal. In 2008, Vennard College closed its doors permanently due to decreasing enrollments and insurmountable financial difficulties.

A more incremental transformation after Vennard's death coincided with Brereton's increasing masculinization thesis that occurred at other religious training schools two decades earlier. Despite Vennard's serving more than three decades as principal, no woman ever again led the school. There is even evidence to suggest that a woman would never have been considered. During a presidential search in the 1960s, a letter soliciting prayer for the next leader, written by the board chair, clearly stated that a *male* leader would be an answer to prayer. "We need your prayers as we seek to find another man to serve as President."[105] This language reflected the board's increasing masculinization. In 1913, three years after CEI opened, its gender ratio stood at 60/40 with six men and four women. By 1948, three years after Vennard's death, the ratio had tipped disproportionately to seventeen men and three women. A decade later, only one woman trustee remained, D. Willia Caffray, Vennard's former student and close friend.[106]

Despite the masculinization trend in later generations, to which even CEI eventually succumbed, the significance of religious training schools to women's vocational education was exceptional. No comparable institution existed during the Progressive Era that provided for the comprehensive educational and religious training of Protestant women. Seminaries, now more than 50 percent women on average, did not welcome women students. Despite their more progressive theological stance, particularly their embrace of historical criticism and evolutionary theories, they lagged behind in seating women in their classrooms. As Brereton commented, women "fared better at Bible schools than at most theological seminaries, where either they were not admitted at all or were relegated to subordinate status."[107] Because of their open policy on gender, at least initially, scores of women enrolled in religious training schools, compared to a few brave ones who matriculated at a seminary. That very accomplishment took its toll on Anna Howard Shaw, the first ordained woman minister in the Methodist Protestant Church, who faced isolation and opposition from the forty-two male students in her class at Boston University School of Theology in 1876. She recalled in her autobiography, *The Story of a Pioneer*, that the class "was composed of forty-two young men and my unworthy self, and before I had been a member of it an hour I realized that women theologians paid heavily for the privilege of being women."[108] Gender discrimination at seminaries had financial ramifications as well because women students did not qualify for the room and board remuneration available to men.[109] As a result, Shaw languished in poverty while in seminary. She skipped meals for prolonged periods to save money, a starvation diet which rendered her susceptible to illness.

Not until the mid-twentieth century would women enroll in seminaries in noticeable numbers. In his monumental work on American theological education, Glenn Miller ties the increase in women seminary students inextricably to the U.S. government rather than to a sudden change in course or principle by seminary administrators. According to Miller, "The GI Bill also had an indirect influence that no one, including the government planners, appeared to have anticipated. By funding the education of men with wives and, in some cases, children, the government changed the character of seminary education. . . . The schools came to see themselves as places for both genders."[110]

Religious training schools, in contrast, catered to men and women with little formal education who wanted to head into full-time Christian work in America and around the world. The curriculum balanced Bible study and practical work in settings where students experienced an internship of sorts in evangelism and religious outreach. One practical type of work site utilized frequently by religious training schools was the rescue homes and missions that opened in droves during the Progressive Era to provide those on the margins with food, clothing, and shelter along with a venue for the gospel message. Women evangelists, ever alert for developing institutions engaged in evangelism, turned their prodigious capabilities and unflagging zeal to opening rescue homes and rescue missions across America, as we discover below.

Martha "Mother" Lee. From *Mother Lee's Experience in Fifteen Years' Rescue Work With Thrilling Incidents of Her Life* (Omaha, NE: Richard Artemus Lee, 1906).

Emma and L. P. Ray. From *Twice Sold, Twice Ransomed: Autobiography of Mr. and Mrs. L. P. Ray* (Chicago: Free Methodist Publishing House, 1926).

4

Soap, Soup, Salvation

Rescue Homes and Rescue Missions

Wearing a long, black dress gathered at the waist and topped with a starched white collarband, a forty-five-year-old woman—whose stern face and tight lips belied her maternal epithet—opened the shuttered door and walked into the dimly lit brothel. Martha "Mother" Lee and her companions had stayed up late to visit in the Omaha slums, knock on doors, distribute gospel tracts, and tell anyone who would listen about "the love of Jesus and His power to save, and how He saved me." Lee entered the brothel's gathering room, took in the scene of young women smoking and drinking, playing cards and reading novels, and boldly declared the religious reason for her visit. Immediately, she heard "the hollow, mocking laugh that went up from nearly every one of the nine throats in the room [that] would have done credit to the inhabitants of the lower regions."[1] As she persisted in telling them of Jesus' love, one woman stammered, "You don't mean to say that God can save such as we are, that there is hope either in this world or the one to come for those fallen as low as we are?" Lee disclosed in her autobiography how that question lingered before her: "Oh, how my heart ached to tell these poor girls to come with me to learn to live for God. But it was as they said, there was no place open to them. They could not do right where they were, so must remain in sin. But from that time we determined to open a place of refuge for just such as these."[2]

Through Lee's gritty determination, she convinced a widow with young children to allow her to set up a rescue home in several unoccupied rooms in the family's home. Soon after, when a nine-room house at 403 Bancroft Street in Omaha became available for rent, she moved there on the east side of town alongside the railroad lines and Missouri river banks. She incorporated her rescue work under Nebraska state laws in 1892.[3] Within a few years, she opened a second rescue home in Wichita, Kansas. Her rescue efforts extended as well to opening a mission in Kansas City, Missouri. Typical of "soap-soup-salvation" rescue missions,[4] her Good Will Mission stood in a dodgy area nicknamed Hell's Half Acre—a "sanctuary for the thugs and drifters who infested the city's nearby train depot and for the barflies and prostitutes who inhabited the area's numerous saloons."[5] Given her proclivity toward rescuing prostitutes, Good Will Mission stood in "plain sight" of "the girls," whom "she could see from the house at all hours of the day and night."[6]

Mother Lee fit the paradigm of rescue workers, women who "were generally not the elite reformers," explains historian Regina Kunzel, but rather represented the "larger 'organized womanhood'" of evangelical Protestant women.[7] Lee came to rescue work in her forties after she was converted, sanctified, and healed. She marked her sanctification by abstaining from pipe smoking, a habit she had enjoyed for twelve years. Her body remained weak from its effects, which in turn hindered her evangelistic work. As she prayed for healing, she recounted what happened: "The healing power went through me, leaving me every whit whole." In response, she dedicated her life to the "rescue of those fallen outcasts" and to the God who had rescued her from spiritual and physical devastation.[8] Similar narratives held true for Emma Whittemore, Emma Ray, Carrie Judd Montgomery, Florence Roberts, and Anna Prosser. Their experience of being healed compelled them into rescue work; their own redemption became the impetus to redeem others. As historian Heather Curtis notes about those who received divine healing, "Personal physical restoration was closely linked with a profound desire to be energetically engaged in serving God and ministering to others."[9]

Rescue work resounded with the maternalist rhetoric and domestic activity utilized by other women reformers in the late nineteenth century. "The concept of maternalism accepted, even idealized, women's traditional role as wife and mother but at the same time insisted that women had a duty to extend their female skills and concerns beyond their own homes," notes historian Elizabeth Clapp.[10] In this regard, many rescue home founders took on the name "mother," like Mother Lee, Mother Whittemore, and Mother Roberts.[11] They decorated rescue institutions to approximate a home-like setting "filled with love and tenderness," as Whittemore suggested.[12] They acted as surrogate mothers to provide "proper instruction and training, including a right religious influence."[13] They taught rescue-home residents how to cook, clean, and sew and young mothers how to feed, clothe, and care for their baby. They provided ongoing religious instruction in prayer and Bible study as part of the daily and weekly routine.

Maternalism and domesticity also characterized Emma Ray's rescue work among African American children in Kansas City. When mothers left for work, the children flocked to Ray, a stay-at-home mom of sorts, who watched them at the mission during the day and who, on Sunday afternoons, invited them back for Sunday School. When she returned to Seattle, her maternalism continued when she invited released prisoners into her home. She cooked meals, washed and mended clothes, made up beds, and insisted that they attend worship; in other words, she mothered them.

This maternal imprint differentiated women evangelists in the Progressive Era in yet another way from their predecessors, who purposefully escaped domesticity to pursue itinerant evangelism. In her work on nineteenth century itinerant women evangelists, Elizabeth Elkin Grammer uses the language of "breaking up housekeeping" to describe how they dismantled the pressing domestic ideology in order to follow God's call to preach. She explains further that "they were compelled by their circumstances to replace the central metaphor of *home* with the countermetaphor of *homelessness* or itinerancy."[14] Jarena Lee, for instance, left home for a week to preach at a venue thirty miles away, even though her son was ill. In her autobiography, she explained that "during the whole time, not a thought of my little son came into my mind; it was hid from me, lest I should have been diverted from the work I had to do, to look after my son." This statement clearly delineated that her work—"the work I had to do"—at least for that week revolved around being an evangelist, not a mother. Then she used the phrase, one that Grammer picked up on, "breaking up housekeeping." Lee wrote, "I now returned home, found all well; no harm had come to my child, although I left it very sick. Friends had taken care of it which was of the Lord. I now began to think seriously of breaking up housekeeping, and forsaking all to preach the everlasting Gospel."[15] In contrast, Mother Lee set up housekeeping and adopted a maternal role in rescue institutions in Kansas, Missouri, and Nebraska. Other women did the same across the country, from Virginia Moss's Door of Hope Mission in North Bergen, New Jersey, to Carrie Judd Montgomery's Beulah Rescue Home in Oakland and, in San Francisco, the People's Mission.

The outreach of these founders of rescue institutions coincided with enormous efforts by many secular and religious organizations in the Progressive Era. In a walk around the block in an urban tenement neighborhood, one might pass a settlement house, a friendly visitor from the Charity Organization Society, and a Salvation Army rescue mission. Each of these offered the destitute, prostitute, addict, and immigrant a new way of life, but their strategy differed, particularly with regard to religion. The settlement-house movement focused on facilitating relationships between settlement workers and their often underprivileged neighbors. Settlement workers, many with a college degree and middle-class upbringing, purposefully took up residence in tenement neighborhoods and worked with residents to develop supportive ventures, from manual job training courses to a safe neighborhood playground.[16] The integration of religion into settlement work became a divisive issue. Many settlement workers, despite the childhood influence of a religious home, eschewed the direct expression of religious sentiments in deference to the interreligious nature of these neighborhoods.[17] "The typical settlement, under American conditions, is one which provides neutral territory traversing all the lines of racial and religious cleavage," wrote the editors of the 1911 *Handbook of Settlements*.[18] A settlement worker who held this opinion, Mary E. McDowell, even though she was a lifelong Methodist, had nothing but disdain for rescue missions. However, other settlement workers, particularly African Americans, took a different stance on religion, argues historian Elisabeth Lasch-Quinn, because "they shared a culture in which religion played a central role." Lasch-Quinn finds that settlement work among African Americans, and also in the South, occurred most often "through missions, institutional churches, or other organizations with a strong religious component."[19] In other words, some settlement workers, like rescue workers, embraced religion as an integral aspect of outreach.

A retreat from anything remotely religious characterized the Charity Organization Society movement (COS). The COS aimed, as its name implied, to organize charity by coordinating the "resources of its community and to refer 'deserving' applicants to the appropriate agency."[20] Its work of visitation and assessment depended on a corps of volunteers known as friendly visitors, many of whom were club women, such as several hundred members of the Chicago Woman's Club.[21] With optimism and pluck, friendly visitors aimed to inculcate a sense of responsibility in the poor and needy for their own welfare because the visitors believed such an attitude would reverse an impoverished situation.

While COS visitors and many settlement workers refrained from integrating religion into their outreach, evangelical rescue workers, like Mother Lee, purposefully reached out to the soul and the body through a combination of evangelism and humanitarianism. Many evangelicals arrived at a brothel or tenement with a religious message, only to realize quickly the value of caring for the body as well. Historian Norris Magnuson confirms Lee's experience and finds a "large body of earnest evangelicals who entered the slums because of their concern for the souls of men and women, but who soon developed wide-ranging social service programs."[22] Those engaged in what he calls "evangelical social work" either launched or expanded their institution building during the Progressive Era. Take the Salvation Army. In a span of two decades after the founder, William Booth, commissioned a group of eight to begin work in the United States, a staggering expanse of institutions had already opened from New York to San Francisco, including "forty-nine men's shelters and five women's shelters; fourteen rescue homes; twenty-three food depots; twenty-three workshops, factories, and labor yards; twenty slum posts; three farm colonies; three hospitals; and two homes for waifs and strays."[23] During her tenure as commander of the Salvation Army in the United States from 1904 to 1934, Evangeline, the youngest of seven Booth children, doubled the number of institutions from approximately two hundred to four hundred.[24] However, in the midst of such institutionalization, she endeavored to keep at the forefront the Army's original evangelistic intention. In her speech before the International Missionary Council, a forerunner of the World Council of Churches, she reiterated the significance of individual salvation to the Army's work: "The question that Salvationists address to the individual is whether he accepts or rejects Christ. Acceptance means that Christ is admitted to and dwells within the soul."[25] As we see here, women evangelists, who engaged in rescue institution building, maintained this evangelistic priority despite the never-ending humanitarian needs of food, clothing, shelter, counseling, and job training.

Evangelism and Humanitarianism

Mother Lee's motivation to launch rescue institutions stemmed from her own dramatic, life-changing conversion experience. As a result, she carried the message of conversion to residents of Omaha's and Kansas City's slums and brothels: "I told them of the love of Jesus and His power to save, and how He saved me."[26] At the same time, she also recognized that ameliorating physical needs through humanitarianism could improve receptivity of the gospel message. To that end, she founded rescue institutions to provide tangible aid for those she encountered in her visitation rounds. Through her institutions, Lee pursued humanitarianism as a means of evangelism.

Iva Durham Vennard held to these same sentiments and set out a clear, no-nonsense strategy for outreach: Engage in humanitarianism as the "bait on the hook" for evangelism. Evangelism, the presentation of the gospel message, came first because she believed that every person ultimately will have to choose between eternal life through salvation in Jesus Christ or eternal damnation. We know she had already come to this conviction before her twenty-first birthday because she presented it in an essay delivered at the Illinois State Normal University's commencement exercises in 1890. In "The Spirit of Negation," she spoke of the conflicted yet inescapable choice between good and evil that pervaded such literary masterpieces as *Paradise Lost*, *Faust*, and the book of Job. "This mighty struggle between good and evil," she declared, "is the essence of all character whether of the race, or of the individual. It is as old as man. It is his life."[27] Using a boat metaphor, she set up the scenario that each individual must make this choice while being transported in lifeboats "launched for Eternity." On each side of the lifeboat, "whirlpools of Temptation" call out to the passengers. She enumerated these temptations as envy and ambition, cowardice and deceit, greed and selfishness.

Continuing on, she declared, "On every side, every craft is threatened. The voyage cannot be abandoned. All have launched for Eternity. They are hurrying to the great Unknown. Is a disaster unavoidable? Must the shattered crack enter the infinite ocean, a wreck? Must life be a tragedy?"[28] These rhetorical questions she answered with a resounding, "No!" because she believed in "the care of the kind Pilot" who guides to safety the ones who choose that route; it is these whom God will "anchor victoriously in the peaceful harbor of Heaven."[29] Amid this nautical scene, the evangelist's duty, according to Vennard, is to warn individuals away from Satan's shore and direct them toward God's safe harbor. One can almost hear the wistful strains of a verse from Philip Bliss's hymn, "Brightly Beams Our Father's Mercy," which he penned from a seafaring illustration by Dwight L. Moody: "Brightly Beams Our Father's Mercy from His lighthouse evermore, / But to us He gives the keeping of the lights along the shore. / Let the lower lights be burning! Send a gleam across the wave! / Some poor struggling, sinking sailor you may rescue, you may save."

Evangelism pointed out the path of "permanent reform."[30] As Vennard would later articulate,

> Important as education and humanitarian relief are, nothing short of the new birth through the Holy Spirit can bring souls into vital union with Christ. And this spiritual life and power is imperative if we hope for *permanent reform*. There is a reason why multitudes are "submerged." Ignorance is one great reason, to be sure, but *sin is at the bottom*, and the same influences that have brought many to pauperism will keep them there unless they are taught to appropriate the Divine Power, which

alone can enable them to conquer. Shiftlessness and drunkenness and immorality will not be cured by anything less than the Atoning Blood."[31]

Even though humanitarianism held second place to evangelism, because it dealt with temporary as opposed to eternal matters, Vennard nevertheless saw it as an integral component of outreach. In other words, she did not care *only* about the soul, an all-too-commonplace stance, according to the Reverend Josiah Strong, Congregational minister, general secretary of the Evangelical Alliance, and early proponent of the Social Gospel. Strong quoted the following remarks spoken by "a prominent representative" of the church: "The church has no business with a man's dirty face; the church has no business with a man's naked back; the church has no business with a man's empty stomach. The Church has just one business with a man, and that is to save his soul."[32] Vennard, too, dismissed such sentiments, noting, "We are using humanitarian methods constantly, and must of necessity do so, to come into contact with the people whom we long to serve. We are caring for their bodies, we are educating their minds, we are helping them in business matters."[33] However, she repeatedly clarified that humanitarianism alone did not suffice. "But if we stop there we have not reached the soul. . . . The enemy is constantly trying to make us content with mere philanthrophy [sic]. But the Spirit of God forces the issue upon us that all this service, Christlike as it is, in its compassionate ministry, is only the bate [sic] on the hook to catch the fish."[34] She continued, "but we have not landed the fish until the individual has been *brought into saving touch with the Lord Jesus*."[35]

While this individualistic approach to evangelism and humanitarianism prevailed among many evangelicals in the Progressive Era, a significant group within American Protestantism championed the social dimensions of Jesus' teachings, known variously as "Social Christianity," "Christian Socialism," or the "Social Gospel."[36] Proponents believed that the Social Gospel held the key, if pursued strategically by the American church, to transforming society and its institutions as well as individuals. Strong, for instance, urged churches to broaden their conception of redemption to encompass the earth itself, yet without forsaking the individual: "As fast as the churches regain Christ's point of view and come to believe that the earth is to be redeemed from its evils, they see, that it is their duty to labor for the realization of Christ's social ideal, and they adapt their methods accordingly; they no longer look upon duty as a circle described around the individual as the center, but rather as an ellipse described around the individual and society as the two foci."[37]

Evidently Vennard mustered appreciation for a particular version of the Social Gospel because she welcomed one of its advocates to Chicago Evangelistic Institute (CEI), the Reverend John Marvin Dean, founder and first president of Northern Baptist Theological Seminary, senior minister at Second Baptist Church of Chicago, and a leader in the Men and Religion Forward Movement, a national, ecumenical effort to rally men and boys to evangelism and social service.[38] Dean's book on the topic, *Evangelism and Social Service*, brought him to her attention. She heaped high praise on his book in CEI's monthly newsletter and invited him to lecture in a sociology class. However, Dean and Vennard did not see completely eye to eye. She had little to say about the social dimension because she targeted the individual. He championed social service precisely because he believed it highlighted the gospel's ramifications for society.[39]

Like Strong, Dean believed that as the church pursued "a social application of Christ's gospel," its "potency" would successfully combat societal injustices, which erupted in poverty, lack of education, worker unrest, and insufficient wages.[40] This potency for social service stems from the same gospel that empowers evangelism. Thus, as his book title declares, he believed in social service *and* evangelism, not social service *or* evangelism. He went on to critique both sides of the either/or approach. The evangelism-only folks purposed to save souls for an eternal life to come in heaven, which, in Dean's opinion, "narrowed and discredited evangelism."[41] Although he does not label this group, he may have had in mind, given his Chicago vantage point and the proximity of Moody Bible Institute, the inheritors of Moody's premillennialism, who believed in Christ's imminent return and God's final judgment upon the world and the unsaved. Social service had no eternal value for a premillennialist; only evangelism mattered, as Moody's infamous quote asserts: "I look upon this world as a wrecked vessel. God has given me a lifeboat and said to me, 'Moody, save all you can.'"[42]

On the other side stood the Modernists, also with a stronghold in the city at the University of Chicago Divinity School, nicknamed "the

Baptist superuniversity."⁴³ Dean denounced Modernists for being "disloyal to the evangelical position" because they remained "uncertain" on pivotal theological loci, such as "revelation, atonement, justification by faith, and the kindred doctrines of grace."⁴⁴ From this inadequate theology, he charged, sprang the Modernists' myopic focus on social service. Despite sharing the Baptist heritage and ordination with Shailer Mathews, a leading Modernist, professor, and dean at the University of Chicago, Dean proposed to counteract his influence by launching Northern Baptist Seminary in 1913 in the basement of the Second Baptist Church in downtown Chicago.⁴⁵ Steering clear of both sides, Dean attempted a middle position that incorporated both social service and evangelism. To encapsulate his approach, he penned a brief creed printed on the book's final page: "I believe in Social Service. I believe in Evangelism. I believe that both are inherent in the very nature of the one indivisible gospel of the grace of God in Christ Jesus. I believe in the gospel."⁴⁶

In tangible ways, he embodied his creed. He mentored a prominent twentieth-century woman evangelist in Baptist circles, Amy Lee Stockton. Stockton grew up in his congregation at San Jose Baptist Church. He recognized and cultivated her speaking abilities, encouraging her to preach at Baptist churches and youth conventions. Unbeknownst to her, before he left for Chicago, he established a fund to cover the costs of her seminary education. When he launched Northern Baptist Seminary, Dean immediately enrolled Stockton as the very first student. As the lone woman in her class, she felt like a misfit and wrote about it later in her autobiography: "My thoughts revert to an afternoon when I sat at my desk quite discouraged. I was homesick. I felt somewhat inadequate to the requirements. My fellow students were all men and they rather resented a woman invading their world."⁴⁷ Nevertheless, she persevered, and on graduation day, she received a telegram from the California Baptist Convention offering her the job of state evangelist for Northern California and western Nevada. She subsequently ventured out as an itinerant evangelist and preached nationwide for more than sixty years.⁴⁸

Dean's commitment to evangelism also marked the seminary's curriculum. Amid Stockton's papers is a one-page chart with the heading: "Reading Courses in Evangelism." Across the top, she wrote,

"Arranged by J.M. Dean for N.B.T.S.," which, without abbreviations, reads "Arranged by John Marvin Dean for Northern Baptist Theological Seminary." The chart delineated four courses annually over a three-year cycle, or twelve total, that included personal evangelism, lives of great soul winners, evangelistic methods, evangelistic sermons, and evangelistic ministry. Reflective of Dean's imprimatur was the course on social service and evangelism, for which his book was required reading. Taken in aggregate, the reading courses added up to a thorough grounding in evangelism for seminary students.

True to his creed, Dean actively engaged in social service. He set up a settlement house in Chicago, the Aiken Institute, through his work at Second Baptist Church. His rationale for the settlement house encapsulated the connection he envisioned between evangelism and social service. "I cannot, however, help but feel that the evangelical church can do both of these services," he wrote. "It can, through its settlement activities, help a whole neighborhood into better living conditions, and it can so infill these social activities with evangelistic passion as to help many of those thus aided on into the fullness of Christ's redemption."[49]

Evidently Vennard found enough camaraderie in Dean's message to invite him to CEI, yet whether she confronted the full import of his commitment to social service remains unknown. In the eight quotes from his book reproduced in CEI's bulletin, *Inasmuch*, not one mentions his extensive condemnation of societal injustices. With rhetorical overtones, he declared over and over that social service cannot cease "until the swollen profits of our vampire department stores show more plainly in living wages . . . until the tired workers are given the seats they pay for in the cars of our dishonest City Railways Company . . . until fifty thousand hard-working people now in this city, under the shadow of a great physical fear of losing their pitiful 'jobs,' no matter how hard they serve at them, are assured by an amended social order of a decent support."[50] Topics such as these remained far from Vennard's conception of rescue work as reaching out to individuals with soap-soup-salvation.

The relationship between evangelism and humanitarianism remains an enduring conundrum. Advocates of evangelism alongside humanitarianism claim that this holistic approach benefits body and soul, not just one or the other. This rationale appears on the current website of the Association of Gospel Rescue Missions: "For more than a century, they [rescue missions] have been keeping watch on the waterfront of despair, and countless men, women, and children have been *saved in every sense of the word*."[51] For critics, evangelism alongside humanitarianism evokes the pejorative term, "rice Christians." They contend that a religious conversion might be conveniently conjured in order to receive the promised incentive. In a retrospect of mission work in his country, a Chinese bishop suggests that the enticement of Western money created superficial Christian converts, or "rice Christians." He writes, "China was the country in which the western missionary societies spent the most money and the field to which they sent the most missionaries. But the number of Christians was never large, and of that number quite a few were 'rice' Christians."[52] As the bishop's comments underscore, the connection between evangelism and humanitarianism remains a conundrum more than a century after Vennard's graduation speech. Yet, as we will see, women evangelists remained quite clear about their strategy of rescue work: humanitarianism as "bait on the hook" for evangelism.

Rescue Missions

Mother Lee came to Kansas City for a time and opened a twenty-four hour rescue mission, Good Will Mission, in 1901. In a square, two-story, frame building on Tenth Street, she fitted up two rooms on the ground floor, one serving as a gathering room flanked by a small bathroom and dressing room in the back, the other housing a kitchen and dining room "where the inmates [prostitutes] of the houses about could come to get a meal or to visit if so inclined."[53] Lee's mission offered food, temporary shelter, and a nightly evangelistic service. This soap-soup-salvation configuration epitomized most rescue missions, like Stranger's Rest Mission on Seattle's waterfront, where Emma Ray regularly volunteered. Stranger's Rest consisted of two unventilated basement rooms partitioned by a door. Bunks and cots for rent at ten or fifteen cents filled one room; in the other stood a lunch counter where coffee, pie, and sandwiches sold for five or ten cents. All the mission's activities—eating, sleeping, singing, preaching, and praying—took place amid unsanitary conditions because the tide rolled into the mission, and with it came the mosquitoes. Ray actually appreciated the mosquitoes, whose bites kept the men awake, despite their fatigued and often drunken state.[54]

Designed to be urban "lighthouses, doors of hope, havens of rest, for the storm-tossed and lost," rescue missions stayed open all night, every night, in destitute, dissolute neighborhoods around the country.[55] On Pacific Street in San Francisco, Carrie Judd Montgomery opened the People's Mission in 1890. She justified the need for the mission with this numerical calculation of nearby dubious establishments: "Radiating two blocks in each direction, we find by actual count, one hundred and fifty-three saloons and dives, forty-one open immoral houses, thirteen houses of assignation, and four large houses of doubtful reputation."[56] Just a few streets over from Lee's Kansas City mission, Emma and L. P. Ray opened a mission in 1902 in "Hick's Hollow," located at the city's North End and central to the business district and streetcar lines.[57] This enclave had the largest number of African American residents in the city, yet only 2 percent of them held white-collar jobs, compared to 29 percent of the whites. Many more African Americans, 46 percent, worked as day laborers or domestic servants, compared to 18 percent of the whites.[58] The subsequent lack of income meant hardship for African American children in Hick's Hollow, as an observer in 1913 explained: "Hundreds of children go to school without enough clothing to keep them warm in the winter time. In cold weather the majority of Negro families huddle around the kitchen fire and live entirely in one room."[59]

Similar to settlement workers who moved into poor neighborhoods, the Rays chose to live at the mission situated on the most disreputable corner in Hick's Hollow and share the same difficult conditions as their neighbors. The Rays, too, walked through mud in winter and summer on streets with no sidewalks and lost sleep due to the noise of all-night gambling games. They lived amid poverty in Hick's Hollow, where "landlords jammed flimsy frame structures onto the hollows' unpaved streets and alleyways. Sanitation facilities were scant, and just a fifth of the buildings were connected to city water mains, so that householders often drew their water from contaminated cisterns or carried it home from nearby saloons. Inevitably, mortality rates in the hollows far exceeded rates for the city as a whole."[60]

The Rays, as poor African Americans in the South, grew up in such conditions. Emma was born in 1859 into slavery and then raised in poverty. After emancipation, her family, alongside other freed slaves, built a Missouri shanty town out of scrap lumber and discarded building materials. To help her family financially, she had to quit school after the fourth grade and go to work as a live-in domestic for a white family. Her husband, L. P., a mulatto—the child of a white master and a slave woman—became an alcoholic at a young age and could not keep a steady job as a stonemason. Their move to Seattle after a devastating fire in 1889 that burned through the downtown district provided a new start for L. P.'s employment and their troubled marriage. At the African Methodist Episcopal Church, they both experienced conversion, and not long after, they were sanctified. Emma linked her sanctification experience to a call to evangelism. She described a jolt like a lightning bolt that struck her head and traveled through her body "from head to foot like liquid fire." She continued, "As my strength began to return, I felt a passion, such a love for souls as I had never felt before. I saw a lost world. My heart became hot. A fire of holy, abiding love for God and souls was kindled at that hour. . . . It was the fire that still burns in my souls this very moment, and I feel it will last until Jesus comes."[61]

The Rays' mission combined humanitarianism with evangelism. For the African American children in Hick's Hollow, they provided clothes, meals, trips to the park in the summer, and a warm place to come in the winter. As Emma recalled,

> Some of these children would come, a half dozen at a time, to our place. . . . Their mothers would leave them without fuel, early in the morning, to go to work, and then they would come into the Mission, poor naked little tots, with their shoes untied and their hair unkempt and ofttimes they would be holding their ragged clothes together with their hands. . . . I remember our first New Year's night. The room was packed with children. We had to keep the windows up and we kept chloride of lime in the room because some of them were so unclean.[62]

The mission also sponsored nightly evangelistic services on the neighborhood's street corners. Emma and L. P. sang and played instruments outside a gathering place—a rooming house, loan office, or saloon—in order to draw a crowd. Then they preached a brief gospel message, followed by a time of prayer. One night, they deliberately interrupted a crap game by forming their song circle at the exact spot where players threw the dice. Emma claimed they were particularly effective: "We had a splendid audience. The Lord helped us to tell them of their sinfulness and how badly they were bringing up their children, and that it was no wonder they were having so much trouble as a people. They believed us. We came away believing that those testimonies would have a lasting effect on those people."[63]

The nightly evangelistic service stood as the centerpiece of a rescue mission. Workers designed it as a one-stop, last-ditch effort to rescue the destitute and outcast. A recurring theme of the service, apropos of the audience in attendance, heralded the rescue of lost sinners. To drive home the message of the lost become found, song leaders had at their disposal a tune, "Feed on Husks No More," with this jaunty chorus about the Prodigal Son (Luke 15:11–32): "I will arise and go at once, / My Father's love implore; Confess my wrong: His pardon seek, / And feed on husks no more."[64] To accompany the songs, most rescue missions, no matter how small in size or depleted in funds, managed to secure an organ. A donation of ten dollars enabled Virginia Moss, a Pentecostal minister and rescue home founder, to buy an organ for her Door of Hope Mission, which opened in the winter of 1906 in a street-level basement room at 700 Fisher Avenue in New Durham, New Jersey. Emma Whittemore, who became an early member of the Christian and Missionary Alliance denomination after an experience of divine healing, sold garage-sale items as a fund-raiser to buy an organ for Jerry McAuley's Water Street Mission in New York City. That same organ continued its usefulness in two more rescue missions before it ended up on a yacht used for outreach to sailors in New York City's harbor.[65]

The composer of the Prodigal Son chorus, Colonel Henry H. Hadley, also wrote the autobiographical words for "He Saves the Drunkard Too."[66] The first two lines offer a brief testimony to his own experience of rescue: "My Saviour can the drunkard save; / For he has rescued me." The next stanzas introduce biblical characters whom Jesus rescued, like the leper, Mary Magdalene, Peter on the waves, and the beggar healed at Jericho. Stanza 6 supplies the rousing finale: "Oh, weary sinner, come to Him; / 'Tis all that thou canst do. / Remember, He alone can keep / And save the drunkard too."[67] Hadley started more than sixty rescue missions after his conversion at Water Street Mission.

New York City's Water Street Mission, founded by Jerry McAuley in 1872, became the catalyst for launching more than one hundred rescue missions around the globe between 1872 and 1892.[68] McAuley had a titillating story that ran the gamut from alcoholism and river thievery to imprisonment in Sing Sing Prison.[69] After his conversion, he founded the mission located in New York City's Lower East Side. During its first year alone, the mission provided twenty-six thousand meals, five thousand lodgings, and services every night of the week.[70] McAuley's successor at Water Street Mission, S. H. Hadley, a former alcoholic converted at Water Street and brother of Colonel Hadley, coordinated rescue missions into a nationwide organization, the International Union of Gospel Missions (IUGM).[71] The first two IUGM presidents, Sidney and Emma Whittemore, invested their considerable tithe and talent into rescue institutions after hearing Jerry McAuley preach at Water Street.[72]

When rescue mission converts like McAuley or the Hadley brothers preached, they told a narrative shared by many in the audience. Words that might have sounded like tacky religious platitudes to others—"The blood of Jesus saved me from a drunkard's grave and a devil's hell"; "I've been trying to get work all day, I couldn't find any but I got a wonderful blessing in my heart"; "Religion has brought me the only peace and satisfaction I've ever had in this life"; or "Since Christ came into my life I'm done with ornaments and clothes"—resonated with honest conviction because they, too, had been prodigals on society's margins.[73] Delia, who became a quintessential, rescue mission evangelist, had no less than three nicknames before her conversion—"The Mystery" because the police could never find her, "the Mulberry Slum Bummer" because she frequented the slum neighborhood along Mulberry Street, and "Blue Bell" because she always wore a blue dress. During a night of visitation by Emma Whittemore, Delia, a twenty-three-year-old woman with facial bruises and patches of missing hair, followed her from door to door, announcing, "I'm neither afraid of man, God nor the devil, and so can go *anywhere*." Before the night ended, Whittemore handed Delia a pink rose with the parting invitation to meet the next night at the mission. Eventually, Delia, still clutching her rose, landed at Whittemore's Door of Hope Mission, where she was "so wondrously rescued of God out of one of the worst dives on Mulberry Street."[74]

For the next eleven months until her death in 1892, Delia spent her days and nights alongside her former Mulberry Street companions, telling them about her conversion. Her funeral, the largest in New York City other than President Grant's, also served an evangelistic purpose. In a letter to Whittemore afterward, a handful of men from Mulberry Street made this pledge: "We *promise* here that we shall at least try and become different men, and do something for ourselves and for our God. We don't say *everyone* will keep his promise, but we *know* there will be a good many who *will* change their lives owing to Delia's sweet happy face that they seen [*sic*] [in her casket] Tuesday." Soon after, they showed up at Whittemore's Door of Hope and spent an afternoon singing hymns and reading the Bible together. A man named Murphy opened a Bible's front cover and read this message in Delia's handwriting: "For Murphy, with regards from Delia. 'Seek first the kingdom of God and His righteousness and all these things shall be added unto you.' Matt. vi:33." In response, according to Whittemore, he confessed, "God be merciful to me a sinner."[75]

While most rescue missions began through the efforts of an individual, like Mother Lee or Jerry McAuley, Anna Prosser undertook a different approach. Prosser, born into a wealthy family and raised a nominal Presbyterian, was healed after suffering as an invalid for ten years due to myriad health issues, including a complete nervous breakdown, internal tumors, and chronic kidney, bowel, and uterine problems. Armed with renewed health and strength, she began to volunteer in a Woman's Christian Temperance Union (WCTU) rescue mission in Buffalo, New York. Within a short time, Prosser also convened a Saturday evening Bible study of "laboring men," which grew from six to more than fifty.[76] Each Christmas, she provided as lavish a feast for them as she could afford from her own resources. After several years, when she felt called to open a new mission, the men in her Bible study elected to go as well and assist her in the work. From then on, when talking about the mission, Prosser used the pronoun "we" to signify the partnership between them: "Finding that the Canal Street Mission was about to be vacated, we concluded to take it, paying all that we could towards rent, etc., and trusting in God to supply any deficiency." Elsewhere, she wrote, "It was good to see my faithful men standing by so heroically in the thickest of the fight, and to watch their steady growth in grace and increasing love for the Word."[77]

Despite testimonies like these, rescue mission founders faced rampant criticism for both their evangelistic objective and humanitarian charity. As mentioned previously, some settlement workers strongly disapproved of rescue mission personnel engaging in evangelism in a tenement neighborhood. Mary E. McDowell, director of the University of Chicago Settlement, drew a sharp contrast between settlement houses and rescue missions when she spoke at the 1908 national conference of Methodist social workers. "Some one has said that where the mission sees sinners, the settlement sees citizens, and that where one believes in converting the individual, the other says the environment also must be converted, believing that pasture is at least as strong, if not stronger, than breed." She then categorically denounced any preconceived agenda, particularly a religious one; instead, she cautioned settlement workers to wait patiently and labor humbly for their neighbors' acceptance. Settlement work, she declared, should aim to have no "definite propaganda" but simply go on "living with folks and responding to their needs as they make demands upon them."[78] McDowell's dismissal of religion as a component of settlement work corresponded with the stance of the National Federation of Settlements (NFS), an organization which she and Jane Addams, among other settlement leaders, helped to found.[79] Still, Addams approached the religious aspect with more nuance than McDowell, suggesting that it was intrinsically embedded in settlement work's humanitarianism. Addressing Christianity in particular, she likened settlement work to Christianity's "impulse to share the lives of the poor, the desire to make social service, irrespective of propaganda, express the spirit of Christ." As such, she portended a "renaissance of the early Christian humanitarianism" in Chicago and throughout the country as the "spiritual force of the settlement movement."[80]

Addams's opinion did not convince Vennard, who founded another settlement house in Chicago, Wayside Settlement, and staffed it as a training ground in practical work for students from Chicago Evangelistic Institute. Vennard had toured several settlement houses in the city, including Hull House, prior to opening Wayside. While she made positive observations about the humanitarian outreach, she noted the absence of "anything distinctively religious," since settlement workers "stop short of a personal Saviour offering a full and free salvation to all to whom it ministers."[81] To the question, Why another settlement in Chicago? she responded with her fishing analogy: "The answer is simple. We have opened 'The Wayside' because we believe that foreigners, poor people, and all classes need salvation. We must do more than serve our people through humanitarian service. These temporal benefits we gladly give, but they are *the bait for our hook*, and we do not feel that we have ever done our best for a family until we have brought them to know Jesus."[82] Thus, consistent with her worldview, any kind of outreach must have evangelism as its raison d'être.

Criticized on the one hand for too much religion, rescue workers met, on the other hand, with disapproval for being indiscriminate in humanitarianism, for not distinguishing between worthy and unworthy recipients among those who showed up at a mission. Josephine Lowell Shaw, founder and long-time director of the New York COS, repeatedly stated her disapproval of this practice. Shaw disdained "the sentimental, morality-laden, and indiscriminate relief" offered by rescue missions; instead, she enthusiastically adhered to COS policy of giving minimal direct relief, and then only to those considered deserving.[83] According to Shaw, "Human nature is so constituted that no man can receive as a gift what he should earn by his own labor without moral deterioration."[84] Armed with this clear purpose and business-like efficiency, COS friendly visitors walked through and systematically observed city neighborhoods to gather information about conditions—"street, alley, and sidewalk conditions; housing, schools, and churches; infant mortality rates, numbers of children, and juvenile delinquency; parks, playgrounds, dance halls, saloons, hotels, jails, and courts."[85] During home visits, they were to notice everything in excruciating detail—"the client's mental and physical condition, the manners of his children and the domestic skills of his wife, his salary, occupation, affiliations, debts, recreational tastes, and personal peccadillos."[86] These close inspections enabled the visitors to recommend appropriate forms of aid, if any, to the deserving and to be the frontline in detecting fraudulent use by "unworthy citizens" who received unnecessary aid.[87] This aspect of the COS sparked condemnation from Jane Addams as well as the poet who composed this lyric: "The organized charity scrimped and iced / In the name of a cautious, statistical Christ."[88]

Undaunted, Shaw challenged the Salvation Army's plan to increase the number of rescue missions in New York City, charging that even more vagrants would come to town for the free food and shelter. In her position as chair of the Committee on Vagrancy of the Conference of Charities,

Shaw held sharp exchanges with Frederick Booth-Tucker, then co-commander of the Salvation Army in the United States. During their dispute, Shaw declared that "a man had no right to be homeless." Booth-Tucker's response was swift and direct: "What can one say to talk like that? I told her men were homeless and would always be so. . . . Men starve while their agents are spending money finding out who they are. . . . We can't find work for men and women in many cases, but we can relieve distress, and that's what we'll go on doing while they go on investigating."[89]

Emma Ray also did not differentiate between recipients as deserving or not. Instead, she generously supplied food, clothing, even shelter in her home, to relative strangers. She invited released prisoners, with whom she became acquainted during her regular visitation rounds at the Seattle jail, to stay at her home until they could find a job and support themselves. This hospitable practice began when she noticed that prisoners who responded to her preaching and "seemed to have a good experience in salvation," would quickly "go down into sin again" once they were released.[90] To reverse this trend, she offered a temporary home, new clothes, a bath, food, some jobs to do, and money for a shave, with the expectation that they would go to church or the rescue mission for services. On one occasion, when she did not have a new coat for one of the men, Emma scrubbed his old coat, which was "so full of vermin." She sang while scrubbing, and as she belted out the chorus, she recalled receiving a great blessing. The man's response was marked. "He stood watching me and helping me get water, and tears came into his eyes as I sang and rubbed. Years after he seemed very grateful, and could never forget what the Lord had wrought in his heart."[91] Thus, despite criticism for being too compassionate or too religious, rescue mission founders and workers like Ray, Lee, Prosser, Montgomery, and Whittemore persevered nonetheless in evangelism and humanitarianism. Several of these women pursued the same strategy in yet another rescue institution—the rescue home—to which we now turn.

Rescue Homes

Because Mother Lee could not shake the prostitute's plaintive words, "There is no place on God's foot-stool for a fallen woman," she ended that night of visitation in the Omaha brothel determined to establish a rescue home where prostitutes and unwed mothers could take refuge. During their stay, "when sheltered and kept from the temptations and allurements and from the associations of those who cause[d] her downfall," she imagined ample opportunities for evangelism.[92] She believed, as did Moody, that no woman could fall beyond the extent of Jesus' forgiveness. "There are some people who believe that these have fallen so low that Christ will pass them by," declared Moody. "But my friends that thought comes from the Evil One. In all this blessed book there is not one, not a solitary one of this class mentioned that ever came to Him but that He received them. Yes, He even went out of His way and sought her out."[93]

Lee's first rescue home opened in 1891 amidst a flurry of such institutions, yet rescue work in America stretched back a century with the founding of moral societies in New England between 1790 and 1815 and Magdalen societies, whose turn of the century work in urban areas focused on rescuing prostitutes.[94] Rescue work took on new life in the 1830s and 1840s owing to the female reform movement in the northeast. "As early as 1842 it [the New England Female Moral Reform Society] opened a Temporary Home for them [prostitutes] and for abandoned women pregnant under the promise of marriage. Three years later, a Strangers' Retreat was opened to provide temporary shelter for young female migrants to Boston."[95] After the Civil War, scattered rescue homes opened under the auspices of Protestant denominations, including the San Francisco Chinese Mission Home for Chinese prostitutes founded in 1874 by the Presbyterian Church.[96] Then, in the mid-1880s, a succession of rescue homes materialized just in New York City alone. The Salvation Army, soon to operate the second largest network of rescue homes, opened its first, Morris Cottage, for "the fallen and the falling," in 1886 in New York City.[97] Under the eight-year leadership of Emma and Frederick Booth-Tucker, the Salvation Army increased rescue homes across America from seven to twenty-one.[98] Emma Whittemore's first Door of Hope also began in New York City and then expanded to sixty more in two decades. She increased that number to almost one hundred by 1930, the year she died.[99]

The largest national chain, the National Florence Crittenton Mission (NFCM), began in 1883, when Charles Crittenton opened his first home for prostitutes at 29 Bleecker Street in New York City's red-light district. He named it Florence Mission in memory of his daughter, who died at a young age. Crittenton, known as the "millionaire evangelist" because of the wealth he accrued through a pharmaceutical company, built an empire of rescue homes while crisscrossing the nation as an itinerant evangelist.[100] Through his association with Frances Willard, he donated $5,000 in 1892 to open five Crittenton homes in partnership with the WCTU, which already had its own assortment of rescue homes.[101] In 1896, the NFCM became the first philanthropic organization to receive a national charter, by an Act of Congress signed by President McKinley.[102]

As the NFCM continued to develop, its outreach shifted from prostitutes to unwed mothers, from rescue homes to maternity homes, from evangelism to social work. Within forty years after first opening Florence Mission as a refuge for prostitutes, the NFCM had evolved into the nation's largest chain of maternity homes with at least one home in seventy-three cities, including several outside of the United States. A NFCM leader explained the shift in these words: "In carrying on the rescue work of the Mission there has been, in the first place, a progressive shift of emphasis from the more fervidly emotional spirit of the earlier evangelistic years to a thorough and careful study of every phase of the problem of helping girls. Undoubtedly this is a reflection of the tendency of the times toward a magnification of the scientific attitude."[103] Regina Kunzel confirms this trend by demonstrating that the evangelical reformers, who answered a religious call to serve in rescue institutions in the early years, collided later on with social workers armed with a scientific, casework approach.[104] Kunzel writes, "Maternity homes—which were once shelters dedicated to the redemption and reclamation of 'fallen women'—were now redefined by social workers as places of scientific treatment. Rather than unfortunate 'sisters to be saved,' unmarried mothers became 'problem girls' to be treated."[105]

While this change marked NFCM in the second generation, Crittenton's initial impetus for rescue work emerged from a personal encounter with two prostitutes during his visitation rounds in New York City. Like Lee, he went out at night in order to visit with prostitutes and tell them of Jesus' love. Visitation thus became the frontline for rescue workers. Whittemore also did nightly visitation in New York City. She believed God prompted her in this direction after she was healed from twelve years of chronic pain and limited mobility caused by a fall that crushed a lower vertebra in her spine: "Suddenly the girls on the street came to my mind so forcibly that it was not difficult to almost imagine I could hear the tramp of numberless feet going straight to perdition."[106] During a brothel visit, Whittemore came face to face with a sixteen-year-old girl wearing a scanty dress and smoking a cigarette. Initially, the teenager mocked Whittemore's gospel talk and deliberately blew smoke in her face. The older woman responded by embracing her and saying, "Child, you have treated me most rudely and you know it. You've laughed, sneered, and ridiculed almost everything I have attempted to say, but tell me dear, tell me truly (pointing to her heart), is there any laughter down there?"[107] Before too long, the teenager showed up at the Door of Hope and experienced a conversion, the happy ending that rescue workers prayed would come true every night during visitation.

To gain easier access to prostitutes' living quarters before they were cleaned up or closed up to visitors, Whittemore dressed as a working-class woman. She offered this description of her visitation clothing:

> Our own dress consisted of a dark calico wrapper with two or three good-sized patches of another colour neatly inserted here and there on the skirt. . . . A blue and white gingham apron was always worn. This, too, had its neat patches. On cold days, we would have a faded old shawl thrown over our shoulders. A plain black straw hat, a bit out of style, had as its only adornment a thin piece of silk twisted around the crown. Our equipment for ministry to the poor souls of Slumdom consisted of a tin pail filled with gruel, soup or tea, and a large package of old clothing done up in newspaper.[108]

Most likely, Whittemore, an honorary staff captain in the Salvation Army, picked up this practice from Evangeline Booth, who, as a teenager, dressed in rags when serving among the poor in London's East End. (Booth later re-created this outreach in a dramatic monologue, "The Commander in Rags.")[109] Female officers of the Army's Slum Brigade, known as "slum sisters," dressed similarly while visiting. Emma Bown and Martha Johnson moved into the Lower East Side of New York City to "set up housekeeping" alongside the poor and destitute.[110] They knocked on doors and offered to clean apartments, prepare food for working parents or the sick, and care for children, invalids, and the elderly; they also initiated conversations about religion and prayed with those they visited. Carrie Judd Montgomery, who partnered with the Army to open a rescue home in Oakland and a rescue mission in San Francisco, worked for a time with "slum sisters" in New York City. She remarked over the different reception that came her way when she dressed in simple attire instead of her finer clothes: "In former years I had had some experience in this kind of work, but had gone on my missionary tours in ordinary dress and had found the dear, erring girls to be shy and unapproachable, and in some cases sullen and reserved. But in the simple garb of the 'slum sisters' I found the warmest welcome from nearly every girl with whom I conversed in the slums."[111]

If visitation rounds identified women ready to be rescued, then the worker's attention turned to the practical matter of finding a suitable structure for the rescue home. It began in tight quarters, like the few spare rooms in a family's home that Lee secured. As soon as possible, the founder relocated the home to a more ideal location away from the city center to a secluded neighborhood or even the countryside. For her second Door of Hope in 1893, Whittemore looked across the Hudson River in Tappan, New York, and found a Dutch cottage-style house complete with broad windows whose upper sashes held tinted squares of glass.[112] Other rescue homes took over a substantial house—with rooms providing a modicum of privacy for the residents—set on a multiacre plot, like Lee's second home in Wichita, Kansas. "The building is of brick, containing nearly forty rooms, with closets, halls, baths and all so convenient and nice, there is no lack of room."[113] Acreage around a home made available a garden plot, or even a working farm, like the Free Methodists' Holmes Home and Hospital in Guthrie, Oklahoma, with its "20 head of cattle, 1 span of mules, 4 horses and 2 colts, 7 hogs, 300 chickens, and an uncounted number of turkeys, geese and ducks."[114]

Running a rescue home required sufficient funds to pay the rent and buy furniture, fuel, food, and other necessities. Meals alone consumed an extravagant amount of ingredients as well as many hours to prepare, cook, serve, and clean. In a nine-month period at the Heartsease Home for Women and Babies in New York City, workers supplied nearly sixteen thousand meals. Feeding the residents, an integral component of rescue work, "is not given much consideration and yet it is one of the most necessary," explained Anne Richardson Kennedy, founder and matron of Heartsease.[115] Finances floundered month to month, and rescue homes remained dependent on donations of clothing, garden seeds, apples, mustard greens, flour, sugar, and buckets of syrup. Even pennies figured largely, as evident in the January 1909 financial report for the Holmes Home and Hospital, which reported a balance of sixty-three pennies once expenditures had been deducted from the month's income.[116] A $12 donation for Whittemore's first Door of Hope came from a group of children who collected as many pennies as each of their ages.

Rescue home founders maintained a frenetic pace from the morning worship service to the midnight knock from a woman seeking shelter. Inbetween came three daily meals to prepare, letters to write for donations or to thank benefactors, babies to wash, feed, and dress, and residents to instruct in basic housekeeping skills. Lee regretted the inordinate amount of time and energy consumed by these tasks rather than time talking to residents about religious matters. While she confessed to discouragement over daily upkeep, she realized that the home had to look attractive, especially to former prostitutes who had enjoyed high standards of comfort in a well-run brothel. "If you get girls that have in sin good rooms and good food with many of the luxuries of life, you cannot put them in bare, cold rooms or set them down to indifferent food. I saw my life work slipping away into mere help for the body and felt I must arouse myself and in some way reach those to whom I am sent." Still, she felt deeply concerned lest the "worldly element might creep in and defeat our plans for the salvation of the souls we were seeking."[117]

In their newsletters and memoirs, rescue home founders penned narratives that assessed the spiritual condition of residents. These frequently conformed to the stylized story of a young, beautiful, fragile woman who fell into addiction or prostitution after desertion by a feckless man, often their betrothed. Once rescued, the resident, often with curious nicknames, such as Wichita Lizzie, Omaha Jack, or Irish Jess, frequently experienced conversion before succumbing to a tragic, early death. Whittemore told the story of "poor motherless" Kittie, who chose prostitution over working "at starvation prices in a store." When rescue workers found her, the "once beautiful" Kittie, who had been "the envy of many in a once most respectable circle of young people," lay in a damp, foul-smelling cellar on a "rude apology for a bed." Her conversion in a Door of Hope occurred not long before she died with "a quiet look of peace that greatly intensified her beauty."[118] Lee introduced her readers to Pretty Cora, "a beautiful young girl with the bloom of her country home still on her cheek," who stayed in the home until she was truly penitent, then returned to her family. However, another former resident, Leslie, had "put off the day of her salvation." She left the home believing she could resist further temptation, but not long after the newspaper reported of her death by poison.[119] Whittemore assessed the conversion rate of residents in numeric terms, roughly 80 percent, noting that of the eighty women who came through the Door of Hope in its first year, only fifteen resumed their "former reckless life."[120] Lee offered a more realistic appraisal; she estimated that only some were saved compared to the many, who even after a stay in her rescue home, "go again into sin."[121]

A very different type of assessment filled the pages of *Some Practical Suggestions on the Conduct of a Rescue Home*, written by Dr. Kate Waller Barrett, longtime NFCM president.[122] Barrett's painstakingly detailed book recounted how to manage a rescue home as a well-run machine. She described washing and then soaking oatmeal overnight to be ready for breakfast, reminding each resident to hang folded pajamas over a chair in the morning to be fresh at night, or handling the decision-making power dynamics between the rescue home board and matron. She standardized schedules, procedures, disciplines, and reward systems to be implemented in every home. Her meticulous organizing prowess garnered for Crittenton homes a reputation as a place of rules and regulations, a notoriety that concerned potential residents who worried about a loss of independence. Barrett remained unmoved by these concerns because she "did not see this as a condemnation of the Crittenton system, but rather of the girls. She believed the girls' objections to the strict regimen prevented them 'from accepting the advice and help that we are willing to give.'"[123]

Lee experienced firsthand the impact of the Crittenton bureaucracy. She had initiated plans to open a rescue home in Kansas City when the Crittenton organization approached her about joining forces. Their offer interested her because she appreciated their commitment to religious instruction through morning and evening services and three Bible studies per week. Each resident received a Bible and was required to memorize a weekly verse. Lee agreed to be the first matron of the Kansas City Crittenton home with "full charge of the inside of the Home," including the "right to teach what seemed best to us."[124] However, the following nonnegotiable condition restricted her oversight: "We were pledged never to deny entrance to any white girl, no matter what she had done, and not to admit a colored girl without permission from the president." Ruminating about this racist condition in her memoir, Lee explained why initially she acquiesced: "This last condition was not in force in our other homes and coming from farther north where there are fewer colored people and less race prejudice, we could not see the need of such a rule, but as we became better acquainted with the girls and saw how they felt about it and hearing that a home for colored girls was being talked of, we thought it might be best at first."[125] Even so, after six months as matron, she cited a growing conviction that she "could not assert our liberty in the Lord or teach as our consciences dictated."[126] She quit the Crittenton home, moved a few streets over and opened Good Will Mission, where she had "liberty" to run it according to her own dictates.

Another rescue home founder, Florence "Mother" Roberts, likewise ended her association with a Crittenton home. Little is known about Roberts with the exception of her autobiography, which covers the fifteen years between her conversion in 1896 to its publication in 1911. She related that God's call to rescue work came as she assisted police in freeing a twelve-year-old girl who had been kidnapped by an older man and forced to submit to "indescribable wickedness."[127] From then on, Roberts resolved "to aid in rescuing the outcast at any cost; to see and love their souls, forgetting the sinning exterior; to help win them to Christ, then encourage and further their advancement; . . . to respond to Christ's call at any and all times, whether that call should be in the highways or hedges, streets or lanes, among rich or poor, the prison boys or the outcast girls."[128] Similar to what we have discussed previously about some evangelist's marriages, tension erupted between Roberts and her husband over her dedication to religious work. In response to his ultimatum—rescue work or him—she chose the former and left her husband and home in Redding, California. Eventually, she took over a fledgling rescue home in San Jose, California, and named it Beth-Adriel, which means "House of the flock of God."[129] A musician and songwriter, Roberts set to verse her intention that Beth-Adriel be a home where any woman, no matter the circumstance, would be welcomed.

> *Verse 1:*
> A poor girl was wand'ring alone on the street
> Of a great busy city, thro' dust and thro' heat,
> With despair in her heart as she walked to and fro,
> When she heard a sweet voice singing softly and low.
>
> *Verse 3:*
> O God, I have sinned, I will do so no more.
> If thou wilt forgive and a sinner restore;
> For the sake of my Savior, for mercy I pray:
> Lord, give me a home with some Christian to stay.[130]

After its incorporation, Roberts's official position as field secretary of Beth-Adriel required her to travel widely to raise donations. Because of this, the home's transition from a rescue to maternity home came as a surprise and disappointment to her. Twice she rescued young women and brought them to Beth-Adriel only to find out later that workers left one outside on the back porch for fear that her venereal disease would put at risk the mothers and babies, and they refused to admit the other. Roberts complained in her memoir that Beth-Adriel "*had never been incorporated for a maternity home.*"[131] Looking at the larger context, however, it is important to note that what happened at Beth-Adriel as well as Crittenton homes occurred in some measure owing to the nationwide increase in premarital pregnancy rates that more than doubled between 1860 and 1910.[132]

Roberts also objected to the heightened scrutiny of the intake procedure that "made it no easy matter for any needy girl to become an inmate of Beth-Adriel."[133] Instead of her open-door policy, new procedures instituted a set of grueling interview questions and a request for money. Again, these changes came to her attention from a disgruntled, potential resident:

"Mrs. Roberts, I've something to ask you. When you persuaded me to come to this place, didn't you tell me I need give only my first name?"

"I did, Amelia," I answered.

"Didn't you say that no questions that might embarrass me would be asked?"

"I certainly did."

"Didn't you say no girl had to sign any papers here, and that if she had no money, the home was free to her?"

"Most assuredly."

"Then—you—lied."[134]

Soon after this conversation, Roberts resigned her position with Beth-Adriel.

Mother Lee and Mother Roberts resisted Crittenton's institutionalism, because they believed that the evangelistic impulse would languish. Yet what seemed to deteriorate more quickly was the institution's longevity. Within a short time, Beth-Adriel ceased to exist as the institution Roberts intended and became a Crittenton maternity home. Likewise, Lee's longest-running institution, the Tinley Rescue Home for Fallen Girls and Women in Omaha, lasted roughly twenty years.[135] This trend, according to NCFM's Barrett, typified unaffiliated institutions. "The mortality among individual rescue homes standing alone, due to local crises, or to a fairly rapid process of going to seed, has been huge indeed. By contrast, the Homes in the Crittenton chain have been able, with a timely helping hand from national headquarters, to weather severe storms of internal dissension, awaken from periods of a still more deadly apathy, and finally expand into a vigorous growth. . . . This same fate would have met every F. C. Home, because *all of them have been reorganized* by the National at least twice and some of them three and four times."[136] Certainly rescue homes attached to a larger organization with a better safety net lasted longer than isolated institutions. Nevertheless, even the NFCM faced more reorganization and eventually ceased to exist independently when, in 1976, it merged into the Child Welfare League of America as the Florence Crittenton Division.[137]

Evaluating the significance and success of rescue homes through extant documents remains problematic. The stories of rescue narrated in the home's publications were mostly penned not by residents but by workers, who presented a "composite image" of the "betrayed and helpless young girl" seduced by a false promise of marriage and "adrift in the city."[138] As Kunzel explains, deciphering what residents themselves experienced requires the complicated, intricate task of piecing together case records, which might have been tampered with, abridged, purposively falsified by the resident, or altered by the home's personnel. She quotes a social worker from 1928 who admitted that "the characters in case records do not speak for themselves. They obtain a hearing only in the translation provided by the language of the social worker."[139]

Contemporary historians evaluate rescue work as eminently unsuccessful in saving prostitutes. Ruth Rosen, for example, cites a settlement worker who made this comment after visiting hundreds of prostitutes: "We reach one in a hundred and try not to be discouraged." Rosen then refers to A. W. Elliot, a clubwoman and president of the Southern California Rescue Mission, who "admitted that she had offered aid to fifteen thousand prostitutes and yet had reformed only one."[140] In a study of rescue work among New York City prostitutes in the 1830s, Carroll Smith-Rosenberg similarly claims that "few prostitutes reformed; fewer still appeared to their benefactresses to have experienced the saving grace of conversion."[141] This perspective certainly tempers Whittemore's overly enthusiastic 80 percent success rate cited earlier.

While rescue home founders focused—perhaps with little success—on the permanent reform of residents through evangelism, at the same time, they raised awareness about human trafficking among their evangelical constituencies, who purposefully shunned establishments connected to sex, alcohol, dancing, or gambling. Along with stories of rescue and conversion, they published stark statistics and startling scenarios in literature sent to churches and benefactors, like this excerpt from the 1907 booklet, *The White Slaves of America*, published by a small Wesleyan/Holiness group in Texas: "Just think, five thousand of the erring girls in Texas only, sixty thousand die every year in the U.S. which makes one hundred and seventy every twenty-four hours or eighty-five every day. It is said, if you place these corpse [sic] one half mile apart, they would reach thirty thousand miles, that is more than encircles the earth."[142] Accompanying the numbers were names, faces, and heart-wrenching stories, all designed to capture the reader's attention, prayers, and donations.

Like many Progressive Era women reformers, including those of the WCTU, rescue home founders did not shy away from condemning the double standard—men will be men, women must be virginal—that mandated women's purity and overlooked men's promiscuity. An anonymous writer in the above booklet declared, "The result is that the whole social system has become depraved."[143] This same writer then turned a critical eye to the church for its false teaching that sin differs depending on gender or, in other words, judging the same sin to be worse if committed by a woman than a man: "Your girls have as good right to curse, blackguard, chew tobacco, smoke cigarettes, drink beer and whiskey and practice unclean and impure habits as your boys have." Lest such activities be encouraged, the sentence continues, "but neither have any right, for God's standard is purity."[144] In other words, they insisted that the gendered double standard in church and society must be replaced by God's standard, which is purity for both men and women.

Another double standard with gender ramifications revolved around starvation wages paid to working women while their male employers prospered. As journalist Jacob Riis noted in his 1890 exposé of New York City tenements, the entrenched economic system caused women's wages to fall lower than men's because women could always resort to prostitution. "It is a known fact," Riis wrote, "that men's wages cannot fall below a limit upon which they can exist, but woman's wages have no limit, since the paths of shame are always open to her."[145] Exacerbating the situation, employers had at their disposal an almost endless supply of potential women employees because more women than ever, nearly six million in the U.S. Census of 1900, earned wages outside the home in the Progressive Era.[146]

Whittemore portrayed the desperation of this pervasive situation through the story of a seventeen-year-old named Julia. After days of searching for a job, she found employment at a large, Brooklyn department store earning the "starvation salary" of $3.00 a week. To make matters worse, the cost of having to "dress in becoming style," as her employer demanded, and the rent for her meager bedroom, left her less than fifty cents per week for food, laundry, and a small, ten-cent bucket of coal on cold days. When Julia's floor supervisor feigned a personal interest in order to lure her to a brothel, she easily fell prey to earning more money through prostitution. As the story's finale, Whittemore drew a direct link between Julia's wages and her turn to prostitution:

> They cannot live decently on what they receive. It is truly heartrending to listen to the stories of how many a girl has been reduced to abject poverty and also robbed of the physical charm that might and should have been hers through the greed of wealthy men. They were willing to work hard, very hard, for an honest livelihood, but while their employers received the homage and compliments of individuals and organizations, these girls whose life-blood was sweated out to produce the wealth, were allowed to languish in conditions of wretchedness on a wage that would not supply a livelihood. Many in desperation have been driven into a life that is worse than death through this gateway of oppression.[147]

While Julia-like stories filled the pages of rescue home publications, women evangelists did not venture into the political arena, as did Jane Addams and other Progressive Era women reformers, in order to strike at the root cause of these injustices. For instance, they did not join the political lobby initiated by women reformers to raise the age of consent or to secure the vote for women.[148] In keeping with their commitment to evangelism, one individual at a time, they devoted themselves instead, as Mother Lee phrased it, "to open a place of refuge for just such as these."

Women in rescue work built homes and missions in order to provide tangible humanitarian relief as an avenue for evangelism. They bolstered their outreach by casting themselves as a mother to the motherless, including the women who would soon be mothers themselves. They provided meals, beds, and spiritual counsel as would a mother. They decorated rescue homes as they would their own homes to attract and retain women on society's margins. They led songs in the rescue mission about the prodigal's returning home, where all would be well. They settled into domesticity, in a manner that seemed to elude women evangelists prior to the Progressive Era, in order to make the gospel message as homey and inviting as possible. These now nearly forgotten rescue institutions that materialized overnight in city basements, rental homes, abandoned churches, and empty factories were mostly stand-alone outposts without oversight from church committees or organizational bureaucracies. Understaffed and chronically underfunded, they nevertheless contributed to the wave of institution building that swept across America and American Christianity during the Progressive Era. Although the work of establishing rescue homes and missions remained distinct, particularly in its maternalist rhetoric and activity, from evangelistic organizations, churches, denominations, and training schools, women evangelists in all these pursuits shifted evangelism from itinerancy to institution building and prepared the way, as we will see in the Conclusion, for the leading woman evangelist and institution builder in the twentieth century, Aimee Semple McPherson.

Angelus Temple, Los Angeles, California. Courtesy of the International Church of the Foursquare Gospel Heritage Archives Department.

Aimee Semple McPherson alongside the dedication plaque for Angelus Temple. Courtesy of the International Church of the Foursquare Gospel Heritage Archives Department.

Conclusion

Nearly twenty years ago, I came across the name Iva Durham Vennard while searching for material on women for an introductory lecture on American evangelism. Scads of resources on a succession of male evangelists, from Jonathan Edwards (1703–58) to Charles Finney (1792–1875) to Dwight Moody (1837–99) to Billy Sunday (1862–1935), to Billy Graham (1918–), I could find. Information on women, I could not, at least during the mid-1990s, when I began my research. No sooner had I scratched the surface on Vennard that I found myself enthralled because of intersections between her life and mine. Methodists from birth, participants in egalitarian marriages (hers nearly a century ago), mothers, teachers, fierce advocates for women in ministry—both of us. Why had no one ever introduced me to Vennard in my Methodist confirmation class or Methodist college or Methodist seminary? Why was I, a Methodist minister, teaching at a Methodist seminary at the time, still unaware of this Methodist foremother, who had trained scores of women evangelists, missionaries, and ministers long before the Methodist church ordained women or Methodist seminaries welcomed them?

I was further hooked when I discovered the love story of her courtship with Thomas Vennard, who wrote a letter in the early 1900s in which he pledged to be her "background of support" if she would marry him. The hook dug even deeper when I read his words, "I may be the janitor of an institution of which you are principal founder and controlling head." His comment turned out to be prophetic. True to his word, Thomas sacrificed his successful architectural career in the Chicago Loop in order to oversee, at minimal cost, building renovations at her school, the Chicago Evangelistic Institute. Hooked completely, I headed full tilt into the world of American women evangelists.

A decade later, I wrote *Turn the Pulpit Loose: Two Centuries of American Women Evangelists*, to recover forgotten women evangelists like Vennard. In that book, I identified, organized, and presented extensive primary source material from eighteen women evangelists. My research required wide-ranging travel to scattered archives, leading me to crisscross North America, from Los Angeles to Cape Breton, Nova Scotia. I spent days sequestered among dusty shelves, scouring files in numbered boxes, bound institutional newsletters, and personal correspondence. The purpose of that book was, on the one hand, to permit these women to speak in their own voices and, on the other, to make available for public use unpublished and previously inaccessible material.

This book does more. The continued recovery of neglected women evangelists remains essential; nonetheless, in this book I propose a revision of American Christianity in the Progressive Era based upon an aggregate of women evangelists across the country, from shore to shore, who settled down, more or less, to build and lead institutions. Their collective yet unchoreographed decision to build institutions to foster the primary expression of American Christianity—evangelism—marked a seismic shift. Evangelism found expression in brick and mortar, uniforms and automobiles, schools and rescue homes—not in preaching and altar calls alone. These institutions popped up in every region of the country, from Elizabeth Baker's Rochester Training School to Florence Crawford's Apostolic Faith Mission in Portland, from Mary Magdalena Tate Lewis's Nashville headquarters to Martha Moore Avery's Catholic Truth Guild in Boston. These institutions occupied the largest American cities—New York City and Chicago—as well as country crossroads in Marion, North Carolina, and Buffalo Gap, Texas. No region escaped their propensity to build institutions.

All sorts of women—black and white, Protestant and Catholic, Pentecostal and Methodist, northern and southern, midwestern and western—pioneered this nationwide shift. They did not wait for a man to step up or a general conference to vote; they simply started. Their efforts were tireless, precariously funded, and persistently underestimated. Still, they proved indefatigable as church planters, denominational executives, training school principals, rescue home matrons, and urban mission founders.

Women Evangelists and Their Male Counterparts

These intrepid pioneers paid a price, typically in their personal life. They negotiated spousal jealousies and parental roles, all the while attempting to live out God's call. Quite a few marriages ended in divorce. Florence Crawford divorced twice, Bishop Tate three times. Alma and Kent White endured a long term separation, which they never resolved. Only one husband among the dozens—Thomas Vennard—broke with traditional expectations and subordinated his career to his wife's in order to assist her work.

In a society that lent negligible support to poor and middle-class women, particularly those who ventured outside the home, some evangelists had to travel with children to evangelistic meetings and to oversee their institutions. This scenario, nevertheless, allowed mothers to continue, if unconventionally, the religious nurture of their children. Other women evangelists opted to leave children in the care of a trusted relative, though as mothers, they agonized over the separation. Alma White, who left her two-year-old son with her mother while he recovered from a serious illness, wrote, "To leave him in care of others was almost like taking a mother's heart from her body, but the Lord had spoken and it would have been perilous to disobey. It was no more than He required of others, and why should I have any controversy."[1] Still, children were no match for God's call. Even White's comment makes clear that obedience to God trumps one's human family. Many women evangelists shared precisely this sentiment.

The pressure was so intense, the personal demands so unrelenting, that some women welcomed widowhood because of the freedom it offered them. Martha "Mother" Lee raised four children singlehandedly once her husband returned home from the Civil War with extensive wounds, both physical and emotional. Lee worked at a variety of ventures to make money for the family's survival until her husband died and her children grew into adulthood. With an empty nest, she turned without hesitation to the rescue of "fallen women" through evangelism and institution building.

The need to negotiate the stress between personal and public life distinguishes these women from their male counterparts. Women took care of both their institutions and their families, while men attended to evangelism in the public arena without the personal distractions of family life. Unencumbered by expectations at home, men followed the demands of their itineraries. Their wives and children fit hand in glove into their schedule, whether by accompanying them or staying home.

Further, men had smoother access than women to the echelons of power—religious, civic, political—in each city that hosted their meetings and to wealthy donors who bankrolled their institutions. Dwight Moody, for instance, rubbed shoulders with the likes of John Wanamaker in Philadelphia and Cyrus McCormick in Chicago. The earnings of Billy Sunday's organization ranked among the wealthiest corporations in the country alongside the likes of Standard Oil and National Cash Register. Deep financial pockets enabled these men to hire more personnel to orchestrate larger meetings, which secured more national publicity and—as a result—a lasting legacy. It should come as no surprise, then, that the names Moody and Sunday are synonymous with American evangelism, while the names Iva Durham Vennard and Mary Magdalena Lewis Tate are largely forgotten. Even in the absence of plentiful resources and powerful patrons, however, these women, more than Moody and Sunday, populated the nation with institutions paid for by penny donations, crates of apples, and used shoes.

Women Evangelists and Their Legacy

Though perhaps without the panache of Moody or Sunday, these women did leave an enduring legacy. Arguably the most illustrious legacy of the shift they promoted from itinerancy to institution building is evident in the rise of Aimee Semple McPherson, whose evangelistic empire emerged as the Progressive Era waned. Her name—and the rumors surrounding it—remain legendary. Her story even made headlines again recently as a Broadway musical. She was, according to the titles of two recent books, "everybody's sister" and the person responsible for "the resurrection of Christian America."[2] Certainly, McPherson was a remarkable evangelist, religious leader, and institution builder. What we now know, however, is that the institutions she built had deep roots in the work of the women evangelists who preceded her. Her success in the following areas rested on the foundations laid by those earlier women.

Evangelistic organization. McPherson began as an itinerant evangelist in 1916, traveling up and down the Eastern Seaboard in a Packard touring gospel car whose front, sides, and headlights sported simple religious phrases in six-inch, block, gold letters—JESUS IS COMING SOON, JESUS SAVES, WHERE WILL YOU SPEND ETERNITY?[3] Along with clothes, bed rolls, cooking utensils, a Corona typewriter, and a tiny organ, the gospel car carried sizeable charts illustrating the roads to heaven and hell. During street meetings, workers hung up the charts from a stand that attached to the car.[4] In this itinerant fashion, McPherson crossed the country with her mother and two children, preaching and distributing literature along the way. When she settled in Los Angeles, in 1922, she set up a permanent evangelistic organization, the Echo Park Evangelistic Association, as a legal entity with established bylaws and property on the corner of Sunset and Glendale and adjacent to Echo Park. "The Evangelistic Association functioned as a holding company—an umbrella organization over the other institutions Sister created over the years," according to biographer Edith Blumhofer.[5]

This same pattern of moving from itinerancy to a multifaceted evangelistic organization was already well established before McPherson began. Recall another Pentecostal woman evangelist, Florence Crawford, for example. After itinerating between Los Angeles and Portland, she launched an evangelistic organization, the Apostolic Faith Mission (AFM), in 1908. From its Portland headquarters, the AFM sent out workers in cars, trucks, boats, and planes to hold evangelistic meetings throughout the Pacific Northwest and across the country. Gospel literature distributed during these evangelistic ventures was written and printed by the AFM. In addition, the organization ran a rescue mission in downtown Portland and a campground on the city's outskirts. Evangelistic organizations like the AFM paved the way for McPherson's institutional accomplishments.

Church and denomination. McPherson built a magnificent church, Angelus Temple, which boasted an unsupported concrete dome standing 110 feet tall and 107 feet wide, painted in light blue interspersed with white clouds, and covering a 5,300-seat auditorium. The denomination she launched in 1927, the International Church of the Foursquare Gospel, ranks as the largest founded by a woman, with over seven million members who gather in nearly 67,000 churches and meeting places in 135 countries.[6] Though outsized, like so many of her initiatives, McPherson's penchant to build a church and found a denomination reflected the sensibilities of her predecessors. Recall Alma White's Pillar of Fire denomination, with its self-contained community—post office, church, store, elementary schools, Bible college, and university—at Zarephath, New Jersey. Or Tate's denomination, which extended across state lines with a bishop assigned to oversee the work in each state. Similarly, Maria Woodworth-Etter, whom McPherson regarded as her mentor, established churches after successful evangelistic meetings in the Midwest. From West Coast to East, from North to South, women evangelists had been launching churches and denominations from the dawn of the Progressive Era.

Religious training school. By the time McPherson opened Echo Park Evangelistic and Missionary Training Institute (later renamed Lighthouse of International Foursquare Evangelism or L.I.F.E.) in 1923, many religious training schools, including those founded by women evangelists, were already in their prime. Their influence is evident in several areas of McPherson's school. L.I.F.E.'s balance between classes, particularly Bible study, and practical work replicated the curricula of already established religious training schools. On a logistical level, like Mattie Perry's Elhanan Training Institute and Jennie Fowler Willing's New York

Evangelistic Training School, L.I.F.E. offered correspondence courses to students who could not attend school four mornings a week, Tuesday through Friday, 9:00 to noon. Similar to schools founded by women evangelists in particular, women as well as men signed up for classes at L.I.F.E. Likewise, for the practical work component, L.I.F.E. students, both men and women, had opportunities to preach at the Friday evening service at Angelus Temple and lead evangelistic meetings and events.[7] Again, McPherson benefited from proven practices instituted by the women who preceded her.

Rescue mission. Open twenty-four hours a day, seven days a week, the Commissary at Angelus Temple was launched in 1927. Within its first five months, people left the Commissary with goods totaling twenty-one thousand cans of food, one thousand bunches of celery, one hundred pies and cakes, and twelve thousand pieces of clothing.[8] During the Great Depression in the 1930s, the demand of over 1.5 million people prompted the addition of a fumigation room, laundry, employment office, nursery, dining hall, and soup kitchen.[9] Famed actor Anthony Quinn once commented, "She [Aimee] literally kept most of that Mexican community alive." He was referring to Mexicans in Los Angeles, who "were terrified of appealing for county help because most of them were in the country illegally."[10] The Commissary also equipped and sent out mobile unit vehicles, packed with basic goods, to help victims of natural disasters, like the 1934 Long Beach earthquake.

The Commissary surpassed the soap-soup-salvation institutions that preceded it, but it did not deviate in purpose or method from them. After all, McPherson's mother was active in the Salvation Army, a leader in rescue mission work in America, and mother and daughter participated together in Army activities. By the turn of the twentieth century, America's cities were already rife with rescue missions, and women evangelists propelled their development. In Kansas City alone, for example, two women established rescue missions in 1902. In Hick's Hollow, Emma and L. P. Ray began a mission for the neighborhood's African American children. Several streets over, in Hell's Half Acre, Martha "Mother" Lee opened a rescue mission near the train depot and across the street from a brothel. These missions, developed in previous decades, provided a foretaste of women's institution building in rescue work which McPherson then developed into the extensive outreach of the Angelus Temple Commissary.[11]

McPherson built an evangelistic empire on the foundations laid by the women we meet in this book. In fact, she outstripped them in her incomparable Hollywood style. By the mid-twentieth century, however, the vigor, intensity, and saturation of women's institution building across the country waned. This impulse did not dry up altogether, but never again would women evangelists found institutions with the same level of industry as those of the Progressive Era. The women who built the "old time religion" from 1890 to 1920 represent the zenith of institution building in the history of American Christianity.[12] For those women evangelists who built institutions after this generation, the focus lay principally on one—the evangelistic organization. Such was the case with evangelist Kathryn Kuhlman, whose Kathryn Kuhlman Foundation coordinated her evangelistic meetings; healing services; a radio program, "Heart-to-Heart"; and a television series, "I Believe in Miracles."[13] This practice continues today, for instance, with evangelistic organizations like Joyce Meyer Ministries and Juanita Bynum Ministries, which promote conferences, media broadcasts, an Internet presence, and book sales.

What dampened women's enthusiasm for building institutions? One factor to consider is the failure of most women evangelists during the Progressive Era to mentor female successors. When the founders died, men rose to prominence in their stead. In subsequent generations, therefore, the commitment to women's leadership and institution-building prowess diminished or died away completely.

Another factor was the emerging opportunities for women in mainline denominations, particularly in licensing and ordination. The Methodist Episcopal Church's vote in 1924, for instance, extended local preacher licenses to women. As these structural inroads continued, women were increasingly able to work within established structures. The push for women's ordination from the 1920s on made many of the institutions women had built during the Progressive Era, such as deaconess training schools, comparatively obsolete.

In evangelicalism and fundamentalism, women held typically female occupations in Christian work as teachers, artists, writers, cooks, pastoral assistants, and music directors.[14] Like their mainline counterparts, they were able to exercise their calling within the confines of established churches, denominations, and parachurch organizations. They did not need to build new institutions in order to be active in Christian work.

Does the demise of institution building require us to conclude that women evangelists of the Progressive Era are simply historical artifacts, women who worked for a generation but left no enduring legacy beyond McPherson? Not at all. One of their legacies was to keep alive prospects for women in religious leadership. When the nation would not permit women to vote, when mainline denominations only begrudgingly allowed laywomen to vote in general church conferences, when a mere handful of women attended seminary, and when women's ordination seemed a pipe dream, they built their own institutions, undeterred by what culture or church had to say about their prescribed roles. In institutions of their own making, they exercised religious leadership as evangelists who led others to religious experiences, as ministers who shepherded congregations and celebrated the sacraments, as bishops who ordained ministers, both female and male, and as theology and Bible teachers, who instructed both men and women. By standing in the pulpit, presiding at the communion table, laying hands on ordinands, teaching classes, and evangelizing the masses, they pioneered women's religious leadership in American Christianity.

Their legacy lies as well in their challenge to patriarchy in American Protestantism. These women broke new ground as religious leaders by building institutions for both women *and* men. Their institutions attracted and enlisted male and female converts. Men and women joined their churches. Men and women sat alongside each other in religious training school classrooms. Men and women filled church leadership positions at all levels. These women evangelists, therefore, rank among the first American women to build—and lead—mixed-gender religious institutions.

Last, their legacy of sacrifice and simplicity provides a challenging model for religious leaders, particularly where finances are concerned. These women did not amass personal wealth from contributions; instead, donations went back into building up their churches, schools, and rescue institutions. Martha Moore Avery dipped into her own personal finances to keep the Catholic Truth Guild afloat. Mattie Perry built her own religious training school from penny donations and used lumber. Even Alma White, who had a knack for real estate purchases, bought properties to be used by the Pillar of Fire rather than herself. Though her denomination owned valuable properties across the country, she lived in a three-room, corner apartment of the administration building at Zarephath.

Women Evangelists: A Final Impression

I have tried in this book to be honest about these women. I have not written hagiography. Instead, at the urging of historian Robert Orsi, I have stopped to explore precisely what is disappointing, even frustrating about these women. Rather than presenting American religious history in a Lake Wobegon manner, where "all women are empowered, all men improved, children nurtured, the universe rendered meaningful," I have taken Orsi's words to heart and written an historical narrative that is "more complex than mastery and triumph."[15] Thus, I have discovered time and again "the everyday tragic" in these flawed yet accomplished women, who pioneered mixed-gender religious institution building. Alma White was often dictatorial. Crawford on divorce and remarriage was hypocritical. Tate, in divorcing her husbands, was puritanical. Martha Moore Avery was egotistical, particularly toward other women. Yet they all shared an unrelenting, exhausting commitment to institution building, and, for a generation, they were builders of the "old time religion" in American Christianity.

Here at the end, we return to the beginning, to Iva Durham Vennard, who, when forced to resign as principal of Epworth Evangelistic Institute by male leaders of St. Louis Methodism, quit that institution but did not quit. With her young son and her husband, who had pledged to work as a janitor in her institution, she moved three hundred miles away to Chicago—and started over.

APPENDIX

Evangelists and Institutions

Evangelists

	DATES	DENOMINATIONS
Jennie Fowler Willing	1834–1916	Methodist
Amanda Berry Smith	1837–1915	African Methodist
Martha Lee	1842–1916	Free Methodist
Jennie Smith	1842–1924	Methodist
Maria Woodworth-Etter	1844–1924	Churches of God, General Conference (Winebrenner)/Pentecostal
Lucy Drake Osborn	1844–1922	Methodist
Anna Prosser	1846–1902	Presbyterian/Methodist
Elizabeth Baker	1849–1915	Methodist/Pentecostal
Emma Whittemore	1850–1931	Christian and Missionary Alliance/Salvation Army
Martha Moore Avery	1851–1929	Roman Catholic
Minnie Draper	1858–1921	Presbyterian/Christian and Missionary Alliance/Assembly of God
Carrie Judd Montgomery	1858–1946	Episcopalian/Christian and Missionary Alliance/Assembly of God
Emma Ray	1859–1930	African Methodist/Free Methodist
Alma White	1862–1946	Methodist/Pillar of Fire
Mary Lee Cagle	1864–1955	Methodist/Church of the Nazarene
Evangeline Booth	1865–1950	Salvation Army
Helen Sunday	1868–1957	Presbyterian
Mattie Perry	1868–1957	Christian and Missionary Alliance
Mary Magdalena Lewis Tate	1871–1930	Methodist / Church of the Living God, the Pillar and Ground of the Truth
Iva Durham Vennard	1871–1945	Methodist
Florence Louise Crawford	1872–1936	Methodist/Apostolic Faith Mission

Virginia Moss	1875–1919	Methodist /Christian and Missionary Alliance/ Assembly of God
Aimee Semple McPherson	1890–1944	Salvation Army/International Church of the Foursquare Gospel
Florence Roberts	N.A.	N.A.

Institutions

Churches (Representative List)

Elizabeth Baker	Elim Tabernacle
Mary Lee Cagle	Buffalo Gap Church
Mary Lee Cagle	Swedonia Church
Florence Louise Crawford	Apostolic Faith Mission
Minnie Draper	Bethel Pentecostal Assembly
Minnie Draper	Ossining Gospel Assembly
Aimee Semple McPherson	Angelus Temple
Carrie Judd Montgomery	Beulah Chapel
Virginia Moss	Beulah Heights Assembly
Mary Magdalena Lewis Tate	Latter Day Saints of the Foundation of True Holiness and Sanctification
Alma White	Alma Temple
Alma White	Zarephath Christian Church
Maria Woodworth-Etter	Woodworth-Etter Tabernacle

Denominations

Mary Lee Cagle	New Testament Church of Christ (merged with the Church of the Nazarene)
Florence Louise Crawford	Apostolic Faith Mission
Aimee Semple McPherson	International Church of the Foursquare Gospel
Mary Magdalena Lewis Tate	Church of the Living God, the Pillar and Ground of the Truth
Alma White	Pillar of Fire

Evangelistic Institutions

Martha Moore Avery	Catholic Truth Guild
Florence Louise Crawford	Apostolic Faith Mission
Aimee Semple McPherson	Echo Park Evangelistic Association
Emma Ray	WCTU Evangelistic Department
Jennie Smith	WCTU Evangelistic Department
Helen Sunday	Billy Sunday Evangelistic Organization
Jennie Fowler Willing	WCTU Evangelistic Department
Maria Woodworth-Etter	Woodworth-Etter Evangelistic Organization

Rescue Homes

Evangeline Booth	The Salvation Army (national network)
Martha Lee	Tinley Rescue Home
Martha Lee	The Home of Redeeming Love
Carrie Judd Montgomery	Beulah Rescue Home
Florence Roberts	Beth-Adriel
Emma Whittemore	Door of Hope (national network)

Rescue Missions

Elizabeth Baker	Faith Mission
Evangeline Booth	The Salvation Army (national network)
Martha Lee	Good Will Mission
Aimee Semple McPherson	Commissary at Angelus Temple
Carrie Judd Montgomery	The People's Mission
Virginia Moss	Door of Hope Mission
Anna Prosser	Canal Street Mission
Emma Ray	Hick's Hollow Mission
Alma White	Peniel Mission

Schools

Elizabeth Baker	Rochester Bible Training School
Minnie Draper	Bethel Bible Training School/Central Bible Institute
Aimee Semple McPherson	L.I.F.E. Bible College
Carrie Judd Montgomery	Shalom Training School
Virginia Moss	Beulah Heights Bible and Missionary Training School
Lucy Drake Osborn	Union Missionary Training Institute
Mattie Perry	Elhanan Training Institute
Iva Durham Vennard	Epworth Evangelistic Institute
Iva Durham Vennard	Chicago Evangelistic Institute/Vennard College
Alma White	Alma White College
Alma White	Belleview College
Alma White	Pentecostal Mission Home
Alma White	Zarephath Bible College
Jennie Fowler Willing	New York Evangelistic Training School

NOTES

Note to the Acknowledgments
1. David Remnick, "Exile on Main Street: Don De Lillo's Undisclosed Underworld," *New Yorker* (September 15, 1997): 43, 47, quoted in Michael Casey, *Strangers to the City: Reflections on the Beliefs and Values of the Rule of Saint Benedict* (Brewster, MA: Paraclete, 2005), 35.

Notes to the Introduction
1. Emma Ray, *Twice Sold, Twice Ransomed: Autobiography of Mr. and Mrs. L. P. Ray* (Chicago: Free Methodist Publishing, 1926), 141.
2. The deaconess movement trained thousands of women in the Progressive Era for religious, medical, and pastoral work. Estimates range to five thousand deaconesses in Methodism alone during the nearly thirty-five years in which Lucy Rider Meyer presided over the influential deaconess training school she founded in 1885—the Chicago Training School for City, Home and Foreign Missions. See Priscilla Pope-Levison, "A 'Thirty Year War' and More: Exposing Complexities in the Methodist Deaconess Movement," *Methodist History* 47:2 (January 2009): 101–16.
3. "Extracts from the Annual Report 1908–09," *Inasmuch* 5 (April 1909): 7.
4. *Minutes of the Forty-third Session of the St. Louis Annual Conference of the Methodist Episcopal Church, Held in Mountain Grove, MO, March 22 to 26, 1911* (Warrensburg, MO: Perry E. Pierce, 1911), 307.
5. Mary Ella Bowie, *Alabaster and Spikenard: The Life of Iva Durham Vennard, D.D., Founder of Chicago Evangelistic Institute* (Chicago: Chicago Evangelistic Institute, 1947), 46.
6. Her biographer summarized her conversation with DeGarmo in the following exchange: "'I've made my choice to be spiritual first,' she said, 'and that means my unswerving allegiance to Christ in every detail.' She had come prepared for opposition and argument, and even rebuke. But she was not at all prepared for his reaction. With his voice full of kindness, he replied, 'I would so much rather you would be a noble woman than a great scholar.'" Bowie, *Alabaster*, 48.
7. Bowie, *Alabaster*, 54.
8. Bowie, *Alabaster*, 54–55.
9. Iva Durham Vennard, *The Evangelism for This Day: An Address* (Chicago: Chicago Evangelistic Institute, 1933), 1.
10. Some historians prefer the terms "revivalism" and "revivalist," as evident in these recent titles: Michael J. McClymond, ed., *Embodying the Spirit: New Perspectives on North American Revivalism* (Baltimore, MD: Johns Hopkins University Press, 2004); Thekla Ellen Joiner, *Sin in the City: Chicago and Revivalism, 1880–1920* (Columbia: University of Missouri Press, 2007); and Benjamin Hartley, *Evangelicals at a Crossroads: Revivalism and Social Reform in Boston, 1860–1910* (Durham: University of New Hampshire Press, 2011). Others, myself included, utilize the terms "evangelism" and "evangelist." See Thomas A.

Robinson and Lanette D. Ruff, *Out of the Mouths of Babes: Girl Evangelists in the Flapper Era* (New York: Oxford University Press, 2012); and Elizabeth Elkin Grammer, *Some Wild Visions: Autobiographies by Female Itinerant Evangelists in 19th Century America* (New York: Oxford University Press, 2003). To confuse further the terminology discussion, Michael McClymond offers what he calls a "new and perhaps more adequate" definition of revivalism. However, his definition applies to evangelism as well: "'Revivalism' is a spiritual movement within Christianity that calls individuals to make a self-conscious decision to repent of sin and believe the gospel, and thereby seeks to bring them an assurance of being in a right or proper relationship with God, and integrate them into a community with other like-minded individuals" (McClymond, *Embodying the Spirit*, 10). My decision to use the words "evangelism" and "evangelist" stems from the fact that it follows the lead of these women; they called themselves evangelists and referred to their religious work as evangelism.

11. Catherine Brekus, *Strangers and Pilgrims: Female Preaching in America, 1740–1845* (Chapel Hill: University of North Carolina Press, 1998), 31.
12. Grammer, *Some Wild Visions*, 21.
13. Brekus, *Strangers and Pilgrims*, 4.
14. Brekus, *Strangers and Pilgrims*; Richard J. Douglass-Chin, *Preacher Woman Sings the Blues: The Autobiographies of Nineteenth-Century African American Evangelists* (Columbia: University of Missouri Press, 2001); Susie Stanley, *Holy Boldness: Women Preachers' Autobiographies and the Sanctified Self* (Knoxville: University of Tennessee Press, 2002); Grammer, *Some Wild Visions*; Chanta Haywood, *Prophesying Daughters: Black Women Preachers and the Word, 1823–1913* (Columbia: University of Missouri Press, 2003); Priscilla Pope-Levison, *Turn the Pulpit Loose: Two Centuries of American Women Evangelists* (New York: Palgrave Macmillan, 2004); Laceye C. Warner, *Saving Women: Retrieving Evangelistic Theology and Practice* (Waco, TX: Baylor University Press, 2007); Matthew Sutton, *Aimee Semple McPherson and the Resurrection of Christian America* (Cambridge, MA: Harvard University Press, 2007); and Robinson and Ruff, *Out of the Mouths of Babes*.
15. Jerald Brauer defines conversion as "a profound, self-conscious, existential change from one set of beliefs, habits, and orientation to a new structure of belief and action." Jerald C. Brauer, "Conversion: From Puritanism to Revivalism," *Journal of Religion* 58 (July 1978): 227.
16. Leonard I. Sweet, "Nineteenth-Century Evangelicalism," in *Encyclopedia of the American Religious Experience: Studies of Traditions and Movements*, ed. Charles H. Lippy and Peter W. Williams (New York: Scribner, 1988), 2:876.
17. D. W. Bebbington, *Evangelicalism in Modern Britain: A History from the 1730s to the 1980s* (Boston: Unwin Hyman, 1989), 2–17, quoted in Mark Noll, *America's God: From Jonathan Edwards to Abraham Lincoln* (New York: Oxford University Press, 2002), 5.
18. David I. Macleod, *Building Character in the American Boy: The Boy Scouts, YMCA, and Their Forerunners, 1870–1920* (Madison: University of Wisconsin Press, 1983), 23.
19. Martin Marty, *Protestantism in the United States: Righteous Empire*, 2nd ed. (Chicago: University of Chicago, 1986), 192. See Horace Bushnell, *Discourses on Christian Nurture* (Boston: Massachusetts Sabbath School Society, 1847).
20. Macleod, *Building Character in the American Boy*, 23. For a discussion of gender and conversion, see Candy Gunther Brown, "Domestic Nurture versus Clerical Crisis: The Gender Dimension in Horace Bushnell's and Elizabeth Prentiss's Critiques of Revivalism," in McClymond, *Embodying the Spirit*, 67–83; and Ann Taves, "Feminization Revisited: Protestantism and Gender at the Turn of the Century," in *Women and Twentieth-Century Protestantism*, ed. Margaret Lamberts Bendroth and Virginia Lieson Brereton (Urbana: University of Illinois Press, 2002), 304–24.

21. Catherine L. Albanese, "Horace Bushnell among the Metaphysicians," *Church History* 79:3 (September 2010): 616.
22. See Dorothy Jean Furnish, "Women in Religious Education: Pioneers for Women in Professional Ministry," in *Women and Religion in America*, vol. 3: *1900–1968*, ed. Rosemary Radford Ruether and Rosemary Skinner Keller (San Francisco: Harper & Row, 1986), 310–17. See also Virginia Lieson Brereton, "Protestant Sunday Schools and Religious Education," in *Encyclopedia of Women and Religion in North America*, ed. Rosemary Skinner Keller and Rosemary Radford Ruether (Bloomington: Indiana University Press, 2006), 2:906–12.
23. Ann Taves, *Fits, Trances, and Visions: Experiencing Religion and Explaining Experience from Wesley to James* (Princeton, NJ: Princeton University Press, 1999), 343.
24. Taves, *Fits, Trances, and Visions*, 342. Further cementing ties between religious education and the progressive wing of Protestant Christianity was the adoption of the interpretive method of higher criticism, "not only in the graduate schools, but in the Sunday Schools of the land." Because of this connection, historian Dorothy Jean Furnish claims that higher criticism had an impact on "a new breed of curriculum writers and teachers." Furnish, "Women in Religious Education," 310.
25. Amanda Smith, *An Autobiography: The Story of the Lord's Dealings with Mrs. Amanda Smith, the Colored Evangelist* (Chicago: Christian Witness, 1921), 47.
26. Martha Moore Avery, Diary, Beaton Institute, University College of Cape Breton.
27. J. A. Wood, *Perfect Love; Plain Things for Those Who Need Them, concerning the Doctrine, Experience, Profession and Practice of Christian Holiness*, rev. ed. (South Pasadena, CA: Published by the author, 1891). The book also held personal significance for Vennard, because at a low period in her life, she happened into a Methodist church on a Sunday morning when Wood preached. After hearing him expound on Matthew 5:8, "Blessed are the pure in heart; for they shall see God," she recalled that "a flood of memories of better days spiritually engulfed her soul, and she resolved to return to the study of the Bible." Bowie, *Alabaster*, 42.
28. Delbert R. Rose, *Vital Holiness: A Theology of Christian Experience* (Minneapolis: Bethany Fellowship, 1975), 50.
29. "Editorial," *Inasmuch* 5:12 (February 1910): 7.
30. William Kostlevy, *Holy Jumpers: Evangelicals and Radicals in Progressive Era America* (New York: Oxford University Press, 2010), 19. Sanctification occupies the middle position between justification and glorification in John Wesley's *ordo salutis*. Justification marks the deliverance from the penalty of sin when one accepts the reconciliation made available through Jesus Christ's death on the cross; sanctification delivers one from the plague of sinning; and glorification marks the final deliverance from the presence of the effects of sin, a state one enters after death. Wesley approached sanctification as a dynamic process of growing into greater love of God and neighbor. He considered love to be at the essence of sanctification: "The humble, gentle, patient love of God and our neighbor, ruling our tempers, words, and actions." John Wesley, "Brief Thoughts on Christian Perfection," in *The Works of the Rev. John Wesley, A.M.*, ed. Thomas Jackson (London: John Mason, 1829), 11:446, quoted in Randy Maddox, "Reconnecting the Means to the End: A Wesleyan Prescription for the Holiness Movement," *Wesleyan Theological Journal* 33:2 (1998): 43.
31. By "instantaneous," Wood meant that "it is instantaneous as a death or a birth, as a washing or refining." He disagreed vociferously with the idea that sanctification could happen gradually. "Can a person successfully seek the gradual attainment of entire sanctification? NO . . . 1. He who seeks a gradual sanctification, seeks necessarily something less than entire sanctification; that is, he does not seek entire sanctification at all." Wood, *Perfect Love*, 82, 80.

32. Iva Durham Vennard, *Upper Room Messages* (Chicago: Chicago Evangelistic Institute, 1916), 114–15.
33. The Wesleyan/Holiness movement emerged in the 1830s within American Methodism during the time of its phenomenal growth upwards to a million members. Several events catalyzed the movement's emphasis on sanctification, or holiness, its more popular synonym. The Tuesday Meetings for the Promotion of Holiness commenced in 1835 in the New York City home of Sarah Worrall Lankford shortly after she experienced entire sanctification. Her sister, Phoebe Palmer, eventually assumed leadership of the weekly meetings and extended their influence nationally and internationally. In 1839, Timothy Merritt founded the premier journal on holiness in the United States, *The Guide to Christian Perfection*, later known as *The Guide to Holiness* under the editorial pen of Palmer. In addition, Merritt's influential book, *The Christian's Manual; a Treatise on Christian Perfection, with Directions for Achieving that State*, published in 1825, consisted of excerpts from John Wesley and John Fletcher on entire sanctification. See also n. 36 below.
34. Noll, *America's God*, 359.
35. About her sanctification experience on her "day of days," July 26, 1837, Palmer wrote: "I now say that I had obtained this blessing, by laying all upon the altar. . . . So long as the offering was kept upon the altar, I saw it to be not only a privilege, but a duty, to believe" (Phoebe Palmer, *The Way of Holiness, with Notes by the Way: Being a Narrative of Religious Experience, Resulting from a Determination to be a Bible Christian* [New York: Piercy & Reed, 1843], 53). For more on her altar metaphor, see Stanley, *Holy Boldness*, 69–79; and Diane Leclerc, *Singleness of Heart: Gender, Sin, and Holiness in Historical Perspective* (Lanham, MD: Scarecrow, 2002), 116–21.
36. John Wesley, "Minutes of Several Conversations," in Jackson, ed., *The Works of the Rev. John Wesley, A.M.*, 8:329, quoted in Donald Dayton, *Theological Roots of Pentecostalism* (Peabody, MA: Hendrickson, 1987), 48. A contemporary of Wesley's, John Fletcher (1729–85), exploited this possibility and presented sanctification as an immediate reception of the Holy Spirit, such as happened at Pentecost. Fletcher made the following comment to differentiate his belief about sanctification from Wesley's: "You will find my views of this matter in Mr. Wesley's sermons on Christian Perfection and on Scriptural Christianity; with this difference, that I would distinguish more exactly between the believer baptized with the Pentecostal power of the Holy Ghost, and the believer who, like the Apostles after our Lord's ascension, is not yet filled with that power" (John Fletcher to Mary Bosanquet, March 7, 1778, reprinted in Luke Tyerman, *Wesley's Designated Successor: The Life, Letters, and Literary Labours of the Rev. John William Fletcher* (London: Hodder & Stoughton, 1882), 411, quoted in Dayton, *Theological Roots of Pentecostalism*, 50). In other words, Fletcher approached sanctification as the "presupposition" rather than the aspiration for the Christian life and moved it closer in proximity to justification in order to impart power to the believer for overcoming sin throughout the entirety of the Christian life. Dayton, *Theological Roots of Pentecostalism*, 69.
37. For a perspective from the Progressive Era, see A. S. Graves, "Wesley's Variations of Belief, and the Influence of the Same on Methodism," *Methodist Review* 69 (1887): 192–211. See also Donald Dayton, "Methodism and Pentecostalism," in *The Oxford Handbook of Methodist Studies*, ed. William J. Abraham and James E. Kirby (New York: Oxford University Press, 2009), 174. This topic continues to be debated among scholars of Methodism. For example, see Laurence W. Wood, *The Meaning of Pentecost in Early Methodism: Rediscovering John Fletcher as John Wesley's Vindicator and Designated Successor*, Kingswood Books (Nashville, TN: Abingdon, 2002); and Randy Maddox, "Wesley's Understanding of Christian Perfection: In What Sense Pentecostal?" *Wesleyan Theological Journal* 34:2 (1999): 78–83.

38. For more on "come-outism," see Melvin E. Dieter, *The Holiness Revival of the Nineteenth Century*, Studies in Evangelicalism, no. 1 (Metuchen, NJ: Scarecrow, 1980), 245–46, 270–73; Charles E. Jones, *Perfectionist Persuasion: The Holiness Movement and American Methodism, 1867-1936*, ATLA (American Theological Library Association) Monograph Series, no. 5 (Metuchen, NJ: Scarecrow, 1974), 55–56, 58–60; and Kostlevy, *Holy Jumpers*, 22–24, 34–36.
39. The Keswick movement in the United States became associated with Oberlin College in Ohio, founded in 1833. Both Asa Mahan, the college's first president, and Charles G. Finney, the first professor of theology and Mahan's successor, experienced sanctification and promoted what came to be known as Oberlin perfectionism. When Mahan retired to England, he associated with the British holiness movement and helped to launch the annual Keswick Convention. Holiness conferences have been held annually in Keswick, a town in Britain's Lake District, since 1875.
40. Leading missionary speakers, like Pandita Ramabai from Pune, India, often addressed the Keswick convention. For more on Ramabai's connection with the holiness movement, see Jay Riley Case, *An Unpredictable Gospel: American Evangelicals and World Christianity, 1812-1920* (New York: Oxford University Press, 2012), 231–55; and Priscilla Pope-Levison, "Holiness and Pentecostal Movements within Methodism," in *The Ashgate Research Companion to World Methodism*, ed. Peter Forsaith, William Gibson, and Martin Wellings (London: Ashgate, 2013), 141–55.
41. Robert Kelso Carter, *The Atonement for Sin and Sickness; or, A Full Salvation for Soul and Body* (Boston: Willard Tract Repository, 1884), 38, quoted in Dayton, *Theological Roots of Pentecostalism*, 130.
42. For a discussion of Aimee Semple McPherson's incorporation of the four-fold gospel as the doctrinal basis of her denomination, the International Church of the Foursquare Gospel, see Matthew Sutton, *Aimee Semple McPherson and the Resurrection of Christian America*, 44–45.
43. Ray, *Twice Sold, Twice Ransomed*, 65.
44. Dayton, *Theological Roots of Pentecostalism*, 94.
45. Stanley, *Holy Boldness*, 93–95.
46. Mary Lee Cagle, *The Life and Work of Mary Lee Cagle: An Autobiography* (Kansas City, MO: Nazarene Publishing House, 1928), 29.
47. Bowie, *Alabaster*, 124.
48. Bowie, *Alabaster*, 145.
49. Another Methodist minister, the Reverend William Nast Brodbeck, launched a nearly identical, not so veiled threat against the deaconess movement: "One thing is certain the deaconess is not a substitute for a pastor, and will mean the destruction of the order for her to take up pastoral lines of work." Rosemary Skinner Keller, "The Deaconess: 'New Woman' of Late Nineteenth Century Methodism" *Explor* 5 (1979): 38.
50. Ann Douglas, *The Feminization of American Culture* (New York: Knopf, 1977), 131.
51. Jean Miller Schmidt, *Grace Sufficient: A History of Women in American Methodism, 1760-1930* (Nashville, TN: Abingdon, 1999), 154.
52. Lewis Curts, ed., *The General Conferences of the Methodist Episcopal Church from 1792 to 1896* (Cincinnati: Curts & Jennings, 1900), 201. This vote also specifically targeted two Methodist women who had submitted applications for ordination to the General Conference that year: Anna Howard Shaw and Anna Oliver. The conference denied their ordinations and revoked their preaching licenses. See Schmidt, *Grace Sufficient*, 185–96.
53. Mark Chaves, *Ordaining Women: Culture and Conflict in Religious Organizations* (Cambridge, MA: Harvard University Press, 1997), 1.
54. Schmidt, *Grace Sufficient*, 158.

55. Rosemary Skinner Keller, "The Organization of Protestant Laywomen in Institutional Churches," in *In Our Own Voices: Four Centuries of American Women's Religious Writing*, ed. Rosemary Skinner Keller and Rosemary Radford Ruether (Louisville, KY: WJK, 1995), 69–70.
56. Mary Lee Cagle, "My Call to the Ministry," in *Women Preachers*, ed. Fannie McDowell Hunter (Dallas: Berachah Printing, 1905), 70.
57. Dana L. Robert, "Protestant Women Missionaries: Foreign and Home," in Keller and Ruether, eds., *Encyclopedia of Women and Religion in North America*, 2:837.
58. Eliza F. Kent, *Converting Women: Gender and Protestant Christianity in Colonial South India* (New York: Oxford University Press, 2004), 113–20.
59. Carolyn DeSwarte Gifford, "Nineteenth- and Twentieth-Century Protestant Social Reform Movements in the United States," in Keller and Ruether, eds., *Encyclopedia of Women and Religion in North America*, 3:1028. In Freedman's words, the female institution-building strategy "helped mobilize women and gained political leverage in the larger society" while, at the same time, maintaining "the positive attraction of the female world of close, personal relationships and domestic institutional structures" (Estelle Freedman, "Separatism as Strategy: Female Institution Building and American Feminism, 1870–1930," *Feminist Studies* 5 (1979): 513, 517). Evelyn Brooks Higginbotham applies Freedman's thesis specifically to a religious organization in the Progressive Era, the women's movement in the Black Baptist Church. See Evelyn Brooks Higginbotham, *Righteous Discontent: The Women's Movement in the Black Baptist Church, 1880–1920* (Cambridge, MA: Harvard University Press, 1993), 79–80.
60. The "Do Everything" policy linked temperance to other reforms for women, from suffrage to dress reform, from equal pay for equal work to equality in church polity. To meet this wide-ranging agenda, the WCTU established departments each with "a band of specialists" dedicated to tackling a single issue (Jennie Fowler Willing, "The Woman's Christian Temperance Union," *Guide to Holiness* [March 1896]: 102). The number of departments would eventually expand to forty-five, and each level—national, state, and local—had departments with a superintendent to oversee it. Wendy Mitchinson claims that this organizational structure made it possible for women from a range of assorted interests to join the WCTU and contribute to its immense growth (Wendy Mitchinson, "The Woman's Christian Temperance Union: A Study in Organization," *International Journal of Women's Studies* 4:2 [1981]: 143–56).
61. Margaret L. Bendroth, "The Search for 'Women's Role' in American Evangelicalism, 1930–1980," in *Evangelicalism and Modern America*, ed. George Marsden (Grand Rapids, MI: Eerdmans, 1984), 124.
62. Kristin Aune, "Evangelical Christianity and Women's Changing Lives," *European Journal of Women's Studies* 15:3 (2008): 282.
63. George M. Marsden, *Reforming Fundamentalism: Fuller Seminary and the New Evangelicalism* (Grand Rapids, MI: Eerdmans, 1987), 2.
64. A partial list of published materials on these movements includes the following: Mary Farrell Bednarowski, "Outside the Mainstream: Women's Religion and Women Religious Leaders in Nineteenth-Century America," *Journal of the American Academy of Religion* 48 (1980): 207–31; Paul K. Conkin, *American Originals: Homemade Varieties of Christianity* (Chapel Hill: University of North Carolina Press, 1997); Sarah Gardner Cunningham, "Christian Science," in Keller and Ruether, eds., *Encyclopedia of Women and Religion in North America*, 2:738–46; Catherine Wessinger, *Women's Leadership in Marginal Religions: Explorations outside the Mainstream* (Urbana: University of Illinois Press, 1993); and Catherine Wessinger, Dell deChant, and William Michael Ashcraft, "Theosophy, New Thought, and New Age Movements," in Keller and Ruether, eds., *Encyclopedia of Women and Religion in North America*, 2:753–68. I did not include Spiritualism, even though women most

often served as the spiritualist medium, because it does not fit the institution-building profile of this study. As historian Ann Braude claims, Spiritualism "never gave rise to permanent institutions of any consequence" (Ann Braude, *Radical Spirits: Spiritualism and Women's Rights in Nineteenth-Century America* [Boston: Beacon Press, 1989], 7). Further, according to Catherine Wessinger, Spiritualism has no individual founder (Wessinger, *Women's Leadership in Marginal Religions*, 60).

65. Cunningham, "Christian Science," 2:740.
66. Cunningham, "Christian Science," 2:742.
67. Wessinger, deChant, and Ashcraft, "Theosophy, New Thought, and New Age Movements," 2:758. See also J. Gordon Melton, "Emma Curtis Hopkins: A Feminist of the 1880s and Mother of New Thought," in Wessinger, *Women's Leadership in Marginal Religions*, 88–101.
68. Because of the book's focus on institution building, some notable women evangelists, such as Maggie Newton van Cott, the first Methodist woman granted a local preacher's license in 1869, and Hannah Whitall Smith, internationally known speaker and author of the bestselling book, *The Christian's Secret of a Happy Life* (Chicago: Fleming H. Revell, 1873), are not included, even though their evangelistic work lasted into the Progressive Era. Their exclusion does not diminish their importance; it simply means they do not showcase the same shift from itinerancy to institution building as the two dozen women evangelists featured in the book.
69. I use the term "Progressive Era" for the straightforward reason expressed by historian Steven J. Diner: "Because historians routinely use this label and readers recognize it more" (Steven J. Diner, *A Very Different Age: Americans of the Progressive Era* [New York: Hill & Wang, 1998], 13). Still, as with any term intended to encapsulate an historical time period, it is problematic. Political scientist Robert Putnam reiterates this point: "Like any historical demarcation, this division is not strict, since developments associated with the Progressive movement had clear antecedents during the earlier period, and developments associated with the Gilded Age persisted into the later period" (Robert D. Putnam, *Bowling Alone: The Collapse and Revival of American Community* [New York: Simon & Schuster, 2000], 367). Because of this, some historians prefer to consider "the period from 1877 through [World War I] as a single historical era" (John D. Buenker, ed., *The Gilded Age and Progressive Era, 1877–1920*, Sources of the American Tradition [Acton, MA: Copley, 2002], 1). Even though I adopt the Progressive Era nomenclature, throughout this book I point out important antecedents before 1890 and look beyond 1920, particularly in the Conclusion, to trace the institutional trajectory and the women's ongoing significance.
70. Michael McGerr, *A Fierce Discontent: The Rise and Fall of the Progressive Movement in America, 1870–1920* (New York: Free Press, 2003), 100.
71. James F. Findlay, *Dwight L. Moody, American Evangelist, 1837–1899* (Chicago: University of Chicago Press, 1969), 309. Lucy Rider Meyer taught Bible in the school during the winter of 1884–85. Her "attempts to interest him [Moody] in the idea of a Bible training school" went unheeded (Schmidt, *Grace Sufficient*, 198). Meyer would launch her own school several months later, the Chicago Training School for City, Home, and Foreign Missions.
72. Findlay, *Dwight L. Moody*, 312.
73. The first summer school attracted college men active in Christian student organizations, like John R. Mott from Cornell University's YMCA. Mott described in a letter home how the school's atmosphere intensified his evangelistic fervor: "Here are 225 young men all of whom are solid Christians and moreover who are all imbued, with the YMCA characteristic—work for souls. I know of no other such meeting in this country at least. They are all impressed with the feeling of responsibility also—I doubt very much if there is a fellow here but what will enter some active religious work" (C. Howard Hopkins, *John R. Mott, 1865–1955: A Biography* [Grand Rapids: William B. Eerdmans, 1979], 26). Mott and ninety-nine others, known as the Mount Hermon Hundred, consecrated themselves to foreign missionary work under the umbrella of

the Student Volunteer Movement for Foreign Missions (SVM). Although Mott never served as a foreign missionary, he galvanized worldwide mission, ecumenism, and evangelism by serving as chair of the SVM for thirty-two years, authoring the best-selling book on the SVM's watchword, *The Evangelization of the World in This Generation* (New York: Student Volunteer Movement for Foreign Missions, 1905), convening the 1910 Edinburgh Missionary Conference, and chairing the Continuation Committee after Edinburgh that evolved into the World Council of Churches. For these and other efforts, he was awarded the 1946 Nobel Peace Prize. In his final public appearance in 1954, he reiterated his enduring commitment to evangelism, fostered at Mount Hermon, with these words, "While life lasts I am an evangelist."

74. Arthur Schlesinger, "A Critical Period in American Religion, 1875-1900," in *Proceedings of the Massachusetts Historical Society* 64 (1932-33): 523-33. Martin Marty and Jean Miller Schmidt developed the metaphor of a two-party system to explain the growing separation between Evangelicals and Progressives that indelibly marked American religion during this time period: "One party, which may be called 'private' Protestantism, seized that name 'evangelical' which had characterized all Protestants early in the nineteenth century. It accented individual salvation out of the world, personal moral life congruent with the ideals of the saved, and fulfillment or its absence in the rewards or punishments in another world in a life to come. The second informal group, which can be called 'public' Protestantism, was public insofar as it was more exposed to the social order and the social destinies of people. Whereas the word 'evangelical' somehow came to be a part of the description of the former group, the word 'social' almost always worked its way into designations of the latter. They pursued a Social Christianity, the social gospel, social service, social realism, and the like" (Marty, *Protestantism in the United States*, 179). See also Jean Miller Schmidt, *Souls or the Social Order: The Two-Party System in American Protestantism* (Brooklyn, NY: Carlson, 1991), xxvi-xxxiii. For a range of responses to the two-party metaphor, see Douglas Jacobsen and William Vance Trollinger, eds., *Re-forming the Center: American Protestantism, 1900 to the Present* (Grand Rapids, MI: Eerdmans, 1998).

75. Sweet, "Nineteenth-Century Evangelicalism," 2:875. Similarly, Marsden comments that evangelical Protestantism "constituted an unofficial religious establishment" (Marsden, *Reforming Fundamentalism*, 4).

76. John D. Buenker, "Introduction to Chapter Six: Innocents on Board: Migrants in Urban-Industrial America," in Buenker, ed., *The Gilded Age and Progressive Era*, 330. See also David H. Bennett, *The Party of Fear: From Nativist Movements to the New Right in American History* (New York: Vintage, 1988), 163-79.

77. Josiah Strong, *Our Country* (1891 ed.), ed. Jurgen Herbst (Cambridge, MA: Harvard University Press, 1963), 52. See also Wendy J. Deichmann Edwards, "Forging an Ideology for American Missions: Josiah Strong and Manifest Destiny," in *North American Foreign Missions, 1810-1914: Theology, Theory, and Policy*, ed. Wilbert R. Shenk (Grand Rapids, MI: Eerdmans, 2004), 163-91.

78. William G. McLoughlin, *Revivals, Awakenings, and Reform: An Essay on Religion and Social Change in America, 1607-1977* (Chicago: University of Chicago Press, 1978), 145.

79. Glenna Matthews, *The Rise of Public Woman: Woman's Power and Woman's Place in the United States, 1630-1970* (New York: Oxford University Press, 1992), 154.

80. J. R. Day, "The Higher Criticism: A Symposium," *Zion's Herald* 71 (March 22, 1893): 89.

81. Ferenc Szasz nods to higher criticism as more problematic for evangelicals than evolution. See Ferenc Szasz, "Protestantism and the Search for Stability: Liberal and Conservative Quests for a Christian America, 1875-1925," in *Building the Organizational Society: Essays on Associational Activities in Modern America*, ed. Jerry Israel (New York: Free Press, 1972), 90-91.

82. Evangeline Booth, "The World's Greatest Romance," in *The Harp and the Sword: Writings and Speeches of Evangeline Cory Booth*, vol. 1, ed. John D. Waldron (New York: Salvation Army, 1992), 167.

83. Sweet, "Nineteenth-Century Evangelicalism," 2:897. On the development of this trend in the earlier part of the century, see Noll, *America's God*, 370–85.
84. William G. McLoughlin, *Modern Revivalism: Charles Grandison Finney to Billy Graham* (New York: Ronald Press, 1959), 168.
85. Sydney E. Ahlstrom, *A Religious History of the American People* (New Haven, CT: Yale University Press, 1972), 744.
86. Ahlstrom, *A Religious History of the American People*, 748.
87. Robert T. Handy, "The Protestant Quest for a Christian America, 1830–1930," *Church History* 22 (March 1953): 10.
88. I made the decision not to devote a chapter to faith homes, even though women founded many of them, like Carrie Judd Montgomery. The primary purpose of a faith home revolved around physical and spiritual healing, not evangelism. Historian Heather Curtis describes the purpose of "houses of healing" as offering "room, board, and an encouraging environment in which to nurture the mental convictions, bodily habits, and spiritual dispositions that made trusting God for healing and acting faith possible" (Heather D. Curtis, *Faith in the Great Physician: Suffering and Divine Healing in American Culture, 1860–1900* [Baltimore, MD: Johns Hopkins University Press, 2007], 141). See also James W. Opp, "Healing Hands, Healthy Bodies: Protestant Women and Faith Healing in Canada and the United States, 1880–1930," in Bendroth and Brereton, ed., *Women and Twentieth-Century Protestantism*, 236–56.

Notes to Chapter 1

1. David Goldstein, "Lay Street Preaching," in *The White Harvest: A Symposium on Methods of Convert Making*, ed. John A. O'Brien (New York: Longmans, Green & Co., 1927), 217. On Catholic motor missions in the decades after the Progressive Era, see Jeffrey D. Marlett, *Saving the Heartland: Catholic Missionaries in Rural America, 1920–1960* (DeKalb: Northern Illinois University Press, 2002), 133–61.
2. For a description of the autovan, see David Goldstein, *Autobiography of a Campaigner for Christ* (Boston: Catholic Campaigners for Christ, 1936), 266; and Debra Campbell, "The Rise of the Lay Catholic Evangelist in England and America," *Harvard Theological Review* 79:4 (1986): 430.
3. Priestly orders, like the Paulists and Redemptorists, had long held evangelistic meetings in the United States, yet the CTG remained unique as an evangelistic organization spearheaded by Catholic laity. A similar venture, the Catholic Evidence Guild, began a year later in Great Britain. See Debra Campbell, "David Goldstein and the Lay Catholic Street Apostolate" (Ph.D. diss., Boston University, 1982), 242–43, and "The Rise of the Lay Catholic Evangelist in England and America," 413–37. For an early account of the Catholic Evidence Guild, see Henry Browne, S.J., *The Catholic Evidence Movement: Its Achievements and Its Hopes* (London: Burns Oates & Washbourne, 1921). See also Debra Campbell, "Catholic Evidence Guild: Towards a History of the Laity," *Heythrop Journal* 30:3 (July 1989): 306–24.

   Secondary materials on Avery and the CTG remain scant. Owen Carrigan's dissertation on Avery, written more than forty years ago, focuses on the fourteen years of her Nationalist and Socialist phases in four of six substantial chapters. In comparison, he devotes only one chapter to her work with the CTG, even though that segment of her life lasted longer. See Owen Carrigan, "Martha Moore Avery: The Career of a Crusader" (Ph.D. diss., University of Maine, Orono, 1966). See also D. Owen Carrigan, "A Forgotten Yankee Marxist," *New England Quarterly* 42:1 (March 1969): 23–43. However, some of Avery's papers that related to the CTG were not yet available for Carrigan's study; they are now housed at the John J. Burns Library, Boston College. Debra Campbell's dissertation on David Goldstein is the most substantive work to explore the CTG and Avery's role

in it. See Campbell, "David Goldstein and the Lay Catholic Street Apostolate." Historian Paula Kane devotes several pages to Avery and the CTG in her book on Boston Catholicism. See Paula Kane, *Separatism and Subculture: Boston Catholicism, 1900–1920* (Chapel Hill: University of North Carolina Press, 1994), 314–17. In a brief reference to the CTG, historian Jeffrey Marlett eliminates Avery completely and simply calls it "David Goldstein's Catholic Truth Guild." See Marlett, *Saving the Heartland*, 137.
4. Martha Moore Avery and David Goldstein, "The Origins, Methods, and Results of the Boston Catholic Truth Guild," Beaton Institute, University College of Cape Breton, 2.
5. Catherine Brekus, *Strangers and Pilgrims: Female Preaching in America, 1740–1845* (Chapel Hill: University of North Carolina Press, 1998).
6. "Woman's Christian Temperance Unions, the National and the World," in *The Encyclopedia of Social Reform*, ed. William D. P. Bliss (New York: Funk & Wagnalls, 1897), 1398.
7. Frances Willard, *Woman in the Pulpit* (Chicago: Woman's Temperance Publishing Association, 1889; reprint, Washington, DC: Zenger, 1978), 57.
8. John J. Burns Library, Boston College. The poem is signed with the name Patrick J. Pendergast. However, I attribute the poem to Avery for the following reasons: the handwriting is Avery's; she often wrote under a male pseudonym; and no one by the name of Pendergast appears in any of the voluminous CTG materials.
9. Jay Dolan, *Catholic Revivalism: The American Experience, 1830–1900* (Notre Dame, IN: University of Notre Dame Press, 1978), 189–92. At the same time, Dolan finds two significant differences between Catholic and Protestant evangelistic meetings. First, because a Catholic parish sponsored the mission, both its location and objective targeted the local church, whereas for Protestant meetings, integrating the local church tended to be a hit-or-miss affair. Sometimes meetings began in the church and then outgrew them, requiring the crowd to move to a tent or a temporary tabernacle. In that case, there might remain only a tangential link to a local church. Second, Dolan noted that only priests could conduct parish missions owing to the central role of the sacraments (Dolan, *Catholic Revivalism*, 196–97). This cleric-centered approach differed from Protestant meetings, where literally anyone, even children converted at a camp meeting, could preach. Orestes Brownson, a well-known convert to Catholicism in the mid-nineteenth century, noted another difference in his 1858 article, "Protestant Revivals and Catholic Retreats." Protestant meetings relied erroneously, in his estimation, on an excess of emotion to awaken response, whereas Catholic meetings, with their instruction in doctrine and liturgical setting with ceremony and sacrament, held any emotional response in balance. See Orestes Brownson, "Protestant Revivals and Catholic Retreats," *Brownson's Quarterly Review* 3 (July 1858): 294–322.
10. Avery and Goldstein, "The Origins, Methods, and Results of the Boston Catholic Truth Guild," 2.
11. "Growth of Democracy Is Subject of Lecture," newspaper clipping, n.d.; Beaton Institute, University College of Cape Breton.
12. David Goldstein and Martha Moore Avery, *Campaigning for Christ* (Boston: Pilot Publishing, 1924), 16, 79. As noted in the introduction, the Protestant minister and reformer Josiah Strong launched precisely the opposite argument about Catholicism in America. As historian Martin Marty explained, "[Josiah] Strong had heard the archbishop of St. Paul announcing the desire to '*make America Catholic.*' This could not be done without bringing the principles of that church into active conflict with those of American government. All who remained loyal to Rome '*would necessarily become disloyal to our free institutions.*'" Martin Marty, *Protestantism in the United States: Righteous Empire*, 2nd ed. (New York: Charles Scribner's Sons, 1986), 160.
13. Carrigan, "Martha Moore Avery," 78.
14. Carrigan, "Martha Moore Avery," 36. Nationalism, a political philosophy, revolved around the principle, set forth in Edward Bellamy's utopian novel, *Looking Backward:*

From 2000–1887 (Boston: Ticknor, 1888), that a "popular government by the equal voice of all for the equal benefit of all . . . should be extended to the economical organization as well; and that the entire capital and labor of nations should be nationalized" (Carrigan, "Martha Moore Avery," 19). On the significance of Bellamy's novel, see Paul T. Phillips, *A Kingdom on Earth: Anglo-American Social Christianity, 1880–1940* (University Park: Pennsylvania State University Press, 1996), 126–27.

15. She became politically active as a member of the Socialist Party, and she was elected several times to the Party's State Central Committee, twice nominated as a delegate to the International Labor Congress and once as a presidential candidate by the National Committee of the Socialist Labor Party at its 1892 national convention. She also ran as the party's candidate for the 1897 Boston School Board election (note in folder; Beaton Institute, University College of Cape Breton).

16. For more on Socialism in the Progressive Era, see Daniel T. Rodgers, *Atlantic Crossings: Social Politics in a Progressive Age* (Cambridge, MA: Belknap Press, 1998), 58; and Lewis L. Gould, *America in the Progressive Era, 1890–1914*, Seminar Studies in History (New York: Pearson Education, 2001), 53, 61, 66–67. Goldstein and Avery's book, *Socialism: The Nation of Fatherless Children*, earned commendation from former president Theodore Roosevelt in an editorial in the *Outlook*, March 20, 1909. See Georgina Pell Curtis, comp. and ed., *The American Catholic Who's Who* (St. Louis: B. Herder, 1911), s.v. "Martha Moore Avery," 15.

17. Mary Harrita Fox, *Peter E. Dietz, Labor Priest* (Notre Dame, IN: University of Notre Dame Press, 1953), 36–37.

18. Kane, *Separatism and Subculture*, 43–44.

19. Kane, *Separatism and Subculture*, 44.

20. Arthur B. Corbett, "The Common Cause Society," *Queen's Work* (March 1915): 147.

21. As an anonymous writer, most likely Avery, explained: "As the society [CCS] was limited in its scope, constitutionally at least, to discussion on Socialism, this was not in full agreement with the desires of Mrs. Avery and Mr. Goldstein, who yearned to proclaim at all times possible, before the public, the truths of the faith" (Avery and Goldstein, "The Origin, Methods, and Results of the Boston Catholic Truth Guild," 2).

22. Walter Elliott, *A Manual of Missions* (Washington, DC: Apostolic Mission House, 1922), 160.

23. Walter Elliott, "The Missionary Outlook in the United States," *Catholic World* 57 (September 1893): 758. For more on Elliott, see Dolan, *Catholic Revivalism*, 50–51, 71, 97, 101–2, 107; and Campbell, "David Goldstein and the Lay Catholic Street Apostolate," 64, 73.

24. Campbell, "The Rise of the Lay Catholic Evangelist in England and America," 423.

25. Historian Kathleen Cummings considers this controversy "one of the most significant episodes in U.S. Catholic history, and its underlying cause—disagreement over what it meant to be Catholic and American—might even be described as the central organizing principle of the discipline" (Kathleen Cummings, *New Women of the Old Faith* [Chapel Hill: University of North Carolina Press, 2009], 7). Of the vast number of resources on the Americanist controversy, particularly helpful are the following: Patricia Byrne, "American Ultramontanism," *Theological Studies* 56 (1995): 301–26; Jay P. Dolan, *The American Catholic Experience: A History from Colonial Times to the Present* (Notre Dame, IN: University of Notre Dame Press, 1992), 294–320; Thomas T. McAvoy, "The Catholic Minority after the Americanist Controversy, 1899–1917: A Survey," *Review of Politics* 21 (1959): 53–82; Donna Merwick, *Boston Priests, 1848–1910: A Study of Social and Intellectual Change* (Cambridge, MA: Harvard University Press, 1973), 147–76; and Thomas E. Wangler, "Americanist Beliefs and Papal Orthodoxy: 1884–1889," *U.S. Catholic Historian* 11 (Summer 1993): 19–35.

26. Leo XIII, *Testem Benevolentiae*, in *The Great Encyclical Letters of Pope Leo XIII* (New York: Benziger Brothers, 1903), 451, quoted in Campbell, "The Rise of the Lay Catholic Evangelist," 425.

27. "The Question Box has the interest of novelty, the brevity of the newspaper paragraph, and the quick change from topic to topic. It answers directly the intellectual and moral difficulties of inquirers, widens their field of study, and brings them in personal contact with a priest" (Bertrand Conway, *Question Box, New Edition: Replies to Questions Received on Missions to Non-Catholics* [New York: Paulist Press, 1929], v). See also Campbell, "The Rise of the Lay Catholic Evangelist in England and America," 417–18. This sort of outreach fit the purpose of the Paulist order, founded in the United States as an apostolate to non-Catholics in 1858 by Isaac Hecker. Hecker, a Catholic convert in the 1850s, a pivotal decade when Orestes Brownson and other prominent intellects joined the Catholic Church, believed that America would one day become the strength of the Catholic Church. To that end, he and five other American-born priests formed the Congregation of St. Paul, or the Paulists, and labored to make America Catholic. In a retrospective moment, Hecker delineated his evangelistic vocation with these words, "It seemed to me in looking back at my career before becoming a Catholic that Divine Providence had led me, as it were, by the hand, through the different ways of error, and made me personally acquainted with the different classes of persons and their wants, of which the people of the United States is composed, in order that having made known to me the truth He might employ me the better to point out to them the way to His Church; that therefore my vocation was to labor for the conversion of my fellow-countrymen" (quoted in Elliott, *A Manual of Missions*, 144).
28. For a longer list of frequently asked questions, see Goldstein and Avery, *Campaigning for Christ*, 67–68.
29. Carrigan, "Martha Moore Avery," 79–81.
30. Letter from Martha Moore Avery to Katherine, August 5, 1924, Beaton Institute, University College of Cape Breton.
31. Elliott, *A Manual of Missions*, 197.
32. Goldstein, "Lay Street Preaching," 223.
33. Letter from Martha Moore Avery to Katherine, October 24, 1922, Beaton Institute, University College of Cape Breton.
34. Campbell, "David Goldstein and the Lay Catholic Street Apostolate," 197.
35. Avery and Goldstein, "The Origins, Methods, and Results of the Boston Catholic Truth Guild," 2.
36. *Muncie Daily News* (September 21, 1885), quoted in Wayne Warner, *The Woman Evangelist: The Life and Times of Charismatic Evangelist Maria B. Woodworth-Etter*, ed. Kenneth E. Rowe and Donald W. Dayton, Studies in Evangelicalism no. 8 (Metuchen, NJ: Scarecrow, 1986), 55.
37. N. A. Trueblood, "The Tipton Trance Meetings," *Kokomo Gazette Tribune* (May 12, 1885): 4, Flower Pentecostal Heritage Center.
38. Maria B. Woodworth, *The Life and Experience of Maria B. Woodworth* (Dayton, OH: United Brethren Publishing House, 1888), 45.
39. Ann Braude, *Radical Spirits: Spiritualism and Women's Rights in Nineteenth-Century America* (Boston: Beacon, 1989), 97.
40. Marty, *Protestantism in the United States*, 83.
41. *Wabash Weekly Courier* (August 21, 1885), front page, Flower Pentecostal Heritage Center.
42. James F. Findlay, *Dwight L. Moody: American Evangelist, 1837–1899* (Chicago: University of Chicago Press, 1969), 227.
43. "I fell under this divine power several times during the meeting, while singing or talking; and sometimes while on my knees I would become rigid and remain in that condition for some time," she explained. "The glory of God would come down like a cloud around me. I seemed to fall into the arms of Jesus. The angels were all around me" (Maria B.

Woodworth, *The Life, Work and Experience of Maria Beulah Woodworth, Evangelist*, rev. ed. [St. Louis: Commercial Printing, 1894], 89).
44. "Mrs. Woodworth in Trance," *Indianapolis Journal* (May 31, 1885): 5, Flower Pentecostal Heritage Center.
45. Maria Woodworth-Etter, *Signs and Wonders*, rev. ed. (New Kensington, PA: Whitaker House, 1997), 53–54.
46. "The Tipton Revival," *Indianapolis Times* (May 7, 1885), front page, Flower Pentecostal Heritage Center.
47. Dr. T. V. Gifford, "Conversion by Trance," *Kokomo Dispatch* (May 7, 1885), 5, Flower Pentecostal Heritage Center.
48. *Muncie Daily News* (September 21, 1885), quoted in Warner, *The Woman Evangelist*, 52.
49. Findlay, *Dwight L. Moody*, 208–9. Findlay details Sankey's contributions to evangelistic meetings in general and Moody's meetings in particular. See Findlay, *Dwight L. Moody*, 205–221.
50. Woodworth, *Life and Experience* (1888), 407.
51. Woodworth *Life and Experience* (1888), 352.
52. "Mrs. Woodworth in Trance," *Indianapolis Journal* (May 31, 1885), 5, Flower Pentecostal Heritage Center.
53. Maria B. Woodworth, *The Life and Experience of Maria B. Woodworth* (Dayton, OH: United Brethren Publishing House, 1885), 28.
54. Woodworth, *Life, Work and Experience*, 97.
55. Maria Woodworth-Etter, *Acts of the Holy Ghost, or The Life, Work, and Experience of Mrs. M. B. Woodworth-Etter, Evangelist* (Dallas: John F. Worley Printing, 1916), 84. See also Warner, *The Woman Evangelist*, 182, n1.
56. Robert Bruce Mullin, *Miracles and the Modern Religious Imagination* (New Haven, CT: Yale University Press, 1996), 91. See also Gary B. Ferngren, "The Evangelical-Fundamentalist Tradition," in *Caring and Curing: Health and Medicine in the Western Religious Traditions*, ed. Ronald L. Numbers and Darrel W. Amundsen (New York: Macmillan, 1986), 493–94.
57. Woodworth, *Life, Work and Experience*, 54. The latter rain metaphor appears several times in the Bible, including Joel 2:23, which is quoted in the story of Pentecost: "O children of Zion, be glad and rejoice in the Lord your God; for he has given the early rain for your vindication, he has poured down for you abundant rain, the early and the later rain, as before" (Acts 2:1–4) Pentecostals concluded that "early rain" pertained to the extraordinary occurrences on the Day of Pentecost and "latter rain" to these sorts of events occurring in their own time, particularly speaking in tongues. See Donald W. Dayton, *Theological Roots of Pentecostalism* (Peabody, MA: Hendrickson, 1987), 24–28.
58. Woodworth, *Life, Work and Experience*, 54.
59. Letters from David Goldstein to M. M. Avery, November 30, 1927, and February, 20, 1922, quoted in Campbell, "David Goldstein and the Lay Catholic Street Apostolate," 203–4.
60. Martha Moore Avery, "Mr. Sunday and the Unitarians," *America*, n.d., John J. Burns Library, Boston College.
61. After the summer season, Goldstein took the CTG on several cross-country trips, beginning in 1918. He traveled with an assistant who helped with the meetings, while Avery remained in Boston.
62. "Increased Throngs at Guild Meetings," *Pilot* (July 26, 1924): 1, John J. Burns Library, Boston College.
63. According to Findlay, "The complexity of his campaigns forced Moody inexorably toward systematization and standardization of procedures" (Findlay, *Dwight L. Moody*, 197). At the same time, Stan Gundry cautions against an overemphasis on Moody's organizational prowess instead of his message. See Stanley N. Gundry, "Demythologizing Moody," in *Mr.*

Moody and the Evangelical Tradition, ed. Timothy George (New York: T & T Clark International, 2004), 20.
64. William G. McLoughlin, *Modern Revivalism: Charles Grandison Finney to Billy Graham* (New York: Ronald Press, 1959), 222.
65. Jean Miller Schmidt, *Souls or the Social Order: The Two-Party System in American Protestantism* (Brooklyn, NY: Carlson, 1991), 99; Thekla Ellen Joiner, *Sin in the City: Chicago and Revivalism, 1880–1920* (Columbia: University of Missouri Press, 2007), 85.
66. Joiner, *Sin in the City*, 106.
67. William G. McLoughlin, *Billy Sunday Was His Real Name* (Chicago: University of Chicago Press, 1955), xvii. A tabernacle, a temporary wooden structure, was constructed in each major city that hosted a Billy Sunday campaign.
68. William A. Sunday and Helen T. Sunday, *The Papers of William and Helen Sunday (1882–1974)*, ed. Robert Shuster, Billy Graham Center Archives, Wheaton College.
69. William A. Sunday and Helen T. Sunday, *The Papers of William and Helen Sunday*.
70. Lyle W. Dorsett, *Billy Sunday and the Redemption of Urban America*, Library of Religious Biography (Grand Rapids, MI: Eerdmans, 1991), 86.
71. Unfortunately, this statistic, cited by Homer Rodeheaver, a longtime worker for the Billy Sunday organization, includes neither the name of the professor of economics who issued the pamphlet with the pertinent statistics nor the name of the eastern university where the professor worked. Homer Rodeheaver, *Twenty Years with Billy Sunday* (Winona Lake, IN: Rodeheaver Hall-Mack Co., 1936), 119.
72. Brekus, *Strangers and Pilgrims*, 257–64.
73. See Priscilla Pope-Levison, *Turn the Pulpit Loose: Two Centuries of American Women Evangelists* (New York: Palgrave Macmillan, 2004), 97–100.
74. *Indianapolis Sentinel* (December 17, 1886), cited in Warner, *The Woman Evangelist*, 132.
75. *Weekly Courier* (Wabash, IN), August 21, 1885, cited in Warner, *The Woman Evangelist*, 133–34. Catherine Brekus notes similarities between nineteenth-century evangelists peddling the gospel and peddlers selling their wares (Brekus, *Strangers and Pilgrims*, 243–55).
76. Woodworth, *Life and Experience* (1888), 329.
77. *Indianapolis Sentinel* (December 9, 1886), cited in Warner, *The Woman Evangelist*, 132.
78. Warner, *The Woman Evangelist*, 138–39.
79. Harry S. Stout, *The Divine Dramatist: George Whitefield and the Rise of Modern Evangelicalism*, Library of Religious Biography (Grand Rapids, MI: Eerdmans, 1991), xxii. See also Brekus, *Strangers and Pilgrims*, 235, 256.
80. Carrigan, "Martha Moore Avery," 131.
81. Martha Moore Avery, "A Call to Catholic Women," *Central-Blatt and Social Justice* (January 1910), Beaton Institute, University College of Cape Breton.
82. Grant Wacker, "Searching for Eden with a Satellite Dish: Primitivism, Pragmatism, and the Pentecostal Character," in *The Primitive Church in the Modern World*, ed. Richard T. Hughes (Urbana: University of Illinois Press, 1995), 147.
83. *A Historical Account of the Apostolic Faith, a Trinitarian-Fundamental Evangelistic Organization: Its Origin, Functions, Doctrinal Heritage and Departmental Activities of Evangelism* (Portland, OR: Apostolic Faith Mission, 1965), 153; and *The Apostolic Faith: History, Doctrine, and Purpose* (Portland, OR: Apostolic Faith Mission, 2005), 101.
84. *Historical Account of the Apostolic Faith*, 158; and "Apostolic Faith Mission Newsletter," 1913, Apostolic Faith Mission Archives.
85. "Apostolic Faith Mission Newsletter," 1915, Apostolic Faith Mission Archives.
86. *The Apostolic Faith: History, Doctrine, and Purpose*, 153.
87. *The Apostolic Faith: History, Doctrine, and Purpose*, 150. In 1930, the AFM bought a second plane, *The Wings of the Morning*, and used it for transporting ministers from city to city to preach and carrying literature from the Portland headquarters to AFM branch churches.

88. *Historical Account of the Apostolic Faith*, 64.
89. *Historical Account of the Apostolic Faith*, 21. See also Estrelda Alexander, "Florence Louise Crawford: The Apostolic Faith Church," in *Limited Liberty: The Legacy of Four Pentecostal Women Pioneers* (Cleveland, OH: Pilgrim, 2008), 39.
90. *Historical Account of the Apostolic Faith*, 208.
91. *The Apostolic Faith: History, Doctrine, and Purpose*, 148.
92. *The Boston Post* (January 30, 1922), Beaton Institute, University College of Cape Breton.
93. Letter from Martha Moore Avery to Katherine, March 15, 1918, Beaton Institute, University College of Cape Breton; italics added.
94. Prominent Catholic groups in Boston that Avery could have joined already existed, like the John Boyle O'Reilly Circle, a well-known Catholic reading circle. She did go once with her godmother and noted it in her 1904 diary: "June 14—1904 Attended the John Boyl O'Riley [*sic*] Reading Circle Reception—My first introduction to Catholic society—I was my godmother's guest" (Martha Moore Avery, Diary, 1904-8, Beaton Institute, University College of Cape Breton). There is no record of a second time. Another possibility was the Catholic Summer School, a Chautauqua-like event for the continuing education of Catholic laity. Avery gave a lecture during the 1909 Summer School, but she never mentioned attending as a participant. (For information on the Catholic Summer School, see Kane, *Separatism and Subculture*, 207-211.) Evidently, she did attend meetings of the Equity Union, an organization whose purpose was "to bring together for mutual work, all people who believe the present competitive system of industry is a violation of the 'Golden Rule'" (note in Avery's papers, Beaton Institute, University College of Cape Breton). However, she received a brusque dismissal in a letter stating that she was no longer welcome at meetings: "We have shown you in many ways that we do not wish you to come to the Equity Union House, but as you persist in coming it is necessary to state the fact in definite terms. . . . Having had full experience of your personality and your methods you will not be permitted to associate yourself with our movement at any point, here or elsewhere" (letter from Morrison I. Swift to Martha Moore Avery, April 23, 1894, Beaton Institute, University College of Cape Breton). Avery's landlady at the time, also an officer in the Equity Union, tried to evict her because of "inharmony." The letter from the landlady included this excerpt: "It is a great disappointment to me! But my experience the past three weeks has forced me to the conclusion that you and I cannot live in the same house. I find so much inharmony that it takes all my energy to simply hold myself anywhere. I am also satisfied that the inharmony is not temporary. Therefore I am compelled to ask you to secure another room ASAP" (letter from L. G. Harding to Martha Moore Avery, December 12, 1894, Beaton Institute, University College of Cape Breton). In response, Avery wrote, "I have none but the best wishes for your success. Meantime I go I come I stay at my pleasure and discretion."
95. *Pilot* (September 5, 1925), quoted in Campbell, "David Goldstein and the Lay Catholic Street Apostolate," 207-8.
96. With this claim, I depart from Owen Carrigan's assertion that Avery's views on women shifted dramatically when she joined the Catholic Church. He writes, "Among the many changes in attitude that accompanied Mrs. Avery's rejection of socialism one of the most significant involved women's rights. She had always been a militant, ambitious individualist who chafed at unequal treatment of females. Yet she completely reversed her position when she became a Catholic and it seemed as if she had changed her character as well" (Carrigan, "Martha Moore Avery," 167-68). Certainly Avery did modify her stance on women's suffrage from supporting it in her Socialist days to actively debating against it once she became Catholic. However, I find her point of view about women's intellectual inferiority to be evident even in the pamphlet she wrote while a Socialist. See Martha Moore Avery, *Woman: Her Quality, Her Environment, Her Possibility* (Boston: Boston Socialist Press, 1903).

97. Avery, *Woman: Her Quality, Her Environment, Her Possibility*, 5.
98. Marcus O'Brien, Ph.D, "A Suggestion of Indian Summer," Beaton Institute, University College of Cape Breton.
99. Letter from Martha Moore Avery to Katherine, April 6, 1908, Beaton Institute, University College of Cape Breton. An advertisement card for her Boston School of Political Economy, formerly the Karl Marx class, contains this phrase: "Where women students are trained to prove that the claims of Socialism are erroneous." Curiously, on another card with the exact same words, one significant word was crossed out—women. Avery's initials and address, written in her handwriting, appear at the top of this second card (cards in folder, Beaton Institute, University College of Cape Breton). She put her preference for male students into practice by working with Richard Dana Skinner to form an intercollegiate club, the American Interuniversity League of Advance and Defense (letter from Martha Moore Avery to Katherine, January 5, 1912, Beaton Institute, University College of Cape Breton), and she worked with Harvard College Catholic boys (letter from Martha Moore Avery to Katherine, October 17, 1912, Beaton Institute, University College of Cape Breton). There is no evidence that she ever mentored college women.
100. Letter from Martha Moore Avery to Katherine, January 27, 1916, Beaton Institute, University College of Cape Breton.
101. Avery, *Woman: Her Quality, Her Environment, Her Possibility*, 6.
102. Letter from Martha Moore Avery to Katherine, May 15, 1925, Beaton Institute, University College of Cape Breton; italics added. The book referenced by Avery is *The White Harvest: A Symposium on Methods of Convert Making*, ed. John A. O'Brien (New York: Longmans, Green, & Co., 1927).
103. Martha Moore Avery, Diary, 1904–8, Beaton Institute, University College of Cape Breton.
104. Letter from Martha Moore Avery to Katherine, June 7, 1929, Beaton Institute, University College of Cape Breton.
105. Martha Moore Avery, Diary, 1904–8, Beaton Institute, University College of Cape Breton.
106. Letter from Martha Moore Avery to Katherine, May 25, 1925, Beaton Institute, University College of Cape Breton. See n. 102 above.
107. Letter from Martha Moore Avery to Katherine, August 12, 1912, Beaton Institute, University College of Cape Breton.
108. Letter from Martha Moore Avery to Katherine, October 30, 1916, Beaton Institute, University College of Cape Breton; italics added.
109. Letter from David Goldstein to Katherine, August 30, 1912, Beaton Institute, University College of Cape Breton.
110. Goldstein, *Autobiography*, 8.
111. Martha Moore Avery, autobiography: "The Long Way Home to Rome," Beaton Institute, University College of Cape Breton.
112. O'Connell watched over Boston Catholicism with tenacity: "Behind his swift and total centralization of the diocese lay the conception of an authoritarian scheme of things that was basically medieval" (Merwick, *Boston Priests*, 177). His oversight included close control of the CTG. See Campbell, "David Goldstein and the Lay Catholic Apostolate," 233–38.
113. Letter from Martha Moore Avery to Katherine, May 7, 1911, Beaton Institute, University College of Cape Breton. Avery had hoped to meet O'Connell's predecessor, Archbishop Williams. In January 1901, before her conversion to Catholicism, she requested an interview to read him her essay, "Harmony-Science-Religion." She held the conviction that her study would "work in the interest of the Institution" and that it would be her "good pleasure" to do so (letter from Martha Moore Avery to Archbishop Williams, January 7, 1901,

Beaton Institute, University College of Cape Breton). Williams declined the interview owing to lack of time (letter from the Most Reverend Archbishop Williams to Martha Moore Avery, January 11, 1901, Beaton Institute, University College of Cape Breton).
114. Letter from Martha Moore Avery to Katherine, October 17, 1912, Beaton Institute, University College of Cape Breton. O'Connell gave her a medallion of himself, the "first one to leave the house," and $100 "to do with as I liked." A year later, he followed through on his promise of financial help and offered to pay her bills after an operation.
115. Thomas O'Connor, *Boston Catholics: A History of the Church and Its People* (Boston: Northeastern University Press, 1998), 224.
116. David Goldstein and Martha Moore Avery, *Bolshevism: Its Cure* (Boston: Boston School of Political Economy, 1919), 32.
117. O'Connell also named the CTG. He vetoed Goldstein's original idea—the Sons, Knights or Advocates of the Church Militant (Campbell, "David Goldstein and the Lay Catholic Street Apostolate," 176). Goldstein then called it the Catholic Propaganda Guild. Again, O'Connell intervened and named it the Catholic Truth Guild, according to Avery. "The name is The Catholic Truth Guild. The Cardinal named it, or rather suggested the word Truth in place of Propaganda" (letter from Martha Moore Avery to Katherine, June 22, 1917, Beaton Institute, University College of Cape Breton).
118. In his autobiography, another CTG assistant, Theodore Dorsey, mentioned that "recruits were added to the staff of speakers" and briefly refers to a training course (Theodore H. Dorsey, *From a Far Country: The Conversion Story of a Campaigner for Christ* [Huntington, IN: Our Sunday Visitor Press, 1939], 161). Campbell claims that O'Connell recommended the training course idea and even appointed an instructor, but it does not appear that the course ever materialized (Campbell, "David Goldstein and the Lay Catholic Street Apostolate," 207; for more on Dorsey's short-lived tenure with Goldstein, see Campbell, "David Goldstein and the Lay Catholic Street Apostolate," 275–81). Campbell offers astute reasons for the small number of CTG workers: "Very few lay persons were attracted to full-time street work during the entire life of the movement. Goldstein and Avery's apostolate demanded a total dedication to the missionary life exhibited by very few in the Catholic laity, especially during the 1920s. Besides, it was not a very realistic vision. Even Goldstein, a young single man with almost no financial obligations, could afford to pursue his rare dream of full-time street lecturing only by contributing all of his assets to the cause and by working as a traveling Knights of Columbus speaker six months of the year" (Campbell, "David Goldstein and the Lay Catholic Street Apostolate," 205–6).
119. Campbell, "The Rise of the Lay Catholic Evangelist," 432.
120. For more on the Catholic Evidence Guild in the United States, see Campbell, "Catholic Evidence Guild," and "The Rise of the Lay Catholic Evangelist," 433–37.
121. Woodworth-Etter, *Acts of the Holy Ghost*, 339.
122. "Divine Healer Tells Why Husband's Ills Defy Her Treatment," *Atlanta Journal* (April 13, 1914), cited in Roberts Liardon, comp., *Maria Woodworth-Etter: The Complete Collection of Her Life Teachings* (Tulsa, OK: Albury Publishing, 2000), 477.
123. "Mrs. Etter Wonderfully Recovered," *Christian Evangel* (January 16, 1915), cited in Liardon, *Maria Woodworth-Etter*, 483.
124. Warner, *The Woman Evangelist*, 261.
125. Woodworth, *Life, Work and Experience*, 282.
126. Woodworth, *Life and Experience* (1888), 509.
127. Woodworth, *Life, Work and Experience*, 263.
128. Her biographer, Wayne Warner, offers a different perspective on this topic with words of praise for her support of women preachers: "During her lifetime Etter arguably opened as many or more doors for women to preach than any other person" (Wayne E. Warner, "Maria B. Woodworth-Etter: Prophet of Equality," in *Portraits of a Generation: Early*

Pentecostal Leaders, ed. James R. Goff and Grant Wacker [Fayetteville: University of Arkansas Press, 2002], 199). Yet in this article, Warner only gives one example of a woman influenced by her—Aimee Semple McPherson. He also quotes Woodworth-Etter's own assertion that through her "God has been raising up men and women by hundreds who have gone out as ministers and evangelists" (Woodworth, *Life, Work and Experiences*, 446, quoted in Warner, "Maria B. Woodworth-Etter," 208). However, because of her propensity to change the story, as she did to expunge Eisenberg's name and contributions, I read these sorts of claims with a hermeneutics of suspicion.
129. Aimee Semple McPherson, *This Is That: Personal Experiences, Sermons and Writings* (Los Angeles: Bridal Call Publishing, 1919), 149.
130. McPherson, *This Is That*, 150. See Warner, *The Woman Evangelist*, 285–87.
131. Jennie Fowler Willing, "Evangelistic Work of the Woman's Christian Temperance Union," *Guide to Holiness* (October 1896): 140. Willing envisioned the Evangelistic Department as "the pivot on which all the other forty departments turn. It is the motor propelling the complex machinery of the powerful organization" (Willing, "Evangelistic Work of the Woman's Christian Temperance Union," 140).
132. Willard, *Woman in the Pulpit*, 58.
133. Elizabeth V. Baker, *Chronicles of a Faith Life* (reprint, New York: Garland Publishing, 1984), 21–22.
134. For more on interracial work in the WCTU, see my two articles: Priscilla Pope-Levison, "Methodist Interracial Cooperation in the Progressive Era: Amanda Berry Smith and Emma Ray," *Methodist History* 49 (January 2011): 68–85, and "Emma Ray in Black and White: The Intersection of Race, Region, and Religion," *Pacific Northwest Quarterly* 102:3 (Summer 2011): 107–16.
135. Adrienne M. Israel, *Amanda Berry Smith: From Washerwoman to Evangelist* (Lanham, MD: Scarecrow, 1998), 97–98.
136. Emma Ray, *Twice Sold, Twice Ransomed: Autobiography of Mr. and Mrs. L. P. Ray* (Chicago: Free Methodist Publishing, 1926), 72.
137. Jennie Smith, *Incidents and Experiences of a Railroad Evangelist* (Washington, DC: Jennie Smith, 1920), 96.
138. Margaret Lamberts Bendroth, *Fundamentalism and Gender: 1875 to the Present* (New Haven, CT: Yale University Press, 1993), 133n52.
139. Bendroth, *Fundamentalism and Gender*, 85.
140. Dorsett, *Billy Sunday*, 106–7.
141. Helen Sunday, *"Ma" Sunday Still Speaks* (Winona Lake, IN: Winona Lake Christian Assembly, 1957), 39–40.
142. Helen Sunday, General Correspondence, in William A. Sunday and Helen Sunday, *The Papers of William and Helen Sunday*. I am grateful to a former student, James G. Mentzer, for this reference.
143. Sunday, *"Ma" Sunday Still Speaks*, 25.
144. Fundamentalism gets its name in part from a set of twelve pamphlets, *The Fundamentals*, beginning in 1910, that addressed the leading theological issues of the day from a conservative, Protestant perspective. The pamphlets focus on what Fundamentalists consider the five nonnegotiable truths about Christianity: virgin birth of Christ, substitutionary atonement (the doctrine that Jesus' death paid the debt for humanity's sin), bodily resurrection of Christ, veracity and supernatural quality of miracles, and inerrancy of the Bible (Bendroth, *Fundamentalism and Gender*, 4). See also George M. Marsden, "Fundamentalism," in *Encyclopedia of the American Religious Experience: Studies of Traditions and Movements*, ed. Charles H. Lippy and Peter W. Williams (New York: Scribner, 1988), 2:947–62.
145. Dorsett, *Billy Sunday*, 160.

146. Helen Sunday, "The Woman Who Didn't Like to Cook," in William A. Sunday and Helen T. Sunday, *The Papers of William and Helen Sunday*.
147. Michael S. Hamilton, "Women, Public Ministry, and American Fundamentalism," *Religion and American Culture* 3 (Summer 1993): 174–75. See also Joiner, *Sin in the City*, 204, 210.
148. Helen Sunday, "Having Faith in Women," in William A. Sunday and Helen T. Sunday, *The Papers of William and Helen Sunday*.
149. Colleen McDannell, *The Christian Home in Victorian America, 1840–1900* (Bloomington: Indiana University Press, 1986), xiii. The mother's role in Christian nurture held such significance that the Methodist deaconess leader, Lucy Rider Meyer, used the "mother in the Church" metaphor to lend legitimacy to deaconess work in the larger world as an extended family of sorts. See Lucy Rider Meyer, "The Mother in the Church," *Methodist Review* 83 (1901): 730.

Notes to Chapter 2

1. *Constitution, Government and General Decree Book of the Church of the Living God, the Pillar and Ground of the Truth, Inc.* (Nashville, TN: New and Living Way Publishing, 1924), 46, quoted in Meharry H. Lewis, ed., *Mary Lena Lewis Tate: Collected Letters and Manuscripts* (Nashville, TN: New and Living Way Publishing, 2003), 137.
2. Lewis, *Mary Lena Lewis Tate: Collected Letters and Manuscripts*, ix.
3. Jarena Lee, *Religious Experience and Journal of Mrs. Jarena Lee, Giving an Account of Her Call to Preach the Gospel* (Philadelphia: Printed and published by Jarena Lee, 1849), 51.
4. Lee, *Religious Experience and Journal*, 27.
5. Catherine Brekus, *Strangers and Pilgrims: Female Preaching in America, 1740–1845* (Chapel Hill: University of North Carolina Press, 1998).
6. Some evangelists, like Methodists Phoebe Palmer and Maggie Newton Van Cott, held meetings in conjunction with Methodist churches or class meetings, which provided a built-in connection to a post-meeting association. John Wesley, the founder of Methodism, instituted class meetings to provide a weekly opportunity for small-group fellowship and accountability through Bible study, prayer, hymn singing, and confession. See Philip F. Hardt, *The Soul of Methodism: The Class Meeting in Early New York City Methodism* (Lanham, MD: University Press of America, 2000); and Thomas Albin, "'Inwardly Persuaded': Religion of the Heart in Early British Methodism," in *"Heart Religion" in the Methodist Tradition and Related Movements*, ed. Richard Steele (Metuchen, NJ: Scarecrow, 2001), 44–45.
7. *Constitution, Government and General Decree Book*, 4. This scene recalls Saint Paula (347–404), who, upon denouncing the world after the death of her husband, left behind four of her five children and embarked upon a penitential life of good works and hospitality in Jerusalem. Only her daughter, Eustochium, went with her. As Paula sailed away, she left her young son, Toxotius, crying on the shore.
8. Lewis, *Mary Lena Lewis Tate: Collected Letters and Manuscripts*, 3.
9. Lewis, *Mary Lena Lewis Tate: Collected Letters and Manuscripts*, 1.
10. George Marsden, *Reforming Fundamentalism: Fuller Seminary and the New Evangelicalism* (Grand Rapids, MI: Eerdmans, 1987), 5.
11. Richard T. Hughes, "The Meaning of the Restoration Vision," in *The Primitive Church in the Modern World*, ed. Richard T. Hughes (Urbana: University of Illinois Press, 1995), x.
12. Robert D. Putnam, *Bowling Alone: The Collapse and Revival of American Community* (New York: Simon & Schuster, 2000), 385. Additional resources consulted on voluntary associations include the following: David T. Beito, *From Mutual Aid to the Welfare State: Fraternal Societies and Social Services, 1890–1967* (Chapel Hill: University of North Carolina Press, 2000); Paul Boyer, *Urban Masses and Moral Order in America, 1820–1920* (Cambridge, MA: Harvard University Press, 1978); Gerald Gamm and Robert D. Putnam, "The Growth of

Voluntary Associations in America, 1840–1940," *Journal of Interdisciplinary History* 29:4 (Spring 1999): 511–57; C. R. Henderson, "The Place and Functions of Voluntary Associations," *American Journal of Sociology* 1 (November 1895): 327–34; Jerry Israel, ed., *Building the Organizational Society: Essays on Associational Activities in Modern America* (New York: Free Press, 1972); Joseph F. Kett, *Rites of Passage: Adolescence in America 1790 to the Present* (New York: Basic Books, 1977); David I. Macleod, *Building Character in the American Boy: The Boy Scouts, YMCA, and Their Forerunners, 1870–1920* (Madison: University of Wisconsin Press, 1983); Mary Ryan, *Civic Wars: Democracy and Public Life in the American City during the Nineteenth Century* (Berkeley: University of California Press, 1997); Arthur Schlesinger, "Biography of a Nation of Joiners," *American Historical Review* 50 (October 1944): 1–25; and Anne Firor Scott, "On Seeing and Not Seeing: A Case of Historical Invisibility," in *Women and Women's Issues*, vol. 12 of *Modern American Protestantism and Its World*, ed. Martin Marty (New York: K. G. Saur, 1993), 18–32.

13. Putnam, *Bowling Alone*, 383. Even though immigration occurred in Northeastern urban centers at a higher rate, the growth rate of voluntary associations did not follow suit. Gamm and Putnam assert that in the first half of the nineteenth century, "an especially high level of associational activity" took place in the Northeast, but this "appears to have dissipated by 1860." They claim that "associational activity in the Northeast dampened, rather than flowered, during the era of intense industrialization, urbanization, and mass immigration" and that "ethnic-based associations" did not show any increase during these same decades (Gamm and Putnam, "The Growth of Voluntary Associations," 538).
14. Henderson, "The Place and Functions of Voluntary Associations," 328–29.
15. Constance Smith and Anne Freedman, *Voluntary Associations: Perspectives on the Literature* (Cambridge, MA: Harvard University Press, 1972), viii.
16. Smith and Freedman, *Voluntary Associations*, 167–69.
17. Schlesinger, "Biography of a Nation of Joiners," 5. For the other authors cited, see n. 12 above.
18. Martin Marty, *Protestantism in the United States: Righteous Empire*, 2nd ed. (New York: Charles Scribner's Sons, 1986), 172. See also Mark A. Noll, *America's God: From Jonathan Edwards to Abraham Lincoln* (New York: Oxford University Press, 2002), 330–64.
19. Ann Taves, *Fits, Trances, and Visions: Experiencing Religion and Explaining Experience from Wesley to James* (Princeton, NJ: Princeton University Press, 1999), 235.
20. Maria B. Woodworth, *The Life, Work and Experience of Maria Beulah Woodworth, Evangelist*, rev. ed. (St. Louis: Commercial Printing, 1894), 126.
21. Grant Wacker, "A Profile of American Pentecostalism," in *Pastoral-Problems In the Pentecostal-Charismatic Movement*, ed. Harold D. Hunter, Thirteenth Annual Conference of the Society for Pentecostal Studies (Cleveland, TN: Society for Pentecostal Studies, 1983), 27.
22. Mary Magdalena Tate, "The Name of the Lord Is a Strong Tower; the Righteous Runneth into It, and Is Safe (Proverbs 18:10)," in Lewis, *Mary Lena Lewis Tate: Collected Letters and Manuscripts*, 22.
23. Lynn S. Neal, "Christianizing the Klan: Alma White, Branford Clarke, and the Art of Religious Intolerance," *Church History* 78:2 (June 2009): 354.
24. Susie C. Stanley, *Feminist Pillar of Fire: The Life of Alma White* (Cleveland: Pilgrim Press, 1993), 98. Stanley explains that "Alma's anti-Catholicism, rather than racism or anti-Semitism, drew her to the Ku Klux Klan" (Stanley, *Feminist Pillar of Fire*, 92). However, as Stanley notes, historian Kathleen Blee disagrees with this assessment. See Stanley, *Feminist Pillar of Fire*, 90–93; and Kathleen Blee, *Women of the Klan: Racism and Gender in the 1920s* (Berkeley: University of California Press, 1991), 53–54, 75–76, 197.
25. Neal, "Christianizing the Klan," 353.
26. Alma White, *The New Testament Church* (Zarephath, NJ: Pillar of Fire, 1929), 245–46. Earlier in the book, she expressed similar sentiments. "But Methodists and other

organizations are not what they used to be. In their apostate condition they are no longer doing the work of the true Church, and God has had to raise up another body to be His representatives" (White, *The New Testament Church*, 79).
27. Letter from F. G. Hamilton to Pillar of Fire, October 16, 1916, Pillar of Fire Archives.
28. Letter from Louisa Gilman to My Dear Friends, December 30, 1916, Pillar of Fire Archives.
29. White, *The New Testament Church*, 388.
30. Alma White, *Looking Back from Beulah* (Denver: Pentecostal Union, 1902), 184.
31. Stanley, *Feminist Pillar of Fire*, 47. Seth Rees's first wife, Hulda, who died in her forties, was also an evangelist and Quaker minister.
32. White, *Looking Back from Beulah*, 381.
33. Alma White, *Demons and Tongues* (Zarephath, NJ: Pillar of Fire, 1910), 76.
34. Alma White, *The Story of My Life and the Pillar of Fire* (Zarephath, NJ: Pillar of Fire, 1943), 5:83.
35. White, *The Story of My Life*, 5:21–22. In another book, she expressed similar considerations: "When one soul-saving vessel has been stranded, God has always raised up another manned by people who were consecrated to die rather than compromise the truth for selfish interests. The Pillar of Fire vessel is floating this banner today over every old wreck that has sailed the seas for the past two hundred years. While we have entered into other men's labors, in the meantime our God is unfolding His word to us, and enriching us with His spiritual treasures. Our storehouses are full of food. The yoke is being broken from those who have long been held in ecclesiastical bondage" (White, *The New Testament Church*, 245–46).
36. The reference to dry bones comes from Ezekiel 37, where the prophet is set down in a valley full of very many, very dry bones. The bones represent Israel's current context of despair: "Then God said to me, 'Mortal, these bones are the whole house of Israel. They say, "Our bones are dried up, and our hope is lost; we are cut off completely"'" (Ezek. 37:11). By evoking this reference, Woodworth-Etter likened the Methodist church's spiritual condition to the dried up bones. As the bones received new life, the same would happen to a church, she claimed, as a result of her meetings.
37. Woodworth, *Life, Work and Experience*, 58.
38. Wayne Warner, *The Woman Evangelist: The Life and Times of Charismatic Evangelist Maria B. Woodworth-Etter*, ed. Kenneth E. Rowe and Donald W. Dayton, Studies in Evangelicalism no. 8 (Metuchen, NJ: Scarecrow, 1986), 17.
39. Woodworth, *Life, Work and Experience*, 45.
40. J. L. Puckett, "A Card from Dr. Puckett," *Kokomo Dispatch* (July 9, 1885): 4, Flower Pentecostal Heritage Center.
41. R. H. Bolton, *Church Advocate* (May 29, 1889), cited in Jon R. Neely, "Maria B. Woodworth-Etter and the Churches of God," *Church Advocate* (August 1975): 6.
42. "More Pastors Needed," *Highways and Hedges* [later *Holiness Evangel*], November 1, 1906, Church of the Nazarene Archives.
43. C. H. Forney, *The History of the Churches of God in the United States of North America* (Findlay, OH: Churches of God Publishing, 1914), 621–22.
44. Neely, "Maria B. Woodworth-Etter," 7.
45. Forney, *History of the Churches of God*, 244.
46. "Lakeview Church," www.lakeviewchurch.org.
47. Maria Woodworth-Etter, *Spirit-Filled Sermons* (Indianapolis: By the author, 1921), 202.
48. Mary Lee Cagle, "My Call to the Ministry," in *Women Preachers*, ed. Fannie McDowell Hunter (Dallas: Berachah Printing, 1905), 70–73.
49. Mary Lee Cagle, *The Life and Work of Mary Lee Cagle: An Autobiography* (Kansas City, MO: Nazarene Publishing House, 1928), 29.

50. C. B. Jernigan, *Pioneer Days of the Holiness Movement in the Southwest* (Kansas City, MO: Pentecostal Nazarene Publishing, 1919), 117.
51. Cagle, *Life and Work*, 60.
52. Jernigan, *Pioneer Days of the Holiness Movement in the Southwest*, 117.
53. Cagle, *Life and Work*, 82.
54. Jernigan, *Pioneer Days of the Holiness Movement*, 116–127.
55. Florence Crawford, "Christian Living," October 11, 1931, quoted in Estrelda Y. Alexander, *Limited Liberty: The Legacy of Four Pentecostal Women Pioneers* (Cleveland, OH: Pilgrim, 2008), 32.
56. Wacker, "A Profile of American Pentecostalism," 33.
57. "Apostolic Faith Mission Newsletter," 1917, Apostolic Faith Church Archives.
58. "Sister Ott's Life Story," n.d., Apostolic Faith Church Archives.
59. *Constitution, Government and General Decree Book*, 48.
60. Craig D. Atwood, "Religion in America," in *Handbook of Denominations in the United States*, 11th ed., ed. Frank S. Mead, Samuel S. Hill, and Craig D. Atwood (Nashville, TN: Abingdon, 2001), 23.
61. *Constitution, Government and General Decree Book*, 6.
62. Grant Wacker, "Searching for Eden with a Satellite Dish: Primitivism, Pragmatism, and the Pentecostal Character," in Hughes, ed., *The Primitive Church in the Modern World*, 141.
63. Lewis, *Mary Lena Lewis Tate: Collected Letters and Manuscripts*, 14.
64. Wacker, "A Profile of American Pentecostalism," 32.
65. Lewis, *Mary Lena Lewis Tate: Collected Letters and Manuscripts*, 17.
66. Meharry H. Lewis, *Mary Lena Lewis Tate: Vision!* (Nashville, TN: New and Living Way Publishing, 2005), 428.
67. Helen Swarth, *My Life in a Religious Commune* (University Park, IA: Vennard College, n.d.), 42.
68. Alma White, *Why I Do Not Eat Meat* (Zarephath, NJ: Pillar of Fire, 1915), 15.
69. White, *Why I Do Not Eat Meat*, 83.
70. White, *Why I Do Not Eat Meat*, 29–30.
71. Ray B. White, comp., *Doctrines and Discipline of the Pillar of Fire Church* (Zarephath, NJ: Pillar of Fire, 1918), 52.
72. Dispensation language became commonplace among nineteenth-century holiness preachers, including Methodist evangelist Phoebe Palmer. In a letter to her sister, Palmer incorporated dispensation language to summarize a camp meeting sermon she preached: "With a feeling of conscious and absolute dependence on the Holy Spirit, we speak of the Christian's high calling—of the glory of the present dispensation, and its responsibilities on individual professors" (Richard Wheatley, *The Life and Letters of Mrs. Phoebe Palmer* [New York: W. C. Palmer, 1881; reprint, New York: Garland, 1984], 319). For more on dispensation language in Methodism, see Donald W. Dayton, *Theological Roots of Pentecostalism* (reprint, Peabody, MA: Hendrickson, 1991), 50–54; Randy Maddox, "Wesley's Understanding of Christian Perfection: In What Sense Pentecostal?" *Wesleyan Theological Journal* 34:2 (1999): 78–83; and Laurence W. Wood, *The Meaning of Pentecost in Early Methodism: Rediscovering John Fletcher as John Wesley's Vindicator and Designated Successor* (Nashville, TN: Abingdon, 2002), 6, 159n2. It is important to clarify that this is not full-fledged dispensationalism, an eschatological system initially constructed by John Nelson Darby (1880–82) and popularized by C. I. Scofield in the Scofield Reference Bible (1909). For more on dispensationalism, see Sydney E. Ahlstrom, *A Religious History of the American People* (New Haven, CT: Yale University Press, 1972), 808–12; Margaret Lamberts Bendroth, *Fundamentalism and Gender, 1875 to the Present* (New Haven, CT: Yale University Press, 1993), 41–53; Virginia Lieson Brereton, *Training God's Army: The American Bible School, 1880–1940* (Bloomington: Indiana University Press, 1990), 16–21; and

Stanley J. Grenz, *The Millennial Maze: Sorting Out Evangelical Options* (Downers Grove, IL: IVP Academic, 1992), 91–125.
73. White, *Why I Do Not Eat Meat*, 19.
74. Florence Crawford, "Holiness unto the Lord," in *Sermons and Scriptural Studies: Book Two*, by Florence Crawford, comp. Raymond Robert Crawford (Portland, OR: Apostolic Faith Mission), 30–33, Apostolic Faith Mission Archives.
75. Florence Crawford, "Entire Sanctification," in *Sermons and Scriptural Studies: Book One*, by Florence Crawford, comp. Raymond Robert Crawford (Portland, OR: Apostolic Faith Mission), 33, Apostolic Faith Archives. Crawford promoted a Keswick understanding of sanctification as the "prerequisite for the Spirit-filled life" (Taves, *Fits, Trances, and Visions*, 334).
76. Florence Crawford, "The Baptism of the Holy Ghost," in Florence Crawford, *Sermons and Scriptural Studies: Book Two*, 70.
77. "Were the Disciples Sanctified before Pentecost?" *Apostolic Faith* 18 (1908): 2, Apostolic Faith Mission Archives.
78. Florence Crawford, "Teaching on the Baptism of the Holy Ghost in the New Testament, Beginning with the Subject of the Latter Rain," July 19, 1921, Apostolic Faith Mission Archives.
79. Lewis, "Introduction," *Mary Lena Lewis Tate: Collected Letters and Manuscripts*, 8.
80. *Constitution, Government and General Decree Book*, 106.
81. Letter from C. M. Fraser to Dear Friends, March 3, 1916, Pillar of Fire Archives.
82. Letter from J. A. Garretson to Dear Pillar of Fire, December 11, 1916, Pillar of Fire Archives.
83. Gertrude Metlen Wolfram, *The Widow of Zarephath: A Church in the Making* (Zarephath, NJ: Pillar of Fire, 1954), 59.
84. Letters from C. M. Fraser to Pillar of Fire, November 10, 15, and 17, 1916, Pillar of Fire Archives.
85. Last minute displacement orders were also received by Helen Swarth, a Pillar of Fire member for many years, who eventually left the denomination. Swarth was later graduated from Chicago Evangelistic Institute while Iva Durham Vennard was principal and became a Church of the Nazarene minister. Swarth wrote about her experience with the Pillar of Fire in a pamphlet titled *My Life in a Religious Commune*.
86. "Who Are the Pillar of Fire?" *Times* (New Brunswick, NJ) (June 25, 1916), in Alma White, *Evangelism*, comp. C. R. Paige and C. K. Ingler (Zarephath, NJ: Pillar of Fire, 1939), 1:14; italics added.
87. White, *The New Testament Church*, 324, 326.
88. Letter from Louisa Gilman to Miss Della Huffman, September 14, 1916, Pillar of Fire Archives.
89. This phrase comes from Phoebe Palmer's book, *The Promise of the Father; or, A Neglected Speciality of the Last Days* (Boston: Henry V. Degen, 1859).
90. See Nancy Hardesty, "Holiness Is Power: The Pentecostal Argument for Women's Ministry," in Hunter, ed., *Pastoral-Problems in the Pentecostal-Charismatic Movement*, 6.
91. This same admonition also applied to men; see *Women Preachers Tract*, Apostolic Faith Mission Archives.
92. "Does God Call Women to Preach the Gospel as Well as Men?" *Apostolic Faith* 18 (1918): 2, Apostolic Faith Mission Archives. See also Vivian Deno, "God, Authority, and the Home: Gender, Race, and U.S. Pentecostals, 1906–1926," *Journal of Women's History* 16:3 (2004): 91–94.
93. Maria Woodworth-Etter, *Signs and Wonders*, rev. ed. (New Kensington, PA: Whitaker House, 1997), 211.
94. Cagle, *Life and Work*, 160–76.
95. "Does God Call Women to Preach the Gospel as Well as Men?" 2.
96. Alma White, *Woman's Chains* (Zarephath, NJ: Pillar of Fire, 1943), 41.

97. White, *Woman's Chains*, 80–81. For more on White's hermeneutics, see Stanley, *Feminist Pillar of Fire*, 98–105.
98. Elizabeth Cady Stanton and the Revising Committee, *The Woman's Bible*, pt. 1, *The Pentateuch* (New York: European Publishing Co., 1895; reprint, Seattle: Coalition Task Force on Women and Religion, 1974), 24–25.
99. Lee Anna Starr, *The Bible Status of Woman* (New York: Fleming H. Revell, 1926).
100. Stanley, *Feminist Pillar of Fire*, 121.
101. *The Pillar of Fire Illustrated* (Zarephath, NJ: Pillar of Fire, 1920), Pillar of Fire Archives.
102. For more on Crawford's legacy for women, see Alexander, *Limited Liberty*, 50–59.
103. Lewis, *Mary Lena Lewis Tate: Collected Letters and Manuscripts*, 27.
104. Meharry H. Lewis, *Mary Lena Lewis Tate: Thundering Daughters, the First One Hundred Years, Ordained Women Preachers in the Church of the Living God, the Pillar and Ground of the Truth, Inc. (A Black Female's Legacy)* (Nashville, TN: New and Living Way Publishing, 2009).
105. Lewis, *Mary Lena Lewis Tate: Collected Letters and Manuscripts*, 18, quoted in Helen M. Lewis and Meharry H. Lewis, *Beauty of Holiness: A Small Catechism of the Holiness Faith and Doctrine* (Nashville, TN: New and Living Way Publishing, 1990). For more on Tate's legacy for women, see Alexander, *Limited Liberty*, 79–87.
106. Lewis, *Mary Lena Lewis Tate: Vision!* 282.
107. For more on the 1931 decision and its aftermath, see *Lewis, Mary Lena Lewis Tate: Vision!* 279–312.
108. Alexander, *Limited Liberty*, 77.
109. Stanley, *Feminist Pillar of Fire*, 117–18.
110. Alexander, *Limited Liberty*, 44.
111. Raymond Robert Crawford, "Memoirs of the Early Days of the Apostolic Faith," December 31, 1951, quoted in Deno, "God, Authority, and the Home," 88.
112. In the *Apostolic Faith*, Crawford included this testimony of her call to move out into other fields of evangelism: "There is no spot on earth so dear to me as this place; but I must go out and tell this story. Souls are perishing far and near. The Lord told me yesterday to go into all the world and preach His Gospel" (Editorial Note, *Apostolic Faith* 1:2 [October 1906]: 3, quoted in David G. Roebuck, "Go and Tell My Brothers: The Waning of Women's Voices in American Pentecostalism," in *Continuity and Change in the Pentecostal and Charismatic Movements*, Twentieth Annual Meeting of the Society for Pentecostal Studies [Dallas, TX: Christ for the Nations Institute, 1990], F-6).
113. See Deno, "God, Authority, and the Home," 94–96.
114. Alexander, *Limited Liberty*, 54.
115. Lewis, *Mary Lena Lewis Tate: Collected Letters and Manuscripts*, 19.
116. Lewis, *Mary Lena Lewis Tate: Collected Letters and Manuscripts*, 20, 46–47.
117. Wacker, "A Profile of American Pentecostalism," 30. The AFM also endured a schism when several male ministers quit to form the Bible Standard Church. That group then renamed themselves the Open Bible Standard Churches, Inc., when it merged with the Open Bible Evangelistic Association, which itself had split previously from Aimee Semple McPherson's International Church of the Foursquare Gospel.
118. For more on this conflict, see Alexander, *Limited Liberty*, 40–41; and Cecil M. Robeck, "Florence Crawford: Apostolic Faith Pioneer," in *Portraits of a Generation: Early Pentecostal Leaders*, ed. James Goff and Grant Wacker (Fayetteville: University of Arkansas Press, 2002), 230–31. The AFM's official statement about the events can be found on its website, "Jesus and the Light of the World: History," www.apostolicfaith.org/OurFaith/History.aspx.
119. Alexander, *Limited Liberty*, 41.
120. "Apostolic Faith Mission Newsletter," n.d., Apostolic Faith Mission Archives.

121. Email to the author from Rick Olson, distribution supervisor, Apostolic Faith Mission.
122. "Apostolic Faith Mission Newsletter," n.d., Apostolic Faith Mission Archives.
123. *The Apostolic Faith: History, Doctrine, and Purpose*, 58–61.
124. This mandate sparked one of several controversies that led to the exit of a group of male pastors and evangelists who formed the Bible Standard Mission. See n. 117 above; and Alexander, *Limited Liberty*, 48.
125. "Sister Ott's Life Story."
126. "Sister Ott's Life Story."
127. William Kostlevy, *Holy Jumpers: Evangelicals and Radicals in Progressive Era America* (New York: Oxford University Press, 2010), 9.
128. Kostlevy, *Holy Jumpers*, 9.
129. Alma White, *The Story of My Life and the Pillar of Fire* (Zarephath, NJ: Pillar of Fire, 1936), 3:340.
130. See Stanley, *Feminist Pillar of Fire*, 59–65; and Kostlevy, *Holy Jumpers*, 122–24.
131. Wolfram, *The Widow of Zarephath*, 34.
132. Author's interview with Zarephath resident, August 21, 2008.
133. "Progress of the Pillar of Fire Work," *Pillar of Fire* (May 15, 1912), 9, Pillar of Fire Archives. Because a large percentage of Pillar of Fire income came from selling literature to the public, White proceeded as quickly as possible to set up printing presses in Denver and London as well.
134. Wolfram, *The Widow of Zarephath*, 164.
135. Letter from Pillar of Fire to Mr. Garringer, November 18, 1916, Pillar of Fire Archives.
136. Helen Swarth explained further what occurred during a prayer siege: "All but absolutely necessary work was laid aside. We spent most of our time in the chapel praying. Simple meals were served [to] those not able to fast but many fasted most of the day or at least one meal. At these times each worker must examine himself or herself thoroughly to make sure of having what we thought we had. The Bishop gave powerful messages on the deceitfulness of the devil in these last days 'deceiving if possible the very elect'" (Swarth, *My Life in a Religious Commune*, 30).
137. Author's interview with Zarephath residents, August 21, 2008.
138. Author's interview with Zarephath residents, August 21, 2008.
139. White, *Woman's Chains*, 85–86. She also made the connection between the decline in propriety of women's fashions and eschatology, specifically the proximity of the end times: "What could be more suggestive of moral and spiritual degeneracy than the brevity of their skirts, their bare arms. Low necks and scanty clothing? Surely the forbearance of the Almighty has well-nigh reached its limit; and yet these things are not taken to heart.... With prophetic vision, Isaiah saw the butterfly age of women, when they would become the victims of foolish fashions designed by commercial men for selfish purposes. Surely there never was a time when there were so many women of the butterfly type. As the Gentile age draws to a close, they are becoming lighter and more frivolous." White, *The New Testament Church*, 309–10.
140. Naomi Wolf, *The Beauty Myth: How Images of Beauty Are Used against Women* (New York: William Morrow, 1991).
141. Letter from Carrie Garretson to Della Huffman, September 19, 1916, Pillar of Fire Archives.
142. Letter from M. G. to Alma White, August 16, 1916, Pillar of Fire Archives.
143. Letter from Louisa Gilman to Della Huffman, September 14, 1916, Pillar of Fire Archives. Helen Swarth summarized how workers handled finances: "A very small percentage of the money taken in was allowed to be kept by the workers for personal expenses. This was the only means of income and for those not able to sell any literature, money was a rare possession. Personal needs were few as all wore uniforms; no luxuries were allowed so there

was little to buy. We even used salt or soda for toothpaste" (Swarth, *My Life in a Religious Commune*, 21).

144. In a 1906 *Atlantic Monthly* article, the writer exuberantly portended that the rapid growth of fraternal societies "shows little indication of ever wielding less power over men's destinies than it does today" (Charles Moreau Harger, "The Lodge," *Atlantic Monthly* [April 1906], 494, quoted in Beito, *From Mutual Aid to the Welfare State*, 16).
145. Beito, *From Mutual Aid to the Welfare State*, 56.
146. Observers of fraternal societies tend to divide them into two types: fraternal secret societies and fraternal benefit societies. The latter are characterized by insurance benefits, the former by ritual and secrecy. See Alvin J. Schmidt, "The Fraternal Context," in *The Greenwood Encyclopedia of American Institutions* (Westport, CT: Greenwood, 1980), s.v. "Fraternal Organizations," 3–20.
147. *Fraternal Monitor* 18 (February 1, 1908): 23, quoted in Beito, *From Mutual Aid to the Welfare State*, 14.
148. Swarth, *My Life in a Religious Commune*, 42.
149. Swarth, *My Life in a Religious Commune*, 18.
150. Robert Orsi, "Dangerous Abuelitas: The Gender of Religious Otherness," *Women and Twentieth Century Protestantism Newsletter* (Winter 1999): 10.
151. Orsi, "Dangerous Abuelitas," 10.

Notes to Chapter 3

1. Mattie Perry, *Christ and Answered Prayer* (Nashville, TN: Benson Printing, 1939), 133–34.
2. Perry, *Christ and Answered Prayer*, 66–67.
3. See Joseph H. Smith, *Training in Pentecostal Evangelism* (Philadelphia: Christian Standard Co., Ltd., 1897).
4. Virginia Lieson Brereton, *Training God's Army: The American Bible School, 1880–1940* (Bloomington: Indiana University Press, 1990), 62.
5. Evelyn Brooks Higginbotham, *Righteous Discontent: The Women's Movement in the Black Baptist Church, 1880–1920* (Cambridge, MA: Harvard University Press, 1993), 214.
6. For a list of religious training schools founded by women that spans a wider chronology than the Progressive Era, see Abraham Ruelas, *Women and the Landscape of American Higher Education: Wesleyan Holiness and Pentecostal Founders* (Eugene, OR: Pickwick, 2010). Women evangelists also dedicated themselves to the education of children. Amanda Berry Smith, for instance, opened the Amanda Smith Orphanage and Industrial Home for Abandoned and Destitute Colored Children in Harvey, Illinois, in 1899. Her institution provided training in basic life skills, such as cooking, cleaning, raising small farm animals, and gardening. At the time, it was "the only Protestant institution for African American children in Illinois" (Nancy A. Hardesty and Adrienne Israel, "Amanda Berry Smith: A 'Downright, Outright Christian,'" in *Spirituality and Social Responsibility: Vocational Vision of Women in the United Methodist Tradition*, ed. Rosemary Skinner Keller [Nashville, TN: Abingdon, 1993], 70). As we saw in Chapter 2, Alma White's commitment to Christian education for youth prompted her to establish eighteen Christian schools in cities across the country.
7. See, e.g., Brereton, *Training God's Army*; Daniel Alan Brown, "A Comparative Analysis of Bible College Quality" (Ph.D. diss., University of California, Los Angeles, 1982); Joel Carpenter, "Fundamentalist Institutions and the Rise of Evangelical Protestantism, 1929–1942," *Church History* 49:1 (March 1980): 62–75; Janette Hassey, *No Time for Silence: Evangelical Women in Public Ministry around the Turn of the Century* (Grand Rapids, MI: Zondervan, 1986); Larry J. McKinney, "The Fundamentalist Bible School as an Outgrowth of the Changing Patterns of Protestant Revivalism, 1882–1920," *Religious Education* 84 (Fall 1989): 589–605; Gary Richard Moncher, "The Bible College and American Moral Culture"

(Ph.D. diss., University of California, Berkeley, 1987); and S. A. Witmer, *Education with Dimension: The Bible College Story* (Manhasset, NY: Channel Press, 1962).
8. Brereton, *Training God's Army*, 131–32. See also Hassey, *No Time for Silence*, 137–43.
9. Nathan Hatch, *The Democratization of American Christianity* (New Haven, CT: Yale University Press, 1989), 211. See also Nathan O. Hatch, "Evangelicalism as a Democratic Movement," in *Evangelicalism and Modern America*, ed. George Marsden (Grand Rapids, MI: Eerdmans, 1984), 79.
10. Aaron I. Abell, *The Urban Impact on American Protestantism, 1865–1900* (London: Archon, 1962), 51. Abell also mentions the Tabernacle Lay College (1872), connected with the Reverend T. DeWitt Talmage's Brooklyn Free Tabernacle and the Training Home for Christian Workers (1870).
11. Jay Riley Case, *An Unpredictable Gospel: American Evangelicals and World Christianity, 1812–1920* (New York: Oxford University Press, 2012), 21.
12. Hatch, *The Democratization of American Christianity*, 216.
13. Brereton, *Training God's Army*, 54.
14. Thekla Ellen Joiner, *Sin in the City: Chicago and Revivalism, 1880–1920* (Columbia: University of Missouri Press, 2007), 45.
15. Joiner, *Sin in the City*, 48.
16. Joiner, *Sin in the City*, 58.
17. Lucy Rider Meyer, *Deaconesses: Biblical, Early Church, European, American: with the Story of the Chicago Training School, for City, Home and Foreign Missions, and the Chicago Deaconess Home*, 2nd ed. (Chicago: Message Publishing Company, 1889). For an early history of Mildmay, see Harriette F. Cooke, *Mildmay; or, The Story of the First Deaconess Institution*, 2nd ed. (London: Eliot Stock, 1893), available at the HathiTrust Digital Library, http://catalog.hathitrust.org/api/volumes/oclc/21254883.html.
18. Catherine M. Prelinger and Rosemary Skinner Keller, "The Function of Female Bonding: The Restored Diaconessate of the Nineteenth Century," in *Women in New Worlds: Historical Perspectives on the Wesleyan Tradition*, vol. 2, ed. Rosemary Skinner Keller, Louise L. Queen, and Hilah F. Thomas (Nashville, TN: Abingdon, 1982), 326.
19. This list of courses comes from an appendix in a book on the early years of the Chicago Training School. See Isabelle Horton, *The Builders: A Story of Faith and Works* (Chicago: Deaconess Advocate, 1910), 205.
20. Meyer, *Deaconesses, Biblical, Early Church, European, American*, 68–69. See also Lucy Rider Meyer, "Deaconesses and the Need," *Message* 5 (1890): 9.
21. Among the seventeen deaconess training schools listed in *The Methodist Year Book 1909*, EEI was the only one to advertise evangelistic training (Stephen Ford, ed., *The Methodist Year Book, 1909* [Cincinnati: Jennings & Graham, 1909], 211).
22. See James Mills Thoburn, *Life of Isabella Thoburn* (New York: Eaton & Mains, 1903). Meyer underscored Thoburn's role in the successful vote: "It was largely by the doctor's earnest advocacy that favorable legislation was secured" (Lucy Rider Meyer, "The Mother in the Church," *Methodist Review* 83 [September 1901]: 728.
23. W. P. Harrison, "The Methodist Deaconess," *Southern Methodist Review* 4 (July 1888): 415.
24. James Mills Thoburn, *The Deaconess and Her Vocation* (New York: Hunt & Eaton, 1893), 123.
25. Thoburn, *The Deaconess and Her Vocation*, 22; italics added. Rosemary Skinner Keller interprets Thoburn from the opposite perspective, claiming that he *did* commend separate spheres for deaconesses by supporting "women's work for women." Keller writes, "Controversy regarding deaconesses arose, however, in determining whether their status was laity or clergy. James Thoburn, an MEC bishop and an advocate of the Chicago Training School, sought to dispel rumors that deaconess work would lead toward ordination. He argued that these women 'speak for Jesus' and were not seeking rights for themselves.

Because deaconess work constituted a sphere 'for women only,' its members were not crossing over the boundary line acceptable to established leaders of the church" (Rosemary Skinner Keller, "Belle Harris Bennett and Lucy Rider Meyer," in *Something More than Human: Biographies of Leaders in American Methodist Higher Education*, ed. Charles E. Cole [Nashville, TN: United Methodist Board of Higher Education and Ministry, 1986], 15). Because Keller did not include footnotes in her article, I could not follow up the sources she consulted. Still, I argue the contrary based upon Thoburn's interpretation of Acts 2, as explained in the chapter, as well as statements that I interpret leaving open the possibility of women being called to the ministry, like the following: "We all believe in the call to what we conventionally denominate the ministry—that is, we believe that God calls men to the distinct work of preaching the word and assuming pastoral oversight of Christian churches. We must not, however, fall into the mistake, which I fear is too common in all the evangelical churches, of assuming that this one call to the ministerial office exhausts the divine prerogative in that direction. If there is any one doctrine clearly taught in the New Testament it is that man must not limit God's prerogative to call whom and when and how he pleases. Men and women have duties imposed upon them in one age to which they are not called in another. *We ought to take a broad view of the whole subject and teach all our people to be prepared to hear the Master's voice at any time or in any place, summoning them forth to new duties and new responsibilities*" (Thoburn, *The Deaconess and Her Vocation*, 114–15); italics added. See also James Mills Thoburn, *The Church of Pentecost* (Cincinnati: Jenning & Pye, 1901), 124.

26. Thoburn, *The Church of Pentecost*, 124. Elaborating more on this sentiment, he wrote, "The vexed question of the right or propriety of women exercising the prophetic gift calls for only a brief word here. The prophet Joel certainly predicted that the daughters should prophesy; the daughters of Philip the evangelist did prophesy; and from the discussion of the question in the First Epistle to the Corinthians it is made abundantly evident that women were accustomed to exercise this gift. . . . The question is happily settling itself, and it seems highly probable that before many years it will cease to be a subject of serious controversy" (Thoburn, *The Church of Pentecost*, 164–65).
27. William F. Oldham, "Thoburn—Mystic, Seer, Prophet, Missionary," *Methodist Review* 106 (March 1923): 189–90.
28. *Minutes of the Thirty-ninth Session of the St. Louis Annual Conference*, held in Clinton, MO, March 20–25, 1907 (Clinton, MO: Republican Printing Co., 1907): back page.
29. "Real, genuine, soul saving work is the fundamental mission of all deaconess work, and no deaconess measures up to her privilege in service or fulfills her responsibility toward God who does not aim persistently at the definite regeneration of her people" (Iva Durham Vennard, "'Help Those Women': XIV. The Evangelistic Department of Deaconess Work," *Inasmuch* 2 (April 1906): 8, MidAmerica Nazarene University Archives.
30. Amos Binney and Daniel Steele, *Binney's Theological Compend Improved*, 2nd ed. (Cincinnati: Curts & Jennings, 1875), 192.
31. Binney and Steele, *Binney's Theological Compend Improved*, 193.
32. Binney and Steele, *Binney's Theological Compend Improved*, 192.
33. "Personals," *Inasmuch* 1 (1905): 8, MidAmerica Nazarene University Archives.
34. Vennard, "Help Those Women," 8.
35. Mary Ella Bowie, *Alabaster and Spikenard: The Life of Iva Durham Vennard, D.D., Founder of Chicago Evangelistic Institute* (Chicago: Chicago Evangelistic Institute, 1947), 136.
36. It is difficult to ascertain Vennard's views on CEI's coeducational student body, because the one cryptic reference in her biography is inextricably linked to those expressed by two men. The reference reads as follows: "During June, also, the Board of Trustees of Chicago Evangelistic Institute was organized and the incorporation details were completed. Dr. Fowler had suggested that C. E. I. be a co-educational school, in which Brother Smith

fully concurred" (Bowie, *Alabaster*, 180). Bowie did not include Vennard's own opinion about this matter.
37. Brown, "A Comparative Analysis of Bible College Quality," 52, 55.
38. Virginia Liseon Brereton, "Preparing Women for the Lord's Work," in *Women in New Worlds: Historical Perspectives on the Wesleyan Tradition*, vol. 1, ed. Hilah F. Thomas and Rosemary Skinner Keller (Nashville, TN: Abingdon, 1981), 179.
39. A. T. Pierson, *The Crisis of Missions* (New York: Robert Carter & Brothers, 1886), 327, quoted in McKinney, "The Fundamentalist Bible School," 604. For a comparative discussion of a seminary versus a religious training school in the Progressive Era, see A. J. Gordon, "Missionary Training Schools, Do Baptists Need Them?" *Baptist Quarterly Review* 12 (January 1890): 69–101. Abell devotes a chapter to the curricular changes that seminaries eventually instituted because they "suffered from too little practical training" (Abell, *The Urban Impact on American Protestantism*, 224–45). However, their curricular transformation emphasized sociology, which many religious training school founders, including Vennard, considered a dangerous, modernist trend.
40. Henry H. Hadley, comp., *Rescue Songs by One Hundred Popular Composers and Gifted Song Writers; Specially Fitted for Rescue Missions and Meetings, Rescue Workers and Evangelists and Revival Services* (New York: Christian Men's Union, 1895).
41. Glenn T. Miller, *Piety and Profession: American Protestant Theological Education, 1870–1970* (Grand Rapids, MI: Eerdmans, 2007), 116–17.
42. Brereton, *Training God's Army*, 156.
43. Miller, *Piety and Profession*, 113. See also Lawrence A. Cremin, *The Transformation of the School: Progressivism in American Education, 1876–1957* (New York: Alfred A. Knopf, 1961); and Thomas E. Woods, *The Church Confronts Modernity: Catholic Intellectuals and the Progressive Era* (New York: Columbia University Press, 2004), 85.
44. Michael McGerr, *A Fierce Discontent: The Rise and Fall of the Progressive Movement in America, 1870–1920* (New York: Free Press, 2003), 109–10. See also Glenda Elizabeth Gilmore, "Responding to the Challenges of the Progressive Era," in *Who Were the Progressives?* Historians at Work Series (Boston: Bedford/St. Martin's, 2002), 16.
45. McGerr, *A Fierce Discontent*, 110. For more on high schools in the Progressive Era, see Claudia Goldin, "America's Graduation from High School: The Evolution and Spread of Secondary Schooling in the Twentieth Century," *Journal of Economic History* 58 (June 1998): 345–74; Claudia Goldin and Lawrence F. Katz, "Human Capital and Social Capital: The Rise of Secondary Schooling in America, 1910–1940," *Journal of Interdisciplinary History* 29:4 (Spring 1999): 683–723; and Edward A. Krug, *The Shaping of the American High School* (New York: Harper & Row, 1964).
46. For more on vocationalism, see Cremin, *The Transformation of the School*, 23–57; Harvey Kantor and David B. Tyack, *Work, Youth, and Schooling: Historical Perspectives on Vocationalism in American Education* (Stanford, CA: Stanford University Press, 1982); Krug, *The Shaping of the American High School*, 217–48; and Jane Bernard Powers, *The "Girl Question" in Education: Vocational Education for Young Women in the Progressive Era* (Washington, DC: Falmer, 1992), 1.
47. Harvey Kantor and David B. Tyack, "Introduction: Historical Perspectives on Vocationalism in American Education," in Kantor and Tyack, *Work, Youth, and Schooling*, 2. See Allen F. Davis, *Spearheads for Reform: The Social Settlements and the Progressive Movement, 1890–1914* (New York: Oxford University Press, 1967), 40–59; Maureen A. Flanagan, "Gender and Urban Political Reform: The City Club and the Woman's City Club of Chicago in the Progressive Era," *American Historical Review* 95 (October 1990): 1039–41; and Marvin Lazerson and W. Norton Grubb, "Introduction," in *American Education and Vocationalism: A Documentary History, 1870–1970*, ed. Marvin Lazerson and W. Norton Grubb, Classics in Education, no. 48 (New York: Teachers College Press, 1974), 17–29.

48. See Melvin Barlow, "The Challenge to Vocational Education," in *The Sixty-fourth Yearbook of the National Society for the Study of Education* (Chicago: University of Chicago Press, 1965), 2–6; Harvey Kantor, "Vocationalism in American Education: The Economic and Political Context, 1880–1930," in Kantnor and Tyack, *Work, Youth, and Schooling*, 14–44; Lazerson and Grubb, "Introduction," 29–32; and Mayor D. Mobley and Melvin L. Barlow, "Impact of Federal Legislation and Policies upon Vocational Education," in *Vocational Education*, ed. Melvin L. Barlow (Chicago: University of Chicago Press, 1965), 186–87, 195–97.
49. "C.E.I. Alumni Offer Tribute to Their Alma Mater," in *Are You Familiar with Chicago Evangelistic Institute?* pamphlet, Billy Graham Center Archives.
50. Chicago Evangelistic Institute, *1916 Yearbook*, 30–32, MidAmerica Nazarene University Archives.
51. Chicago Evangelistic Institute, *1916 Yearbook*, 33.
52. Elizabeth Baker, "Bible Training School," *Trust* (September 1912): 10, Flower Pentecostal Heritage Center.
53. Chicago Evangelistic Institute, *1916 Yearbook*, 30.
54. "Christian Workers' Course," Correspondence Department, Chicago Evangelistic Institute, 5, B. L. Fisher Library Archives, Asbury Theological Seminary.
55. For more on higher criticism, see W. G. Kummel, *The New Testament: The History and Investigation of Its Problems* (Nashville, TN: Abingdon, 1972); and Stephen Neill, *The Interpretation of the New Testament, 1861–1961* (New York: Oxford University Press, 1964). For more on higher criticism in seminaries, see Miller, *Piety and Profession*, 112.
56. This wording comes from an advertisement for Zarephath Bible Institute. See Alma White, *Looking Back from Beulah* (Zarephath, NJ: Pillar of Fire, 1929), 384.
57. Iva Durham Vennard, "2 Timothy 2:15," *Heart and Life* 9 (November 1919): 4.
58. Letter from Iva Durham Vennard to John Paul, January 6, 1922, B. L. Fisher Library Archives, Asbury Theological Seminary; italics added.
59. Greg Schneider constructs what I consider a false dichotomy between Vennard and Meyer, despite their disagreement over historical criticism. Building upon their respective connection to two opposing camps within Methodism, he places Vennard with the holiness folk, labeling her an evangelist, and Meyer with the mainstream connectional folk, labeling her an educationalist (Greg Schneider, "'Heart Religion' on the Divide," in *"Heart Religion" in the Methodist Tradition and Related Movements*, ed. Richard Steele (Lanham, MD: Scarecrow, 2001), 127–74). What complicates this dichotomy is that both women remained simultaneously evangelists and educationalists, to use Schneider's terms. Along with her commitment to evangelism, Vennard was an educationalist who founded two schools. Similarly, Meyer, an educationalist, not only put a high premium on evangelism herself but also trained deaconesses in evangelism at her school. See Priscilla Pope-Levison, "The Deaconess Disorder: Lucy Rider Meyer and Iva Durham Vennard," consultation on "The Significance of Wesleyan Thought for the 21st Century," conference at Asbury College, Wilmore, KY, 2001, and "'A Thirty Year War' and More: Exposing Complexities in the Methodist Deaconess Movement," *Methodist History* 47:2 (January 2009): 101–16.
60. Horton, *The Builders: A Story of Faith and Works*, 213–14. See also Mary Agnes Dougherty, "The Methodist Deaconess: 1885–1919: A Study in Religious Feminism" (Ph.D. diss., University of California, Davis, 1979), 180.
61. Isabelle Horton, *High Adventure: Life of Lucy Rider Meyer* (New York: Methodist Book Concern, 1928), 323.
62. Letter from Iva Durham Vennard to John Paul, 1.
63. James Orr, "Preface," *Problem of the Old Testament, Considered with Reference to Recent Criticism* (1906; reprint, New York: Charles Scribner's Sons, 1917), xiv–xv. In his review of Orr's book, Kemper Fullerton calls the tone of the book "admirable" (Kemper Fullerton, "The Bross Prize," *American Journal of Theology* 10:4 (October 1906): 705.

64. Chicago Evangelistic Institute, *1916 Yearbook*, 32.
65. Perry, *Christ and Answered Prayer*, 307.
66. Joanne Carlson Brown, "Jennie Fowler Willing (1834–1916): Methodist Churchwoman and Reformer" (Ph.D. diss., Boston University, 1983), 37.
67. Jennie Fowler Willing, "Historical Department, Lesson I," *Open Door* 1 (January–February 1909): 33. For instance, the answer supplied for the first question is this: "The commonly received date of the creation of man is about 4004 B. C." (Jennie Fowler Willing, "Our Course of Bible Study. Historical Department. Lesson I. Answers," *Open Door* 1:2 [March–April 1909]: 19).
68. Jennie Fowler Willing, "Our Non-resident Class. Conditions of Membership in the Class," *Open Door* 3:1 (October 1905): 27.
69. Jennie Fowler Willing, "The World's Evangelistic Training School," *Guide to Holiness* (January 1898): 23.
70. Willing, "The World's Evangelistic Training School," 23. Willing's training school closed in 1910 when the Pennsylvania Railroad Company tore down its building to construct tunnels underneath the property.
71. Chicago Evangelistic Institute, *1916 Yearbook*, 39–40.
72. Lucy Drake Osborn, "The Union Missionary Training Institute," pamphlet (Brooklyn, NY: Union Missionary Training Institute, 1899), 24, Burke Library at Union Theological Seminary, Columbia University Libraries.
73. Chicago Evangelistic Institute, "Financial Summary," *Heart and Life* 2 (December 1912 and January 1913): 14–15, B. L. Fisher Library Archives, Asbury Theological Seminary.
74. Mary E. Hopkins, *As I Remember: Precious Memories of Belleview* (Seattle: Mary E. Hopkins, 1970), 34–35.
75. Lucy Drake Osborn, *Heavenly Pearls Set in a Life: A Record of Experiences and Labors in America, India and Australia* (New York: Fleming H. Revell, 1893), 288.
76. Perry, *Christ and Answered Prayer*, 157.
77. Perry, *Christ and Answered Prayer*, 183.
78. Chicago Evangelistic Institute, "God Answers Prayer," *Heart and Life* 2 (December 1912 and January 1913): 8.
79. Brereton, *Training God's Army*, 49–51.
80. Lewis Curts, ed., *The General Conferences of the Methodist Episcopal Church from 1792 to 1896* (Cincinnati: Curts & Jennings, 1900), 201.
81. Bowie, *Alabaster*, 182.
82. John L. Rury, *Education and Women's Work: Female Schooling and the Division of Labor in Urban America, 1870–1930* (Albany: State University of New York Press, 1991), 19, 4.
83. See Kathleen S. Hurty, "Protestant Women's Colleges in the United States," in *Encyclopedia of Women and Religion in North America*, ed. Rosemary Skinner Keller and Rosemary Radford Ruether (Bloomington: Indiana University Press, 2006), 2:912–23.
84. Barbara Kuhn Campbell, *The "Liberated" Woman of 1914: Prominent Women in the Progressive Era*, Studies in American History and Culture, no. 6 (Ann Arbor, MI: UMI Research Press, 1979), 26. See also Linda K. Kerber, *Toward an Intellectual History of Women: Essays by Linda K. Kerber* (Chapel Hill: University of North Carolina Press, 1997), 230.
85. See Higginbotham, *Righteous Discontent*, 31–40.
86. Debra Campbell, "American Catholic Women, 1900–1965," in Keller and Ruether, eds., *Encyclopedia of Women and Religion in North America*, 1:192. See also Tracy Schier, "Catholic Women's Colleges in the United States," in Keller and Ruether, eds., *Encyclopedia of Women and Religion in North America*, 2:881–89. On the founding of Trinity College, another early Roman Catholic women's college, see Kathleen Sprows Cummings, *New Woman of the Old Faith: Gender and American Catholicism in the Progressive Era* (Chapel Hill: University of North Carolina Press, 2009), and "The 'New Woman' at the

'University': Gender and American Catholic Identity in the Progressive Era," in *The Religious History of American Women: Reimagining the Past*, ed. Catherine A. Brekus (Chapel Hill: University of North Carolina Press, 2007), 206–31.

87. Kathryn Kish Sklar, *Florence Kelley and the Nation's Work: The Rise of Women's Political Culture, 1830–1900* (New Haven, CT: Yale University Press, 1995), 50. Despite myriad advances and achievements, this same generation was "haunted" by Edward Clarke's medical prognosis of the inherent danger to women's wombs for childbearing caused by too much education. In his highly influential book, *Sex in Education*, Clarke expressed particular concern for women's participation in a coeducational curriculum on the grounds that it would deplete a woman's energy for childbearing (Edward H. Clarke, *Sex in Education; or, A Fair Chance for the Girls* [Boston: James R. Osgood, 1873], 125–26, quoted in Sklar, *Florence Kelley and the Nation's Work*, 52–53). This line of reasoning coincided with the popular conjecture among physicians that women contracted diseases when engaged in unfeminine endeavors, such as when "sexually aggressive, intellectually ambitious, and defective in proper womanly submission and selflessness" (Ann Douglas Wood, "'The Fashionable Diseases': Women's Complaints and Their Treatment in Nineteenth-Century America," in *Clio's Consciousness Raised: New Perspectives on the History of Women*, ed. Mary Hartman and Lois W. Banner [New York: Harper & Row, 1974], 8). Although subsequent studies disparaged these myths, they loomed over women "haunted by the 'clanging chains' of the gloomy specter of Clarke's book and did not themselves know 'whether women's health could stand that strain of education.'" Sklar adapted a quote from M. Carey Thomas (Sklar, *Florence Kelley and the Nation's Work*, 53).
88. The slogan, bantered about by Progressive Era educational reformers, that encapsulated the idea of matching education to presumed vocational destiny was "social efficiency." For more on social efficiency, see Rury, *Education and Women's Work*, 8–9, 134, 212.
89. National Education Association, "The Vocational Education of Females," in *American Education and Vocationalism*, 115. As women's work opportunities expanded, two additional vocational tracks were developed: trade education for industrial work, and commercial education for office work. For statistics on female vocations from 1890 to 1909, see Mary A. LaSelle and Katherine E. Wiley, *Vocations for Girls* (Chicago: Houghton Mifflin, 1913), 102–4. See also Ileen A. DeVault, "'Give the Boys a Trade': Gender and Job Choice in the 1980s," in *Work Engendered: Toward a New History of American Labor*, ed. Ava Baron (Ithaca, NY: Cornell University Press, 1991), 191–215.
90. Albert H. Leake, *The Vocational Education of Girls and Women* (New York: Macmillan, 1918), v–vi.
91. Daniel E. Albrecht, "The Life and Ministry of Carrie Judd Montgomery," (master's thesis, Western Evangelical Seminary, 1984), 87.
92. Osborn, "The Union Missionary Training Institute," 9.
93. Hassey, *No Time for Silence*, 44.
94. Brereton, *Training God's Army*, 131–32; and Hassey, *No Time for Silence*, 137–43.
95. Brereton, *Training God's Army*, 132.
96. Brereton, *Training God's Army*, 131–32.
97. Brereton's one and only reference to Vennard, whose four decades as principal of a religious training school were among the longest, does not relate to either EEI or CEI but, rather, to her annual practice of beginning each new year with a biblical verse that guided her throughout the year (Brereton, *Training God's Army*, 60).
98. Chicago Evangelistic Institute, "Acquainting You with Chicago Evangelistic Institute," 5, B. L. Fisher Library Archives, Asbury Theological Seminary.
99. "In this, Mrs. Vennard stated that our present enrollment numbers 112. Of this number 58 are young women and 54 young men. We feel that this is especially gratifying as it indicates a better balance between men and women than in any previous year" (Chicago

Evangelistic Institute, Meeting Minutes of the Executive Committee of the Board of Trustees, November 26, 1926, 1, B. L. Fisher Library Archives, Asbury Theological Seminary).
100. Iva Durham Vennard, "Highlights of the Year: Doctor Vennard's Family Letter," *Heart and Life* 26 (July 1940): 19–20.
101. Letter from Iva Durham Vennard to John Paul, 1.
102. Letter from Iva Durham Vennard to John Paul, 4.
103. Miller, *Piety and Profession*, 41.
104. "While we do not expect to enter the lists in rivalry against the great theological seminaries and may never call our Post Graduate Department by the name of seminary, it is our conviction that this department should be made so strong and complete in its theological courses that *students taking this degree with us will have no need of further training in the theological seminaries*" (Minutes of the Executive Committee Meeting of the Board of Trustees, 1). Twenty years later, she still referenced the theological seminary as a comparison for CEI's educational level. In 1940, in a Thursday morning chapel message, she explained her reasons for not "trying for credentials" as a seminary. "The thing for us to do was to major on the one thing. That is what the Bible college is for. It is technical. The reason we don't meet the requirements as a theological seminary, such a school must have a denomination back of it and you must meet that standard of that denominational course of study. We do not want any one denomination back of us. We will teach the Bible and truths from the Wesleyan standard point of interpretation as I have said before" (Iva Durham Vennard, "Chapel Message," May 9, 1940, 2, B.L. Fisher Library Archives, Asbury Theological Seminary Archives). The following poignant phrase, included in a 1945 advertisement, in which CEI is compared to a seminary, prompts further reflection on whether Vennard ever fully relinquished the seminary dream: the Bible College meets "the need of young men and women who have had a collegiate training, or sufficient other scholastic work, who desire this technical course for the ministry. *Its courses are similar to those of a theological seminary*, but subjects are presented without the dangers of destructive criticism" (Chicago Evangelistic Institute, *1945 Yearbook*, 4–5, MidAmerica Nazarene University Archives; italics added).
105. Letter from Earle J. Stine, Jr., to an unnamed friend, 2, B. L. Fisher Library Archives, Asbury Theological Seminary.
106. Vennard College, *Vennard Vision*, 1958; MidAmerica Nazarene University Archives.
107. Brereton, *Training God's Army*, 129.
108. Anna Howard Shaw, *Anna Howard Shaw: The Story of a Pioneer*, William Bradford Collection, ed. Barbara Brown Zikmund (reprint, Cleveland, OH: Pilgrim Press, 1994), 82–83. The difficulties continued with Shaw's tumultuous path to ordination. After she was graduated from seminary at age thirty-one, she served as minister of a church in East Dennis, Cape Cod. However, when she applied for ordination to the New England Conference of the MEC, the bishop denied her request, even though she already had a local preacher's license and had been approved for ordination by the conference's examining committee. Shaw would go on to become the first American woman to hold simultaneous degrees in theology and medicine and to serve as president of the National American Woman Suffrage Association from 1904 to 1915.
109. Beverly Zink-Sawyer, *From Preachers to Suffragists: Woman's Rights and Religious Conviction in the Lives of Three Nineteenth-Century American Clergywomen* (Louisville, KY: WJK, 2003), 113.
110. Miller, *Piety and Profession*, 656.

Notes to Chapter 4

1. Richard Artemus Lee, *Mother Lee's Experience in Fifteen Years' Rescue Work with Thrilling Incidents of Her Life* (Omaha, NE: Richard Artemus Lee, 1906), 35–36.

2. Lee, *Mother Lee's Experience*, 35–36.
3. A decade later, a benefactor, Samuel Tinley, bought the home, enlarged it to include four city lots and three small houses, and set up Lee as superintendent of the Tinley Rescue Home for Fallen Girls and Women.
4. This was a common motto for rescue missions (see Lee, *Mother Lee's Experience*, 26; and Ronald W. Fagan, "Skid-Row Rescue Missions: A Religious Approach to Alcoholism," *Journal of Religion and Health* 28:2 [Summer 1987]: 153, 169). Rescue missions have since moved beyond "soap-soup-salvation" to offer a more extensive program of humanitarian outreach: "Today, the mission must be able to change from this single purpose role to a versatile facility caring for . . . displaced families, the drifting or throwaway teen, the unemployed, the handicapped . . . the discarded old and sick . . . [and] women" (Fagan, "Skid-Row Rescue Missions," 154). See also Jim Varnhagen, "Setting the Oppressed Free: New York City Rescue Mission," in *Signs of Hope in the City: Ministries of Community Renewal*, ed. Robert D. Carle and Louis A. Decaro (Valley Forge, PA: Judson, 1999), 237–40.
5. Sherry Lamb Schirmer, *A City Divided: The Racial Landscape of Kansas City, 1900–1960* (Columbia: University of Missouri Press, 2002), 34.
6. Lee, *Mother Lee's Experience*, 149.
7. Regina G. Kunzel, *Fallen Women, Problem Girls: Unmarried Mothers and the Professionalization of Social Work, 1890–1945* (New Haven, CT: Yale University Press, 1993), 10.
8. Lee, *Mother Lee's Experience*, 32.
9. Heather D. Curtis, *Faith in the Great Physician: Suffering and Divine Healing in American Culture, 1860–1900* (Baltimore, MD: Johns Hopkins University Press, 2007), 168; cf. 164–65.
10. Elizabeth J. Clapp, *Mothers of All Children: Women Reformers and the Rise of Juvenile Courts in Progressive-Era America* (University Park: Pennsylvania State University Press, 1998), 3.
11. On the incorporation of images, themes, and appellations of motherhood in rescue work by Protestant evangelical women, see Katherine G. Aiken, *Harnessing the Power of Motherhood: The National Florence Crittenton Mission, 1883–1925* (Knoxville: University of Tennessee Press, 1998); and Regina G. Kunzel, "The Professionalization of Benevolence: Evangelicals and Social Workers in the Florence Crittenton Homes, 1915 to 1945," *Journal of Social History* 22 (Fall 1988): 24, 30–31. Evangeline Booth took the motherhood image even further and adopted it as a metaphor for Jesus Christ. "'As a Mother'—He [Jesus] will dry your tears. There is a mother's forgiveness," and "As a mother Christ will put his children to sleep" (Evangeline Booth, "As a Mother," Salvation Army Archives). Jonathan Butler explores themes of motherhood, sentimentalism, and middle-class family ideals in the sermons of late-nineteenth century male evangelists, including Dwight Moody. See Jonathan M. Butler, *Softly and Tenderly Jesus Is Calling: Heaven and Hell In American Revivalism, 1870–1920*, Chicago Studies in the History of American Religion, ed. Jerald C. Brauer and Martin E. Marty (New York: Carlson Publishing, 1991), 143–62.
12. F. A. Robinson, ed., *Mother Whittemore's Modern Miracles* (Toronto: Missions of Biblical Education, 1931), 48.
13. For the role of nineteenth-century mothers in religious instruction, see Colleen McDannell, *The Christian Home in Victorian America* (Bloomington: Indiana University Press, 1986), 114, 132.
14. Elizabeth Elkin Grammer, *Some Wild Visions: Autobiographies by Female Itinerant Evangelists in 19th Century America* (New York: Oxford University Press, 2003), 34.
15. Jarena Lee, *The Life and Religious Experience of Jarena Lee, A Coloured Lady, Giving an Account of Her Call to Preach the Gospel* (Philadelphia: Printed and published by Jarena Lee, 1836), 22.
16. In aggregate, 90 percent of settlement workers had attended college, over 80 percent finished a bachelor's degree, and over 50 percent had done graduate work (Allen F. Davis,

Spearheads for Reform: The Social Settlements and the Progressive Movement, 1890–1914 [New York: Oxford University Press, 1967], 33–34). Elisabeth Lasch-Quinn critiques contemporary scholarship of the settlement movement for its exclusion of the South and especially of African Americans (Elisabeth Lasch-Quinn, *Black Neighbors: Race and the Limits of Reform in the American Settlement House Movement, 1890–1945* [Chapel Hill: University of North Carolina Press, 1993], 3–5).

17. Eleanor J. Stebner, "The Settlement House Movement," in *Encyclopedia of Women and Religion in North America*, ed. Rosemary Skinner Keller and Rosemary Radford Ruether (Indianapolis: Indiana University Press, 2006), 3:1063. For a discussion of sectarian settlement houses with a decidedly religious purpose and strategy, see Stebner, "The Settlement House Movement," 1063–64. Benjamin L. Hartley analyzes the evangelistic goals of the Methodist's University Settlement in Boston in *Evangelicals at a Crossroads: Revivalism and Social Reform in Boston, 1860–1910* (Durham: University of New Hampshire, 2011), 151–55.

18. Robert A. Woods and Albert J. Kennedy, eds., *Handbook of Settlements* (Philadelphia: Russell Sage Foundation, 1911), v.

19. Lasch-Quinn, *Black Neighbors*, 7.

20. Kunzel, *Fallen Women*, 37. In his comprehensive book on the history, growth, and method of the charity organization movement, Frank Watson offered this definition of the COS: "A device to aid all who will work together to find out, need by need, what is the best way out of a given difficulty, best for those on whom the need presses most heavily and best for the community at large; and to aid in seeing each problem through to a final solution, including the removal of all preventable causes of poverty, either by measures the society launches itself or by measures it stimulates others to launch" (Frank D. Watson, *The Charity Organization Movement in the United States* [New York: Macmillan, 1922], 106). On the COS and its influential predecessors, see Roy Lubove, *The Professional Altruist: The Emergence of Social Work as a Career, 1880–1930* (Cambridge, MA: Harvard University Press, 1965), 2–5. The COS, launched in 1877, was well established by the turn of the century with one hundred fifty societies across the country, a number that would double again within two decades (Kenneth L. Kusmer, "The Functions of Organized Charity in the Progressive Era: Chicago as a Case Study," *Journal of American History* 60 (December 1973): 658; and Watson, *The Charity Organization Movement in the United States*. For a study of organized charity programs in smaller cities, see John T. Cumbler, "The Politics of Charity: Gender and Class in Late 19th Century Charity Policy," *Journal of Social History* 14 (Fall 1980): 99–111.

21. Elizabeth Clapp notes the connection between two committees of the Chicago Woman's Club—the Philanthropy Committee and the Reform Committee—and the COS movement in Chicago (Clapp, *Mothers of All Children*, 25, 27). These women imbibed the noblesse oblige message proclaimed from the pulpit as well as the pages of *Godey's Lady's Book*, which exhorted leisure-class women "to venture into even the most unsavory places" in order to contribute a measure of civilization and improvement (Kathleen D. McCarthy, *Noblesse Oblige: Charity and Cultural Philanthropy in Chicago, 1849–1929* [Chicago: University of Chicago Press, 1982], 17–18).

Visitation in impoverished areas traces a long history in the United States. In New York City, as Carroll Smith-Rosenberg attests, visitation began in the early nineteenth century under the auspices of the Young Men's Missionary Society of New York and the Female Missionary Society. Ward Stafford, a missionary for the Female Missionary Society, encouraged the organization's members to visit the city's wards in a systematic fashion, providing "temporal and religious philanthropy." Members provided "temporal aid, clothing, and food for the sick and hungry" and integrated a religious component through prayer and Bible distribution (Carroll Smith-Rosenberg, *Religion and the Rise of the American City: The New York City Mission Movement, 1812–1870* [Ithaca, NY: Cornell University Press, 1971], 57–58).

22. Norris Magnuson, *Salvation in the Slums: Evangelical Social Work, 1865-1920*, ATLA (American Theological Library Association) Monograph Series, no. 10 (Metuchen, NJ: Scarecrow, 1977), ix. Magnuson argues that Timothy Smith's thesis—revivalism and the quest for Christian perfection, as demonstrated in substantial social reform efforts, stood out as the two endeavors animating American Christianity in the first half of the nineteenth century—holds up through the Progressive Era (Timothy L. Smith, *Revivalism and Social Reform* [New York: Harper & Row, 1957]). Aaron Abell's book on a similar theme covers numerous organizations and movements, including the YMCA and YWCA, city churches with established urban mission centers, the Social Christianity movement, the Salvation Army, and mainline theological seminaries, all of which embraced some sort of relationship between evangelism and humanitarianism (Aaron I. Abell, *The Urban Impact on American Protestantism, 1865-1900* [London: Archon, 1962]). Curiously, Abell's earlier study appears only once in Magnuson's book, despite widespread overlap in chronology, organization, and topic.

More recently, Hartley considers the juxtaposition of revivalism and social reform in Boston during the same decades covered by Abell and Magnuson. Hartley argues that an eclectic group of Boston evangelicals, with Methodists and holiness folk at the center, pursued an agenda of revivalism and social reform based upon "their desire for sanctification in themselves as well as their city to more perfectly reflect God's will as they understood it" (Benjamin L. Hartley, *Evangelicals at a Crossroads: Revivalism and Social Reform in Boston, 1860-1910* [Durham: University of New Hampshire Press, 2011], 3). As the Progressive Era advanced, this two-fold agenda disintegrated, according to Hartley, owing to differences over the specific practice of both endeavors: "People who had previously walked side by side began to go in markedly different directions owing to a whole assortment of ideas and strategies surrounding their revivalism and social reform efforts" (Hartley, *Evangelicals at a Crossroads*, 3).

23. Diane Winston, *Red-Hot and Righteous: The Urban Religion of The Salvation Army* (Cambridge, MA: Harvard University Press, 1999), 120. See also Lillan Taiz, *Hallelujah Lads and Lasses: Remaking the Salvation Army in America, 1880-1930* (Chapel Hill: University of North Carolina Press, 2001), 105-8.

24. Winston, *Red-Hot and Righteous*, 171. For these statistics, Winston references Edward McKinley, *Somebody's Brother: A History of the Salvation Army Men's Social Service Department, 1891-1985*, Studies in American Religion, vol. 21 (Lewiston, NY: 1986), 69-71. William Booth catapulted the Army's investment in institution building after he, with the help of W. T. Stead, journalist and author of *If Christ Came to Chicago! A Plea for the Union of All Who Love in the Service of All Who Suffer* (Chicago: Laird & Lee, 1894), researched, wrote, and published *In Darkest England, and the Way Out* (London: Salvation Army) in 1890. What commenced in the Army's outreach as a result of this book, according to Paul Phillips, was a "burst of social service on a par with the most successful Social Christian enterprises of the late 1800s" (Paul T. Phillips, *A Kingdom on Earth: Anglo-American Social Christianity, 1880-1940* [University Park: Pennsylvania State University Press, 1996], 97). Booth himself launched "The Salvation Army Social Campaign" to promote, among other objectives, the renovation of city shelters into city colonies, where the poor and destitute could find employment along with Christian compassion and the gospel message. Such efforts prompted even Friedrich Engels to commend the Army's work among the poor because it "revives the propaganda of early Christianity, appeals to the poor as the elect, fights capitalism in a religious way, and thus fosters an element of early Christian class antagonism" (Frederick Coutts, *Bread for My Neighbour: An Appreciation of the Social Influence of William Booth* [London: Hodder & Stoughton, 1978], 11, quoted in William Kostlevy, *Holy Jumpers: Evangelicals and Radicals in Progressive Era America* [New York: Oxford University Press, 2010], 12).

25. Evangeline Booth, "Missionary, IMC (International Missionary Council)," Salvation Army Archives. Simultaneous with this "ambitious program of social and spiritual work," as historian Diane Winston notes, the Army "sought spiritual conversion first and foremost, [though] they tended the body as well as the soul" (Winston, *Red-Hot and Righteous*, 122, 108).
26. Lee, *Mother Lee's Experience*, 35.
27. Iva Durham Vennard, "The Spirit of Negation," April 17, 1890, 6, MidAmerica Nazarene University Archives. Even Walter Rauschenbusch, a leading Social Gospel theologian, expressed similar sentiments: "Spiritual regeneration is the most important fact of any life history. A living experience of God is the crowning knowledge attainable to a human mind. Each one of us needs the redemptive power of religion for his own sake, for on the tiny stage of the human soul all the vast world tragedy of good and evil is re-enacted" (Walter Rauschenbusch, *Christianizing the Social Order* [New York: Macmillan, 1912], 104, quoted in Winthrop S. Hudson, "Walter Rauschenbusch and the New Evangelism," *Religion in Life* 30 [Winter 1960–61]: 419).
28. Vennard, "The Spirit of Negation," 1.
29. Vennard, "The Spirit of Negation," 1–2.
30. The Salvation Army also adopted the phrase "permanent reform"; according to historian Herbert Wisbey, "Constant effort was expended to help the girls experience conversion, for it was believed that only this would ensure their permanent reformation" (Herbert A. Wisbey, *Soldiers without Swords: A History of the Salvation Army in the United States* [New York: Macmillan, 1955], 100). Yet providing a refuge until "permanent reform" happened could be a long time. "Placements in the homes and refuges were lengthy, because the process of reclamation was slow. During the nineteenth century the average commitment approached two years. Disposition records indicated that four or five year terms were not uncommon" (Michael W. Sedlak, "Young Women and the City: Adolescent Deviance and the Transformation of Educational Policy, 1870–1960," *History of Education Quarterly* 23 (Spring 1983): 7.
31. "Epworth Settlement," *Inasmuch* 1 (July 1905): 5–6.
32. Josiah Strong, *Religious Movements for Social Betterment* (New York: Baker & Taylor, 1900), 34–35.
33. Iva Durham Vennard, "The Evangelistic Department of Deaconess Work," *Inasmuch* 2 (April 1906): 8.
34. Vennard, "The Evangelistic Department of Deaconess Work," 8. This same terminology endures decades later. See Fagan, "Skid-Row Rescue Missions," 160.
35. Iva Durham Vennard, "Studies in Missionary Problems and Methods," *Heart and Life* 10 (October 1920): 6–7.
36. For a discussion of these terms, see Janet F. Fishburn, "The Social Gospel as Missionary Ideology," in *North American Foreign Missions, 1810–1914: Theology, Theory, and Policy*, ed. Wilbert R. Shenk (Grand Rapids, MI: Eerdmans, 2004), 225–28; and Phillips, *A Kingdom on Earth*, xvi–xx. Additional secondary resources on the Social Gospel include Butler, *Softly and Tenderly Jesus Is Calling*; Wendy J. Deichmann Edwards and Carolyn De Swarte Gifford, eds., *Gender and the Social Gospel* (Urbana: University of Illinois, 2003); Robert T. Handy, ed., *The Social Gospel in America, 1870–1920: Gladden, Ely, Rauschenbusch* (New York: Oxford University Press, 1966); C. Howard Hopkins, *The Rise of the Social Gospel in American Protestantism, 1865–1915* (New Haven, CT: Yale University Press, 1940); Hudson, "Walter Rauschenbusch and the New Evangelism"; Magnuson, *Salvation in the Slums*; Jean Miller Schmidt, *Souls or the Social Order: The Two-Party System in American Protestantism* (Brooklyn, NY: Carlson Publishing, 1991); and Kenneth Smith and Leonard Sweet, "Shailer Mathews: A Chapter in the Social Gospel Movement," *Foundations* 18:3 (1975): 219–37.

37. Strong, *Religious Movements for Social Betterment*, 21.
38. Dean's book dedication reads: "To the incomparable fellowship, my comrades of 'Team Three' of the Men and Religion Forward Movement." Following a list of ten names, he concluded: "Every man a bond-servant of both evangelism and social service, this little book is affectionately inscribed" (John Marvin Dean, *Evangelism and Social Service* [Philadelphia: Griffith & Rowland, 1913], frontispiece). Secondary sources on the movement include L. Dean Allen, *Rise Up, O Men of God: The Men and Religion Forward Movement and Promise Keepers* (Macon, GA: Mercer University Press, 2002); and Gail Bederman, "'The Women Have Had Charge of the Church Work Long Enough': The Men and Religion Forward Movement of 1911–1912 and the Masculinization of Middle-Class Protestantism," *American Quarterly* 41:3 (September 1989): 432–65. See also a volume of addresses given at the Buffalo Conference of the Men and Religion Forward Movement on October 25 and 26, 1910, in Fayette L. Thompson et al., *Men and Religion* (New York: Young Men's Christian Association, 1911).
39. The term "social service" held prominence in the Men and Religion Forward Movement (see Fayette L. Thompson, "Men and Religion: The Program," in Thompson et al., *Men and Religion*, 8). Even though Dean stressed the social aspects of the gospel, he purposefully did not adopt the term "Social Gospel." His book's first sentence reads: "There is no social gospel." Continuing on, he wrote, "To speak of a social gospel argues that there are various gospels. . . . But ever since Calvary there has been but one gospel—the proclaiming of a redemption that has to do both with the individual and society, both with the Jew and the nations, both with man's relationship to this world and the world to come." He repeated the same a few lines later: "It is not an individualistic gospel. It is not a social gospel. It is the one all-comprehensive gospel of the grace of God" (Dean, *Evangelism and Social Service*, 11).
40. Dean, *Evangelism and Social Service*, 14–16. He included a poem by the Reverend Frank Mason North in the book's frontispiece. North, a Methodist minister, chaired the Church and Modern Industry committee for the newly formed, national ecumenical organization, the Federal Council of Churches (FCC); served as the FCC's president for four years; and drafted its influential "Social Creed of the Churches." Two stanzas in particular from North's poem, better known as the hymn "Where Cross the Crowded Ways of Life," delineate the social implications of the Christian gospel:
    In haunts of wretchedness and need, / On shadowed thresholds dark with fears,
    From paths where hide the lures of greed, / We catch the vision of Thy tears. . . .
    O Master, from the mountainside, / Make haste to heal these hearts of pain,
    Among these restless throngs abide, / Oh, tread the city's streets again.
    For more on the Federal Council of Churches, see Hopkins, *The Rise of the Social Gospel in American Protestantism*, 302–17; Mary L. Mapes, "Visions of a Christian City: The Politics of Religion and Gender in Chicago's City Missions and Protestant Settlement Houses, 1886–1929" (Ph.D. diss., Michigan State University, 1998), 125–69; and Schmidt, *Souls or the Social Order*, 119–36.
41. Dean, *Evangelism and Social Service*, 38.
42. Butler, *Softly and Tenderly Jesus Is Calling*, 98.
43. Smith and Sweet, "Shailer Mathews: A Chapter in the Social Gospel Movement," 234.
44. Dean, *Evangelism and Social Service*, 55.
45. Mathews, who served as professor and dean from 1908 to 1933, developed with his colleagues a theological approach known as "The Chicago School" or "Scientific Modernism." He defined Modernism as "the use of scientific, historical, social method in understanding and applying evangelical Christianity to the needs of living persons" (Shailer Mathews, *The Faith of Modernism* [New York: Macmillan, 1924], 34–35). Despite Dean's charge, Mathews referred to himself as an evangelical and spoke to the necessity of

a personal relationship with God: "Nothing is more fatal to the spirit of genuine religion than the substitution of scientific method for personal fellowship with God" (Shailer Mathews, "The Historical Study of Religion," in *A Guide to the Study of the Christian Religion*, ed. Gerald B. Smith [Chicago: University of Chicago Press, 1916], 25, quoted in John S. Reist, "The Dread of the Father: An Analysis of the Theological Method of Shailer Matthews," [sic] *Foundations* 8 [July 1965]: 241). For more on "The Chicago School," see W. Creighton Peden, "The Chicago School (1906–1926) in American Religious Thought and Its Contribution to a Better Understanding of Ultimate Reality and Meaning of Human Experience," *Ultimate Reality and Meaning* 6 (March 1983): 51–79. Additional sources on Shailer Mathews include his autobiography, *New Faith for Old: An Autobiography* (New York: Macmillan, 1936); W. Creighton Peden, "Shailer Mathews," in *Makers of Christian Theology in America*, ed. Mark G. Toulouse and James O. Duke (Nashville, TN: Abingdon, 1997), 392–98; Reist, "The Dread of the Father," 239–55; and Smith and Sweet, "Shailer Mathews: A Chapter in the Social Gospel Movement," 219–37. Glenn T. Miller summarizes the conflict between conservatives in the Northern Baptist denomination and the University of Chicago in *Piety and Profession: American Protestant Theological Education, 1870–1970* (Grand Rapids, MI: Eerdmans, 2007), 407–21.

According to Dean's protégé, Stockton, he hoped to "combat modernism's destructive teaching" by offering a seminary that was "founded on the Rock, Christ Jesus, and in its teaching never deviating from the infallible Word of God" (Amy Lee Stockton, "Autobiography," 18, Northern Baptist Theological Seminary Archives). See also Miller, *Piety and Profession*, 409; and James D. Mosteller, "Something Old—Something New: The First Fifty Years of Northern Baptist Theological Seminary," *Foundations* 8 (January 1965): 26–30.

46. Dean, *Evangelism and Social Service*, 69.
47. Stockton, "Autobiography," 20.
48. For many years, she worked alongside musician Rita Gould; together they formed the Stockton Gould evangelistic team. In 1950, Stockton received an honorary doctor of divinity degree from her alma mater, Northern Baptist Theological Seminary. The seminary also selected her to receive—posthumously—the Alumna of the Year Award in 1988. In her booklet, "The Word of the Woman" (Northern Baptist Theological Seminary Archives), she articulated a biblical defense of women's preaching. John Marvin Dean also pursued full-time evangelistic work after resigning from Second Baptist Church in 1917. I am grateful to my friend and former colleague, David Scholer, for acquainting me with Stockton and making her materials available.
49. Dean, *Evangelism and Social Service*, 7.
50. Dean, *Evangelism and Social Service*, 15.
51. "Association of Gospel Rescue Missions," www.agrm.org.
52. K. H. Ting, "Retrospect and Prospect," *International Review of Mission* 70 (April 1981): 27. The same claim is made about missionaries in other countries. In an anthropological study of missionary work in postcolonial Zaire, Raija Warkentin states: "There is little doubt that missionaries used material gifts to facilitate acceptance of their spiritual message." Warkentin cites the term "rice Christians" in this quote about missionaries and education, the primary arena in which material incentives were invoked: "In postcolonial Zaire, the government paid the wages for schoolteachers, but the missions acted as buffers for the uncertain delivery of funds to schools. They did this on the condition that the schools upheld Christian rules of conduct for their teachers and staff. The Protestant mission leader called those who converted to Christianity in order to obtain material goods 'rice Christians'" (Raija Warkentin, "Begging as Resistance: Wealth and Christian Missionaries in Postcolonial Zaire," *Missiology: An International Review* 29 [April 2001]: 146, 149). See also Dana Robert, "Shifting Southward: Global Christianity since 1945," *International Bulletin of Missionary Research* 24 (April 2000): 50–54, 56–58; and G. Jan van

Butselaar, "Christian Conversion in Rwanda: The Motivations," *International Bulletin of Missionary Research* 5 (July 1981): 111–13. This same criticism appears in a study of rescue missions in the United States. See Fagan, "Skid-Row Rescue Missions, 160.
53. Lee, *Mother Lee's Experience*, 149.
54. Emma J. Ray, *Twice Sold, Twice Ransomed: Autobiography of Mr. and Mrs. L. P. Ray* (Chicago: Free Methodist Publishing, 1926), 154. A more recent study claims that standing during the congregational singing keeps people awake. Fagan, "Skid-Row Rescue Missions," 161.
55. "Rescue Mission Work," *Christian Alliance* (May 1892): 376. A historian of the International Union of Gospel Missions cites this purpose statement for a rescue mission: " . . . believing that the best way to change a community is by changing the lives of the individual and using the material and physical needs of the people as an opportunity to effect their salvation through the acceptance of Jesus Christ as Savior and believing that changed and redeemed individuals will in time change and redeem a community" (William E. Paul, *The Romance of Rescue* [n.p.: n.p., 1948], 115–16.
56. Carrie Judd Montgomery, *"Under His Wings": The Story of My Life* (Oakland, CA : Office of Triumphs of Faith, 1936), reprinted as *The Life and Teaching of Carrie Judd Montgomery*, in *"The Higher Christian Life": Sources for the Study of the Holiness Pentecostal, and Keswick Movements*, ed. Donald W. Dayton (New York: Garland Publishing, 1985),141.
57. Hick's Hollow ranked highest in African American population (38 percent) and number of African American households (446) in Kansas City (Kevin Fox Gotham, *Race, Real Estate, and Uneven Development: The Kansas City Experience, 1900–2000* [Albany: State University of New York Press, 2002], 32).
58. Schirmer, *A City Divided*, 38.
59. Asa Martin, *Our Negro Population: A Sociological Study of the Negroes of Kansas City* (Kansas City, MO: Franklin Hudson, 1913), 11.
60. Schirmer, *A City Divided*, 37.
61. Ray, *Twice Sold, Twice Ransomed*, 63.
62. Ray, *Twice Sold, Twice Ransomed*, 118.
63. Ray, *Twice Sold, Twice Ransomed*, 144.
64. These three verses constitute the rest of the song:
    Verse 1:
    O'er squander'd wealth and wasted years / In sin and folly past,
    A wretched starving prodigal / Awoke to mourn at last.
    He pressed his weary throbbing brow / And thro' his tears he said,
    "I spurned the home I might have shar'd, / And now I starve for bread."
    Verse 2:
    Forsaken, friendless, clothed in rags, / And poor as poor can be;
    To lowest menial service brought, / A tyrant's slave was he;
    He turned disgusted from the swine / That he so long had fed;
    "I can not from my Father stay." / With firm resolve he said.
    Verse 3:
    I thought the world was what I dream'd, / My heart obeyed its call;
    But now I find its fleeting joys / Are wormwood after all.
    Be warn'd, oh, gay and thoughtless ones, / That to the whirlwind sow,
    Let's hasten back to Father now, / He's coming; let us go.
    (H. H. Hadley, comp., *Rescue Songs by One Hundred Popular Composers and Gifted Song Writers; Specially Fitted for Rescue Missions and Meetings, Rescue Workers and Evangelists and Revival Services* [New York: Christian Men's Union, 1893], no. 64)
Robert Lowry composed another popular hymn on the Prodigal Son, "Where Is My Wandering Boy Tonight?" At Water Street Mission, this chorus about the Prodigal Son

was often sung, "Calling now to thee, prodigal, Calling now to thee; / Thou hast wandered far away, But he's calling now to thee" (Helen Campbell, *Darkness and Daylight, or Lights and Shadows of New York Life* [Hartford, CT: Hartford Publishing, 1896], 64). For a more recent study of gospel songs and sermons presented at rescue missions, see Fagan, "Skid-Row Rescue Missions," 161–67.
65. Delores T. Burger, *Women Who Changed the Heart of the City: The Untold Story of the City Rescue Mission Movement* (Grand Rapids, MI: Kregel, 1997), 55.
66. For more on the Hadley brothers, see Magnuson, *Salvation in the Slums*, 9–13.
67. Hadley, *Rescue Songs*, no. 113.
68. Magnuson, *Salvation in the Slums*, 10. Water Street Mission is featured in this late nineteenth- century book: Campbell, *Darkness and Daylight*. The mission continues today, more than a century later, as the New York City Rescue Mission (www.nycrescue.org). For more on its ministry, see Varnhagen, "Setting the Oppressed Free," 235–45. A significant rescue mission that preceded Water Street in New York City by more than two decades was Five Points Mission founded in 1850. Historian Timothy Smith lauded Five Points for initiating "Protestant institutional work in the slums" (Smith, *Revivalism and Social Reform*, 170). See also Abell, *The Urban Impact on American Protestantism*, 35–36; Barbara J. Berg, *The Remembered Gate: Origins of American Feminism, The Woman and the City, 1800–1860* (New York: Oxford University Press, 1978), 227–29; Magnuson, *Salvation in the Slums*, 10; and Smith-Rosenberg, *Religion and the Rise of the American City*, 225–44. On yet another early rescue mission, see Benjamin L. Hartley, "Philadelphia's 'Five Points': Evangelism and Social Welfare at the Bedford Street Mission," *Methodist History* 48:1 (October 2009): 10–22.
69. R. M. Offord, ed., *Jerry McAuley, His Life and Work* (New York: New York Observer, 1885), 9–47.
70. Magnuson, *Salvation in the Slums*, 48.
71. Magnuson, *Salvation in the Slums*, 12. For a history of IUGM into the 1940s, see Paul, *The Romance of Rescue*. The International Union of Gospel Missions continues today as the Association of Gospel Rescue Missions (AGRM). Its website (www.agrm.org) offers a brief history and timeline of IUGM.
72. Emma described the first evangelistic meeting she attended at Water Street. Robinson, *Mother Whittemore's Modern Miracles*, 21.
73. William Plummer Black, "Rescue Missions of Seattle" (master's thesis, University of Washington, 1926), 86.
74. Emma Whittemore, "Snatched as a Brand from the Burning," *Christian Alliance and Missionary Weekly* (July 1891): 10. See also Emma Whittemore, *Delia; Formerly the Blue-Bird of Mulberry Bend* (New York: Door of Hope, 1893); and Robinson, *Mother Whittemore's Modern Miracles*, 128–31. For before-and-after pictures of Delia—before and after her conversion—see Curtis, *Faith in the Great Physician*, 179–80; and Robinson, *Mother Whittemore's Modern Miracles*, 128.
75. Emma Whittemore, "Out of Darkness into Light," *Christian Alliance and Missionary Weekly* (December 1892): 377–78.
76. Anna Prosser, *From Death to Life* (Chicago: Evangel Publishing, 1911), 68.
77. Prosser, *From Death to Life*, 71–72.
78. Mary E. McDowell, "The Value of a Social Settlement in an Industrial Neighborhood," in *The Socialized Church: Addresses before the First National Conference of the Social Workers of Methodism, St. Louis, November 17–19, 1908*, ed. Worth M. Tippy (New York: Eaton & Mains, 1909), 136–37.
79. Lasch-Quinn argues that the NFS's exclusionary policy on religion "contributed to the organization's elitism and eventual decline" (Lasch-Quinn, *Black Neighbors*, 47). The issue of religion (or not) in the settlement movement, both white and African American, constitutes a major theme in Lasch-Quinn's book.

80. Jane Addams, *Twenty Years at Hull House* (New York: Macmillan, 1939), 122, 124. See also R. A. R. Edwards, "Jane Addams, Walter Rauschenbusch, and Dorothy Day: A Comparative Study of Settlement Theology," in *Gender and the Social Gospel*, 150–57.
81. Iva Durham Vennard, "The Wayside," *Heart and Life Bulletin* 1 (October and November 1911): 12.
82. Iva Durham Vennard, "Wayside Notes," *Heart and Life Bulletin* 1 (October and November 1911): 15.
83. Kunzel, *Fallen Women*, 37. On the reluctance of the COS to distribute direct aid, see Lori D. Ginzberg, *Women and the Work of Benevolence: Morality, Politics, and Class in the 19th-Century United States* (New Haven, CT: Yale University Press, 1990), 196–97. In her influential, turn-of-the-century book, Mary Richmond, a leader in the COS in several cities, offered six principles about when, how, and to whom to give relief (Mary Richmond, *Friendly Visiting among the Poor: A Handbook for Charity Workers* [1899], reprinted in the Patterson Smith Reprint Series in Criminology, Law Enforcement, and Social Problems [Montclair, NJ: Patterson Smith, 1969], 149–65). See also Elizabeth N. Agnew, "Shaping a Civic Profession: Mary Richmond, the Social Gospel, and Social Work," in *Gender and the Social Gospel*, 116–35. Even many orphanages in the Progressive Era operated on the "deserving" principle and "chose to admit only children whose parents were 'deserving'" (Nurith Zmora, *Orphanages Reconsidered: Child Care Institutions in Progressive Era Baltimore* [Philadelphia: Temple University Press, 1994], 13).
84. Quoted in Lubove, *The Professional Altruist*, 7.
85. Maureen A. Flanagan, "Gender and Urban Political Reform: The City Club and the Woman's City Club of Chicago in the Progressive Era," *American Historical Review* 95 (October 1990): 1047.
86. McCarthy, *Noblesse Oblige*, 132.
87. Winston, *Red-Hot and Righteous*, 106.
88. Max Siporin, "Mary Richmond, A Founder of Modern Social Work," in Richmond, *Friendly Visiting among the Poor*, x.
89. *New York Times*, February 7, 1897, 9, quoted in Winston, *Red-Hot and Righteous*, 129. See also Magnuson, *Salvation in the Slums*, xiii–xvi. According to Lasch-Quinn, settlement workers also criticized the COS for focusing "on the needy individual rather than trying to alter social conditions" (Lasch-Quinn, *Black Neighbors*, 50).
90. Ray, *Twice Sold, Twice Ransomed*, 74.
91. Ray, *Twice Sold, Twice Ransomed*, 229.
92. This quote comes from a sermon preached by Lee's son, Richard, who followed his mother into rescue work. He likened the rescue home to the shrub in the wilderness under which Hagar put her son, Ishmael, after Abraham and Sarah cast them out (Gen. 21:14–20): "The Rescue Home is as a shrub in a desert or wilderness under which any girl who will may come and be; and as God heard the cry of the lad, so God will hear the cry of those who repent of their sins and turn away from their wrong doings. He will have mercy on them and save them" (Lee, *Mother Lee's Experience*, 201). Historian Peggy Pascoe offers insight into the term "rescue home": "It conveyed the two goals Protestant women had for home mission projects: on the one hand, they wanted to 'rescue' women who had been the victims of male abuse; on the other, they wanted to inculcate in all women their particular concept of the Christian 'home'" (Peggy Pascoe, *Relations of Rescue: The Search for Female Moral Authority in the American West, 1874–1939* [New York: Oxford University Press, 1990], 76).
93. Butler, *Softly and Tenderly Jesus Is Calling*, 149.
94. See David J. Pivar, *Purity Crusade, Sexual Morality, and Social Control* (Westport, CT: Greenwood, 1973), 25–27; Robert E. Riegel, "Changing American Attitudes toward Prostitution (1800–1920)," *Journal of the History of Ideas* 29 (July–September 1968):

443–44; Steven Ruggles, "Fallen Women: The Inmates of the Magdalen Society Asylum in Philadelphia, 1836–1908," *Journal of Social History* 16 (Summer 1983): 65–82; and Smith-Rosenberg, *Religion and the Rise of the American City*, 97–124.
95. Daniel S. Wright, *"The First of Causes to Our Sex": The Female Moral Reform Movement in the Antebellum Northeast, 1843–1848*, Studies in American Popular History and Culture (New York: Routledge, 2006), 165–66.
96. For more on this home and three others in the American West, see Pascoe, *Relations of Rescue*.
97. Wisbey, *Soldiers without Swords*, 99–100; and Kunzel, *Fallen Women*, 14. See also Edward H. McKinley, *Marching to Glory: The History of the Salvation Army in the United States of America, 1880–1980* (San Francisco: Harper & Row, 1980), 54–55; Taiz, *Hallelujah Lads and Lassies*, 40–41; and Winston, *Red-Hot and Righteous*, 156–58. Winston notes that the Army defined "fallen women" loosely to include "drunks, drug addicts, and homeless women as well as prostitutes" (Winston, *Red-Hot and Righteous*, 157).
98. Winston, *Red-Hot and Righteous*, 156.
99. Magnuson, *Salvation in the Slums*, 21. The name "Door of Hope" comes from Hosea 2:15: "And I will give her vineyards from thence and the Valley of Achor as a Door of Hope; and she shall sing there as in the days of your youth" (Robinson, *Mother Whittemore's Modern Miracles*, 60).
100. For more on Charles Crittenton, see Aiken, *Harnessing the Power of Motherhood*, 1–32.
101. Studies of WCTU rescue homes include Sherilyn B. Brandenstein, "The Colorado Cottage Home," *Colorado Magazine* 53:3 (1976): 229–42; Joan Jacobs Brumberg, "'Ruined' Girls: Changing Community Responses to Illegitimacy in Upstate New York, 1890–1920," *Journal of Social History* 18 (Winter 1984): 247–72; and Pascoe, *Relations of Rescue*. For more on the WCTU's Department of Social Purity, see Ruth Bordin, *Women and Temperance: The Quest for Power and Liberty, 1873–1900* (Philadelphia: Temple University Press, 1981), 110–11; Pivar, *Purity Crusade*, 110–17; and Frances E. Willard, *Glimpses of Fifty Years: The Autobiography of an American Woman* (Chicago: Woman's Temperance Publication Association, 1889), 418–29.
102. Otto Wilson, *Fifty Years' Work with Girls, 1883–1933: A Story of the Florence Crittenton Homes* (Alexandria, VA: National Florence Crittenton Mission, 1933), 45.
103. Wilson, *Fifty Years' Work with Girls*, 7–8.
104. By the term "evangelical reformer," Kunzel refers to self-identified evangelicals who "came to maternity homes after 'hearing the call' and described their commitment to rescue work as religiously inspired and motivated" (Kunzel, *Fallen Women*, 10). Scholarship on the emergence of social work in the Progressive Era is extensive. Helpful sources include Robert Bremner, *From the Depths: The Discovery of Poverty in the United States* (New York: New York University Press, 1956); Clarke A. Chambers, "Toward a Redefinition of Welfare History," *Journal of American History* 73 (September 1986): 407–33; Mary Agnes Dougherty, "The Methodist Deaconess, 1885–1919: A Study in Religious Feminism" (Ph.D. diss., University of California, Davis, 1979); Kunzel, *Fallen Women*; Lubove, *The Professional Altruist*; and Phillips, *A Kingdom on Earth*.
105. Kunzel, *Fallen Women*, 2. See also Aiken, *Harnessing the Power of Motherhood*, xvii.
106. Robinson, *Mother Whittemore's Modern Miracles*, 41. Whittemore exemplifies the paradigm of many invalids "who had previously given little thought to the question of God's calling upon their lives [but who] now found themselves confronted with an understanding of Christian ethics that demanded their full, active participation in some form of 'godly' work on behalf of others. . . . Many previously incapacitated invalids pioneered or participated in urban ministries, temperance movements, foreign missions, and even dress reform campaigns" (Curtis, *Faith in the Great Physician*, 168–69; see also 109–10, 178–82).
107. Robinson, *Mother Whittemore's Modern Miracles*, 43–44.

108. Robinson, *Mother Whittemore's Modern Miracles*, 156.
109. For a full description of the performance, see Winston, *Red-Hot and Righteous*, 143–46.
110. Like Whittemore, Bown also described their clothing in detail: "We purchased enough calico to make dresses for ourselves and an apron each. We bought little brown sailor hats and trimmed them very plainly with black and green. These we purposed to wear instead of the regular uniform, which we laid aside entirely until at some future day it would seem appropriate to wear it again. Our 'ammunition to war' consisted of a broom, a scrubbing brush, a pail, and a Bible" (Winston, *Red-Hot and Righteous*, 69). For more on slum sisters, see Abell, *The Urban Impact on American Protestantism*, 126–28; McKinley, *Marching to Glory*, 55–56; Wisbey, *Soldiers without Swords*, 101–2; Taiz, *Hallelujah Lads and Lasses*, 41–43 and 128–30; and Winston, *Red-Hot and Righteous*, 67–76.
111. Montgomery, *The Life and Teachings of Carrie Judd Montgomery*, 146–47.
112. Emma Whittemore, "The Opening of Door of Hope, No. 2, June 1, 1893," *Christian Alliance* (July 1893): 28.
113. Lee, *Mother Lee's Experience*, 91.
114. Mary McReynolds, *Redeeming Love: The Legacy of the Deaconess Ladies* (Oklahoma: n.p., [2000?]), 43.
115. Annie Richardson Kennedy, *The Heartsease Miracle* (New York: Heartsease Publications, 1920), 81.
116. McReynolds, *Redeeming Love*, 4.
117. Lee, *Mother Lee's Experience*, 147, 103.
118. Emma Whittemore, "At the Gateway, or How Kitty Was Saved," *Christian Alliance* (January 1892): 28.
119. Lee, *Mother Lee's Experience*, 83, 78.
120. Emma Whittemore, "The Door of Hope," *Christian Alliance* (October 1891): 2.
121. Lee, *Mother Lee's Experience*, 78.
122. Kate Waller Barrett, *Some Practical Suggestions on the Conduct of a Rescue Home* (Washington, DC: National Florence Crittenton Mission, 1903), reprinted in the Women in America from Colonial Times to the 20th Century Series (New York: Arno Press, 1974), 54–55. For more on Barrett and her influence on the NFCM, see Aiken, *Harnessing the Power of Motherhood*, 33–66.
123. Aiken, *Harnessing the Power of Motherhood*, 96.
124. Lee, *Mother Lee's Experience*, 102–3.
125. Lee, *Mother Lee's Experience*, 103. See *Florence Crittenton Bulletin* 4 (January 1929): 5; cited in Kunzel, *Fallen Women*, 28–29. In another article, Kunzel traces the "white only" admission policies of most maternity homes into the 1940s and 1950s (Regina Kunzel, "Pulp Fictions and Problem Girls: Reading and Rewriting Single Pregnancy in the Postwar United States," *American Historical Review* [December 1995]: 1484–85).
126. Lee, *Mother Lee's Experience*, 135.
127. Florence Roberts, *Fifteen Years with the Outcast* (Anderson, IN: Gospel Trumpet, 1912), 224–31.
128. Roberts, *Fifteen Years with the Outcast*, 34.
129. Roberts, *Fifteen Years with the Outcast*, 224–25.
130. Roberts, *Fifteen Years with the Outcast*, 222.
131. Roberts, *Fifteen Years with the Outcast*, 251.
132. Aiken, *Harnessing the Power of Motherhood*, 70. See also Pascoe, *Relations of Rescue*, 18; and Daniel Scott Smith and Michael S. Hindus, "Premarital Pregnancy in America 1640–1971: An Overview and Interpretation," *Journal of Interdisciplinary History* 5 (Spring 1975): 537–70.
133. Roberts, *Fifteen Years with the Outcast*, 279.
134. Roberts, *Fifteen Years with the Outcast*, 355.

135. No extant records exist for the home after 1916, according to Gary Rosenberg, archivist, Douglas County Historical Society, Library Archives Center, Omaha, NE.
136. Wilson, *Fifty Years' Work with Girls*, 43; italics added.
137. Aiken, *Harnessing the Power of Motherhood*, 212.
138. Pascoe, *Relations of Rescue*, 59.
139. Ernest W. Burgess, "What Social Case Records Should Contain to be Useful for Sociological Interpretation," *Social Forces* 6 (June 1928): 527, quoted in Kunzel, *Fallen Women*, 7. Despite this stated difficulty, Kunzel's study, more than any other, excels in giving voice to residents' experience of rescue homes, owing to the close read of case histories and statements. From these sources, Kunzel makes the following claim: "A rich and largely unexamined set of documents, case records reveal unmarried mothers as active and resourceful agents rather than as docile recipients of the reforming intentions of evangelical women and social workers" (Kunzel, *Fallen Women*, 7). See also Pascoe, *Relations of Rescue*, 75–76.
140. Ruth Rosen, *The Lost Sisterhood: Prostitution in America, 1900–1918* (Baltimore, MD: Johns Hopkins University Press, 1982), 64–65.
141. Smith-Rosenberg, *Religion and the Rise of the American City*, 111.
142. Rest Cottage Association, *The White Slaves of America: A Book on Rescue Work* (Pilot Point, TX: Evangel Publishing Co., 1907), 18. For more on this holiness group, see C. B. Jernigan, *Pioneer Days of the Holiness Movement in the Southwest* (Kansas City, MO: Pentecostal Nazarene Publishing, 1919).
143. Rest Cottage Association, *The White Slaves of America*, 59. In an encyclopedia entry on the WCTU, the Purity Department's statement of purpose included this task: "It seeks to establish a single code of morals, and to maintain the law of purity as equally binding upon men and women" (*The Encyclopedia of Social Reform*, ed. William D. P. Bliss [New York: Funk & Wagnalls, 1897], 1399).
144. Rest Cottage Association, *The White Slaves of America*, 59.
145. Jacob Riis, *How the Other Half Lives: Studies among the Tenements of New York* (New York: Charles Scribner's Sons, 1890), 234. See also Jane Addams, *A New Conscience and an Ancient Evil* (New York: Macmillan, 1912).
146. Rheta Childe Dorr, "What Eight Million Women Want," quoted in *The Progressive Movement, 1900–1915*, ed. Richard Hofstadter (Englewood Cliffs, NJ: Prentice-Hall, 1963), 84. According to Dorr, "Between 1890 and 1900 the number of women in industry increased faster than the number of men in industry. It increased faster than the birth rate" (84).
147. Robinson, *Mother Whittemore's Modern Miracles*, 184.
148. For political activities of women reformers connected to prostitution and the sexual double standard, see Rosen, *The Lost Sisterhood*, 54–61.

Notes to the Conclusion

1. Alma White, *Truth Stranger than Fiction: God's Lightning Bolts* (Zarephath, NJ: Pentecostal Union, 1914), 48. Even a century later, this situation remains imperative for women who are mothers, spouses, and religious leaders. According to Catherine Wessinger, "The question of how to balance their professional leadership with marriage and child rearing will remain an issue for American women religious leaders" (Catherine Wessinger, "Women's Religious Leadership in the United States," in *Religious Institutions and Women's Leadership: New Roles inside the Mainstream*, ed. Catherine Wessinger [Columbia: University of South Carolina Press, 1996], 13).
2. Edith Blumhofer, *Aimee Semple McPherson: Everybody's Sister* (Grand Rapids, MI: Eerdmans, 1993); and Matthew A. Sutton, *Aimee Semple McPherson and the Resurrection of Christian America* (Cambridge, MA: Harvard University Press, 2007).
3. "Pentecostal Gospel Auto News," *Bridal Call* (November 1918): 10.

4. "Gospel Auto News," *Bridal Call* (January 1919): 10.
5. Blumhofer, *Aimee Semple McPherson*, 190.
6. These statistics are available on the Foursquare Church's website at www.foursquare.org.
7. As a result, after graduation, both genders fanned out to organize Angelus Temple branch churches in other cities, though women outnumbered the men. In 1929, women constituted the majority of the four hundred ordained ministers in McPherson's denomination (Sutton, *Aimee Semple McPherson*, 210).
8. "The Commissary," *Bridal Call* (March 1928): 16.
9. Sutton, *Aimee Semple McPherson*, 189.
10. Sutton, *Aimee Semple McPherson*, 196.
11. In a technical sense, McPherson did not found a rescue *home*. She did, however, host an improvised one whenever a pregnant woman showed up at her parsonage doorstep across the courtyard from Angelus Temple. The mother-to-be received a welcome and a bed alongside McPherson's daughter, and practical care continued after birth with baby furniture, clothes, and child care provided by widows in the Angelus Temple congregation (Sutton, *Aimee Semple McPherson*, 63).
12. This next generation of women evangelists "reinvented" themselves, a phenomenon historian Catherine Brekus finds to be commonplace: "Throughout most of American history, female preaching has been characterized not by upward progress, but by discontinuity and reinvention." Comparing the women in her study to the next generation, Brekus states, "Even as one chapter in the history of female preaching came to an end in the 1840s, another one was just beginning" (Catherine Brekus, *Strangers and Pilgrims: Female Preaching in America, 1740–1845* [Chapel Hill: University of North Carolina Press, 1998], 339). Her statement underscores the ongoing shifts among generations of American women preachers and evangelists. Women in the early to mid-nineteenth century preached and then moved on to the next venue, without convening their converts together. The next generation of women evangelists, in keeping with Progressive Era impulses, shifted the strategy from itinerancy to building and leading institutions. Then, in the mid-twentieth century, there was another "reinvention," to a multifaceted evangelistic organization.
13. In similar fashion, the Billy Graham Evangelistic Association oversaw every aspect of a crusade, including "promotion, accounting, spiritual counseling, literature, follow-up, mobilization of prayer and church support" (William Martin, *A Prophet with Honor: The Billy Graham Story* [New York: William Morrow, 1991], 608).
14. Margaret Bendroth, *Fundamentalism and Gender: 1875 to the Present* (New Haven, CT: Yale University Press, 1993), 74–76.
15. Robert Orsi, "Dangerous Abuelitas: The Gender of Religious Otherness," *Women and Twentieth Century Protestantism Newsletter* (Winter 1999): 10.

BIBLIOGRAPHY

Archives
Apostolic Faith Mission Archives, Portland, OR
Beaton Institute, University College of Cape Breton, Sidney, NS
Billy Graham Center Archives, Wheaton College, Wheaton, IL
Burke Library at Union Theological Seminary, Columbia University Libraries, New York
Church of the Nazarene Archives, Kansas City, MO
Fisher Library Archives, Asbury Theological Seminary, Wilmore, KY
Flower Pentecostal Heritage Center, Springfield, MO
John J. Burns Library, Boston College, Chestnut Hill, MA
MidAmerica Nazarene University Archives, Olathe, KS
Northern Baptist Theological Seminary Archives, Lombard, IL
Pillar of Fire Archives, Zarephath, NJ
Pitts Theological Library, Special Collections, Emory University, Atlanta, GA
Salvation Army Archives, Alexandria, VA

Primary Sources
Addams, Jane. *A New Conscience and an Ancient Evil*. New York: Macmillan, 1912.
———. "Subjective Necessity for Social Settlements." *Forum* 14 (November 1892): 345–58.
———. *Twenty Years at Hull House*. New York: Macmillan, 1939.
Avery, Martha Moore. "A Call to Catholic Women." *Central-Blatt and Social Justice* (January 1910). Beaton Institute, University College of Cape Breton.
———. Diary. Beaton Institute. University College of Cape Breton.
———. "Mr. Sunday and the Unitarians." *America*, n.d. John J. Burns Library, Boston College.
———. "The Long Way Home to Rome." Autobiography. Beaton Institute. University College of Cape Breton.
———. *Woman: Her Quality, Her Environment, Her Possibility*. Boston: Boston Socialist Press, 1903.
Avery, Martha Moore, and David Goldstein. *Bolshevism: Its Cure*. Boston: Boston School of Political Economy, 1919.
———. *Campaigning for Christ*. Boston: Pilot Publishing, 1924.
———. "The Origins, Methods, and Results of the Boston Catholic Truth Guild." Beaton Institute, University College of Cape Breton.
Baker, Elizabeth V. "Bible Training School." *Trust* (September 1912): 10.
———. *Chronicles of a Faith Life*. Christian Higher Life Series. New York: Garland, 1984.
Barrett, Kate Waller. *Some Practical Suggestions on the Conduct of a Rescue Home*. Washington, DC: National Florence Crittenton Mission, 1903. Reprinted in Women in America from Colonial Times to the 20th Century Series. New York: Arno Press, 1974.
Binney, Amos, and Daniel Steele. *Binney's Theological Compend Improved*. 2nd ed. Cincinnati: Curts & Jennings, 1875.

Black, William Plummer. "Rescue Missions of Seattle." Master's thesis. University of Washington, 1926.
Bliss, William D. P., ed. "Woman's Christian Temperance Unions, the National and the World." In *The Encyclopedia of Social Reform*, 1398. New York: Funk & Wagnalls, 1897.
Booth, Evangeline. "As a Mother." Salvation Army Archives.
———. "Missionary, IMC (International Missionary Council)." Salvation Army Archives.
———. *Toward a Better World*. Garden City, NY: Doubleday, Doran & Co., 1928.
———. "The World's Greatest Romance." In *The Harp and the Sword: Writings and Speeches of Evangeline Cory Booth*, vol. 1, ed. John D. Waldron, 160–68. New York: Salvation Army, 1992.
Boswell, Charles M. "Rescue Missions." Leaflet 6, ser. A. Philadelphia: Board of Home Missions and Church Extension of the Methodist Episcopal Church. Pitts Theological Library, Special Collections, Emory University.
Brownson, Orestes. "Protestant Revivals and Catholic Retreats." *Brownson's Quarterly Review* 3 (July 1858): 294–322.
Burgess, Ernest W. "What Social Case Records Should Contain to Be Useful for Sociological Interpretation." *Social Forces* 6 (June 1928): 524–32.
Bushnell, Horace. *Discourses on Christian Nurture*. Boston: Massachusetts Sabbath School Society, 1847.
Buxton, Arthur. "The Automobile as Advertiser: A New Way of Attracting Attention." *Scientific American* (March 25, 1911): 301–2.
Cagle, Mary Lee. *The Life and Work of Mary Lee Cagle: An Autobiography*. Kansas City, MO: Nazarene Publishing House, 1928.
———. "My Call to the Ministry." In *Women Preachers*, ed. Fannie McDowell Hunter, 70–74. Dallas: Berachah Printing, 1905.
Campbell, Helen. *Darkness and Daylight, or Lights and Shadows of New York Life*. Hartford, CT: Hartford Publishing, 1896.
Carter, Robert Kelso. *The Atonement for Sin and Sickness; or, A Full Salvation for Soul and Body*. Boston: Willard Tract Repository, 1884.
Census of Religious Bodies, 1926. *Pillar of Fire: Statistics, Denominational History, Doctrine, and Organization*. Washington, DC: U.S. Government Printing Office, 1928.
Chicago Evangelistic Institute, *1916 Yearbook*. MidAmerica Nazarene University Archives.
———. *1945 Yearbook*. MidAmerica Nazarene University Archives.
———. "Acquainting You with Chicago Evangelistic Institute." B. L. Fisher Library Archives, Asbury Theological Seminary.
———. "C.E.I. Alumni Offer Tribute to Their Alma Mater." *Are You Familiar with Chicago Evangelistic Institute?* Billy Graham Center Archives.
———. "Christian Workers' Course." Correspondence Department, Chicago Evangelistic Institute. B. L. Fisher Library Archives, Asbury Theological Seminary.
———. "Financial Summary." *Heart and Life* 2 (December 1912 and January 1913): 14–15.
———. "God Answers Prayer." *Heart and Life* 2 (December 1912 and January 1913): 8.
Clarke, Edward H. *Sex in Education; or, A Fair Chance for the Girls*. Boston: James R. Osgood, 1873.
Cole, Mary. *Trials and Triumphs of Faith*. Anderson, IN: Gospel Trumpet Co., 1914.
Constitution, Government and General Decree Book of the Church of the Living God, the Pillar and Ground of the Truth, Inc. Nashville, TN: New and Living Way, 1924.
Conway, Bertrand. *Question Box, New Edition: Replies to Questions Received on Missions to Non-Catholics*. New York: Paulist Press, 1929.
Corbett, Arthur B. "The Common Cause Society." *Queen's Work* (March 1915): 147.
Crawford, Florence. "The Baptism of the Holy Ghost." In *Sermons and Scriptural Studies: Book Two*, by Florence Crawford, comp. Raymond Robert Crawford. Portland, OR: Apostolic Faith. Apostolic Faith Church Archives.
———. "Does God Call Women to Preach the Gospel as Well as Men?" *Apostolic Faith* 18 (1918): 2. Apostolic Faith Church Archives.

———. "Entire Sanctification." In *Sermons and Scriptural Studies: Book One*, by Florence Crawford, comp. Raymond Robert Crawford. Portland, OR: Apostolic Faith. Apostolic Faith Church Archives.

———. "Teaching on the Baptism of the Holy Ghost in the New Testament, Beginning with the Subject of the Latter Rain." July 19, 1921. Apostolic Faith Mission Archives.

Crittenton, Charles N. *The Brother of Girls: The Life Story of Charles N. Crittenton as Told by Himself*. Chicago: World's Events Co., 1910.

Curtis, Georgiana Pell, comp. and ed. "Martha Moore Avery." *The American Catholic Who's Who*. St. Louis: B. Herder, 1911.

Curts, Lewis, ed. *The General Conferences of the Methodist Episcopal Church from 1792 to 1896*. Cincinnati: Curts & Jennings, 1900.

Day, J. R. "The Higher Criticism: A Symposium." *Zion's Herald* 71 (March 22, 1893): 89.

Dean, John Marvin. *Evangelism and Social Service*. Philadelphia: Griffith & Rowland, 1913.

Dorr, Rheta Childe. *What Eight Million Women Want*. Boston: Small, Maynard & Co., 1910.

Dorsey, Theodore H. *From a Far Country: The Conversion Story of a Campaigner for Christ*. Huntington, IN: Our Sunday Visitor Press, 1939.

Duff, Mrs. E. S. *Redeemed by the Blood*. Cincinnati, OH: God's Revivalist, 1905.

Dunning, Jane. *Brands from the Burning: An Account of a Work among the Sick and Destitute in Connection with Providence Mission New York City*. New York: J. W. Pratt, 1877.

Edholm, Charlton. *The Traffic in Girls and Work of Florence Crittenton Missions*. Chicago: Woman's Temperance Publishing Association, 1893.

Elliott, Walter. *A Manual of Missions*. Washington, DC: Apostolic Mission House, 1922.

———. "The Missionary Outlook in the United States." *Catholic World* 57 (September 1893): 757–69.

Flatbush, Adda M. *Methods and Results of Rescue Work, from an Experience of Ten Years*. Kansas City, MO: Hudson-Kimberly, 1901.

Ford, Stephen, ed. *The Methodist Year Book, 1909*. Cincinnati: Jennings & Graham, 1909.

Forney, C. H. *The History of the Churches of God in the United States of North America*. Findlay, OH: Churches of God Publishing, 1914.

Fullerton, Kemper. "The Bross Prize." *American Journal of Theology* 10:4 (October 1906): 705.

Godbey, William B. *Woman Preacher*. Louisville, KY: Pentecostal Publishing, 1891.

Goldstein, David. *Autobiography of a Campaigner for Christ*. Boston: Catholic Campaigners for Christ, 1936.

———. "Lay Street Preaching." In *The White Harvest: A Symposium on Methods of Convert Making*, ed. John A. O'Brien, 209–38. New York: Longmans, Green & Co., 1927.

Gordon, A. J. "Missionary Training Schools, Do Baptists Need Them?" *Baptist Quarterly Review* 12 (January 1890): 69–101.

Graves, A. S. "Wesley's Variations of Belief, and the Influence of the Same on Methodism." *Methodist Review* 69 (1887): 192–211.

Hadley, Henry H., comp. *Rescue Songs by One Hundred Popular Composers and Gifted Song Writers; Specially Fitted for Rescue Missions and Meetings, Rescue Workers and Evangelists and Revival Services*. New York: Christian Men's Union, 1895.

Harrison, W. P. "The Methodist Deaconess." *Southern Methodist Review* 4 (July 1888): 415.

Horton, Isabelle. *The Builders: A Story of Faith and Works*. Chicago: Deaconess Advocate, 1910.

———. *High Adventure: Life of Lucy Rider Meyer*. New York: Methodist Book Concern, 1928.

Hunter, Fannie McDowell, ed. *Women Preachers*. Dallas: Berachah Printing, 1905.

Jernigan, C. B. *Pioneer Days of the Holiness Movement in the Southwest*. Kansas City, MO: Pentecostal Nazarene Publishing, 1919.

Kennedy, Annie Richardson. *The Heartsease Miracle*. New York: Heartsease Publications, 1920.

LaSelle, Mary A., and Katherine E. Wiley. *Vocations for Girls*. Chicago: Houghton Mifflin, 1913.

Leake, Albert H. *The Vocational Education of Girls and Women*. New York: Macmillan, 1918.

Lee, Jarena. *Religious Experience and Journal of Mrs. Jarena Lee, Giving an Account of Her Call to Preach the Gospel*. Philadelphia: Printed and published by Jarena Lee, 1849.
Lee, Richard Artemus. *Mother Lee's Experience in Fifteen Years' Rescue Work with Thrilling Incidents of Her Life*. Omaha, NE: Richard Artemus Lee, 1906.
Loud, Grover. *Evangelized America*. New York: Dial, 1928.
Martin, Asa. *Our Negro Population: A Sociological Study of the Negroes of Kansas City*. Kansas City, MO: Franklin Hudson, 1913.
Mathews, Shailer. *The Faith of Modernism*. New York: Macmillan, 1924.
———. "The Historical Study of Religion." In *A Guide to the Study of the Christian Religion*, ed. Gerald B. Smith, 19–80. Chicago: University of Chicago Press, 1916.
———. *New Faith for Old: An Autobiography*. New York: Macmillan, 1936.
———. "The Significance of the Church to the Social Movement." *American Journal of Sociology* 4 (July 1898–May 1899): 603–20.
McDowell, Mary E. "The Value of a Social Settlement in an Industrial Neighborhood." In *The Socialized Church: Addresses before the First National Conference of the Social Workers of Methodism, St. Louis, November 17–19, 1908*, ed. Worth M. Tippy, 131–48. New York: Eaton & Mains, 1909.
McPherson, Aimee Semple. *The Personal Testimony and Life of Aimee Semple McPherson*. Chicago: Pentecostal Herald, 1915.
———. *This Is That: Personal Experiences, Sermons and Writings*. Los Angeles: Bridal Call Publishing, 1919.
Meyer, Lucy Rider. *Deaconesses, Biblical, Early Church, European, American: With the Story of the Chicago Training School, for City, Home and Foreign Missions, and the Chicago Deaconess Home*, 2nd ed. Chicago: Message Publishing Company, 1889.
———. "The Mother in the Church." *Methodist Review* 83 (September 1901): 716–32.
Minutes of the Forty-third Session of the St. Louis Annual Conference of the Methodist Episcopal Church, Held in Mountain Grove, MO, March 22 to 26, 1911. Warrensburg, MO: Perry E. Pierce, 1911.
Montgomery, Carrie Judd, *The Life and Teachings of Carrie Judd Montgomery*. Oakland, CA: Office of Triumphs of Faith, 1936. Reprinted in *"The Higher Christian Life": Sources for the Study of the Holiness Pentecostal and Keswick Movements*, ed. Donald W. Dayton. New York: Garland Publishing, 1985.
"More Pastors Needed." *Highways and Hedges* (later *Holiness Evangel*) (November 1, 1906). Church of the Nazarene Archives.
Moss, Virginia. *Following the Shepherd*. North Bergen, NJ: Beulah, 1923.
Oldham, William F. "Thoburn—Mystic, Seer, Prophet, Missionary." *Methodist Review* 106 (March 1923): 189–90.
Osborn, Lucy Drake. *Heavenly Pearls Set in a Life: A Record of Experiences and Labors in America, India and Australia*. New York: Fleming H. Revell, 1893.
———. *Light on Soul Winning*. New York: Fleming H. Revell, 1911.
Palmer, Phoebe. *The Promise of the Father; or, A Neglected Speciality of the Last Days*. Boston: Henry V. Degen, 1859.
———. *The Way of Holiness, with Notes by the Way: Being a Narrative of Religious Experience, Resulting from a Determination to be a Bible Christian*. New York: Piercy & Reed, 1843.
Perry, Mattie. *Christ and Answered Prayer*. Nashville, TN: Benson Printing, 1939.
Pierson, A. T. *The Crisis of Missions*. New York: Robert Carter & Brothers, 1886.
Pillar of Fire. *Catechism of the Pillar of Fire Church*. Denver, CO: Pillar of Fire, 1948.
———. *The Pillar of Fire Illustrated*. Zarephath, NJ: Pillar of Fire, 1920.
Prosser, Anna W. *From Death to Life: An Autobiography*. Chicago: Evangel Publishing, 1911.
Puckett, J .L. "A Card from Dr. Puckett." *Kokomo Dispatch* (July 9, 1885): 4. Flower Pentecostal Heritage Center.
Rauschenbusch, Walter. *Christianizing the Social Order*. New York: Macmillan, 1912.
———. "The New Evangelism." *Independent* (May 12, 1904): 1–6.

Ray, Emma J. *Twice Sold, Twice Ransomed: Autobiography of Mr. and Mrs. L. P. Ray.* Chicago: Free Methodist Publishing House, 1926.
Rest Cottage Association. *The White Slaves of America: A Book on Rescue Work.* Pilot Point, TX: Evangel, 1907.
Richmond, Mary. *Friendly Visiting among the Poor: A Handbook for Charity Workers* (1899). Reprinted in Patterson Smith Reprint Series in Criminology, Law Enforcement, and Social Problems. Montclair, NJ: Patterson Smith, 1969.
——. *The Good Neighbor in the Modern City.* Philadelphia: J. B. Lippincott Co., 1913.
Riis, Jacob. *How the Other Half Lives: Studies among the Tenements of New York.* New York: Charles Scribner's Sons, 1890.
Roberts, Florence. *Fifteen Years with the Outcast.* Anderson, IN: Gospel Trumpet, 1912.
Robinson, F. A., ed. *Mother Whittemore's Modern Miracles.* Toronto: Missions of Biblical Education, 1931.
Rodeheaver, Homer. *Twenty Years with Billy Sunday.* Winona Lake, IN: Rodeheaver Hall-Mack, 1936.
Rosenberg, Charles, and Carroll Smith-Rosenberg, eds. *The Prostitute and the Social Reformer: Commercial Vice in the Progressive Era.* Reprint, New York: Arno, 1974.
Smith, Amanda. *An Autobiography: The Story of the Lord's Dealings with Mrs. Amanda Smith, the Colored Evangelist.* Chicago: Christian Witness, 1921.
Smith, Jennie. *From Baca to Beulah.* Philadelphia: Garrigues Brothers, 1880.
——. *Incidents and Experiences of a Railroad Evangelist.* Washington, DC: Jennie Smith, 1920.
——. *Valley of Baca: A Record of Suffering and Triumph.* Philadelphia: Garrigues Brothers, 1876.
Smith, Joseph H. *Training in Pentecostal Evangelism.* Philadelphia: Christian Standard, 1897.
Stanton, Elizabeth Cady and the Revising Committee, *The Woman's Bible.* Pt. 1, *The Pentateuch.* New York: European Publishing Co., 1895. Reprint, Seattle: Coalition Task Force on Women and Religion, 1974.
Starr, Lee Anna. *The Bible Status of Woman.* New York: Fleming H. Revell, 1926.
Strong, Josiah. *The New Era.* New York: Baker & Taylor, 1893.
——. *Our Country: Its Possible Future and Its Present Crisis.* New York: Baker & Taylor, 1885.
——. *Religious Movements for Social Betterment.* New York: Baker & Taylor, 1900.
——. *The Twentieth-Century City.* New York: Baker & Taylor, 1898.
Sunday, Helen. *"Ma" Sunday Still Speaks.* Winona Lake, IN: Winona Lake Christian Assembly, 1957.
Sunday, William A., and Helen T. Sunday, *The Papers of William and Helen Sunday (1882–1974),* ed. Robert Shuster. Billy Graham Center Archives, Wheaton College.
Swarth, Helen. *My Life in a Religious Commune.* University Park, IA: Vennard College, n.d. MidAmerica Nazarene University Archives.
Thoburn, James Mills. *The Church of Pentecost.* Cincinnati: Jenning & Pye, 1901.
——. *The Deaconess and Her Vocation.* New York: Hunt & Eaton, 1893.
——. *Life of Isabella Thoburn.* New York: Eaton & Mains, 1903.
Thompson, Fayette L., et al. *Men and Religion.* New York: Young Men's Christian Association, 1911.
Trueblood, N. A. "The Tipton Trance Meetings." *Kokomo Gazette Tribune* (May 12, 1885): 4. Flower Pentecostal Heritage Center.
Vennard College. *Vennard Vision.* 1958. MidAmerica Nazarene University Archives.
Vennard, Iva Durham. "2 Timothy 2:15." *Heart and Life* 9 (November 1919): 4.
——. "Chapel Message." (May 9, 1940), 2. B. L. Fisher Library Archives, Asbury Theological Seminary.
——. *The Evangelism for This Day: An Address.* Chicago: Chicago Evangelistic Institute, 1933. B. L. Fisher Library Archives, Asbury Theological Seminary.
——. "Extracts from the Annual Report, 1908–09." *Inasmuch* 5 (April 1909): 7. MidAmerica Nazarene University Archives.
——. "'Help Those Women': XIV. The Evangelistic Department of Deaconess Work." *Inasmuch* 2 (April 1906): 8. MidAmerica Nazarene University Archives.

———. "Highlights of the Year: Doctor Vennard's Family Letter." *Heart and Life* 26 (July 1940): 19–20. B. L. Fisher Library Archives, Asbury Theological Seminary.
———. "The Spirit of Negation." (April 17, 1890): 6. MidAmerica Nazarene University Archives.
———. *Upper Room Messages*. Chicago: Chicago Evangelistic Institute, 1916.
———. "The Wayside." *Heart and Life* 1 (October and November 1911): 12. B. L. Fisher Library Archives, Asbury Theological Seminary.
———. "Wayside Notes." *Heart and Life* 1 (October and November 1911): 15. B. L. Fisher Library Archives, Asbury Theological Seminary.
Wheatley, Richard. *The Life and Letters of Mrs. Phoebe Palmer*. New York: W. C. Palmer, 1881. Reprint, New York: Garland, 1984.
Wheaton, Elizabeth. *Prisons and Prayer, or A Labor of Love*. Tabor, IA: Chas. M. Kelley, 1906.
White, Alma. *Demons and Tongues*. Zarephath, NJ: Pillar of Fire, 1936.
———. *Evangelism*, comp. C. R. Paige and C. K. Ingler. Vol. 1. Zarephath, NJ: Pillar of Fire, 1939.
———. *Looking Back from Beulah*. Denver: Pentecostal Union, 1902.
———. *The New Testament Church*. Zarephath, NJ: Pillar of Fire, 1929.
———. *The Story of My Life and the Pillar of Fire*. Vol. 5. Zarephath, NJ: Pillar of Fire, 1943.
———. *Why I Do Not Eat Meat*. Zarephath, NJ: Pillar of Fire, 1915.
———. *Woman's Chains*. Zarephath, NJ: Pillar of Fire, 1943.
White, Ray B., comp. *Doctrines and Discipline of the Pillar of Fire Church*. Zarephath, NJ: Pillar of Fire, 1918.
Whittemore, Emma. "At the Gateway, or How Kitty Was Saved." *Christian Alliance* (January 1892): 28.
———. *Delia; Formerly the Blue-Bird of Mulberry Bend*. New York: Door of Hope, 1893.
———. "The Door of Hope." *Christian Alliance* (October 1891): 2.
———. "The Opening of Door of Hope, No. 2." *The Christian Alliance* (July 1893): 28.
———. "Out of Darkness into Light." *Christian Alliance and Missionary Weekly* (December 1892): 377–78.
———. *Promoted! Or, A Brief Life Sketch of P. Cameron Scott*. New York: Door of Hope, 1897.
———. "Snatched as a Brand from the Burning." *Christian Alliance and Missionary Weekly* (July 1891): 10.
Willard, Frances E. *Glimpses of Fifty Years: The Autobiography of an American Woman*. Chicago: Woman's Temperance Publication Association, 1889.
———. *Woman and Temperance*. Hartford, CT: Park Publishing, 1883. Reprint, New York: Arno Press, 1972.
———. *Woman in the Pulpit*. Chicago: Woman's Temperance Publishing Association, 1889. Reprint, Washington, DC: Zenger, 1978.
Willing, Jennie Fowler. "Evangelistic Work of the Woman's Christian Temperance Union." *Guide to Holiness* (October 1896): 141, 143.
———. "Historical Department, Lesson I." *Open Door* 1 (January–February 1909): 33.
———. *How to Save Souls*. Chicago: Christian Witness Co., 1909.
———. "Our Course of Bible Study. Historical Department. Lesson I. Answers." *Open Door* (March–April 1909): 19.
———. "Our Non-resident Class. Conditions of Membership in the Class." *Open Door* (October 1905): 27.
———. "The Woman's Christian Temperance Union." *Guide to Holiness* (March 1896): 102.
———. "The World's Evangelistic Training School." *Guide to Holiness* (January 1898): 23.
Winslow, Anna J. *Jewels from My Casket*. N.p.: Anna J. Winslow, 1910.
Wood, J. A. *Perfect Love; Plain Things for Those Who Need Them, concerning the Doctrine, Experience, Profession and Practice of Christian Holiness*. South Pasadena, CA: Published by the author, 1891.
Woods, Robert A., and Albert J. Kennedy, eds. *Handbook of Settlements*. Philadelphia: Russell Sage Foundation, 1911.

Woodworth, Maria B. *The Life and Experience of Maria B. Woodworth*. Dayton, OH: United Brethren Publishing House, 1885.
———. *The Life and Experience of Maria B. Woodworth*. Dayton, OH: United Brethren Publishing House, 1888.
———. *The Life, Work and Experience of Maria Beulah Woodworth, Evangelist*. St. Louis: Commercial Printing, 1894.
Woodworth-Etter, Maria. *Acts of the Holy Ghost, or The Life, Work, and Experience of Mrs. M. B. Woodworth-Etter, Evangelist*. Dallas: John F. Worley Printing, 1916.
———. *Spirit-Filled Sermons*. Indianapolis: by the author, 1921.

Secondary Sources

Abell, Aaron I. *The Urban Impact on American Protestantism, 1865–1900*. London: Archon, 1962.
Adams, David K., and Cornelis A. van Minnen. *Religious and Secular Reform in America: Ideas, Beliefs, and Social Change*. New York: New York University Press, 1999.
Agnew, Elizabeth N. "Shaping a Civic Profession: Mary Richmond, the Social Gospel, and Social Work." In *Gender and the Social Gospel*, ed. Wendy J. Deichmann Edwards and Carolyn De Swarte Gifford, 116–35. Urbana: University of Illinois Press, 2003.
Ahlstrom, Sydney E. *A Religious History of the American People*. New Haven, CT: Yale University Press, 1972.
Aiken, Katherine G. *Harnessing the Power of Motherhood: The National Florence Crittenton Mission, 1883–1925*. Knoxville: University of Tennessee, 1998.
Albanese, Catherine L. "Horace Bushnell among the Metaphysicians." *Church History* 79:3 (September 2010): 614–53.
Albin, Thomas. "'Inwardly Persuaded': Religion of the Heart in Early British Methodism." In *"Heart Religion" in the Methodist Tradition and Related Movements*, ed. Richard Steele, 33–66. Metuchen, NJ: Scarecrow, 2001.
Albrecht, Daniel E. "Carrie Judd Montgomery: Pioneering Contributor to Three Religious Movements." *Pneuma* (Fall 1986): 101–19.
———. "The Life and Ministry of Carrie Judd Montgomery." Master's thesis. Western Evangelical Seminary, 1984.
Alexander, Estrelda. *Limited Liberty: The Legacy of Four Pentecostal Women Pioneers*. Cleveland, OH: Pilgrim, 2008.
Alexander, Estrelda, and Amos Yong, eds. *Philip's Daughters: Women in Pentecostal-Charismatic Leadership*. Eugene, OR: Pickwick, 2009.
Allen, L. Dean. *Rise Up, O Men of God: The Men and Religion Forward Movement and Promise Keepers*. Macon, GA: Mercer University Press, 2002.
Andrews, William L. *Sisters of the Spirit: Three Black Women's Autobiographies of the Nineteenth Century*. Bloomington: Indiana University Press, 1986.
Armitage, Susan. "Women and Men in Western History: A Stereoptical Vision." *Western Historical Quarterly* 16 (October 1985): 381–91.
Atwood, Craig D. "Religion in America." In *Handbook of Denominations in the United States*, 11th ed., ed. Frank S. Mead, Samuel S. Hill, and Craig D. Atwood, 15–24. Nashville, TN: Abingdon, 2001.
Aune, Kristin. "Evangelical Christianity and Women's Changing Lives." *European Journal of Women's Studies* 15:3 (2008): 277–94.
Bacon, Margaret Hope. *Mothers of Feminism: The Story of Quaker Women in America*. San Francisco: Harper & Row, 1986.
Baker, Elizabeth V. *Chronicles of a Faith Life*. Reprint, New York: Garland Publishing, 1984.
Banner, Lois W. "Religious Benevolence as Social Control: A Critique of an Interpretation." *Journal of American History* 60:1 (June 1973): 23–41.
Barfoot, Charles H., and Gerald T. Sheppard. "Prophetic vs. Priestly Religion: The Changing Role of Women Clergy in Pentecostal Churches." *Review of Religious Research* 22 (September 1980): 2–17.

Barlow, Melvin and the National Society for the Study of Education Yearbook Committee. *The Sixty-fourth Yearbook of the National Society for the Study of Education.* Chicago: University of Chicago Press, 1965.

Baron, Ava. *Work Engendered: Toward a New History of American Labor.* Ithaca, NY: Cornell University Press, 1991.

Bassard, Kathryn Clay. *Spiritual Interrogations: Culture, Gender, and Community in Early African American Women's Writing.* Princeton, NJ: Princeton University Press, 1999.

Bassett, Paul Merritt. "The Fundamentalist Leavening of the Holiness Movement, 1914-1940, The Church of the Nazarene: A Case Study." *Wesleyan Theological Journal* 13 (Spring 1978): 65-91.

Bebbington, D. W. *Evangelicalism in Modern Britain: A History from the 1730s to the 1980s.* Boston: Unwin Hyman, 1989.

Bederman, Gail. "'The Women Have Had Charge of the Church Work Long Enough': The Men and Religion Forward Movement of 1911-1912 and the Masculinization of Middle-Class Protestantism." *American Quarterly* 41:3 (September 1989): 432-65.

Bedford, Henry F. *Socialism and the Workers in Massachusetts, 1886-1912.* Amherst, MA: University of Massachusetts Press, 1966.

Bednarowski, Mary. "Outside the Mainstream: Women's Religion and Women Religious Leaders in 19th Century America." *Journal of the American Academy of Religion* 48 (June 1980): 207-31.

Behan, Warren Palmer. "An Introductory Survey of the Lay Training School Field." *Religious Education* 11 (1916): 47-49.

Beito, David T. *From Mutual Aid to the Welfare State: Fraternal Societies and Social Services, 1890-1967.* Chapel Hill: University of North Carolina Press, 2000.

Bendroth, Margaret Lamberts. *Fundamentalism and Gender, 1875 to the Present.* New Haven, CT: Yale University Press, 1993.

———. "The Search for 'Women's Role' in American Evangelicalism, 1930-1980." In *Evangelicalism and Modern America,* ed. George Marsden, 122-34. Grand Rapids, MI: Eerdmans, 1984.

Bendroth, Margaret Lamberts, and Virginia Lieson Brereton, eds. *Women and Twentieth-Century Protestantism.* Urbana: University of Illinois Press, 2002.

Bennett, David H. *The Party of Fear: From Nativist Movements to the New Right in American History.* New York: Vintage, 1988.

Berg, Barbara J. *The Remembered Gate: Origins of American Feminism, the Woman and the City, 1800-1860.* New York: Oxford University Press, 1978.

Blair, Karen. *The Clubwoman as Feminist: True Womanhood Redefined, 1868-1914.* New York: Holmes & Meier Publishers, 1980.

Blee, Kathleen. *Women of the Klan: Racism and Gender in the 1920s.* Berkeley: University of California Press, 1991.

Blumhofer, Edith W. *Aimee Semple McPherson: Everybody's Sister.* Grand Rapids, MI: Eerdmans, 1993.

———. "A Confused Legacy: Reflections on Evangelical Attitudes toward Ministering Women in the Past Century." *Fides et Historia* 22 (Winter-Spring 1990): 49-61.

Blumhofer, Edith W., and Randall Balmer, eds. *Modern Christian Revivals.* Urbana: University of Illinois, 1993.

Blumhofer, Edith W., Russell P. Spittler, and Grant Wacker, eds. *Pentecostal Currents in American Protestantism.* Urbana: University of Illinois Press, 1999.

Bordin, Ruth. *Women and Temperance: The Quest for Power and Liberty, 1873-1900.* Philadelphia: Temple University Press, 1981.

Bowie, Mary Ella. *Alabaster and Spikenard: The Life of Iva Durham Vennard D.D., Founder of Chicago Evangelistic Institute.* Chicago: Chicago Evangelistic Institute, 1947.

Boyer, Paul. *Urban Masses and Moral Order in America, 1820-1920.* Cambridge, MA: Harvard University Press, 1978.

Brandenstein, Sherilyn B. "The Colorado Cottage Home." *Colorado Magazine* 53:3 (1976): 229-42.

Brantley, Clovis A. *God Can: A Study of Rescue Mission Work*. Atlanta: Home Mission Board, Southern Baptist Convention, 1946.
Brasher, Brenda E. *Godly Women: Fundamentalism and Female Power*. New Brunswick, NJ: Rutgers University Press, 1998.
Braude, Ann. *Radical Spirits: Spiritualism and Women's Rights in Nineteenth-Century America*. Boston: Beacon, 1989.
———. "Women's History IS American Religious History." In *Retelling U.S. Religious History*, ed. Thomas A. Tweed, 87–107. Berkeley: University of California Press, 1997.
Brauer, Jerald C. "Conversion: From Puritanism to Revivalism." *Journal of Religion* 58 (July 1978): 227–43.
Brekus, Catherine A. ed. *The Religious History of American Women: Reimaging the Past*. Chapel Hill: University of North Carolina Press, 2007.
———. *Strangers and Pilgrims: Female Preaching in America, 1740–1845*. Chapel Hill: University of North Carolina Press, 1998.
———. "Studying Women and Religion: Problems and Possibilities." *Criterion* 32 (Autumn 1993): 24–28.
Bremner, Robert. *From the Depths: The Discovery of Poverty in the United States*. New York: New York University Press, 1956.
Brereton, Virginia Lieson. *From Sin to Salvation: Stories of Women's Conversions, 1800 to the Present*. Bloomington: Indiana University Press, 1991.
———. "Preparing Women for the Lord's Work." In *Women in New Worlds: Historical Perspectives on the Wesleyan Tradition*, vol. 1, ed. Hilah F. Thomas and Rosemary Skinner Keller, 178–99. Nashville, TN: Abingdon, 1981.
———. *Training God's Army: The American Bible School, 1880–1940*. Bloomington: Indiana University Press, 1990.
Brown, Candy Gunther. *The Word in the World: Evangelical Writing, Publishing, and Reading in America, 1789–1880*. Chapel Hill: University of North Carolina Press, 2004.
Brown, Daniel Alan. "A Comparative Analysis of Bible College Quality." Ph. D. dissertation. University of California, Los Angeles, 1982.
Brown, Earl Kent. *Women of Mr. Wesley's Methodism*. New York: Edwin Mellen, 1983.
Brown, Joanne Carlson. "Jennie Fowler Willing (1834–1916): Methodist Churchwoman and Reformer." Ph.D. dissertation. Boston University, 1983.
Browne, Henry. *The Catholic Evidence Movement: Its Achievements and Its Hopes*. London: Burns Oates & Washbourne, 1921.
Brumberg, Joan Jacobs, "'Ruined Girls': Changing Community Responses to Illegitimacy in Upstate New York, 1890–1920." *Journal of Social History* 18 (Winter 1984): 247–72.
Buenker, John D. *The Gilded Age and the Progressive Era*. Armonk, NY: Sharpe Reference, 2005.
———, ed. *The Gilded Age and Progressive Era, 1877–1920*. Sources of the American Tradition. Acton, MA: Copley, 2002.
Burger, Delores T. *Women Who Changed the Heart of the City: The Untold Story of the City Rescue Mission Movement*. Grand Rapids, MI: Kregel, 1997.
Butler, Anthea D. *Women in the Church of God in Christ: Making a Sanctified World*. Chapel Hill: University of North Carolina Press, 2007.
Butler, Jonathan M. *Softly and Tenderly Jesus Is Calling: Heaven and Hell in American Revivalism, 1870–1920*, 143. New York: Carlson Publishing, 1991.
Byrne, Patricia. "American Ultramontanism." *Theological Studies* 56 (1995): 301–26.
Cain, Madelyn. *The Childless Revolution*. Cambridge, MA: Perseus, 2001.
Calhoun, Charles W., ed. *The Gilded Age: Essays on the Origins of Modern America*. Wilmington, DE: Scholarly Resources, 1996.
Campbell, Barbara Kuhn. *The "Liberated" Woman of 1914: Prominent Women in the Progressive Era*. Studies in American History and Culture, no. 6. Ann Arbor, MI: UMI Research Press, 1979.

Campbell, Debra. "American Catholic Women, 1900–1965." In *Encyclopedia of Women and Religion in North America*, ed. Rosemary Skinner Keller and Rosemary Radford Ruether, 1:187–99. Bloomington: Indiana University Press, 2006.
———. "Catholic Evidence Guild: Towards a History of the Laity." *Heythrop Journal* 30:3 (July 1989): 306–24.
———. "A Catholic Salvation Army: David Goldstein, Pioneer Lay Evangelist." *Church History* 52:3 (September 1983): 322–32.
———. "David Goldstein and the Lay Catholic Street Apostolate." Ph.D. dissertation. Boston University, 1982.
———. "The Rise of the Lay Catholic Evangelist in England and America." *Harvard Theological Review* 79:4 (1986): 413–37.
Carpenter, Delores Causion. "Black Women in Religious Institutions: A Historical Summary from Slavery to the 1960s." *Journal of Religious Thought* 46:2 (Winter–Spring 1989–90): 7–27.
Carpenter, Joel. "Fundamentalist Institutions and the Rise of Evangelical Protestantism, 1929–1942." *Church History* 49:1 (March 1980): 62–75.
———. *Revive Us Again: The Reawakening of American Fundamentalism*. New York: Oxford University Press, 1997.
Carrigan, Owen. "A Forgotten Yankee Marxist." *New England Quarterly* 42:1 (March 1969): 23–43.
———. "Martha Moore Avery: The Career of a Crusader." Ph.D. dissertation. University of Maine, Orono, 1966.
Case, Jay Riley. *An Unpredictable Gospel: American Evangelicals and World Christianity, 1812–1920*. New York: Oxford University Press, 2012.
Chambers, Clarke A. "Toward a Redefinition of Welfare History." *Journal of American History* 73 (September 1986): 407–33.
Chaves, Mark. *Ordaining Women: Culture and Conflict in Religious Organizations*. Cambridge, MA: Harvard University Press, 1997.
Chilcote, Paul Wesley. *John Wesley and the Women Preachers of Early Methodism*. Metuchen, NJ: Scarecrow, 1991.
Clapp, Elizabeth J. *Mothers of All Children: Women Reformers and the Rise of Juvenile Courts in Progressive-Era America*. University Park: Pennsylvania State University Press, 1998.
Collier-Thomas, Bettye. *Daughters of Thunder: Black Women Preachers and Their Sermons, 1850–1979*. San Francisco: Jossey-Bass, 1998.
Conkin, Paul K. *American Originals: Homemade Varieties of Christianity*. Chapel Hill: University of North Carolina Press, 1997.
Conway, Jill. "Women Reformers and American Culture, 1870–1930." *Journal of Social History* 5 (Winter 1971–72): 164–77.
Cott, Nancy. "Comment on Karen Offen's 'Defining Feminism: A Comparative Historical Approach.'" *Signs* 15 (1989): 203–5.
Coutts, Frederick. *Bread for My Neighbour: An Appreciation of the Social Influence of William Booth*. London: Hodder & Stoughton, 1978.
Cremin, Lawrence A. *The Transformation of the School: Progressivism in American Education, 1876–1957*. New York: Alfred A. Knopf, 1961.
Crouse, Eric R. *Revival in the City: The Impact of American Evangelists in Canada*. Montreal: McGill-Queen's University Press, 2005.
Cumbler, John T. "The Politics of Charity: Gender and Class in Late 19th Century Charity Policy." *Journal of Social History* 14 (Fall 1980): 99–111.
Cummings, Kathleen Sprows. "The 'New Women' at the 'University': Gender and American Catholic Identity in the Progressive Era." In *The Religious History of American Women: Reimagining the Past*, ed. Catherine A. Brekus, 206–31. Chapel Hill: University of North Carolina Press, 2007.
———. *New Women of the Old Faith: Gender and American Catholicism in the Progressive Era*. Chapel Hill: University of North Carolina Press, 2009.

Cunningham, Sarah Gardner. "Christian Science." In *Encyclopedia of Women and Religion in North America*, ed. Rosemary Skinner Keller and Rosemary Radford Ruether, 2:738–46. Bloomington: Indiana University Press, 2006.
Curtis, Heather D. *Faith in the Great Physician: Suffering and Divine Healing in American Culture, 1860–1900*. Baltimore, MD: Johns Hopkins University Press, 2007.
Davidson, Phebe. *Religious Impulse in Selected Autobiographies of American Women (c. 1630–1983): Uses of the Spirit*. Lewiston, NY: Mellen, 1993.
Davis, Allen F. *American Heroine: The Life and Legend of Jane Addams*. New York: Oxford University Press, 1973.
———. *Spearheads for Reform: The Social Settlements and the Progressive Movement, 1890–1914*. New York: Oxford University Press, 1967.
Dayton, Donald. "Methodism and Pentecostalism." In *The Oxford Handbook of Methodist Studies*, ed. William J. Abraham and James E. Kirby, 171–87. New York: Oxford University Press, 2009.
———. *Theological Roots of Pentecostalism*. Peabody, MA: Hendrickson, 1987.
Dayton, Donald, and Lucille Sider Dayton. "'Your Daughters Shall Prophesy': Feminism in the Holiness Movement." *Methodist History* 14 (January 1976): 67–92.
DeBerg, Betty. *Ungodly Women: Gender and the First Wave of American Fundamentalism*. Minneapolis: Fortress, 1990.
DeGraaf, Lawrence B. "Race, Sex and Region: Black Women in the American West, 1850–1920." *Pacific Historical Review* 49:2 (May 1980): 285–313.
Deno, Vivian. "God, Authority, and the Home: Gender, Race, and U.S. Pentecostals, 1906–1926." *Journal of Women's History* 16:3 (2004): 91–94.
DeVault, Ileen A. "'Give the Boys a Trade': Gender and Job Choice in the 1980s." In *Work Engendered: Toward a New History of American Labor*, ed. Ava Baron, 191–215. Ithaca, NY: Cornell University Press, 1991.
Dieter, Melvin Easterday. *The Holiness Revival of the Nineteenth Century*. Studies in Evangelicalism, no. 1. Metuchen, NJ: Scarecrow, 1980.
Diner, Steven J. *A Very Different Age: Americans of the Progressive Era*. New York: Hill & Wang, 1998.
Dolan, Jay P. *The American Catholic Experience: A History from Colonial Times to the Present*. Notre Dame, IN: University of Notre Dame Press, 1992.
———. *Catholic Revivalism: The American Experience, 1830–1900*. Notre Dame, IN: University of Notre Dame Press, 1978.
Dorsett, Lyle W. *Billy Sunday and the Redemption of Urban America*. Library of Religious Biography. Grand Rapids, MI: Eerdmans, 1991.
Dougherty, Mary Agnes. "The Methodist Deaconess, 1885–1919: A Study in Religious Feminism." Ph.D. dissertation. University of California, Davis, 1979.
Douglas, Ann. *The Feminization of American Culture*. New York: Knopf, 1977.
Douglass-Chin, Richard J. *Preacher Woman Sings the Blues: The Autobiographies of Nineteenth-Century African American Evangelists*. Columbia: University of Missouri Press, 2001.
Edwards, Wendy J. Deichmann. "Forging an Ideology for American Missions: Josiah Strong and Manifest Destiny." In *North American Foreign Missions, 1810–1914: Theology, Theory, and Policy*, ed. Wilbert R. Shenk, 163–91. Grand Rapids, MI: Eerdmans, 2004.
Edwards, Wendy J. Deichmann, and Carolyn De Swarte Gifford, eds. *Gender and the Social Gospel*. Urbana: University of Illinois Press, 2003.
Elshtain, Jean Bethke. *Public Man, Private Woman: Women in Social and Political Thought*. Princeton, NJ: Princeton University Press, 1981.
Epstein, Barbara Leslie. *The Politics of Domesticity: Women, Evangelism, and Temperance in the Nineteenth Century*. Middletown, CT: Wesleyan University Press, 1981.
Epstein, Daniel Mark. *Sister Aimee: The Life of Aimee Semple McPherson*. New York: Harcourt Brace Jovanovich, 1993.

Fagan, Ronald W. "Skid-Row Rescue Missions: A Religious Approach to Alcoholism." *Journal of Religion and Health* 28:2 (Summer 1987): 153–71.
Ferngren, Gary B. "The Evangelical-Fundamentalist Tradition." In *Caring and Curing: Health and Medicine in the Western Religious Traditions*, ed. Ronald L. Numbers and Darrel W. Amundsen, 486–513. New York: Macmillan, 1986.
Findlay, James. *Dwight L. Moody, American Evangelist, 1837–1899.* Chicago: University of Chicago Press, 1969.
Fishburn, Janet F. "The Social Gospel as Missionary Ideology." In *North American Foreign Missions, 1810–1914: Theology, Theory, and Policy*, ed. Wilbert R. Shenk, 218–42. Grand Rapids, MI: Eerdmans, 2004.
Flanagan, Maureen A. "Gender and Urban Political Reform: The City Club and the Woman's City Club of Chicago in the Progressive Era." *American Historical Review* 95:4 (October 1990): 1032–50.
Flowers, Elizabeth Hill. *Into the Pulpit: Southern Baptist Women and Power since World War II.* Chapel Hill: University of North Carolina Press, 2012.
Folbre, Nancy. *The Invisible Heart: Economics and Family Values.* New York: New Press, 2001.
Fox, Mary Harrita. *Peter E. Dietz, Labor Priest.* Notre Dame, IN: University of Notre Dame Press, 1953.
Fox-Genovese, Elizabeth. "Religion and Women in America: An Introduction." In *World Religions in America*, ed. Jacob Neusner, 223–32. Louisville, KY: WJK, 1994.
———. "Two Steps Forward, One Step Back: New Questions and Old Models in the Religious History of American Women." *Journal of the American Academy of Religion* 55 (1987): 211–33.
Freedman, Estelle. "Separatism as Strategy: Female Institution Building and American Feminism, 1870–1930." *Feminist Studies* 5 (Fall 1979): 512–29.
Furnish, Dorothy Jean. "Women in Religious Education: Pioneers for Women in Professional Ministry." In *Women and Religion in America*, vol. 3: *1900–1968*, ed. Rosemary Radford Ruether and Rosemary Skinner Keller, 310–17. San Francisco: Harper & Row, 1986.
Gamm, Gerald, and Robert D. Putnam. "The Growth of Voluntary Associations in America, 1840–1940." *Journal of Interdisciplinary History* 29:4 (Spring 1999): 511–57.
George, Timothy, ed. *Mr. Moody and the Evangelical Tradition.* New York: T & T Clark International, 2004.
Getz, Gene A. *MBI: The Story of Moody Bible Institute.* Chicago: Moody, 1986.
Gifford, Carolyn DeSwarte. "Nineteenth- and Twentieth-Century Protestant Social Reform Movements in the United States." In *Encyclopedia of Women and Religion in North America*, ed. Rosemary Skinner Keller and Rosemary Radford Ruether, 3:1021–38. Bloomington: Indiana University Press, 2006.
Giggie, John M. *After Redemption: Jim Crow and the Transformation of African American Religion in the Delta, 1875–1915.* New York: Oxford University Press, 2008.
Gilmore, Glenda Elizabeth. "Responding to the Challenges of the Progressive Era." In *Who Were the Progressives?* ed. Glenda Elizabeth Gilmore. Historians at Work Series. Boston: Bedford/St. Martin's, 2002.
Ginzberg, Lori D. *Women and the Work of Benevolence: Morality, Politics, and Class in the 19th-Century United States.* New Haven, CT: Yale University Press, 1990.
Goen, C.C. "Fundamentalism in America." In *American Mosaic: Social Patterns of Religion in the United States*, ed. Phillip Hammond and Benton Johnson, 85–93. New York: Random House, 1970.
Goff, James R., and Grant Wacker, eds. *Portraits of a Generation: Early Pentecostal Leaders.* Fayetteville: University of Arkansas Press, 2002.
Goldin, Claudia. "America's Graduation from High School: The Evolution and Spread of Secondary Schooling in the Twentieth Century." *Journal of Economic History* 58 (June 1998): 345–74.
Goldin, Claudia, and Lawrence F. Katz. "Human Capital and Social Capital: The Rise of Secondary Schooling in America, 1910–1940." *Journal of Interdisciplinary History* 29:4 (Spring 1999): 683–723.

Goode, Gloria Davis. "Preachers of the Word and Singers of the Gospel: The Ministry of Women among Nineteenth-Century African-Americans." Ph.D. dissertation. University of Pennsylvania, 1990.
Gotham, Kevin Fox. *Race, Real Estate, and Uneven Development: The Kansas City Experience, 1900–2000*. Albany: State University of New York, 2002.
Gould, Lewis L. *America in the Progressive Era, 1890–1914*. Seminar Studies in History. New York: Pearson Education, 2001.
Grammer, Elizabeth Elkin. *Some Wild Visions: Autobiographies by Female Itinerant Evangelists in Nineteenth-Century America*. New York: Oxford University Press, 2003.
Grenz, Stanley J. *The Millennial Maze: Sorting Out Evangelical Options*. Downers Grove, IL: IVP Academic, 1992.
Griffith, R. Marie. *God's Daughters: Evangelical Women and the Power of Submission*. Berkeley: University of California Press, 1997.
Griffith, R. Marie, and Barbara Dianne Savage, eds. *Women and Religion in the African Diaspora: Knowledge, Power, and Performance*. Baltimore, MD: Johns Hopkins University Press, 2006.
Gundry, Stanley N. "Demythologizing Moody." In *Mr. Moody and the Evangelical Tradition*, ed. Timothy George, 13–29. New York: T & T Clark International, 2004.
Haarsager, Sandra. *Organized Womanhood: Cultural Politics in the Pacific Northwest, 1840–1920*. Norman: University of Oklahoma Press, 1997.
Hackett, David G. "Gender and Religion in American Culture, 1870–1930." *Religion and American Culture* 5 (Summer 1994): 127–57.
Hamilton, Michael S. "Women, Public Ministry, and American Fundamentalism." *Religion and American Culture* 3 (Summer 1993): 171–96.
Handy, Robert T. "The Protestant Quest for a Christian America." *Church History* 22 (March 1953): 8–20.
———, ed. *The Social Gospel in America, 1870–1920: Gladden, Ely, Rauschenbusch*. New York: Oxford University Press, 1966.
Hard, William. "Chicago's Five Maiden Aunts." *American Magazine* 62 (September 1906): 481–89.
Hardesty, Nancy A. "Holiness Is Power: The Pentecostal Argument for Women's Ministry." In *Pastoral-Problems in the Pentecostal-Charismatic Movement*, ed. Harold D. Hunter, Thirteenth Annual Conference of the Society for Pentecostal Studies, 1–15. Cleveland, TN: Society for Pentecostal Studies, 1983.
———. *Women Called to Witness: Evangelical Feminism in the Nineteenth Century*. Nashville, TN: Abingdon, 1984.
———. *Your Daughters Shall Prophesy: Revivalism and Feminism in the Age of Finney*. Brooklyn, NY: Carlson, 1991.
Hardt, Philip F. *The Soul of Methodism: The Class Meeting in Early New York City Methodism*. Lanham, MD: University Press of America, 2000.
Harris, Barbara, and McNamara, JoAnn, eds. *Women and the Structure of Society: Selected Research from the Fifth Berkshire Conference on the History of Women*. Durham, NC: Duke University Press, 1984.
Hartley, Benjamin L. *Evangelicals at a Crossroads: Revivalism and Social Reform in Boston, 1860–1910*. Durham: University of New Hampshire, 2011.
———. "Philadelphia's 'Five Points': Evangelism and Social Welfare at the Bedford Street Mission." *Methodist History* 48:1 (October 2009): 10–22.
———. "Salvation and Sociology in the Methodist Episcopal Deaconess Movement." *Methodist History* 40:3 (April 2002): 182–97.
Harvey, Paul. *Through the Storm, through the Night: A History of African American Christianity*. Lanham, MD: Rowman & Littlefield Publishers, 2011.
Hassey, Janette. *No Time for Silence: Evangelical Women in Public Ministry around the Turn of the Century*. Grand Rapids, MI: Zondervan, 1986.

Hatch, Nathan. *The Democratization of American Christianity*. New Haven, CT: Yale University Press, 1989.
Haywood, Chanta. *Prophesying Daughters: Black Women Preachers and the Word, 1823–1913*. Columbia: University of Missouri Press, 2003.
Helly, Dorothy O., and Susan M. Reverby, eds. *Gendered Domains: Rethinking Public and Private in Women's History: Essays from the Seventh Berkshire Conference on the History of Women*. Ithaca, NY: Cornell University Press, 1992.
Henderson, C. R. "The Place and Functions of Voluntary Associations." *American Journal of Sociology* 1 (November 1895): 327–34.
Higginbotham, Evelyn Brooks. *Righteous Discontent: The Women's Movement in the Black Baptist Church, 1880–1920*. Cambridge, MA: Harvard University Press, 1993.
Hofstadter, Richard, ed. *The Progressive Movement, 1900–1915*. Englewood Cliffs, NJ: Prentice-Hall, 1963.
Hopkins, C. Howard. *John R. Mott, 1865–1955, A Biography*. Grand Rapids, MI: Eerdmans, 1979.
———. *The Rise of the Social Gospel in American Protestantism, 1865–1915*. Yale Studies in Religious Education. New Haven, CT: Yale University Press, 1940.
Hopkins, Mary E. *As I Remember: Precious Memories of Belleview*. Seattle: Mary E. Hopkins, 1970.
Houchins, Sue, ed. *Spiritual Narratives*. New York: Oxford University Press, 1988.
Hudson, Winthrop S. "Walter Rauschenbusch and the New Evangelism." *Religion in Life* 30 (Winter 1960–61): 412–30.
Hughes, Richard T. "Preface: The Meaning of the Restoration Vision." In *The Primitive Church in the Modern World*, ed. Richard T. Hughes, ix–xviii. Urbana: University of Illinois Press, 1995.
Humez, Jean. "'My Spirit Eye': Some Functions of Spiritual and Visionary Experiences in the Lives of Five Black Women Preachers, 1810–1880." In *Women and the Structure of Society*, ed. Barbara Harris and JoAnn McNamara, 129–43. Durham, NC: Duke University Press, 1984.
Hurty, Kathleen S. "Protestant Women's Colleges in the United States." In *Encyclopedia of Women and Religion in North America*, ed. Rosemary Skinner Keller and Rosemary Radford Ruether, 2:912–23. Bloomington: Indiana University Press, 2006.
Ingersol, Stan. "Burden of Dissent: Mary Lee Cagle and the Southern Holiness Movement." Ph.D. dissertation. Duke University, 1989.
———. "The Ministry of Mary Lee Cagle: A Study in Women's History and Religion." *Wesleyan Theological Journal* (Spring–Fall 1993): 176–98.
Ingersoll, Julie. *Evangelical Christian Women: War Stores in the Gender Battles*. New York: New York University Press, 2003.
Israel, Adrienne M. *Amanda Berry Smith: From Washerwoman to Evangelist*. Lanham, MD: Scarecrow, 1998.
Israel, Jerry, ed. *Building the Organizational Society: Essays on Associational Activities in Modern America*. New York: Free Press, 1972.
Jacobsen, Douglas, ed. *A Reader in Pentecostal Theology: Voices from the First Generation*. Bloomington: Indiana University Press, 2006.
Jacobsen, Douglas, and William Vance Trollinger, eds. *Re-forming the Center: American Protestantism, 1900 to the Present*. Grand Rapids, MI: Eerdmans, 1998.
James, Janet Wilson, ed. *Women in American Religion*. Philadelphia: University of Pennsylvania Press, 1980.
Jelinek, Estelle C., ed. *Women's Autobiography: Essays in Criticism*. Bloomington: Indiana University Press, 1980.
Jensen, Richard. "Family, Career, and Reform: Women Leaders of the Progressive Era." In *The American Family in Social-Historical Perspective*, ed. Michael Gordon, 267–80. New York: St. Martin's, 1973.
Joiner, Thekla Ellen. *Sin in the City: Chicago and Revivalism, 1880–1920*. Columbia: University of Missouri Press, 2007.

Jones, Charles E. *Perfectionist Persuasion: The Holiness Movement and American Methodism, 1867-1936*. ATLA (American Theological Library Association) Monograph Series, no. 5. Metuchen, NJ: Scarecrow, 1974.
Juster, Susan. "'In a Different Voice': Male and Female Narratives of Religious Conversion in Post-Revolutionary America." *American Quarterly* 41 (March 1989): 34-62.
Kane, Paula M. *Separatism and Subculture: Boston Catholicism, 1900-1920*. Chapel Hill: University of North Carolina Press, 1994.
Kanter, Rosabeth Moss. *Commitment and Community: Communes and Utopias in Sociological Perspective*. Cambridge, MA: Harvard University Press, 1972.
Kantor, Harvey. "Vocationalism in American Education: The Economic and Political Context, 1880-1930." In *Work, Youth, and Schooling: Historical Persepectives on Vocationalism in American Education*, ed. Harvey Kantnor and David B. Tyack, 14-44. Stanford, CA: Stanford University Press, 1982.
Karson, Marc. *American Labor Union and Politics, 1900-1918*. Carbondale: Southern Illinois University Press, 1958.
Keeling, Annie. *Eminent Methodist Women*. London: Charles H. Kelly, 1889.
Keller, Rosemary Skinner. "The Deaconess: 'New Woman' of Late Nineteenth Century Methodism." *Explor* 5 (1979): 33-40.
———, ed. *Spirituality and Social Responsibility: Vocational Vision of Women in the United Methodist Tradition*. Nashville, TN: Abingdon, 1993.
———. "Women and the Nature of Ministry in the United Methodist Tradition." *Methodist History* 22 (January 1984): 99-114.
Keller, Rosemary Skinner, Ann Braude, Maureen Ursenbach Beecher, and Elizabeth Fox-Genovese. "Forum: Female Experience in American Religion." *Religion and American Culture* 5 (Winter 1995): 1-12.
Keller, Rosemary Skinner, and Rosemary Radford Ruether, eds. *Encyclopedia of Women and Religion in America*. 3 vols. San Francisco: Harper & Row, 1981-86.
———. *In Our Own Voices: Four Centuries of American Women's Religious Writing*. Louisville, KY: WJK, 1995.
Kennelly, Karen. *American Catholic Women: A Historical Exploration*. New York: Macmillan, 1989.
Kent, Eliza F. *Converting Women: Gender and Protestant Christianity in Colonial South India*. New York: Oxford University Press, 2004.
Kerber, Linda K. *Toward an Intellectual History of Women: Essays by Linda K. Kerber*. Chapel Hill: University of North Carolina Press, 1997.
Kerber, Linda K., Alice Kessler-Harris, and Kathryn Kish Sklar, eds. *U.S. History as Women's History: New Feminist Essays*. Chapel Hill: University of North Carolina Press, 1995.
Kett, Joseph F. *Rites of Passage: Adolescence in America 1790 to the Present*. New York: Basic Books, 1977.
Kostlevy, William, ed. *Historical Dictionary of the Holiness Movement*. Historical Dictionaries of Religions, Philosophies, and Movements, no. 36. Lanham, MD: Scarecrow, 2001.
———. *Holy Jumpers: Evangelicals and Radicals in Progressive Era America*. New York: Oxford University Press, 2010.
Koven, Seth, and Sonya Michel. *Mothers of a New World: Maternalist Politics and the Origins of Welfare States*. New York: Routledge, 1992.
———. "Womanly Duties: Maternalist Politics and the Origins of Welfare States in France, Germany, Great Britain, and the United States, 1880-1920." *American Historical Review* 95 (October 1990): 593-618.
Kreutziger, Sarah Sloan. "Going on to Perfection: The Contribution of Wesleyan Theological Doctrine of Entire Sanctification to the Value Base of American Professional Social Work through the Lives and Activities of 19th Century Evangelical Women Reformers." D.S.W. dissertation. Tulane University, 1991.

Krug, Edward A. *The Shaping of the American High School*. New York: Harper & Row, 1964.
Kull, Irving S., ed. *New Jersey: A History*, vol. 4. New York: American Historical Society, 1930.
Kummel, W. G. *The New Testament: The History and Investigation of Its Problems*. Nashville, TN: Abingdon, 1972.
Kunzel, Regina G. *Fallen Women, Problem Girls: Unmarried Mothers and the Professionalization of Social Work, 1890–1945*. New Haven, CT: Yale University Press, 1993.
———. "The Professionalization of Benevolence: Evangelicals and Social Workers in the Florence Crittenton Homes, 1915 to 1945." *Journal of Social History* 22 (Fall 1988): 21–43.
———. "Pulp Fictions and Problem Girls: Reading and Rewriting Single Pregnancy in the Postwar United States." *American Historical Review* (December 1995): 1465–87.
Kusmer, Kenneth. "The Function of Organized Charity in the Progressive Era: Chicago as a Case Study." *Journal of American History* 60 (December 1973): 657–78.
Larson T.A. "Dolls, Vassals and Drudges: Pioneer Women in the West." *Western Historical Quarterly* 3 (January 1972): 5–16.
Lasch-Quinn, Elisabeth. *Black Neighbors: Race and the Limits of Reform in the American Settlement House Movement, 1890–1945*. Chapel Hill: University of North Carolina Press, 1993.
Lawless, Elaine J. *Handmaidens of the Lord: Pentecostal Women Preachers and Traditional Religion*. Philadelphia: University of Pennsylvania Press, 1988.
Lawrence, Evan Jerry. "Alma White College: A History of Its Relationship to the Development of the Pillar of Fire." Ed.D. dissertation. Columbia University, 1966.
Lazerson, Marvin, and W. Norton Grubb. "Introduction." In *American Education and Vocationalism: A Documentary History, 1870–1970*, ed. Marvin Lazerson and W. Norton Grubb, 1–50. New York: Teachers College Press, 1974.
Lebsock, Suzanne. "Women and American Politics: 1880–1920." In *Women, Politics, and Change*, ed. Louise Tilly and Patricia Gurin, 35–62. New York: Russell Sage Foundation, 1990.
Leclerc, Diane. *Singleness of Heart: Gender, Sin, and Holiness in Historical Perspective*. Lanham, MD: Scarecrow, 2002.
Lee, Shayne, and Phillip Luke Sinitiere. *Holy Mavericks: Evangelical Innovators and the Spiritual Marketplace*. New York: New York University Press, 2009.
Lewis, Meharry H. *Beauty of Holiness: A Small Catechism of the Holiness Faith and Doctrine*. Nashville, TN: New and Living Way, 1990.
———. *Mary Lena Lewis Tate: Thundering Daughters, the First One Hundred Years, Ordained Women Preachers in the Church of the Living God, the Pillar and Ground of the Truth, Inc. (A Black Female's Legacy)*. Nashville, TN: New and Living Way, 2009.
———. *Mary Lena Lewis Tate: Vision!* Nashville, TN: New and Living Way, 2005.
———, ed. *Mary Lena Lewis Tate: Collected Letters and Manuscripts*. Nashville, TN: New and Living Way, 2003.
Lindley, Susan Hill. *"You Have Stept Out of Your Place": A History of Women and Religion in America*. Louisville, KY: WJK, 1996.
Loewenberg, Bert James, and Ruth Bogin, eds. *Black Women in Nineteenth-Century American Life: Their Words, Their Thoughts, Their Feelings*. University Park: Pennsylvania State University Press, 1976.
Lubove, Roy. *The Professional Altruist: The Emergence of Social Work as a Career, 1880–1930*. Cambridge, MA: Harvard University Press, 1965.
Macleod, David I. *The Age of the Child: Children in America, 1890–1920*. New York: Twayne, 1998.
———. *Building Character in the American Boy: The Boy Scouts, YMCA, and Their Forerunners, 1870–1920*. Madison: University of Wisconsin Press, 1983.
Maddox, Randy. "Reconnecting the Means to the End: A Wesleyan Prescription for the Holiness Movement." *Wesleyan Theological Journal* 33:2 (1998): 29–66.
———. *Responsible Grace: John Wesley's Practical Theology*. Nashville, TN: Kingswood, 1994.

———. "Wesley's Understanding of Christian Perfection: In What Sense Pentecostal?" *Wesleyan Theological Journal* 34:2 (1999): 78–83.
Maffly-Kipp, Laurie F., Leigh Eric Schmidt, and Mark R. Valeri. *Practicing Protestants: Histories of Christian Life in America, 1630–1965*. Baltimore, MD: Johns Hopkins University Press, 2006.
Magnuson, Norris. *Salvation in the Slums: Evangelical Social Work, 1865–1920*. ATLA (American Theological Library Association) Monograph Series, No. 10. Metuchen, NJ: Scarecrow, 1977.
Mapes, Mary L. "Visions of a Christian City: The Politics of Religion and Gender in Chicago's City Missions and Protestant Settlement Houses, 1886–1929." Ph.D. dissertation. Michigan State University, 1998.
Marlett, Jeffrey D. *Saving the Heartland: Catholic Missionaries in Rural America, 1920–1960*. DeKalb: Northern Illinois University Press, 2002.
Marsden, George M. "Fundamentalism." In *Encyclopedia of the American Religious Experience: Studies of Traditions and Movements*, ed. Charles H. Lippy and Peter W. Williams, 2:947–62. New York: Scribner, 1988.
———. *Reforming Fundamentalism: Fuller Seminary and the New Evangelicalism*. Grand Rapids, MI: Eerdmans, 1987.
Marty, Martin. *Protestantism in the United States: Righteous Empire*, 2nd ed. New York: Charles Scribner's Sons, 1986.
Matthews, Glenna. *The Rise of Public Woman: Woman's Power and Woman's Place in the United States, 1630–1970*. New York: Oxford University Press, 1992.
McAvoy, Thomas T. "The Catholic Minority after the Americanist Controversy, 1899–1917: A Survey." *Review of Politics* 21 (1959): 53–82.
McCarthy, Kathleen, ed. *Lady Bountiful Revisited: Women, Philanthropy and Power*. New Brunswick, NJ: Rutgers University Press, 1991.
———. *Noblesse Oblige: Charity and Cultural Philanthropy in Chicago, 1849–1929*. Chicago: University of Chicago Press, 1982.
McClymond, Michael J., ed. *Embodying the Spirit: New Perspectives on North American Revivalism*. Baltimore, MD: Johns Hopkins University Press, 2004.
McDannell, Colleen. *The Christian Home in Victorian America, 1840–1900*. Bloomington: Indiana University Press, 1986.
———. *Material Christianity: Religion and Popular Culture in America*. New Haven, CT: Yale University Press, 1995.
McGee, Gary B. *Miracles, Missions, and American Pentecostalism*. American Society of Missiology Series, no. 45. Maryknoll, NY: Orbis, 2010.
———. "Three Notable Women in Pentecostal Ministry." *A/G Heritage* (Spring 1985–86): 3–5, 12, 16.
McGerr, Michael. *A Fierce Discontent: The Rise and Fall of the Progressive Movement in America, 1870–1920*. New York: Free Press, 2003.
McKinley, Edward H. *Marching to Glory: the History of the Salvation Army in the United States of America*, 1880–1980. San Francisco: Harper & Row, 1980.
———. *Somebody's Brother: A History of The Salvation Army Men's Social Service Department, 1891–1985*. Studies in American Religion, vol. 21. Lewiston, NY: Edwin Mellen, 1986.
McKinney, Larry J. "The Fundamentalist Bible School as an Outgrowth of the Changing Patterns of Protestant Revivalism, 1882–1920." *Religious Education* 84 (Fall 1989): 589–605.
McLoughlin, William G. *Billy Sunday Was His Real Name*. Chicago: University of Chicago Press, 1955.
———. *Modern Revivalism: Charles Grandison Finney to Billy Graham*. New York: Ronald Press, 1959.
———. *Revivals, Awakenings, and Reform: An Essay on Religion and Social Change in America, 1607–1977*. Chicago: University of Chicago Press, 1978.

McReynolds, Mary. *Redeeming Love: The Legacy of the Deaconess Ladies*. Oklahoma: n.p., [2000?].
Merwick, Donna. *Boston Priests, 1848-1910: A Study of Social and Intellectual Change*. Cambridge, MA: Harvard University Press, 1973.
Miller, Glenn T. *Piety and Profession: American Protestant Theological Education, 1870-1970*. Grand Rapids, MI: Eerdmans, 2007.
Mitchell, Michele. *Righteous Propagation: African Americans and the Politics of Racial Destiny After Reconstruction*. Chapel Hill: University of North Carolina Press, 2004.
Mitchinson, Wendy. "The Woman's Christian Temperance Union: A Study in Organization." *International Journal of Women's Studies* 4:2 (1981): 143-56.
Moloney, Deirdre M. *American Catholic Lay Groups and Transatlantic Social Reform in the Progressive Era*. Chapel Hill: University of North Carolina Press, 2002.
Moncher, Gary Richard. "The Bible College and American Moral Culture." Ph.D. dissertation. University of California, Berkeley, 1987.
Mosteller, James D. "Something Old—Something New: The First Fifty Years of Northern Baptist Theological Seminary." *Foundations* 8 (January 1965): 26-48.
Mountford, Roxanne. *The Gendered Pulpit: Preaching in American Protestant Spaces*. Carbondale: Southern Illinois University Press, 2003.
Mullin, Robert Bruce. *Miracles and the Modern Religious Imagination*. New Haven, CT: Yale University Press, 1996.
Neal, Lynn S. "Christianizing the Klan: Alma White, Branford Clarke, and the Art of Religious Intolerance." *Church History* 78:2 (June 2009): 350-78.
Neely, Jon R. "Maria B. Woodworth-Etter and the Churches of God." *Church Advocate* (August 1975): 2-7.
Neill, Stephen. *The Interpretation of the New Testament, 1861-1961*. New York: Oxford University Press, 1964.
Noll, Mark A. *America's God: From Jonathan Edwards to Abraham Lincoln*. New York: Oxford University Press, 2002.
Noll, William. "Women as Clergy and Laity in the 19c Methodist Protestant Church." *Methodist History* 15 (January 1977): 107-21.
O'Connor, Thomas. *Boston Catholics: A History of the Church and Its People*. Boston: Northeastern University Press, 1998.
Offen, Karen. "Defining Feminism: A Comparative Historical Approach." *Signs* 14 (1988): 119-57.
Offord, R. M., ed. *Jerry McAuley, His Life and Work*. New York: New York Observer, 1885.
O'Neill, William. *Divorce in the Progressive Era*. New Haven, CT: Yale University Press, 1967.
Opp, James W. "Healing Hands, Healthy Bodies: Protestant Women and Faith Healing in Canada and the United States, 1880-1930." In *Women and Twentieth-Century Protestantism*, ed. Margaret Lamberts Bendroth and Virginia Lieson Brereton, 236-56. Urbana: University of Illinois Press, 2002.
Orr, James. *The Problem of the Old Testament, Considered with Reference to Recent Criticism*. Originally published 1906. Reprint, New York: Charles Scribner's Sons, 1917.
Orsi, Robert, "Dangerous Abuelitas: The Gender of Religious Otherness." *Women and Twentieth Century Protestantism Newsletter* (Winter 1999): 8-11.
———. *The Madonna of 115th Street: Faith and Community in Italian Harlem, 1880-1950*. New Haven, CT: Yale University Press, 1985.
Overton, Betty. "Black Women Preachers: A Literary View." *Southern Quarterly* 23 (Spring 1985): 157-66.
Painter, Nell Irvin. *Standing at Armageddon: The United States, 1877-1919*. New York: W. W. Norton, 2008.
Pascoe, Peggy. *Relations of Rescue: The Search for Female Moral Authority in the American West, 1874-1939*. New York: Oxford University Press, 1990.

Paul, William E. *The Romance of Rescue*. N.p.: n.p., 1948.
Peden, W. Creighton. "The Chicago School (1906–1926) in American Religious Thought and Its Contribution to a Better Understanding of Ultimate Reality and Meaning of Human Experience." *Ultimate Reality and Meaning* 6 (March 1983): 51–79.
———. "Shailer Mathews." In *Makers of Christian Theology in America*, ed. Mark G. Toulouse and James O. Duke, 392–98. Nashville, TN: Abingdon, 1997.
Peterson, Carla L. *"Doers of the Word": African American Writers and Speakers in the North, 1830–1880*. New York: Oxford University Press, 1995.
Phillips, Paul T. *A Kingdom on Earth: Anglo-American Social Christianity, 1880–1940*. University Park: Pennsylvania State University Press, 1996.
Pivar, David J. *Purity Crusade: Sexual Morality and Social Control, 1868–1900*. Westport, CT: Greenwood, 1973.
Pope-Levison, Priscilla. "Emma Ray in Black and White: The Intersection of Race, Region, and Religion." *Pacific Northwest Quarterly* (Summer 2011): 107–16.
———. "Holiness and Pentecostal Movements within Methodism." In *The Ashgate Research Companion to World Methodism*, ed. Peter Forsaith, William Gibson, and Martin Wellings, 141–55. London: Ashgate, 2013.
———. "Methodist Interracial Cooperation in the Progressive Era: Amanda Berry Smith and Emma Ray." *Methodist History* 49 (January 2011): 68–85.
———. "Revivalism." In *Encyclopedia of Women and Religion in North America*, ed. Rosemary Skinner Keller and Rosemary Radford Ruether, 416–24. Bloomington: Indiana University Press, 2006.
———. "'A Thirty Year War' and More: Exposing Complexities in the Methodist Deaconess Movement." *Methodist History* 47:2 (January 2009): 101–16.
———. *Turn the Pulpit Loose: Two Centuries of American Women Evangelists*. New York: Palgrave Macmillan, 2004.
Porterfield, Amanda. *Feminine Spirituality in America: From Sarah Edwards to Martha Graham*. Philadelphia : Temple University Press, 1980.
Powers, Jane Bernard. *The "Girl Question" in Education: Vocational Education for Young Women in the Progressive Era*. Washington, DC: Falmer, 1992.
Prelinger, Catherine M., and Rosemary Skinner Keller. "The Function of Female Bonding: The Restored Diaconessate of the Nineteenth Century." In *Women in New Worlds*, vol. 2, ed. Rosemary Skinner Keller, Louise L. Queen, and Hilah F. Thomas, 318–37. Nashville, TN: Abingdon, 1982.
Putnam, Robert. *Bowling Alone: The Collapse and Revival of American Community*. New York: Simon & Schuster, 2000.
Rack, H. D. "Domestic Visitation: A Chapter in Early Nineteenth Century Evangelism." *Journal of Ecclesiastical History* 24 (October 1973): 357–76.
Reist, John S. "The Dread of the Father: An Analysis of the Theological Method of Shailer Mathews." *Foundations* 8 (July 1965): 239–55.
Riegel, Robert E., "Changing American Attitudes toward Prostitution (1800–1920)." *Journal of the History of Ideas* 29 (July–September 1968): 437–52.
Riess, Steven. *Touching Base: Professional Baseball and American Culture in the Progressive Era*. Urbana: University of Illinois Press, 1999.
Robeck, Cecil M. "Florence Crawford: Apostolic Faith Pioneer." In *Portraits of a Generation: Early Pentecostal Leaders*, ed. James R. Goff and Grant Wacker, 219–35. Fayetteville: University of Arkansas Press, 2002.
Robert, Dana L. *American Women in Mission: A Social History of Their Thought and Practice*. Macon, GA: Mercer University Press, 1996.
———. "Protestant Women Missionaries: Foreign and Home." In *Encyclopedia of Women and Religion in North America*, ed. Rosemary Skinner Keller and Rosemary Radford Ruether, 2:834–43. Bloomington: Indiana University Press, 2006.

———. "Shifting Southward: Global Christianity since 1945." *International Bulletin of Missionary Research* 24 (April 2000): 50–58.
Roberts, Liardon, comp. *Maria Woodworth-Etter: The Complete Collection of Her Life Teachings*. Tulsa, OK: Albury Publishing, 2000.
Robertson, Darrel M. *The Chicago Revival, 1876: Society and Revivalism in a Nineteenth-Century City*. Metuchen, NJ: Scarecrow, 1989.
Robinson, Thomas A., and Lanette D. Ruff. *Out of the Mouths of Babes: Girl Evangelists in the Flapper Era*. New York: Oxford University Press, 2012.
Rodgers, Daniel T. *Atlantic Crossings: Social Politics in a Progressive Age*. Cambridge, MA: Belknap Press, 1998.
Roebuck, David G. "Go and Tell My Brothers: The Waning of Women's Voices in American Pentecostalism." In *Continuity and Change in the Pentecostal and Charismatic Movements*, Twentieth Annual Meeting of the Society for Pentecostal Studies, F1–F19. Dallas, TX: Christ for the Nations Institute, 1990.
———. "Pentecostal Women in Ministry: A Review of Selected Documents." *Perspectives in Religious Studies* 16 (Spring 1989): 29–44.
Rose, Delbert R. *Vital Holiness: A Theology of Christian Experience*. Minneapolis: Bethany Fellowship, Inc., 1975.
Rosen, Ruth. *The Lost Sisterhood: Prostitution in America, 1900–1918*. Baltimore, MD: Johns Hopkins University Press, 1982.
Rotella, Elyce J. *From Home to Office: U.S. Women at Work, 1870–1930*. Ann Arbor, MI: UMI Research Press, 1981.
Rothman, Sheila M. *Woman's Proper Place: A History of Changing Ideals and Practices, 1870 to the Present*. New York: Basic Books, 1978.
Rudy, Willis. "From Normal School to Multi-purpose College." *History of Education Quarterly* (Summer 1980): 241–46.
Ruelas, Abraham. *Women and the Landscape of American Higher Education: Wesleyan Holiness and Pentecostal Founders*. Eugene, OR: Pickwick, 2010.
Ruggles, Steven. "Fallen Women: The Inmates of the Magdalen Society Asylum in Philadelphia, 1836–1908." *Journal of Social History* 16 (Summer 1983): 65–82.
Rury, John L. *Education and Women's Work: Female Schooling and the Division of Labor in Urban America, 1870–1930*. Albany: State University of New York Press, 1991.
Ryan, Mary P. *Civic Wars: Democracy and Public Life in the American City during the Nineteenth Century*. Berkeley: University of California Press, 1997.
———. *Cradle of the Middle Class: The Family in Oneida County, New York, 1790–1865*, Interdisciplinary Perspectives on Modern History. New York: Cambridge University Press, 1981.
———. *Women in Public: Between Banners and Ballots, 1825–1880*. Baltimore, MD: Johns Hopkins University Press, 1990.
Sadovnik, Alan, and Susan Semel. *Founding Mothers and Others: Women Educational Leaders during the Progressive Era*. New York: Palgrave, 2002.
Sanders, Cheryl J. *Saints in Exile: The Holiness-Pentecostal Experience in African American Religion and Culture*. New York: Oxford University Press, 1996.
Scanzoni, Letha Dawson, and Susan Setta. "Women in Evangelical, Holiness, and Pentecostal Traditions." In *Women and Religion in America*, vol. 3, *1900–1968*, ed. Rosemary Skinner Keller and Rosemary Radford Ruether, 223–65. San Francisco: Harper & Row, 1986.
Schier, Tracy. "Catholic Women's Colleges in the United States." In *Encyclopedia of Women and Religion in North America*, ed. Rosemary Skinner Keller and Rosemary Radford Ruether, 2:881–89. Bloomington: Indiana University Press, 2006.
Schirmer, Sherry Lamb. *A City Divided: The Racial Landscape of Kansas City, 1900–1960*. Columbia: University of Missouri Press, 2002.

Schlesinger, Arthur, Jr. "Biography of a Nation of Joiners." *American Historical Review* 50 (October 1944): 1–25.

———. "A Critical Period in American Religion, 1875–1900." *Proceedings of the Massachusetts Historical Society* 64 (1932–33): 523–47.

Schmidt, Alvin J. *Fraternal Organizations. The Greenwood Encyclopedia of American Institutions.* Westport, CT: Greenwood, 1980.

Schmidt, Jean Miller. "Denominational History When Gender Is the Focus: Women in American Methodism." In *Reimagining Denominationalism*, ed. Robert Bruce Mullin and Russell A. Richey, 203–21. New York: Oxford University Press, 1994.

———. *Grace Sufficient: A History of Women in American Methodism, 1760–1939.* Nashville, TN: Abingdon, 1999.

———. "Reexamining the Public/Private Split: Reforming the Continent and Spreading Scriptural Holiness." In *Perspectives on American Methodism: Interpretive Essays*, ed. Russell Richey, Kenneth Rowe, and Jean Miller Schmidt, 228–47. Nashville, TN: Kingswood, 1993.

———. *Souls or the Social Order: The Two-Party System in American Protestantism.* Brooklyn, NY: Carlson Publishing, 1991.

Schneider, A. Gregory. "'Heart Religion' on the Divide." In *"Heart Religion" in the Methodist Tradition and Related Movements*, ed. Rick Steele, 127–74. Lanham, MD: Scarecrow, 2001.

———. *The Way of the Cross Leads Home: The Domestication of American Methodism.* Bloomington: Indiana University Press, 1993.

Scott, Anne Firor. *Making the Invisible Woman Visible.* Urbana: University of Illinois Press, 1984.

———. *Natural Allies: Women's Associations in American History.* Women in American History. Urbana: University of Illinois Press, 1991.

———. "On Seeing and Not Seeing: A Case of Historical Invisibility." *Journal of American History* 71:1 (1984): 8–10.

Scott, Joan. "Gender: A Useful Category of Historical Analysis." *American Historical Review* 91 (December 1985): 1053–75.

Seath, William. *A Study of Rescue Missions.* Chicago: Chicago Christian Industrial League, 1954.

Sedlak, Michael W. "Young Women and the City: Adolescent Deviance and the Transformation of Educational Policy, 1870–1960." *History of Education Quarterly* 23 (Spring 1983): 1–28.

Selles, Johanna M. *The World Student Christian Federation, 1895–1925: Motives, Methods, and Influential Women.* Eugene, OR: Wipf & Stock, 2011.

Shaw, Anna Howard. *Anna Howard Shaw: The Story of a Pioneer.* William Bradford Collection, ed. Barbara Brown Zikmund. Cleveland, OH: Pilgrim Press, 1994.

Sheehan, Nancy. "'Women Helping Women': The WCTU and the Foreign Population in the West, 1905–1930." *International Journal of Women's Studies* 6 (November–December 1983): 395–441.

Sklar, Kathryn Kish. "A Call for Comparisons." *American Historical Review* 95:4 (October 1990): 1109–14.

———. *Florence Kelley and the Nation's Work: The Rise of Women's Political Culture, 1830–1900.* New Haven, CT: Yale University Press, 1995.

———. "Hull House in the 1890s: A Community of Women Reformers." *Signs* 10 (Summer 1985): 658–77.

Smith, Constance, and Anne Freedman. *Voluntary Associations: Perspectives on the Literature.* Cambridge, MA: Harvard University Press, 1972.

Smith, Daniel Scott, and Michael S. Hindus. "Premarital Pregnancy in America, 1640–1971: An Overview and Interpretation." *Journal of Interdisciplinary History* 5 (Spring 1975): 537–70.

Smith, Kenneth, and Leonard Sweet. "Shailer Mathews: A Chapter in the Social Gospel Movement." *Foundations* 18:3 (1975): 219–37.

Smith, Timothy. *Revivalism and Social Reform.* Nashville, TN: Abingdon, 1957.

Smith-Rosenberg, Carroll. *Religion and the Rise of the American City: The New York City Mission Movement, 1812–1870*. Ithaca, NY: Cornell University Press, 1971.
Soden, Dale. *The Rev. Mark Matthews: An Activist in the Progressive Era*. Seattle: University of Washington Press, 2000.
Stanley, Susie C. *Feminist Pillar of Fire: The Life of Alma White*. Cleveland, OH: Pilgrim Press, 1993.
———. *Holy Boldness: Women Preachers' Autobiographies and the Sanctified Self*. Knoxville: University of Tennessee Press, 2002.
———. "The Promise Fulfilled: Women's Ministries in the Wesleyan/Holiness Movement." In *Religious Institutions and Women's Leadership: New Roles inside the Mainstream*, ed. Catherine Wessinger, 139–57. Columbia: University of South Carolina Press, 1996.
———. "'Tell Me the Old Old Story': An Analysis of Autobiographies by Holiness Women." *Wesleyan Theological Journal* 29 (Spring–Fall 1994): 7–22.
Stebner, Eleanor J. "The Settlement House Movement." In *Encyclopedia of Women and Religion in North America*, ed. Rosemary Skinner Keller and Rosemary Radford Ruether, 3:1059–68. Indianapolis: Indiana University Press, 2006.
Stelzle, Charles. "The Evangelist in Present-Day America." *Current History* 35 (November 1931): 224–28.
Stephens, Randall. *The Fire Spreads: Holiness and Pentecostalism in the American South*. Cambridge, MA: Harvard University Press, 2008.
Storms, Jeannette. "Carrie Judd Montgomery: The Little General." In *Portraits of a Generation: Early Pentecostal Leaders*, ed. James R. Goff and Grant Wacker, 271–87. Fayetteville: University of Arkansas Press, 2002.
Stout, Harry S. *The Divine Dramatist: George Whitefield and the Rise of Modern Evangelicalism*. Library of Religious Biography. Grand Rapids, MI: Eerdmans, 1991.
Strong, Doug. *They Walked in the Spirit: Personal Faith and Social Action in America*. Louisville, KY: WJK, 1997.
Sutton, Matthew. *Aimee Semple McPherson and the Resurrection of Christian America*. Cambridge, MA: Harvard University Press, 2007.
———. "Clutching to 'Christian' America." *Journal of Policy History* 17:3 (July 2005): 308–38.
Sweet, Leonard I. *The Minister's Wife: Her Role in Nineteenth-Century American Evangelicalism*. Philadelphia: Temple University Press, 1983.
———. "Nineteenth-Century Evangelicalism." In *Encyclopedia of the American Religious Experience: Studies of Traditions and Movements*, ed. Charles H. Lippy and Peter W. Williams, 875–99. New York: Scribner, 1988.
Sweet, William Warren. *Revivalism in America: Its Origin, Growth and Decline*. New York: Charles Scribner's Sons, 1944.
Synan, Vinson. *The Holiness-Pentecostal Tradition: Charismatic Movements in the Twentieth Century*. Grand Rapids, MI: Eerdmans, 1997.
———, ed. *Aspects of Pentecostal-Charismatic Origins*. Plainfield, NJ: Logos, 1975.
Szasz, Ferenc M. *The Divided Mind of Protestant America, 1880–1930*. Tuscaloosa: University of Alabama Press, 1982.
———. "Protestantism and the Search for Stability: Liberal and Conservative Quests for a Christian America, 1872–1925." In *Building the Organizational Society: Essays on Associational Activities in Modern America*, ed. Jerry Israel, 88–102. New York: Free Press, 1972.
Taiz, Lillan. *Hallelujah Lads and Lasses: Remaking the Salvation Army in America, 1880–1930*. Chapel Hill: University of North Carolina Press, 2001.
Tappan, Richard E. "The Dominance of Men in the Domain of Women: The History of Four Protestant Church Training Schools, 1880–1918." Ed.D. dissertation. Temple University, 1979.
Taves, Ann. "Feminization Revisited: Protestantism and Gender at the Turn of the Century." In *Women and Twentieth-Century Protestantism*, ed. Margaret Lamberts Bendroth and Virginia Lieson Brereton, 304–24. Urbana: University of Illinois Press, 2002.

———. *Fits, Trances, and Visions: Experiencing Religion and Explaining Experience from Wesley to James*. Princeton, NJ: Princeton University Press, 1999.
———. "Women and Gender in American Religion(s)." *Religious Studies Review* 18 (October 1992): 263–70.
Taylor, Quintard. "Blacks in the American West: An Overview." *Western Journal of Black Studies* 1 (March 1977): 4–10.
———. "The Emergence of Black Communities in the Pacific Northwest, 1864–1910." *Journal of Negro History* 64 (Fall 1979): 346–51.
Thomas, Hilah, Rosemary Skinner Keller, and Louise L. Queen, eds. *Women in New Worlds: Historical Perspectives on the Wesleyan Tradition*. 2 vols. Nashville, TN: Abingdon, 1982.
Ting, K. H. "Retrospect and Prospect." *International Review of Mission* 70 (April 1981): 25–42.
Tomko, Linda J. *Dancing Class: Gender, Ethnicity, and Social Divides in American Dance, 1890–1920*. Bloomington: Indiana University Press, 1999.
Tucker, Cynthia Grant. *Prophetic Sisterhood: Liberal Women Ministers of the Frontier, 1880–1930*. Boston: Beacon, 1990.
Valenze, Deborah. *Prophetic Sons and Daughters*. Princeton, NJ: Princeton University Press, 1985.
van Butselaar, Jan. "Christian Conversion in Rwanda: The Motivations." *International Bulletin of Missionary Research* 5 (July 1981): 111–13.
Varnhagen, Jim. "Setting the Oppressed Free: New York City Rescue Mission." In *Signs of Hope in the City: Ministries of Community Renewal*, ed. Robert D. Carle and Louis A. Decaro, 235–45. Valley Forge, PA: Judson, 1999.
Wacker, Grant. *Heaven Below: Early Pentecostals and American Culture*. Cambridge, MA: Harvard University Press, 2001.
———. "The Holy Spirit and the Spirit of the Age in American Protestantism, 1880–1910." In *New and Intense Movements*, vol. 11 of *Modern American Protestantism and Its World*, ed. Martin Marty, 181–198. New York: K. G. Saur, 1993.
———. "A Profile of American Pentecostalism." In *Pastoral Problems in the Pentecostal-Charismatic Movement*, ed. Harold D. Hunter, Thirteenth Annual Conference of the Society for Pentecostal Studies, 1–47. Cleveland, TN: Society for Pentecostal Studies, 1983.
———. "Searching for Eden with a Satellite Dish: Primitivism, Pragmatism, and the Pentecostal Character." In *The Primitive Church in the Modern World*, ed. Richard T. Hughes, 139–66. Urbana: University of Illinois Press, 1995.
Wallace, James A. "Reconsidering the Parish Mission." *Worship* 67:4 (July 1993): 340–51.
Wangler, Thomas E. "Americanist Beliefs and Papal Orthodoxy: 1884–1889." *U.S. Catholic Historian* 11 (Summer 1993): 19–35.
Warkentin, Raija. "Begging as Resistance: Wealth and Christian Missionaries in Postcolonial Zaire." *Missiology: An International Review* 29 (April 2001): 146–49.
Warner, Laceye C. *Saving Women: Retrieving Evangelistic Theology and Practice*. Waco, TX: Baylor University Press, 2007.
Warner, Wayne E. *Maria Woodworth-Etter: For Such a Time as This*. Gainesville, FL: Bridge-Logos, 2004.
———. "Maria B. Woodworth-Etter: Prophet of Equality." In *Portraits of a Generation: Early Pentecostal Leaders*, ed. James R. Goff and Grant Wacker, 199–216. Fayetteville: University of Arkansas Press, 2002.
———. *The Woman Evangelist: The Life and Times of Charismatic Evangelist Maria B. Woodworth-Etter*. Studies in Evangelicalism, no. 8. Metuchen, NJ: Scarecrow, 1986.
Watson, Frank D. *The Charity Organization Movement in the United States*. New York: Macmillan, 1922.
Weber, Timothy P. *Living in the Shadow of the Second Coming: American Premillennialism, 1875–1925*. Chicago: University of Chicago Press, 1987.

Weisenfeld, Judith, and Richard Newman, eds. *This Far by Faith: Readings in African-American Women's Religious Biography*. Columbia: University of South Carolina Press, 1996.

Wessinger, Catherine, ed. *Religious Institutions and Women's Leadership: New Roles inside the Mainstream*. Columbia: University of South Carolina Press, 1996.

———. *Women's Leadership in Marginal Religions: Explorations outside the Mainstream*. Urbana: University of Illinois Press, 1993.

Wessinger, Catherine, Dell deChant, and William Michael Ashcraft. "Theosophy, New Thought, and New Age Movements." In *Encyclopedia of Women and Religion in North America*, ed. Rosemary Skinner Keller and Rosemary Radford Ruether, 2:753–68. Indianapolis: Indiana University Press, 2006.

Wills, David W. "Aspects of Social Thought in the African Methodist Episcopal Church, 1884–1910." Ph.D. dissertation. Harvard University, 1977.

Wilson, Otto. *Fifty Years' Work with Girls, 1883–1933: A Story of the Florence Crittenton Homes*. Alexandria, VA: National Florence Crittenton Mission, 1933.

Winston, Diane. "Living in the Material World: Salvation Army Lassies and Urban Commercial Culture, 1880–1918." In *Faith in the Market: Religion and the Rise of Urban Commercial Culture*, ed. John M. Giggie and Diane Winston, 13–36. New Brunswick, NJ: Rutgers University Press, 2002.

———. *Red-Hot and Righteous: The Urban Religion of the Salvation Army*. Cambridge, MA: Harvard University Press, 1999.

Wisbey, Herbert A. *Soldiers without Swords: A History of the Salvation Army in the United States*. New York: Macmillan, 1955.

Witmer, S. A. *Education with Dimension: The Bible College Story*. Manhasset, NY: Channel Press, 1962.

Wolf, Naomi. *The Beauty Myth: How Images of Beauty Are Used against Women*. New York: William Morrow, 1991.

Wolfram, Gertrude Metlen. *The Widow of Zarephath: A Church in the Making*. Zarephath, NJ: Pillar of Fire, 1954.

Wood, Ann Douglas. "'The Fashionable Diseases': Women's Complaints and Their Treatment in Nineteenth-Century America." In *Clio's Consciousness Raised: New Perspectives on the History of Women*, ed. Mary Hartman and Lois W. Banner, 1–22. New York: Harper & Row, 1974.

Wood, Laurence W. *The Meaning of Pentecost in Early Methodism: Rediscovering John Fletcher as John Wesley's Vindicator and Designated Successor*. Nashville, TN: Abingdon, 2002.

Woods, Thomas E. *The Church Confronts Modernity: Catholic Intellectuals and the Progressive Era*. New York: Columbia University Press, 2004.

Wright, Daniel S. *"The First of Causes to Our Sex": The Female Moral Reform Movement in the Antebellum Northeast, 1843–1848*. Studies in American Popular History and Culture. New York: Routledge, 2006.

Young, Warren Cameron. *Commit What You Have Heard: A History of Northern Baptist Theological Seminary, 1913–1988*. Wheaton, IL: Harold Shaw, 1988.

Zink-Sawyer, Beverly. *From Preacher to Suffragists: Woman's Rights and Religious Conviction in the Lives of Three Nineteenth-Century American Clergywomen*. Louisville, KY: WJK, 2003.

Zmora, Nurith. *Orphanages Reconsidered: Child Care Institutions in Progressive Era Baltimore*. Philadelphia: Temple University Press, 1994.

INDEX OF NAMES AND SUBJECTS

Addams, Jane, 19, 156, 157, 170. *See also* Hull House
African Americans, 61–62, 68, 71, 81, 98, 108, 151–52; children, missions for, 5, 141, 151–52, 212n6; colleges, 130; discrimination against, 165, 230n125; in social work, 143
African Methodist Episcopal Church (AME), 7, 13, 152
Ahlstrom, Sydney, 22–23
Aiken Institute, 149. *See also* Dean, John Marvin
Alma White College, 91, 113. *See also* White, Alma
altar, 10, 56, 57, 61, 62, 68, 80, 112, 118, 174
American Association of Women Preachers, 133–34
American Bible Society, 118
Angelus Temple, 178; Commissary, 179–80. *See also* International Church of the Foursquare Gospel; McPherson, Aimee Semple
Anthony, Susan B., 37
Apostolic Faith, 95, 99
Apostolic Faith Mission (AFM), 5, 13, 23; annual camp meeting, 100–101; founded, 47, 69; gospel grenades, 48–49; headquarters, 99; schisms, 210n117; street meetings, 28–29; transportation, 47–49, 200n87; on women preachers, 92. *See also* Crawford, Florence Louise
Asher, Virginia, 62. *See also* Billy Sunday Evangelistic Organization
Association of Gospel Rescue Missions (AGRM), 149, 227n71
Atlanta Female Baptist Seminary, 130
autobiography, 5, 45, 55, 57–58, 68, 136, 153, 165
Avery, Katherine (Rev. Mother St. Mary), 52–54, 55

Avery, Martha Moore, 5, 13, 23, 27–28, 39, 53, 65, 201n94; on Billy Sunday, 41–42; Catholic Truth Guild, 30–36, 42, 50–56, 182, 197n21; conversion to Catholicism, 8, 30–31; correspondence, 52–54, 55; and David Goldstein, 30–31, 53–54; involvement with Socialism 32, 46, 197n15, 201n94; pseudonyms, 29–30, 36, 51–52, 196n8; on women, 51–52, 201n94, 202n99; and William O'Connell, 55, 203n114
Avery, Millard, 54–55
Azusa Street Mission, 5, 12, 40, 69, 82, 86, 96–99. *See also* Seymour, William

Baker, Elizabeth, 24, 62, 113, 123, 174; call to preach, 59–60. *See also* Rochester Bible Training School
baptism, 77, 79, 82, 101. *See also* Holy Spirit: baptism of
Baptist Missionary Training School, 114
Baptists, 76, 148
Barrett, Kate Waller, 164, 167. *See also* National Florence Crittenton Mission
Belleview College, 91, 113. *See also* White, Alma
Bendroth, Margaret, 16, 62
Bennett College, 130
Beth-Adriel, 166–67. *See also* Roberts, Florence
Bethel Bible School, 12
Bethel Bible Training School, 113. *See also* Draper, Minnie
Beulah Heights Bible and Missionary Training School, 113. *See also* Moss, Virginia
Beulah Rescue Home, 142. *See also* Montgomery, Carrie Judd

Bible, the, 1, 6, 18, 20, 21, 22, 24, 31, 72, 77, 85, 90–94, 113, 116, 122, 123, 129, 133, 134; study of, 20, 70, 112, 120, 122, 123, 126, 127, 137, 165, 178. See also biblical figures; biblical interpretation; women preachers: biblical defense of. See also Index of Scripture References
Bible Institute of Los Angeles, 113
Bible Standard Church, 210n117
Bible Work of Chicago, 115. See also Dryer, Emma
biblical figures, 4; Adam, 85, 94; Anna, 91; beggar at Jericho, 153; Deborah, 91; disciples, 101; Elijah, 91; Esther, 91; Eve, 85, 94; Huldah, 91; John the Baptist, 74; Mary Magdalene, 91, 153; Mary, mother of Jesus, 87; Paul, 72, 91, 93, 118, 123; Peter, 91, 153; Philip's daughters, 91, 117; Phoebe, 91; Priscilla, 91; Samaritan woman, 91; Satan, 94, 145, 154, 159; Timotheus, 72
biblical interpretation, 22–23, 72: spiritual application method, 123. See also higher criticism; inerrancy
Billy Sunday Evangelistic Organization, 23, 44–45, 176; role of women in, 29, 62. See also Asher, Virginia; Saxe, Grace; Sunday, Billy; Sunday, Helen
Binney, Amos, 118
Black Baptist Church, 113, 192n59
Blavatsky, Helena, 17
Blumhofer, Edith, 177
Bolshevism: Its Cure, 55. See also Avery, Martha Moore; Goldstein, David
Booth, Catherine, 11
Booth, Evangeline, 11; denounces higher criticism, 22; as Salvation Army U.S. commander, 144, 161. See also Salvation Army
Booth, William, 9, 11, 222n24
Booth-Tucker, Emma, 159
Booth-Tucker, Frederick, 158, 159. See also Salvation Army
Boston Bible Training School, 129
Boston, city of, 4, 5, 18, 28, 31–32, 41, 45, 47, 50, 53, 54–55, 60, 129, 159, 174, 199n61, 201n94, 202n112, 222n22
Boston College, 8, 50
Boston Commons, 4, 28, 32, 45
Boston University School of Theology, 136. See also seminaries
Bown, Emma, 161
Brauer, Jerald, 188n15

Brekus, Catherine, 4, 28
Brereton, Virginia, 113–14, 115, 132–33, 135, 136
Brodbeck, William Nast, 191n49
Brownson, Henry, 33
Brownson, Orestes, 33, 196n9, 198n27
Bryn Mawr College, 130
Buffalo, city of, 3, 155
Buffalo Gap (TX), city of, 81, 175
Bushnell, Horace, 7, 8, 74
Bynum, Juanita, 180

Caffray, D. Willia, 133–34, 136
Cagle, Henry C., 81
Cagle, Mary Lee, 11, 24, 80–81; call to preach, 15, 80; conversion of, 80; founded churches, 68; sanctification of, 13, 80
Campbell, Debra, 36
camp meetings, 2, 10, 36, 39, 46, 72, 81, 82, 100–101, 112
Canal Street Mission, 155. See also Prosser, Anna
Carrigan, Owen, 201n96
Carter, R. Kelso, 12
Catholic Evidence Guild, 56, 195n3
Catholic Truth Guild (CTG), 5, 8, 23, 27–36, 41–42, 43, 51, 195n3; naming of, 203n117; patriotism of, 55–56; publicity, 46–47. See also Avery, Martha Moore; Goldstein, David
Catholicism, Roman, 5, 8, 13, 21, 28, 30, 36, 41, 52, 65, 198n27; Americanist controversy, 34; criticized by Protestants, 73; and democracy, 31–32; healing shrines, 12; and immigration, 21; nineteenth-century parish missions, 30, 35–36; women's colleges, 130
Charity Organization Society (COS), 142, 143; criticized, 228n89; founding and aims, 157–58, 221n20; friendly visitors, 142–43, 157
Chaves, Mark, 15
Chicago Bible Society, 115. See also Dryer, Emma
Chicago, city of, 2, 19, 44, 48, 114, 115, 119, 127, 134–35, 147–49, 156, 174–75, 176, 182, 221n21
Chicago Evangelistic Institute (CEI), 2, 119, 122–25, 127, 128, 130, 133–35, 147, 156, 174. See also Vennard, Iva Durham
Chicago Training School for City, Home,

and Foreign Missions, 114, 115, 187n2, 193n71, 213n19, 213n25. *See also* Meyer, Lucy Rider
Chicago Woman's Club, 143, 221n21
Chicago World's Fair, 33, 43
Child Welfare League of America, 167
Christian and Missionary Alliance, 12, 131. *See also* Simpson, Albert B.
Christian Science Theological Seminary, 18. *See also* Church of Christ (Scientist); Hopkins, Emma Curtis
Church of Christ (Scientist), 12, 17, 18. *See also* Eddy, Mary Baker
Church of the Living God, the Pillar and Ground of the Truth, 13; "Decree Book," 84, 87–88; "Do Rights" bands, 67, 70, 83; founded, 67, 69–70, 83–84; headquarters, 98; incorporated, 84. *See also* New and Living Way Publishing Company; Tate, Mary Magdalena Lewis
Church of the Nazarene, 81. *See also* Cagle, Mary Lee
Churches of God, General Conference (Winebrenner), 58, 77–78, 79. *See also* Eisenberg, Emma; Woodworth-Etter, Maria
Cincinnati, city of, 48, 71, 88
Civil War, 15, 121, 130, 159, 176
Clapp, Elizabeth, 141
Clarendon Street Baptist Church, 129. *See also* Gordon, Adoniram J.
Clarke, Branford, 73. *See also* Ku Klux Klan; White, Alma
Clarke, Edward, 218n87
College of Notre Dame, 130
Columbian Catholic Congress, 33
come-outers, 11, 191n38. *See also* Wesleyan/Holiness movement
Common Cause Society, 32–33, 51, 52, 54. *See also* Avery, Martha Moore; Goldstein, David
communism, 101–2, 105–6
Congregationalism, 7, 20
conversion, 18, 163–64, 168; at the meetings of Maria Woodworth-Etter, 39–40; conflict in American Christianity over, 6–8; definition of, 188n15; gradual, 6–7; as moment of salvation, 7; and reason, 8, 30; of women evangelists, 7, 8. *See also* individual listings by name
Corbett, Arthur B., 56

correspondence courses, 126–27, 179
Cotton, John, 4
Crawford, Florence Louise, 5, 13, 23, 24, 28, 65, 81–83, 174; children, 49, 96–98; on divorce and remarriage, 108, 175, 182; founded Apostolic Faith Mission, 47–50, 69; on male headship, 92, 96; marital history, 97–98; publishing, 99–100, 211n133; on sanctification, 86; on women, 93, 95
Crawford, Frank, 97
Crawford, Mildred, 96, 97
Crawford, Raymond, 49, 97, 98
Crawford, Virginia, 96, 97
Crittenton, Charles, 159–60. *See also* National Florence Crittenton Mission
Cummings, Kathleen, 197n25
Curtis, Heather, 141, 191n88

Darwin, Charles, 21, 74
Dayton, Donald, 13
deaconesses, 14, 180; duties of, 116–19; as evangelists, 3, 6, 116–18, 133, 213n21, 216n59; male pastors' reaction to, 14, 191n49, 213n25; in the Methodist Episcopal Church, 116; as pastors, 119; in the Pillar of Fire, 95; training and oversight of, 1–2, 115–16, 187n2. *See also* Chicago Training School for City, Home, and Foreign Missions; Epworth Evangelistic Institute; Methodist Deaconess Bureau; Meyer, Lucy Rider; Mildmay; Vennard, Iva Durham
Dean, John Marvin, 147–49, 224n39, 225n45, 225n48
Debs, Eugene, 32
Declaration of Independence, 31
DeGarmo, Charles, 2, 187n6
democracy, 31–32
Demons and Tongues, 75. *See also* White, Alma
denominations, 67–69, 81, 83–98; defined, 83; separation from, 70; as voluntary associations, 71; on women in leadership, 91. *See also* individual listings by name
Denver, city of, 69, 71, 74, 88–89, 91, 102, 107, 128, 211n133
Dewey, John, 19
dispensations: in Alma White's teaching, 85–86; in Phoebe Palmer's teaching, 92, 208n72

divorce among women evangelists, 97, 175; of Florence Crawford, 97–98, 108, 182; of Maria Woodworth-Etter, 46; of Mary Magdalena Lewis Tate, 69, 84, 97, 108
Dolan, Jay, 30, 35, 39, 196n9
Door of Hope Mission, 24, 142, 153, 154, 155, 159, 161–64. *See also* Whittemore, Emma
Dorsey, Theodore, 203n118
Douglas, Ann, 14
Draper, Minnie, 113
Dryer, Emma, 115. *See also* Bible Work of Chicago; Chicago Bible Society
Durham, Iva May. *See* Vennard, Iva Durham
Dyer, Mary, 4. *See also* Quakers

Echo Park Evangelistic Association, 177. *See also* International Church of the Foursquare Gospel; McPherson, Aimee Semple
ecumenism, 30
Eddy, Mary Baker, 12, 17, 18. *See also* Church of Christ (Scientist)
education, religious, 7, 189n24. *See also* Sunday school
Edwards, Jonathan, 173
Eisenberg, Emma, 57–58, 204n128. *See also* Churches of God, General Conference (Winebrenner)
Elaw, Zilpha, 28, 68
Elhanan Training Institute, 5, 111–12, 114, 120; correspondence courses, 126; volunteer labor, 128. *See also* Perry, Mattie
Elliott, Walter, 33, 35. *See also* Paulists
Emmanuel movement, 12
Episcopal Church in America, 12
Epworth Evangelistic Institute (EEI), 1–2, 3, 14, 112, 182: conflict at, 5–6, 9, 14, 119, 182; curriculum, 6–7, 116–19. *See also* Vennard, Iva Durham
Equal Rights Amendment, 95
Etter, Samuel, 56–57. *See also* Woodworth-Etter, Maria
Evangelical Alliance, 20, 146
evangelicalism, 6–7, 16–18, 20–22, 132, 143, 180
evangelism: call to, 3, 4, 15, 59–60, 63 (*see also individual evangelist by name*); defined, 187–88n10; ecstasy and, 36; and humanitarianism, 24, 143, 144–50, 152, 156, 158; in meetings, 3, 9–10, 18, 20, 23, 28, 29, 30, 57, 68, 108, 112, 114, 134, 141–42, 152–53, 175, 178; music in, 39–40, 70, 80 (*see also* songs); nineteenth-century, 4, 28, 30, 33, 36, 68–69; organizations for, 18, 23, 27–63 (*see also* institution building); and patriotism, 27–28, 55; training for, 3, 19; transportation in, 4, 24, 27, 47–49
evolutionary theory, 21–23, 124, 126, 136

Fall, the, 93, 126
Federal Council of Churches, 224n40
Feick, August, 57
feminism, 55
Findlay, James, 39, 199n63
Finney, Charles G., 37, 191n39
First Nationalist Club, 32. *See also* Avery, Martha Moore; nationalism
Five Points Mission, 227n68
Fletcher, John, 190n33, 190n36
Florence Mission, 160. *See also* Crittenton, Charles; National Florence Crittenton Mission
foot washing, 82–83
Foote, Julia, 68
Ford, Henry, 19
Fordham University, 51, 53
fraternalism. *See* voluntary associations
Free Methodism, 11, 13, 80, 162
Freedman, Anne, 71
Freedman, Estelle, 16, 192n59
fundamentalism, 64, 180, 204n144
fund-raising, 5, 42–43, 45–46, 49, 61, 112, 115, 128, 153, 163, 181
Furnish, Dorothy Jean, 189n24

Gamm, Gerald, 72
Garrett Bible Institute, 125. *See also* Chicago Training School for City, Home, and Foreign Missions
gender: conflict in American Christianity over, 6, 14–19; double standard, 169; in education, 130–31; equality, 93–95, 108; in religious training schools, 113–14, 118–19, 129–37
GI Bill, 136
glorification, 189n30
glossolalia, 12, 13, 40, 75, 86, 199n57
God, 10, 22, 37, 57, 60, 64, 68, 73, 75, 76, 79, 80, 86, 96, 111, 119, 123, 128, 139, 140, 145, 147, 154, 166, 169, 175
Goldstein, David, 41, 203n117, 203n118; and Martha Moore Avery, 23, 27, 28, 30, 34, 35–36, 50, 53, 55, 65; correspondence, 54;

solo work, 199n61. *See also* Catholic Truth Guild
Good Will Mission, 140, 150, 165. *See also* Lee, Martha
Gordon, Adoniram J., 113, 129. *See also* Clarendon Street Baptist Church
Gordon Bible College (Gordon College), 113
gospel autovans, 24, 177, 178; of the Apostolic Faith Mission, 47–48; of the Catholic Truth Guild, 27–28, 30, 49, 56
gospel tracts. *See* religious literature
gospel wagons, 24, 47–48
Gould, Rita, 225n48. *See also* Stockton, Amy Lee
Graham, Billy, 64
Grammer, Elizabeth Elkin, 141–42
Great Britain, 19
Great Depression, 179
Green, Maud, 51
Guide to Holiness, The, 10, 190n33
Gundry, Stan, 199n63

Hadley, Henry H. 120, 153, 154
Hadley, Samuel H. (S. H.), 154
Hamilton, Michael, 64
Handbook of Settlements, The, 142
Harper, Frances, 60
Harris, Robert L. (R.L.), 80
Harvard University, 50
Hassey, Janette, 132, 133
headship, male, 65, 92–93, 96
healings, 12, 56–57, 84; Anna Prosser, 155; at Azusa Street, 82; Emma Whittemore, 153, 160–61; Jennie Smith, 61; Martha Lee, 140–41; Mary Magdalena Lewis Tate, 84; places of, 12, 195n88; and sanctification, 11–12; at Woodworth-Etter meetings, 39–40
heaven, 38, 55, 86, 145
Hecker, Isaac, 198n27. *See also* Paulists
hell, 7, 34, 38, 55, 80
Hell's Half Acre, 140, 179. *See also* Kansas City
Henderson, Charles R. (C.R.), 71
Hick's Hollow, 151–52, 179, 226n57. *See also* Ray, Emma
Higginbotham, Evelyn Brooks, 113
higher criticism (historical criticism), 21–22, 94, 123–26, 136, 189n24, 194n81; adopted by Elizabeth Cady Stanton, 94
holiness. *See* sanctification

Holiness Church of Christ, 81. *See also* Cagle, Mary Lee
holiness movement. *See* Keswick movement; Wesleyan/Holiness movement
Holmes Home and Hospital, 162, 163
Holy Spirit (Ghost), 38, 40–41, 67, 92, 93, 145; baptism of, 11, 12–13, 82, 84, 86–87; in sanctification, 9, 190n36; in signs and wonders, 40
home economics, 131, 132
Home of the Evangelists, 114
Hopkins, Emma Curtis, 17–18
Hopkins Metaphysical Association, 18
Hull House, 19, 156. *See also* Addams, Jane; settlement house movement
human trafficking, 168
Hunter, Fannie McDowell, 81
Hutchinson, Anne, 4

Illinois State Normal University, 2, 115, 121, 144
immigration, 20, 121
Inasmuch (publication), 1, 119, 128, 149. *See also* Epworth Evangelistic Institute
India, 12, 16
Indianapolis, city of, 57, 58, 68, 77, 79
inerrancy, 94. *See also* biblical interpretation
institution building, 4–5, 174–82; benefits for women, 192n59; fundraising for, 45; inclusion of men in, 16; overseas, 16; and revivals, 23; succession to leadership, 51, 65, 96, 108, 180; types of institutions, 16–17, 23, 177–80
International Church of the Foursquare Gospel, 12, 178, 191n42. *See also* McPherson, Aimee Semple
International Missionary Council, 144
International Union of Gospel Missions (IUGM), 154, 227n71
Internet, the, 180
Ireland, John, 33–34
itinerancy, 4–5, 28, 30, 67–68, 141–42; transition from, to institution building, 4, 108, 171, 177
Itinerant Institute on Evangelism, 112. *See also* Smith, Joseph H.

Jacksonville, city of, 57, 88, 105
Jesus Christ, 4, 9, 11–12, 30, 40, 64, 75, 87, 100, 125, 139, 144, 146, 148, 152, 153, 154, 156, 159, 165, 166; atonement of, 9; birth of, 31; crucifixion of, 86; as the Good Shepherd, 75

Johnson, Martha, 161
justification, 10, 86–87, 189n30, 190n36. See also conversion

Kansas City, 5, 24, 140, 151–52
Keller, Rosemary Skinner, 213n25
Keswick movement, 11, 191n39; on sanctification, 13
Knock Chapel. See healings: places of
Ku Klux Klan, 35, 73, 108. See also Clarke, Branford; White, Alma
Kuhlman, Kathryn, 30, 180
Kunzel, Regina, 140, 160, 168

Lakeview Church (Indianapolis, IN), 79. See also Woodworth-Etter Tabernacle
Lankford, Sara Worrall, 190n33
Lasch-Quinn, Elizabeth, 143
latter rain, 41, 199n57
Lawrence, Arlene White, 95, 96
Leake, Albert H., 131
Lee, Jarena, 28, 67–68, 141–42
Lee, Martha, 11, 24, 141, 155, 170, 179; and Crittenton maternity home, 164–65, 167; evangelism and humanitarianism, 143, 144, 158; family, 176; rescue mission work, 139–40, 142, 150, 158–59, 163, 167. See also Good Will Mission; Tinley Rescue Home for Fallen Girls and Women
Leo XIII (pope), 32, 34
Lewis, David, 70
Lewis, Felix, 70, 97
Lewis, Helen, 96
Lewis, Meharry, 85, 96
Lewis, Walter, 97
Lighthouse of International Foursquare Evangelism (L.I.F.E.), 178–79. See also McPherson, Aimee Semple
Livermore, Harriet, 28, 68
London, city of, 60, 69, 88, 161, 211n133
Lord's Supper, the, 82–83, 181
Los Angeles, city of, 12, 40, 58, 69, 81, 88, 97–98, 99, 174, 177, 179
Lourdes. See healings: places of
Lucy Perry Noble Institute for Women, 16
Lum, Clara, 96, 99

Magdalen societies, 159
Magnuson, Norris, 143
Mahan, Asa, 191n39
Marion (NC), city of, 5, 111–12, 175

marriage, 69, 108, 174, 176, 182. See also individual evangelists by name
Marsden, George, 17, 70
Marty, Martin, 37
Marxism, 32
Massachusetts Metaphysical College, 18. See also Eddy, Mary Baker
maternalism, 141–42, 171; of women evangelists, 64–65
Mathews, Shailer, 124, 148, 224n45
McAuley, Jerry, 153, 154. See also Water Street Mission
McClymond, Michael, 188n10
McCormick, Cyrus, 176
McDowell, Mary E., 143, 156
McLoughlin, William, 21, 22
McPherson, Aimee Semple, 12, 24–25, 41, 58–59, 177–81, 191n42, 204n128. See also Angelus Temple; International Church of the Foursquare Gospel; Lighthouse of International Foursquare Evangelism
McRobbie, James, 89–90
Men and Religion Forward Movement, 147
Merritt, Timothy, 190n33
Methodism, 10, 11, 38
Methodist Deaconess Bureau, 3, 112
Methodist Episcopal Church (MEC), 21, 116, 119, 130, 134, 173–74; 1880 General Conference of, 14, 180; 1904 General Conference of, 2; 1924 General Conference of, 180; conflict with Wesleyan/Holiness movement, 11; critiqued by women evangelists, 73–74, 76; ordination of women, 14–15, 129; sanctification and the, 10; Woman's Division, 122
Methodist Protestant Church, 95, 136
Metropolitan Church Association, 101, 102
Meyer, Joyce, 180
Meyer, Lucy Rider, 115–16, 124–25, 133, 187n2, 193n71, 205n149, 216n59. See also Chicago Training School for City, Home, and Foreign Missions
middle class, 72, 79
Mildmay, 115
Miller, Glenn, 136
miracles, 40–41
mission organizations, 15, 129, 150
missionaries, 15–16, 24, 81, 111, 112, 114, 122, 127, 129, 132, 133–34, 150, 174
Missionary Training College for Home and Foreign Missions, 113. See also Simpson, Albert B.

INDEX OF NAMES AND SUBJECTS >> 263

Mitchinson, Wendy, 192n60
Modernists, 7, 147–48, 224n45
Montgomery, Carrie Judd, 12, 24, 113, 140, 195n88; evangelism and humanitarianism, 158; founds Beulah Rescue Home and People's Mission, 142, 151, 162; founds Shalom Training School, 131
Moody, Dwight L., 19–20, 22, 43, 113, 145, 159, 173; at the 1893 World's Fair, 43; and Emma Dryer, 115; family, 65; influential connections, 176; meetings, 39, 42–43, 198n63; premillennialism, 147; sermons, 38
Moody, Emma, 65
Moody Bible Institute, 20, 113, 114, 115; women in, 132
moral societies, 159
Morris Cottage, 159. *See also* Salvation Army
Moss, Virginia, 24, 113, 142; founds Open Door Mission, 153
Mott, John R., 193–94n73. *See also* Northfield Conference; Student Volunteer Movement for Foreign Missions
Mount Hermon School for Boys, 20. *See also* Moody, Dwight L.
Mountain Lake Park campground, 112
Mukti Mission, 12
music, 36, 40, 61, 62, 82–83, 89, 91, 127, 153. *See also* songs

National Baptist Convention, 113
National Camp Meeting Association, 9
National Cash Register, 45
National Federation of Settlements (NFS), 156
National Florence Crittenton Mission (NFCM), 159–60; bureaucracy and rules, 164–66; merged into Child Welfare League of America, 167
National Training School for Women and Girls, 113
nationalism, 196n14. *See also* First Nationalist Club
New and Living Way Publishing Company, 98. *See also* Church of the Living God, the Pillar and Ground of the Truth
New England Female Moral Reform Society, 159
New Testament Church of Christ, 11; founded, 80; becomes Holiness Church of Christ, 81. *See also* Cagle, Mary Lee
New Thought, 17; ordination of women in, 18. *See also* Hopkins, Emma Curtis

New York City, 43–44, 57, 62–63, 113, 114, 127, 153–55, 157, 159–62, 168, 169, 175, 190n33, 221n21, 227n68
New York City Rescue Mission, 227n68
New York Evangelistic Training School, 113. *See also* Willing, Jennie Fowler
New York's Neighborhood Guild and College Settlement, 19
Nineteenth Amendment, 19, 94. *See also* women's suffrage
Noll, Mark, 10
normal schools, 120–21
North Bergen, city of, 142
Northern Baptist Theological Seminary, 147–49. *See also* Dean, John Marvin
Northfield Conference, 20. *See also* Moody, Dwight L.
Northfield Seminary, 20. *See also* Moody, Dwight L.
Northwestern Bible and Missionary Training School, 113
Noyes, John Humphrey, 101. *See also* Oneida Community

Oakland, city of, 24, 37, 46, 131, 142, 162
Oberlin College, 191n39
O'Connell, William, 28, 32, 55, 202n112, 203n117; and Catholic Truth Guild, 45, 203n114
old time religion, 4, 21, 22, 102, 180
Oldham, William F., 117
Oliver, Anna, 191n52
Omaha, city of, 24
Oneida Community, 101. *See also* Noyes, John Humphrey
ordo salutis, 86–87, 189n30
Orr, James, 125
Orsi, Robert, 108–9, 182
Osborn, Lucy Drake, 113; finances, 128; founds Union Missionary Training Institute, 114
Ott, Elsie, 83, 100–101
Our Country: Its Possible Future and Its Present Crisis, 21. *See also* Strong, Josiah

pacifism, 85
Paino, Lydia, 57
Palmer, Phoebe, 93, 190n33, 205n6, 208n72; on sanctification, 10–11, 92. *See also* dispensations
Pantheism, 8

Paul, John, 124, 125, 134
Paulists, 33, 35, 195n3, 198n27; at the 1893 World's Fair, 34
Pentecost, day of, 91–92, 105, 117, 190n36, 199n57
Pentecostal Mission Home, 113. *See also* White, Alma
Pentecostal Union Church, 74. *See also* Pillar of Fire
Pentecostalism, 5, 12, 30, 41, 47, 60, 199n57
People's Mission, 142, 151. *See also* Montgomery, Carrie Judd
Perfect Love, 9; influence on Iva Durham Vennard,189n27
Perry, Mattie, 5, 10, 12, 24, 182; founds Elhanan Training Institute, 111–12, 114, 129; develops correspondence courses, 126; fund-raising, 128
Philadelphia School of the Bible, 113
Philomatheia Club, 50–51. *See also* Avery, Martha Moore
Pierson, Arthur T., 120
Pillar of Fire, 11; disciplinary actions, 88, 105; education, 90–91; finances, 211n143; founded, 69, 74; headquarters at Zarephath, 73, 89–90, 91, 101–8, 178; on women, 95; uniforms, 88, 105, 230n110; vegetarianism, 24, 73, 85, 86, 107; workers, 88–91, 102–7. *See also* White, Alma
Pittsburgh, city of, 48
Portland, city of, 5, 47, 48–50, 69, 82, 96, 98–100, 174, 177–78, 200n87
poverty, 136, 145, 151–52
prayer meetings, 10, 68, 103, 76–77, 129, 152
premillennialism, 147
Presbyterianism, 13, 64; women's ordination, 15
Progressive Era, 4–6, 8, 14, 19–20, 23, 25, 28, 68, 71, 106, 114, 121, 130–32, 136–37, 141–43, 159–60, 169–71, 174, 177, 178, 180–81
Prosser, Anna, 140, 158; mission work, 155. *See also* Canal Street Mission
prostitution, 115, 140, 150, 158–65, 168–70, 176
publicity, 42–43; in newspapers, 38–39, 46–47
Puritans, 4
Putnam, Robert D., 72

Quakers, 4, 38
Question Box, 34, 198n27. *See also* Catholic Truth Guild; Paulists
Quinn, Anthony, 179
Quiz Period, 34–35. *See also* Catholic Truth Guild

Radcliffe College, 50, 130
radio, 69, 180
Rauschenbusch, Walter, 19
Ray, Emma, 5, 11, 24, 140, 179; on baptism of the Holy Spirit, 12–13, 152; evangelism and humanitarianism, 158; family, 151–52; maternalism, 141; mission at Hick's Hollow, 151–53; Woman's Christian Temperance Union work, 60–61, 62; Stranger's Rest Mission, 150–51
Ray, Lloyd P. (L. P.), 61, 152–53, 179
Rees, Frida, 74
Rees, Seth, 74
Religious Education Association, 7
religious literature, 35, 42, 48–50, 59, 61, 99–100
religious training schools, 81, 90, 111–137; compared to seminaries and normal schools, 120–21, 124, 134, 136; curriculum of, 112, 122–25; denominational support for, 129–130; finances, 127–29; gender in, 131; legacy of women evangelists, 178–79; list of, 113; masculinization of, 56–57, 95, 97, 113–14, 132–33, 135–36, 180; other types of training schools, 113; role of Dwight L. Moody in, 115, 132; students in, 120; vocational education in, 120–27. *See also individual listings by name*
rescue homes, 24, 158–71; goals of, 228n92. *See also individual listings by name*
rescue missions, 81, 127, 134, 150–58; different from settlement work, 143, 156; as legacy of women evangelists, 179–82; of the New Testament Church of Christ, 81; purpose of, 226n55; of the Woman's Christian Temperance Union, 155; workers in, 143, 161–62, 230n110. *See also individual listings by name*
revivalism. *See* evangelism
revivals, 22–23
Revolutionary War, 30
Riis, Jacob, 169
Riley, William Bell, 113
Roaring Twenties, 24
Roberts, Florence, 24, 140, 141, 165–67. *See also* Beth-Adriel
Rochester Bible Training School, 60, 113, 123, 174. *See also* Baker, Elizabeth

Rodeheaver, Homer, 200n71. See also Billy Sunday Evangelistic Organization
Rosen, Ruth, 168
Ryan, Mary, 72

sacraments. See baptism; Lord's Supper, the
Salt Lake City, 48
Salvation Army, 9, 11, 22, 142, 179; attire of rescue workers, 161–62; in conflict over rescue work, 157–58; expansion of rescue work, 143–44, 159. See also Booth, Evangeline
San Francisco Chinese Mission Home, 159
San Francisco, city of, 142, 143, 151, 162
San Jose Baptist Church, 148. See also Dean, John Marvin
sanctification, 18, 81, 189n30; conflict in American Christianity over, 6, 9–14; definition, 12–13; and healing, 11–12; instantaneous, 9, 189n31; of women evangelists, 2, 13. See also individual listings by name
Sankey, Ira, 22, 39. See also Moody, Dwight L.
Saxe, Grace, 62. See also Billy Sunday Evangelistic Organization
Scarritt Bible and Training School, 112
Schlesinger, Arthur, 20, 72
Schneider, Greg, 216n59
Scofield, Cyrus I. (C. I.), 113
Seattle, city of, 5, 48, 60, 61, 141, 150, 152, 158
Second Baptist Church of Chicago, 147–49; 225n48. See also Aiken Institute; Dean, John Marvin
seminaries, 7, 134–37, 148–49, 173, 181. See also religious training schools: compared to seminaries and normal schools
settlement house movement, 19, 116, 121; in Chicago, 127, 149, 156; contrasted with rescue missions, 156–57; education of settlement workers, 220n16; relation to religion, 19, 142–43. See also individual listings by name
Seventh Day Adventism, 17
Seymour, William, 98, 99. See also Azusa Street Mission
Shalom Training School, 113, 131. See also Montgomery, Carrie Judd
Shaw, Anna Howard, 136, 191n52, 219n108
Shaw, Josephine Lowell, 157. See also Charity Organization Society
Simpson, Albert B., 12, 113. See also Christian and Missionary Alliance
sin, 6, 68, 140, 153, 158
Sinclair, Upton, 19
Skinner, Richard Dana, 202n99
Sklar, Kathryn Kish, 130
slavery, 151–52
Slum Brigade (slum sisters), 161. See also Salvation Army
Smith, Amanda Berry, 10; conversion of, 7, 8; founds an orphanage, 212n6; involvement with Woman's Christian Temperance Union, 60, 62
Smith, Constance, 71
Smith, Gipsy, 41
Smith, Hannah Whitall, 193n68
Smith, Jennie, 10, 61–62. See also Woman's Christian Temperance Union
Smith, Joseph H., 2, 112
Smith College, 130
Smith-Hughes Act, 122
Smith-Rosenberg, Carroll, 168
social efficiency, 218n88
Social Gospel, 19, 223n27; defined, 146–47; and John Marvin Dean, 224n39
Socialism, 31, 32, 34, 51–52, 55, 197n15, 197n21
Somerset, Lady Henry, 60
Somerset Christian College, 91, 107. See also White, Alma
songs: "Brightly Beams Our Father's Mercy," 145; "Feed on Husks No More," 153; "He Saves the Drunkard Too," 153; Holy Name hymn, 28; "May I Know Thy Voice," 120; "A Poor Girl was Wand'ring Alone on the Street," 166; "Standing on the Promises," 12; "When the Saints are Marching In," 82; "Where Cross the Crowded Ways of Life," 224n40; "Where Is My Wandering Boy Tonight?" 226n64. See also music
Southern California Rescue Mission, 168
speaking in tongues. See glossolalia
Spelman College, 130
Spiritualism, 37, 192–93n64
St. Louis, city of, 1–2, 6, 9, 14, 37, 41, 57, 68, 71, 77, 112, 117, 119, 130, 182
Standard Oil Company, 45
Stanley, Susie, 13, 73
Stanton, Elizabeth Cady, 37, 94. See also Woman's Bible, The
Starr, Lee Anna, 95
Stockton, Amy Lee, 148–49, 225n48

Stranger's Rest Mission, 150–51. *See also* Ray, Emma
Strong, Josiah: on Catholicism, 196n12; on immigration, 20–21; proponent of Social Gospel, 146
Student Volunteer Movement for Foreign Missions, 194n73. *See also* Moody, Dwight L.; Mott, John R., Northfield Conference
Sunday, Billy, 29, 44, 59, 62–63, 173; critiqued by Martha Moore Avery, 41; rise to renown, 43. *See also* Billy Sunday Evangelistic Organization
Sunday, Helen, 13; as business manager, 13, 23, 29, 43–45, 62–63; as a fundamentalist, 64; called to preach, 63; licensed to preach, 64; *Ma Sunday's Column*, 64; "Ma" Sunday Still Speaks, 64; on women, 64–65. *See also* Billy Sunday Evangelistic Organization
Sunday school, 14, 68, 76, 98, 127, 141
Swarth, Helen, 209n85
Swarthmore College, 2
Sweet, Leonard, 6
Swift, Eva, 16

Tacoma, city of, 48
Tate, Mary Magdalena Lewis, 13, 24, 67; authority of, 87–88; condemns denominations, 72; healing, 83–84; marital history, 69, 108, 175, 182; sanctification, 84; on women, 96. *See also* Church of the Living God, the Pillar and Ground of the Truth
Taves, Ann, 7, 72
Taylor University, 124, 125
television, 180
Ten Commandments, 31
tenements, 57, 127, 142, 143, 144, 151, 154, 156, 169
Testem Benevolentiae, 34
Theosophy, 17
Third Great Awakening, 21. *See also* revivals
Thoburn, Isabella, 116
Thoburn, James, 116–17
Thurman, Lucy, 61
Tinley Rescue Home for Fallen Girls and Women, 167. *See also* Lee, Martha
Torrey, Reuben A. (R. A.), 113
Towle, Nancy, 28, 68
training schools. *See* religious training schools

Tuesday Meetings for the Promotion of Holiness, 10
Tyng, Stephen H., 114

Union Missionary Training Institute, 113, 114, 128; gender in, 132. *See also* Osborn, Lucy Drake
Unitarianism, 8
United States Steel, 45
University of Chicago Divinity School, 124, 147–48
University of Chicago Settlement, 156. *See also* McDowell, Mary E.
unwed mothers, 24, 159, 160

Van Cott, Maggie Newton, 14, 193n68, 205n6
Vancouver, city of, 48
Vassar College, 130
Vennard, Iva Durham, 1–3, 4, 8–10, 14, 24, 112, 129, 133, 135, 173, 182, 187n6; called to evangelism, 3; conversion, 1; on evangelism and humanitarianism, 144–47, 149; family, 121, 174–75; founds Chicago Evangelistic Institute, 119, 127, 130, 134–35; founds Epworth Evangelistic Institute, 116–19; founds Wayside Settlement, 156; and Garrett Bible Institute, 125; and historical criticism, 125; opposition to, 2–3; sanctification of, 2, 9
Vennard, Thomas, 174, 175
Vennard College. *See* Chicago Evangelistic Institute
visitation, 42, 59, 62, 115, 116, 127, 139, 142–143, 144, 157, 158, 160–62, 221n21
vocation, defined, 122
vocational education: pioneered by women evangelists, 24; in public schools, 113–114, 131–32; in religious training schools, 120–27
voluntary associations, 15, 70–71, 77, 106–7

Wacker, Grant, 47
wages, 147, 169–70
Wanamaker, John, 43, 176
Warner, Wayne, 203–4n128
Washington, George, 28
Water Street Mission, 153, 154, 227n68. *See also* McAuley, Jerry
Waukesha, city of, 101
Way of Holiness, The, 10. *See also* Palmer, Phoebe

Wayside Settlement, 156. *See also* Vennard, Iva Durham
Wellesley College, 2, 130
Welsh Revival, 12
Wesley, John, 10, 79, 189n30, 190n33, 205n6
Wesleyan/Holiness movement, 9, 190n33; disputes over sanctification, 10–11, 13
White, Alma, 10, 11, 24, 97, 107–8, 182; condemns glossolalia, 75; family, 74–75, 95–96, 175; founds Christian schools, 212n6; founds Pillar of Fire, 68–69; leadership style, 88–89; ordination of, 74; poetry by, 93–94, 104; sanctification, 74; supports Ku Klux Klan, 73, 108. *See also* dispensations; Pillar of Fire
White, Arthur, 89, 97
White, Ellen, 17
White, Kent, 74–75, 175
White, Ray, 97
Whitefield, George, 46, 79
Whittemore, Emma, 12, 24, 140, 141; evangelism and humanitarianism, 158; healing, 153; rescue work, 154–55, 160–61, 162; writes about her work, 163–64, 169–70. *See also* Door of Hope Mission
Whittemore, Sidney, 154
Willard, Frances, 16, 29, 59, 160. *See also* Woman's Christian Temperance Union
Willing, Jennie Fowler, 10, 14, 24, 59, 62, 113, 126–27, 178, 204n131; local preacher's license, 129. *See also* New York Evangelistic Training School
Wolf, Naomi, 105
Wolfram, Gertrude Metlen, 89
Woman in the Pulpit, 59. *See also* Willard, Frances
Woman's Bible, The, 94. *See also* Stanton, Elizabeth Cady
Woman's Christian Temperance Union (WCTU), 16, 169; departments of, 192n60; "Do Everything" policy, 16, 192n60; Evangelistic Department, 23, 29, 59–62, 123, 204n131; interracial cooperation in, 60–62; rescue mission, 155; rescue homes, 160. *See also* Willard, Frances
women bishops, 67, 88, 95, 96, 148
women preachers, 14–15, 17, 59–60, 95, 173; biblical defense of, 91–93; opponents, 14, 74, 81. *See also individual listings by name*
women's ordination, 14–15, 18; opposition to, 191n52. *See also* Methodist Episcopal Church; Presbyterianism
women's religious authority, 18, 65, 87–88, 91–96
women's separate sphere, 1, 14, 118
women's suffrage, 19, 37, 55, 94, 181. *See also* Nineteenth Amendment
Women's Temperance Crusade, 16
Wood, John A. (J. A.), 9, 189n27, 189n30
Woodworth, Philo, 40, 46, 56; as business manager, 45–46; divorced and remarried, 46
Woodworth-Etter, Maria, 22, 23, 24, 28, 30, 36–42, 50, 56–59, 65, 68, 203n128; autobiographies of, 57–58; condemns denominations, 72, 76; deaths of children, 69; divorced, 46; founds churches, 68; Pentecostalism of, 30, 41; trances, 37–38
Woodworth-Etter Tabernacle, 57, 79
working class, 121, 160
Workmen's Circle, 106
World War I, 85
Wright, Frank Lloyd, 19

Young Men's Christian Association (YMCA), 6, 193n73, 222n22

Zarephath. *See* Pillar of Fire: headquarters
Zarephath Bible College, 113. *See also* White, Alma

INDEX OF SCRIPTURE REFERENCES

Numbers in boldface indicate biblical chapters and verses.

Genesis **1–3**, 93; **1–11**, 126; **1:29–30**, 85; **2:4b–25**, 91; **2:18**, 93; **21:14–20**, 228n92
Exodus **20**, 31
Deuteronomy **5**, 31
1 Kings **17:8–9**, 101
Ezekiel **37:11**, 207n36
Hosea **2:15**, 229n99
Joel **2:23**, 199n57; **2:28–32**, 91
Matthew **5:8**, 189n27; **6:33**, 155; **23:19**, 10
Luke **15:11–32**, 153; **24:49**, 92
John **4**, 91; **10:11–18**, 75
Acts **1**, 91; **1:13**, 87; **2**, 86, 87, 214n25; **2:1–4**, 199n57; **2:16**, 91; **2:17**, 117; **2:17–18**, 117; **2:44–47**, 105; **10:34**, 96; **16:9–15**, 118; **21:1–4**, 199n57; **21:9**, 117
Romans **16:1–7**, 118; **16:12–15**, 118
1 Corinthians **14:33b–35**, 118; **14:33b–36**, 91; **14:34**, 92, 93
Galatians **3:28**, 91, 96
Philippians **4:3**, 91
1 Tim **2:11–15**, 91; **2:12**, 92; **2:14**, 92; **3:15**, 72

ABOUT THE AUTHOR

Priscilla Pope-Levison is Professor of Theology and Assistant Director of Women's Studies at Seattle Pacific University. Her previous books include *Sex, Gender, and Christianity*; *Turn the Pulpit Loose: Two Centuries of American Women Evangelists*; *Return to Babel: Global Perspectives on the Bible*; *Jesus in Global Contexts*; and *Evangelization in a Liberation Perspective*.

www.ingramcontent.com/pod-product-compliance
Lightning Source LLC
Chambersburg PA
CBHW020359080526
44584CB00014B/1096